P9-APS-431

PATRICK LEIGH FERMOR
A Life in Letters

PATRICK LEIGH FERMOR
A Life in Letters

Selected and edited by
ADAM SISMAN

NEW YORK REVIEW BOOKS

New York

THIS IS A NEW YORK REVIEW BOOK
PUBLISHED BY THE NEW YORK REVIEW OF BOOKS
435 Hudson Street, New York, NY 10014
www.nyrb.com

Letters of Patrick Leigh Fermor copyright © 1940–2010 by the Estate of Patrick Leigh Fermor
Compilation, notes, introduction, and editorial matter copyright © 2016 by Adam Sisman
All rights reserved.

First published in Great Britain in 2016 by John Murray (Publishers), an Hachette UK Company

A catalog record for this book is available from the Library of Congress.

ISBN 978-1-68137-156-6
Available as an electronic book; ISBN 978-1-68137-157-3

Printed in the United States of America on acid-free paper.
10 9 8 7 6 5 4 3 2 1

In memory of Robyn Sisman

CONTENTS

INTRODUCTION

The letters in this volume span seventy years, from February 1940 to January 2010. The first was written ten days before Patrick Leigh Fermor's twenty-fifth birthday, when he was an officer cadet, hoping for a commission in the Guards. He had hurried back to England from Rumania in September 1939, expecting to die within weeks of being sent into action, like a junior officer in the First World War. The last two were written on the same day in 2010, when Paddy (as he called himself, and almost everyone else called him) was ninety-four, a widower, very deaf, and suffering from tunnel vision, which made it hard for him to read even his own handwriting. His voice was already hoarse from the throat cancer which would kill him seventeen months later. But these last letters, like the first and most of the others printed here, exude a zest that was characteristic. From first to last, Paddy's letters radiate warmth and gaiety. Often they are decorated with witty illustrations and enhanced by comic verse. Sometimes they contain riddles and cringe-causing puns.

Although, as I have mentioned, he was only twenty-four when he wrote the first letter in this volume, one of the two achievements for which he is best known was already behind him. Paddy had set out at the age of eighteen to walk to Constantinople (as he called it), after a premature exit from his boarding school (which would honour him later in life as 'a free spirit'). He left England early in December 1933, and arrived at his destination just over twelve months later, on New Year's Eve 1934. In the course of this 'Great Trudge' across Europe, he slept under the stars and in schlosses, dossed down in hostels, awoke more than once with a hangover in the houses of strangers, sat round a campfire singing songs with shepherds, frolicked with peasant girls and played bicycle polo with his host. He observed customs and practices that dated back to the Middle Ages, many of which were about to vanish for ever – swept away, first by the catastrophe of war and then by Communism. As Paddy puts it in one of these letters, 'a sudden Dark Age descended that nobody was ready for'. He would give an account of his experiences in what became a trilogy of much admired books, which remained incomplete at his death: *A Time of Gifts* (1977), *Between the Woods and the Water* (1986), and the posthumously published *The Broken Road* (2013).

Paddy would spend the late 1930s oscillating between Greece, Rumania, France and England. In the late summer of 1938, before leaving for Rumania, he left with a friend in London two trunks, which were subsequently lost with their contents, among them notebooks he had kept on his walk and letters home to his mother. The loss helps to explain why there are no pre-war letters in this volume. Nor are there more than a couple from the war itself. Rather than going into the Guards, which had rated his capabilities as 'below average', Paddy had been snapped up by the Intelligence Corps, on the basis of the fact that he spoke German, Rumanian and Greek; and after being evacuated first from mainland Greece and then from Crete as the Germans invaded, he had been infiltrated back on to Crete to operate under cover, liaising with the local resistance. It was during this period, as Paddy made regular clandestine visits to German-occupied Crete from his base in Cairo, that he planned and executed the abduction of an enemy general, the other achievement for which he is best known. The second letter in this volume, written to the mother of his second-in-command, Billy Moss, refers to this daring exploit, albeit discreetly.

After the war Paddy worked for the British Council in Athens for just over a year – his only period of peacetime employment, as it would turn out, which ended in his dismissal. It became quickly apparent that he was 'unfit for office work'. Included here is a letter written during a lecture tour of Greece undertaken on behalf of the British Council, and another to Lawrence Durrell in which he complains at being let go, prompting a rare lapse into profanity.

The rest of his long life was spent as a writer. Before the war he was already pursuing literary projects, and had translated a novel from French into English; after leaving the British Council, he accepted an invitation to write the captions for a book of photographs of the

Caribbean, a task that grew into a full-length book, *The Traveller's Tree*, published in 1950. (Paddy would invariably exceed any word limit he was given, just as he could never keep to a deadline.) From then on, though often short of money, he seems never to have considered any other form of work. His experiences in the Caribbean inspired him to write a novel (his only work of fiction), *The Violins of Saint-Jacques* (1953). He was already working on a book drawing on his travels in Greece, part autobiographical, part ethnographical, which grew into two volumes: *Mani* (1958) and *Roumeli* (1966).

One of the surprises of these letters is to find how much recognition mattered to him. In a letter to Colin Thubron, written towards the end of his life, Paddy admits to feeling 'rather gloomy' at not being included in a list of the greatest writers since the war. His habitual procrastination, and his apparent readiness to allow himself to be distracted by the smallest thing, suggests a dilettante. But the letters tell a different story, of a writer always anxious at his lack of progress, guilty at his failure to fulfil his commitments, and perpetually trying to do better. This is the refrain of Paddy's letters to his publisher, 'Jock' Murray, over a period of more than forty years. At Christmas 1984, for example, Paddy tells two friends that he has deferred a visit to London because he cannot face Jock while his book remains unfinished. Even after Jock's death, when Paddy was in his eighties, he felt it necessary to apologise to Jock's son for his presence in England by marking his letter 'NO SKULKING'.

At the beginning of his career Paddy had been encouraged by Harold Nicolson to aim high, and he strove to produce the masterpiece that Nicolson (and no doubt others) thought him capable of. Some thought that he achieved this in *A Time of Gifts*. Yet even the acclaim this book and its successor attracted was double-edged, because it called attention to the fact that the story was incomplete. There was public as well as private pressure on him to finish the trilogy; an article in *Le Monde* mocked him as 'L'Escargot des Carpathes' ('The Snail of the Carpathians'), a soubriquet that he ruefully accepted. The unfinished work hung around his neck to the end, weighing him down. Even in the last letter reproduced here, written long since everyone else had given up hope of the third volume, Paddy reports that he has recently resumed work on it 'after a long pause'.

Paddy's domestic arrangements were unusually chaotic, even by the standards of a freelance writer. For one thing, he found it hard to resist the lure of society, and was capable of travelling across a continent for a party. He seemed unable to concentrate on work in London, and sought out retreats in order to write free of distraction. He became adept at cadging houses from friends: Lady Diana Cooper's farmhouse in Bognor, Niko Ghika's mansion on Hydra, Barbara Warner's cottage in Pembrokeshire, Sir Walter and Lady Smart's manor-house in the Eure. Being usually alone in such places, he wrote to his friends, often inviting them to stay (which somewhat defeated the object). After the war he formed a permanent bond with Joan Rayner, who became his lifelong partner, and, eventually, his wife; but they spent much of the time apart, especially in the first two decades of their relations. This of course meant that they often wrote to each other. Paddy called himself 'Mole' and Joan 'Muskin'. His letters to Joan reveal an aspect of his character that he normally kept hidden, his slides into gloom and depression. He depended on her, not only for encouragement and emotional support, but also for practical and indeed financial assistance. Joan was unquestionably the most important woman in his life. It is appropriate that there are more letters in this volume to her than to any other correspondent.

But before Joan, there was Balasha, whom he had met in Athens in the spring of 1935. Though sixteen years older than him, she was still in her prime, and they fell in love – or, as Paddy might have put it, became 'terrific pals'. They were together almost five years, until separated by the coming of war: after 1939, they would not see each other again for more than a quarter of a century. By the time they renewed contact, Paddy was in love with Joan. Yet Balasha Cantacuzène had been his first love, and seems to have retained a special place in his heart. His earliest post-war letter to her, written over the Easter weekend of 1946, may never have been sent, for reasons we can only speculate about; but it is known that he sent her a letter the following year. She tried to escape from Rumania, but was detained and sent back, and soon afterwards she and her sister were brutally evicted from their ancestral home. Her life afterwards was hard. In 1965 Paddy was able to travel to Rumania, and visited Balasha and her sister after dark, because it was dangerous for Rumanians to be seen to consort with anyone from the

West. Paddy, himself still youthful and vigorous at fifty, was shocked by Balasha's appearance: she was now an old woman, losing her teeth and her hair, the wreck of her former self. His subsequent letters to her reproduced in this volume are written with gallantry and consideration: one has the sense that he is trying to include her in his life, even at long distance.

Joan recognised the sentimental importance of Balasha to Paddy, and wrote to her affectionately as if to a member of the family. She also tolerated Paddy's lovers, and even his casual encounters with prostitutes, confident that he would never leave her. Included in this volume are love letters (some quite frisky) to two younger girlfriends, Lyndall Birch and Ricki Huston. One hilarious letter to the latter refers to the potentially awkward subject of infestation with 'crabs' (pubic lice).

As well as such love affairs, Paddy maintained several long-term friendships with women, conducted largely by letter. Though platonic, there was an element of courtly love in them; it is significant that his ladies were all well born. Among his best letters are those to Lady Diana Cooper (twenty-three years his senior) and to Ann Fleming (twenty-nine years), both of whom he always addressed as 'darling'. In 1980 Paddy dug out his letters from Diana Cooper and reread them, a correspondence that by that time had lasted almost three decades. He was very moved, he told her, 'by this record of shared delights and trust, confidence, warmth and loving friendship, and can't believe my luck, unfaltering for all these years, and still prospering in such a marvellous, happy and treasured bond, light as garlands, as lasting as those hoops of Polonius'. Another long-term correspondence was with Deborah, Duchess of Devonshire ('Debo'), youngest of the lively Mitford sisters, five years his junior. Some believed that Paddy and Debo had once had an affair, but those who knew them best doubted this. In 2008, the correspondence between them over the previous half-century was published as *In Tearing Haste*, edited by Charlotte Mosley. In one of the two subsequent letters published here for the first time, Paddy tells her that he has been 'dipping furtively into *In Tearing Haste*, and enjoying it *almost* as if it was a total stranger and laughing at all the jokes'. Also included are three letters from that book – apart from the two letters to George Seferis, the only letters in this volume that have been previously published in full, though extracts from some of them have been quoted in Artemis Cooper's authorised biography, *Patrick Leigh Fermor: An Adventure* (2012). The witty parody of John Betjeman's verse on pages 85–6 has appeared in a specialist journal, but this is the first time it has been made more widely available.

In the late 1940s, when writing *The Traveller's Tree*, Paddy sought sanctuary in a succession of monasteries in northern France, an experience which itself would provide a subject for a short book, *A Time to Keep Silence* (1957). Reproduced here is a series of letters from these monasteries which gives a vivid picture of monastic life. Writing the letters, and observing how the monks lived, prompted Paddy into reflections on spiritual questions, unusual subjects for him, at least in correspondence. He would return to his favourite monastery, Saint-Wandrille, several times over the next decade. Another, more temporary refuge was the 'stupendous' castle of Passerano, inland from Rome (from its battlements the dome of Saint Peter's was just discernible on the horizon), which he took for the summer of 1959. Paddy had sewn 'a vast heraldic banner, several yards square', to adorn one wall at the end of a large banqueting hall. He was tempted to fly it from the highest tower, as he admitted in a letter to Jock Murray. 'Then, when the Black Castellan of Passerano displays his gonfalon from the battlements, the peasants of the valley can hide their cattle and douse their lights and bolt up their dear ones!' To balance this attack of *folie de grandeur*, he explained that the living conditions were primitive, since the castle had not been inhabited for five hundred years. 'There is no sanitation at all. It's all fieldwork under the trees, and the only lighting is by oil-lamp.'

Yet another refuge was Easton Court at Chagford, an hotel on the edge of Dartmoor run by an unconventional American woman and her English beau. Easton Court had been discovered by Evelyn Waugh, who wrote several of his books there; other writers had followed, including Paddy's friends John Betjeman and Patrick Kinross. From the late 1940s until the early 1960s Paddy stayed often at 'Chaggers', from which he wrote several of the letters included here. He went there to write; though another attraction of the hotel was that it offered the possibility of riding to hounds over the moor with the local hunt three times a week. Here and elsewhere, are lyrical descriptions of nature – riding home at dusk, striding along a ridge, driving into the dawn.

As all this suggests, Paddy rarely stayed in one place long. In fact, he did not have a permanent home until he was almost fifty, in 1964, when he and Joan bought a piece of land overlooking the sea in the Mani, beneath the towering Taygetus mountains near the village of Kardamyli, and began building a house. Letters included here describe the search for a site, negotiations to purchase the land, and plans for the house itself and the surrounding garden. For the first year or two at Kardamyli Paddy and Joan bivouacked in tents as the land was cleared and the house was built. Paddy took a keen interest in every detail of the design and construction, a further distraction from his writing, as he acknowledges in an apologetic letter to Jock Murray. Work on the house would not be complete until the end of the decade.

Letters provided a lifeline from this isolated spot. In an era when international telephoning was difficult and expensive, Paddy and Joan kept their friendships in good repair by correspondence. And, at least for Paddy, it went further than this. Letters were a means of reaching out to those whose company he enjoyed, of making convivial connection across the void. Paddy seems to relish the contact with those to whom he is writing, even if it is only on paper. He is psychologically and often emotionally engaged with his correspondent. At times one senses that Paddy is writing to raise his spirits, as if he knows that his imaginative construction of those of whom he is fond will bring him comfort and cheer.

Some of their friends came to visit, bringing more than a whiff of glamour to this remote region. A letter here describes the arrival of the shipping tycoon Stavros Niarchos by helicopter, which created a sensation when it landed in the Kardamyli market square. Twice Lady Diana Cooper whisked Paddy off for a cruise of the Aegean in Niarchos's second best yacht, *Eros II*. Others came to stay, sometimes for weeks at a time, visitors ranging from John Betjeman to Bruce Chatwin. But much of the time Paddy and Joan were alone at Kardamyli, with just each other and their cats for company, enjoying simple pleasures such as swimming and reading. One letter here tells of surfacing after diving into the sea and almost colliding with a kingfisher, which Paddy watched from a floating position for twenty minutes or so. Another tells of losing his way on an evening walk in the mountains, fighting through the maquis and stumbling down a deep ravine as night fell, trying to stave off panic.

Plenty of stories are recounted in these letters, often very funny ones: an evening with the eccentric Lady Wentworth, then in her eighties, who insisted that her young male guests join her at billiards, and trounced them; the hunt for Byron's slippers in one of the remotest regions of Greece; a disastrous visit to Somerset Maugham's Villa Mauresque. The incongruity of a film crew, headed by the maverick director John Huston, and a starry cast that included Trevor Howard, Juliette Gréco and Errol Flynn, on location in darkest Africa is explored in three letters from a former French colonial territory, now Cameroon. Paddy was there in his temporary capacity as screenwriter, since he had adapted the novel on which the film was based for the screen. Another letter relates the shooting of *Ill Met by Moonlight*, the film based on the story of General Kreipe's abduction. On location in the French Alps Paddy met a screen version of himself. 'It was all pretty queer,' he writes to Debo Devonshire. 'Dirk Bogarde, the actor who is doing one in the film, is absolutely charming – slim, handsome, nice speaking-voice and manner, a super-gent, the ghost of oneself twelve years ago.'

It would be foolish to deny that Paddy had a romantic interest in aristocracy, and all its paraphernalia: genealogy, heraldry, and the rest. Yet if this was snobbery, it was of a comparatively innocuous kind. There was nothing oleaginous in Paddy's relations with his betters. Nor was there any superciliousness towards the lower classes. Paddy was at ease in any company: he could walk into a simple taverna and soon have everyone singing. He took delight in servants who spoke their minds to their masters, such as the Marquess of Bath's butler, whose pointed remarks to His Lordship are repeated here in a letter to Joan. Paddy's letters contain glimpses of the great and the good: a walk in the woods with Harold Macmillan, or conversation over dinner with Camilla Parker-Bowles, for example; but also of the humble: a 'picknick' with the stonemasons at Kardamyli, or a day spent with a lonely cham-bermaid in Saint-Émilion. In a letter to Xan Fielding early in 1972, Paddy reports on a long 'colloquy' in a pub in the Bogside area of 'Free Derry', with a spokesman for the Provisional IRA ('Don't open your mouth on the way out, for Christ's sake!', were the IRA man's parting words), before going on to spend a few days at Chatsworth. Two more different worlds could scarcely be imagined.

'He was the most English person I ever met,' recalled Agnes 'Magouche' Phillips, later Xan Fielding's second wife: 'Everything was *ripping*, and there was more talk of P. G. Wodehouse than of Horace or Gibbon.' Indeed, Paddy himself was something of a Wodehouse hero, in his boyish manner, his innocence, his gentleness, his playfulness with language, his sense of fun, and his tendency to get into scrapes, particularly when driving. (Letters here describe a crash when his car turned over, bashing a wall to escape a head-on collision, and the car being destroyed by a bomb.) There is an absence of malice in his writing, and a related unwillingness to offend. Several letters in this volume express anxiety that casual comments made in private correspondence may wound if broadcast. Towards the end of his life he began to edit those of his own letters in his possession, censoring passages that might cause upset, and adding the occasional explanatory note for his biographer, Artemis Cooper.

Paddy was a philhellene, who lived in Greece for most of his life. Among the letters here are accounts of exuberant jamborees with his old comrades from the Cretan resistance, most of them simple shepherds, with whom he felt the kind of kinship that can be formed only when men experience tragedy and danger together. In Athens after the war Paddy formed close and enduring friendships with Greek artists and intellectuals, especially the poet George Seferis, the painter Niko Ghika and the 'Colossus' of letters, George Katsimbalis; but in the mid 1950s these became strained by the Cyprus emergency. This was 'an argument among friends': two nations, Britain and Greece, which had enjoyed a long history as allies. It was understandable that Greeks should feel a claim on British sympathies, since only a decade earlier, in 1940–1, they had been the only other people fighting Axis troops on the continent of Europe. Paddy felt a conflict of loyalties, between the country of his birth and the country he had made his home. The enmity was such that he felt obliged to quit Greece for a while. His distress is expressed in agonised letters written at the time to his Greek friends, to Lawrence Durrell, and to others.

In general, Paddy was not a political person. An instinctive, old-fashioned conservative, he took little interest in politics except when it touched him in some way. As a young man travelling through Germany in the mid 1930s he had disliked the Nazis he encountered because of their crudeness and their anti-Semitism, but he was indifferent to their rhetoric. In 1967 he reacted cautiously to the military takeover in Greece, the so-called 'Colonels' coup'. In a letter to Joan, who was in England at the time, he suggests that she may know more about what is happening than he does. 'All my spontaneous sympathies (in spite of my official views generally) are against the coup,' he wrote, 'largely because those in the provinces who welcome it are . . . the people one likes least in Greece.' During the regime of 'the Colonels' he became friendly with Tzannis Tzannetakis, then in political exile, and a prominent politician (briefly prime minister) once democracy had been restored.

Paddy was certainly no xenophobe. In a letter written to Rudi Fischer in October 2001 after the attack on the twin towers in New York, he dissents from the description of the terrorists as 'cowards', and refers to President Bush's call for a 'crusade' as a 'gaffe'.

Paddy's magpie mind is evident in his letters. Before setting out on his 'Great Trudge' he had packed *The Oxford Book of English Verse* in his rucksack, and on the walk had committed much to memory, so that he could recite great chunks of poetry, more or less accurately, at will. He would continue to read widely throughout his life, and was able to retain much: repeatedly topping up a cornucopia of knowledge that overflowed into his correspondence. 'I wonder if you fully realised that Harun-al-Rashid sent an elephant called Abulahaz as a present to Charlemagne in AD 802?' Paddy began one letter to Diana Cooper. Perhaps she did realise this, but then again, perhaps she didn't. In another letter to her, Paddy points to 'the enormous amount of buried quotation' in Raymond Asquith's letters to his wife, 'which must mean a vast quantity of shared poetry which was in daily use, and pointless if the other correspondent couldn't spot it'. There is an enormous amount of buried quotation in Paddy's letters too, and one suspects that a significant proportion of this went unrecognised by their recipients. Undoubtedly some will have escaped the editor of this volume.

The letters themselves tell us something of the circumstances in which they were written. The first of Paddy's letters to Balasha in this volume was begun on Easter Saturday, sitting at a café by the waterside; the first letter to Joan was written at a desk in his bedroom at the monastery of Saint-Wandrille, and he stays up until 4.00 in the morning to finish it. Just as Paddy finishes a long letter to his lover Lyndall Birch on an hotel terrace, a gust of wind sweeps the sheets off the table, and he scrambles to save them, 'before they took wing over the balustrade down through the circling wood pigeons to lose themselves below among the ilexes and elderflowers'. Once Paddy was settled at Kardamyli, he seems to have developed a routine of rising early to work, writing letters in the afternoon; they often refer to the need to finish before the post departs ('dashing for the post'). A postscript to a letter to Balasha tells how he had strolled into the village to post it and then reopened the envelope, after finding letters from her waiting there: he explains that he is 'scribbling this in the *kafeneion*, but must stop it now and post it, as the postman is rolling his eyes and tapping his fingers in mock impatience!'

Almost all of Paddy's letters were written by hand, though a handful were then corrected and typed. Some are very long, ten tightly written pages or more; many of those included in this volume have been edited to remove ephemeral content or other material of little interest to the general reader. A few have been edited to half their original length, or even less.

The 174 letters included in this volume have been selected from a hoard (scattered across six countries) at least ten times their number. The standard is such that another editor might have chosen 174 different letters to make a selection of equal quality – and perhaps more will be published in due course. Undoubtedly further letters survive which this editor has not seen, and of course many more must have been discarded or lost over the years. A rough estimate suggests that Paddy wrote between five and ten thousand letters in his adult lifetime. That is an average of several letters a week – and of course, there would have been many weeks when he could not have written any, so the rest of the time he must have been writing more. When one reflects on this, what is most striking is the sheer amount of time and effort Paddy devoted to writing letters. Since many of them record his unhappiness at failing to fulfil his promises to his publisher (not to mention his bank manager), one is forced to conclude that writing letters took up time he could have spent writing books. But was this such a bad thing? Of course, it was regrettable that Paddy never completed his trilogy, and perhaps sadder still that the evening of his life was darkened by anxiety about the unfinished work.

Yet we may take a different view. The letters may sometimes be penned in haste (or even 'in tearing haste'), but they are written in a free-flowing prose that is easier and more entertaining to read than the baroque style of his books, which can seem convoluted and overworked. I would argue that Paddy's correspondence is part of his *oeuvre*, worthy to take its place alongside the work that he published in his lifetime. Now that we can read his letters at length, we can judge their worth. At their best, they are as good as any in the language. They are utterly distinctive: Paddy's personality shines through them. His letters are exhilarating; to borrow an expression he liked to use, they are absolutely 'tip-top'.

ACKNOWLEDGEMENTS

I should like to thank Patrick Leigh Fermor's literary executors – Artemis Cooper, Olivia Stewart and Colin Thubron – for asking me to undertake this work. Each has helped me in various ways, and I am extremely grateful to all three of them. I am especially grateful to Artemis Cooper for her assistance throughout. As Paddy's biographer she knows more about my subject than anyone else alive.

I am also grateful to Artemis for reading the text of this book and providing me with her comments and corrections – as did John Julius Norwich. Since he was the first person to read this book in draft, his enthusiastic comments were particularly encouraging. Two other readers performed this invaluable service for me: Charlotte Mosley, editor of *In Tearing Haste*, Paddy's correspondence with Debo Devonshire, answered some detailed queries and provided useful general recommendations; and my old friend Henry Woudhysen provided pages of detailed notes, demonstrating once again that he is not only a fine scholar but also an excellent editor. Colin Thubron and William Blacker read the proofs, and saved me from several blunders. I must state, however, that any mistakes in the book are my sole responsibility.

In compiling a volume of this kind an editor incurs many debts. My hunt for Paddy's letters has ranged across two continents, and taken me to locations I should otherwise never have seen – a castle perched on a cliff in Tuscany, an apartment overlooking the Tiber in Rome, a romantic Wiltshire garden, the terrace of one of England's grandest houses; and many other interesting locations. I remember, in particular, a day in a Budapest flat with the late Rudi Fischer and his wife Dagmar, who fortified me throughout with strudel and Transylvanian schnapps (tuica). I also recall lunch at a taverna in Athens where the two of us consumed three carafes of retsina. I am grateful to all those who made me welcome, listed below. I am especially grateful to Myrto Kaouki

and Irini Geroulanou of the Benaki Library for allowing me to stay at
Paddy's house at Kardamyli, and to Elpida Beloyannis for making my
stay so comfortable.

I want to thank the following individuals for supplying me with
letters: William Blacker, Hugh and Gabriella Bullock, Max Egremont,
Dagmar von Errfa, the late Rudi Fischer, Denise Harvey, Philippa Jellicoe,
George Katsimbalis Jr., John Julius Norwich, Janetta Parladé, David
Pryce-Jones, Avi Sharon, Ann Shukman and Petros Tzannetakis. A private
collector in Scotland allowed me to transcribe a manuscript letter to
Harold Nicolson in his possession. Lyndall Passerini-Hopkinson (Lyndall
Birch) patiently answered my queries about Paddy's letters to her. Dr
Christine Kenyon Jones kindly gave me advice on Byron's portraits.

I am grateful to Ioanna Providi, former archivist at the Ghika Gallery
in Athens and editor of a forthcoming volume of correspondence
between Paddy and Niko Ghika, for showing me a selection of letters
from the work, and for allowing me to print three of them in this
book; and to her successor Ioanna Moraiti for facilitating this. I am
grateful also to Anna Londou, stepdaughter of George Seferis, and to
Professor Fotios Dimitrakopoulos and Vassiliki D. Lambropoulou, editors
of a volume of correspondence between Paddy, Joan and Seferis published
in 2007 by the Cyprus Research Centre, for permission to publish two
letters from that volume.

I particularly want to thank David McClay and his colleagues at
the National Library of Scotland, where Paddy's archive is kept, as
part of the John Murray archive. David exudes energy and enthusiasm,
and has been exceptionally helpful to me in all sorts of ways. I should
like to acknowledge the work of David's colleague Graham Stewart,
who compiled the inventory of Paddy's archive; and Simon Fenwick,
who did much of the initial sorting and sifting. I should also like to
thank the following archivists and archives for supplying me with
copies of Paddy's letters and giving me permission to publish them:
John Frederick and the Special Collections and University Archives
of the McPherson Library of the University of Victoria, for access to
the papers of John Betjeman; the Special Collections Research Center,
Morris Library, Southern Illinois University, Carbondale, for access to
the Lawrence Durrell Papers; the estate of Enrica Soma Huston; Gayle

Richardson of the Huntington Library in California for access to Patrick Kinross's papers; Helen Marchant, James Towe and the Mitford Archive at Chatsworth for access to the papers of the late Dowager Duchess of Devonshire, and her sister Nancy Mitford; the Rare Books and Special Collections of Princeton University Library, for access to the papers of Raymond Mortimer; Peter Monteith and the Provost and Fellows of King's College, Cambridge, for access to the papers of Frances Partridge and 'Dadie' Rylands; and Elizabeth L. Garver of the Harry Ransom Center, The University of Texas at Austin, for access to the papers of Freya Stark.

I want to extend special thanks to John and Virginia Murray for their hospitality at the John Murray building in Albemarle Street during the days when I was there. It seemed appropriate to be reading Paddy's letters to John's father in the very room where Paddy himself had often laboured on his own manuscripts. If I needed inspiration, his portrait by Derek Hill hung on the staircase outside.

I am much indebted to Peter Mackridge, Emeritus Professor of Modern Greek at Oxford, who translated all Paddy's Greek and provided me with transcriptions.

I also want to thank Ceri Evans for her stalwart help with the transcription. Much of what she typed might as well have been written in Rumanian in that it was so far from her own experience, but she did an excellent job all the same.

I should like to thank Roland Philipps for his calm editorial guidance; Caroline Westmore for her assured and skilful handling of the mechanics of turning the typescript into a printed book; Juliet Brightmore for expert picture research; Hilary Hammond for copyediting and making helpful suggestions; Jane Birkett for proofreading; and my old friend Douglas Matthews, for compiling the index. I also wish to thank my agent, Andrew Wylie, and Tracy Bohan of the Wylie Agency, for their steadfast support.

EDITORIAL NOTE

Readers should be aware that Paddy's letters are not necessarily reproduced in full: I have chosen to omit long travelogues and the more mundane passages which often refer to practical arrangements of ephemeral interest. Excisions are indicated by ellipses. I have taken it upon myself to correct Paddy's spelling errors, particularly in the use of foreign words and names, though I decided to retain his delightful spelling of 'picknick'. I have also standardised his somewhat erratic punctuation. As he himself would frequently lament, his handwriting is notoriously difficult to decipher, so I have sometimes been obliged to resort to guesswork, and no doubt my guesses have been wrong on occasion. A few words have remained stubbornly illegible. I have used square brackets for simple translations or other brief expository material, to avoid unnecessary annotation. Words that Paddy underlined are usually presented in italics, to conform to standard publishers' practice. My own footnotes are listed numerically at the end of each letter; I have retained a few of Paddy's footnotes, which are indicated with an asterisk and printed at the foot of the page.

Most of the quotations in my introductory passages are taken from Ben Downing's interview, which appeared after Paddy's death in the *Paris Review*; or from the volume of correspondence between Paddy and Debo Devonshire, published under the title *In Tearing Haste*. Short profiles of the people mentioned most often in the letters, including most of the addressees, are provided in a *dramatis personae* at the end of the book.

THE LETTERS

Paddy was twenty-four years old, and on a mushroom-gathering picnic in Rumania, when he heard the news that Germany had invaded Poland. He hurried back to England to enlist. Many years later he told his biographer that he came home in 1939 expecting to die. 'I had read somewhere that the average life of an infantry officer in the First World War was eight weeks, and I had no reason to think that the odds would be much better in the Second. So I thought I might as well die in a nice uniform.' Claiming Irish descent, he inveigled his way into the Irish Guards. 'I joined "the Micks" in the ranks in 1939, same day as Iain Moncreiffe and other friends, though he was in the Scots Guards,' he later explained (PLF to Rudi Fischer, 2 February 1982). 'It was the first time future Guards officers went through the ranks, and a very good idea, though it was tremendously tough. We were all from the five Guards regiments – Grenadier, Coldstream, Scots, Irish and Welsh – trained in a squad of thirty at the Gd's Depot at Caterham by the Coldstream. All had been fixed up before joining through mild pull etc., I'm sorry to say.'

The letter that follows was written to a fellow recruit while Paddy was in hospital recovering from a bout of severe pneumonia which had almost killed him. Adrian Pryce-Jones (1919–68) was the younger son of a colonel in the Coldstream Guards. His brother Alan, later a travel writer and journalist, had been briefly engaged to Joan Eyres Monsell, Paddy's post-war companion and, eventually, his wife.

To Adrian Pryce-Jones   Redhill County Hospital
1 February 1940   Earlswood Common
                                   Redhill
                                   Surrey

My dear Adrian,

    I liked your letter, and it really was kind of you to write at such a moment of stress. God, how pleased you must have been to have escaped from that jail. My fate is positively tragic. Apparently, as I have missed over five weeks' training through illness, the authorities are regretfully obliged to *backsquad* me; that is, I am to wait till they are at the six and a half weeks (the next Brigade Squad), finish with them and proceed with them to Sandhurst for the April intake. Isn't this wretched? I am more vexed and disappointed than I can say; obviously, because it means the Depot for three weeks, and a long pointless wait before that, but still more because I would have so loved being at Sandhurst with you and our other friends. A still graver reason for concern presents itself: as the Irish Guards have only twelve vacancies, all being competed for in your course, my commission with them may be jeopardised, as there are fifteen candidates, and I don't suppose they can very well hold one up for me, as there is such a crush. It may turn out all right, but if it doesn't it will be very sad and disappointing. I can't think of any other regiment I would like to join; and anyway, it would be wretched to be gazetted out of the Brigade. Why did I ever fall sick?

Really, you know, owing to those butcher boys at the Depot hospital, I very nearly died. I felt myself all through one night at the brink of turning into a lump of carrion. Luckily, all goes well now, and I am feeling very well, though I must remain here[1] another fortnight . . .

But that is enough about the horrid Depot, which you are probably beginning to forget. I want to know all about Sandhurst, if you can extricate yourself for half an hour from the maelstrom and write a fruity letter – uniform – who is there – juicy bits of scandal etc. – other candidates for our Regiments etc. Are you enjoying it? It must be silk and satin after Caterham. Please tell me all.

Here, life flows by in a mild lotus-eating atmosphere. Lots of books and fruit and flowers, in the middle of which I lie pale and endearing, with an attendant chorus of surprisingly personable and charming nurses. I have invented a fascinating brave, hurt, bittersweet expression, with eyebrows wrinkled up over a twisted smile, and I use this on them whenever I want some special favour. (Lights on late, drink etc.). It works every time. Family have been here several times, also sweet Prue Branch and Guy,[2] the ones I told you about. Last night something marvellous happened. I am just being tucked up for the night, when I hear strange foreign noises outside the door, which opens, and in bursts Anne-Marie Callimachi,[3] followed by Costa.[4] She was dressed in black satin and dripping with mink, with pearls and diamonds crusted at every possible point, topped by the maddest Schiaparelli hat I've ever seen. Then Costa, who is very dark, with a huge grin, and quite white hair at the age of thirty. He was dressed in a bright green polo jersey over which he wore a very long black new coat with an immense astrakhan collar: both laden with huge presents. The nurses were struck dumb. Shrill squeals burst from us all, and then we were gabbling the parleyvoo like apes. The nurses fled in disorder. Then of course, they couldn't get a taxi as Anne-Marie had left Rolls Royces etc. in London; but they had their luggage, and stopped the night at the hospital! We all pretended they were married, so the Sister, with girlish squeaks, got their room ready, with screens coyly arranged between the beds. By this time Costa was telephoning the Ritz to say Her Highness wouldn't be back that night, his voice echoing down all the passages. The sensation in the hospital was absolutely phenomenal. Huge princely coronets on the luggage – such nighties! Slippers! Oh!! The hospital hasn't recovered yet, and my glamour-value among the nurses is at fever pitch.

It was great fun. We talked and laughed idiotically late into the night, Anne-Marie narrating her latest experiences, which, as usual, were quite extraordinary. I dramatised the Depot to them. I told them about you, and as they know your brother Alan well, Anne-Marie was very curious to know what you were like. I said you were just a naughty little jazz-baby. Nothing could have intrigued her more.

They left this morning, Anne-Marie leaving a munificent cheque for the Hospital Fund, which I tendered with a languid gesture to the head doctor. Their passage will not be forgotten for *ages*!

Alors, mon petit Adrien, te voilà déjà presqu'un petit officier dans la Garde Galloise! Ce que vous devez rigoler là-bas, vous autres. Oh la la! Je me rouge de jalousie. Je vous emmerde! Et royalement![5]

My address during my sick leave is at my sister's: c/o Mrs
Fenton, St Arild's House, Kington, near Thornbury, Gloucestershire.
Don't forget to send your civilised address when you write. I will
be a day or two in London before going to my bucolic retreat. We
might meet and make whoopee. Helen Hardinge[6] suggested I
might go and stay a bit at Windsor, but it isn't supposed to be
frightfully healthy there, so I don't think I will. May go to the
Sitwells for a bit.[7]

Remember me affectionately to Desmond and Trevor and Iain[8]
and Hal & Michael, Nevill, Douglas, Jeremy, and all the boys. I can't
tell you how I will miss being with you all there. Pity Holland[9] &
the wicked Baron aren't there too!

Every kind of good wish to yourself, *mon petit*, and very much
luck for a successful course at Sandhurst.

Love Paddy

---

[1] In hospital.

[2] Flying Officer Guy Rawstron Branch (b. 1913) and his wife, Lady Prudence, née
Pelham, daughter of the 6th Earl of Chichester. They were married the previous March.
PLF and his Rumanian lover, Princess Balasha Cantacuzène, had stayed with Branch's
family when they visited London in 1937. Just over six months after this letter was
written Branch would be dead, killed in action over the English Channel during the
Battle of Britain.

[3] The Rumanian Princess Anne-Marie Callimachi, a cousin of PLF's lover, Balasha
Cantacuzène.

[4] The Greek photographer Costa Achillopoulos, later PLF's collaborator on *The
Traveller's Tree* (1950).

[5] 'Now, my dear Adrian you are already almost an officer in the Welsh Guards. What
fun you lot must be having down there. *Oh la la!* I am *red* with envy. Up yours.
And royally!'

[6] The wife of Sir Alec Hardinge, Private Secretary to King George VI. The Hardinges
had an apartment in Windsor Castle. It was through them that PLF had wangled his
way into the Irish Guards.

[7] After PLF had been introduced by Costa Achillopoulos to Sacheverell 'Sachie' Sitwell
and his wife Georgia in 1937, he spent many happy weekends at Weston Hall, their
Jacobean house in Northamptonshire.

[8] Iain Moncreiffe (1919–85), later Sir Iain Moncreiffe of that Ilk, MP and genealogist.

[9] Antony Holland (see note 5 on page 92).

It is in time of war that the public school system that so many of you laugh at, is really put to the test. You may scoff at Latin and Greek, Virgil and Homer, but its value is character training . . .

On his recovery, Paddy expected to become a regular officer with the Irish Guards. But it did not turn out this way. 'When I was finishing my recruit time at the Depot, I had tempting promises of future exciting intelligence work in Greece, and like a fool, talked about it.' The Intelligence Corps was very interested in the fact that he spoke French, German, Rumanian and Greek, despite his 'below average' record. 'The Col. of the Micks, who I knew quite well (Tom Vesey), had me up to Birdcage Walk (Wellington Barracks) and asked me if this was true. I said it was, and he was very cutting about it. "What's the point of us training you as an ensign if you go buggering off on some ghastly Intelligence rubbish?" I was given a week to decide. If I hung on with the Micks as an officer, I would, morally, have been bound to eschew all tempting "I" offers. So, most reluctantly, I went into the Intelligence Corps. Very unhappy, because I loved the Irish Guards. But I was much more use where I went, as it turned out, than I would have been as an ensign in the Brigade' (PLF to Rudi Fischer, 2 February 1982). Paddy was posted to Greece, and, after the Axis invasion, to Egypt, from which he was infiltrated on to the island of Crete, to work with the resistance against the German occupiers.

Natalie Moss was the mother of Paddy's wartime comrade Billy Moss, his second-in-command in the daring and successful operation to capture General Kreipe.

To Natalie Moss
15 November 1944   In the Wilds[1]

Dear Mrs Moss,

I do hope you got a letter I wrote to you this summer in hospital,[2] and thank you very much for your kind telegram. It *was* nice of you to send it, and I do hope Billy thanked you for it as I asked him to, as I couldn't write at the time.

Unfortunately, when I was let out of hospital, Billy had left on a fresh adventure, that we had planned to carry out together, but which I was too ill to take part in. He carried it out most brilliantly and bravely, and, as you will have heard, has been recommended for a very well-deserved bar to his MC. Meanwhile, I went to stay with Lady Spears, our minister to Syria's wife,[3] in the cool mountains near Beirut, and just as I was finishing my stay, who should arrive by plane but Billy, just arrived back from our island hunting-ground,[4] where he had ambushed a German column, knocked out ten trucks, killed forty Germans, and taken fifteen prisoners. Finally an armoured car appeared, which Billy put out of action by climbing on the back and throwing hand-grenades down the turret until the cannon stopped firing. It was a really splendid and brave achievement.

From Beirut we drove off to Damascus together, and spent a very happy and gay five days there and in Beirut, after which we flew back to Cairo, and returned to our home – 'Tara'[5] – of which you must have heard so much! We share it with Sophie Tarnowska,[6] Billy McLean[7] and David Smiley.[8] But Bill had to leave soon, and I a month later, so now poor Sophie is holding the fort all alone. She is a most charming girl and looks after our comic household of rather wild young men like a very responsible younger sister. I left for the place where Bill and I caught the Hun General three weeks ago, and am writing from there. Billy is absolutely all right, and will probably be back in 'Tara' soon. I hope to meet him there for Christmas.

Billy is a really magnificent chap, and it would be hard to think of anyone more universally loved in the Middle East. He is one of the few really great friends I have made during the war, and this island seems very bleak without his gay company.

You must not get worried if you hear from him only irregularly, as posts are sometimes difficult from these out of the way places. Perhaps you have news of him already. If not I'm sure you very soon will. Thank you again for your kind sympathy while I was ill, and every kind wish.

 Yrs very sincerely
 Paddy L-F

[1] Soldiers on active service were forbidden to reveal their location.

[2] 'The rigors of a year and a half of Cretan cave life, it seems, suddenly struck me with an acute rheumatic infection of the joints, akin to paralysis. After two months in a Cairo hospital – where King Farouk once kindly sent me a magnum of champagne – I was sent to convalesce in Lebanon.'

3 Lady Spears (1886–1968), the American novelist Mary Borden. Known as 'May', she was married to Major-General Sir Edward Spears (1886–1974), diplomat, army officer and MP, noted for his role as a liaison officer between British and French forces in two world wars.

4 Crete.

5 A spacious villa on Gezira Island, inhabited by a group of high-spirited Special Operations Executive (SOE) officers and named by them 'Tara' after the title used by the High Kings of Ireland. 'With its ballroom and a piano borrowed from the Egyptian Officers' Club, and funded by our vast accumulations of back pay, it became famous – or notorious – for the noisiest and most hilarious parties in wartime Cairo. At one of these, fired by the tinkle of a dropped glass, everyone began throwing their glasses through the windows until not a pane was left.'

6 Countess Zofia Roza Maria Jadwiga Elzbieta Katarzyna Aniela Tarnowska (1917–2009), known as 'Sophie', later Mrs Billy Moss. She and her first husband, a cousin, had been forced to flee their native Poland after the German invasion in 1939. She lived at Tara with a fictitious chaperone, Madame Khayatt, who supposedly suffered from 'distressingly poor health' and thus was always indisposed when visitors called.

7 Lieutenant Colonel Neil Loudon Desmond 'Billy' McLean DSO (1918–86), SOE officer, and later an MP.

8 Colonel David de Crespigny Smiley MC and Bar (1916–2009), special forces and intelligence officer.

In 1935, at the age of twenty, Paddy had fallen in love with Marie-Blanche Cantacuzène, known as 'Balasha'. Sixteen years his senior, Balasha was a princess from one of the great dynasties of eastern Europe, married to a Spanish diplomat, who had left her for another woman. She and Paddy met in Athens, and spent the next eighteen months in Greece, before making their way by steamer to Constanța, on the Black Sea, and thence by train and coach inland to the dales of eastern Moldavia, where Balasha's family owned 'a rambling, down-at-heel country house' called Băleni. 'It was surrounded by hills and trees and full of books, there was snow on the windowsills all winter, and outdoors meant sleighs or horses: a Tolstoy or Turgenev kind of life. The family were Moldavian Cantacuzènes, and, as in certain spheres in pre-revolutionary Russia, French was the language used. They were civilised, warm-hearted, amusing people, and devoted to literature . . .'

'It was a magical house, and the time I spent in it seemed to take the place of the university I was missing; I read more there, and in several languages, than anywhere else in my life. I don't think it is entirely the decades of patina which may have accumulated between now and my early

twenties which makes me say that the charm, intelligence, humour, fun, and
range and stimulus of conversation at Băleni equal anything I can remember
since.'

Paddy wrote the letter that follows on a table by the water's edge, overlooking the narrow channel that flows between the Greek island of Poros
and the mainland of the Peloponnese; on the other side of the channel a
path runs uphill to the watermill of Lemonodassos, where he had spent
two 'blissful summers' with Balasha ten years before, reading, painting and
swimming. The two lovers had last seen each other in September 1939. Now,
almost seven years later, he was in love with another woman, though he still
felt loyal towards Balasha. This letter tries to make sense of his conflicting
feelings. It seems probable that it was never sent.

To Balasha Cantacuzène
Easter Saturday 1946   Poros

My own darling,

The clock has suddenly slipped back ten years, and here I am
sitting in front of our café in the small square, at a green-topped
iron table on one of those rickety chairs. The marble-lantern, with
its marine symbols – anchors and dolphins – is within reach of
my arm; the drooping tree has been cut down. But the same old
men, in broad shady hats, snowy *fustanellas* [skirt-like garments
traditionally worn by men in southern Europe] and moustaches, sit
conversing quietly over their *narghiléhs* [shisha pipes]. They all bowed
and greeted me warmly, but soberly as if I had seen them only
yesterday; my hand still aches from the iron grasp of Christo, the
smiling Mongolian *kafedzi* [café-proprietor] – 'Where's Kyria
Balasha? How is she?' they all cry. – Mitso the boatman, Spiro's
coumbáros [god-brother] at the grocer's shop, the man at the *zacharo-
plasteion* [shop selling sweet cakes], the barber, the chaps in the little
walled restaurant, and a dozen whiskered friends – especially Tomás,
the one armed forest-guard, all down here for the Easter ceremonies.
Loud shrieks of delight from Uncle Alcibiades's daughter, married
now. Best of all, three tall young men – guess who? Niko, Yanni and
Andrea, and a strapping Tasso in his teens. Spiro is up at the mill,

with thirteen-year-old Kosta and Katrina, and, isn't it amazing?, ten-years-old Evtychia! Devout Marina is across the water at Galata, busy at her religious observances. Stop! Who do you think has just come and sat at my table, flinging an affectionate arm round my shoulders? Yanni, our boatman, who taught us the names of the winds, and always rowed us to Plaka. His brother Mitso told him I was here. He is a sailor now, veteran of countless battles, and as charming and gay and simple as ever and sends heaps of love to you. Ἔ! Ἡ Μπαλάσσα! Ἡ Μπαλάσσα! Τι καλὴ γυναίκα! ['Ah! Balasha! Balasha! What a nice lady!'] They all adore us both here, and are real friends.

I arrived last night, and have not been to the hill yet. I am going today with Yanni and tomorrow for Easter Sunday, where Spiro is going to roast a huge lamb, and all our friends will assemble from the lemon-forest to eat it. I'll take a camera with me, and send you lots of photographs.

A caïque brought me here – the *Hydra*, the *Pteroti*, and *Avli* were sunk by the Germans – and it was very beautiful. I missed you dreadfully, Balasha darling, as we slid over those silk-smooth waters between dreaming islands: the same soft air caressed our arms and hands and temples, the same light wind carried the smell of pine-needles and thyme to one's nostrils, and I had the same argonaut plus conquistador feeling of being the first traveller to cross these ancient waters and gulfs and lagoons. The moment the caïque anchored at the quay, I jumped ashore, and walked to the monastery, along that lovely road winding under the pines overhanging the steep timbered cliffs, and the broken rocks half sunk in blue-green water, the lulling sound of whose splash and murmur reached us through the pine-branches. All at once the white monastery came into sight, and I was walking past the trickling spring, and the ravine full of plane-trees and fig-trees, and up the worn steps to the terrace with its one cypress, the sea, the sphinx-rock and the castle island beyond, and the *vounò* [mountain], with the mill glimmering palely in its cloud of olives and lemons and cypresses and walnut-trees. The courtyard of the monastery, with its thick round arches and cypress-shaded church and

luminous walls, snowy and cream-coloured and blue in shadow, was
heavy with the scent of orange-blossom. As I left, the first cuckoo,
alarming and strange, called from the woods above. The light failed
along the road back . . . You divined more than saw, the trees and
rocks, and the poppies in the young grass. The streets were empty
in Poros – the whole village was in church for the Entombment,
and the streets and stucco houses and white staircases were quiet
under thousands of low and bright stars, the lights sinking still
reflections into the windless water. Later, from the window of the
Averoff Hotel – where the toothless crone used to cackle us a
welcome – I watched the hundreds of candles of the Epitaphios
procession[1] crawl along the sea-path from Galata, the reflections of
fireworks flowering and fading and the drone of chanting, faintly
crossing the water.

It is seven in the morning now, and all glitters and dances under a
clear sky. Through the masts of the caïques, the Argive mountains unfold,
the fleece of the olive trees grey-green and silver and gold where the
sun touches them, the hollows and branching stream-beds a cloudy
purple. Gulls float idly over the caïque sails.

Easter Sunday
Darling, I am again at the *narghiléh* café, quiet, happy, sun-
drenched, and filled with the most terrific '*dor*' [longing] for you.
Yesterday, I got Yanni to row me to the bay of Artemis, and lay in
the sun all the afternoon, watching the shadows change on the
island. Towards dusk, I shook myself, and walked through the
wood where the white horse used to gallop aimlessly, and I used
to talk of half-submerged vessels. Then through that sloping
golden glade to the minute church, the narrow path till the place
where the donkey used to pace round and round, drawing up the
water, and up through the lemon-groves, to the mill. My darling,
it was a moment I had been aching for, and, of course, dreading,
for the last six years but, Boodle,[2] there it was, as if nothing *had*
changed; I stood and watched through the branches: Marina busy
at the oven, Spiro, cheeks puffed with feigned and endearing
exertion, emptying lemons into huge baskets – τὰ καλάθια – and

a boy and a girl that I recognised as Kosta and Katrina, helping
him. You can imagine the cries of welcome when I ventured onto
the terrace, Marina smiling with her hands crossed on her apron,
Spiro laughing and gesticulating with clownish glee. Evtychia is a
thoughtful little girl of ten with dark bobbed hair and a mauve
jersey. When kisses and greetings were over, all the talk was of
you. 'When is she coming?' I said, Soon. We sat on the wall and
talked for hours, (Kosta, still with those affectionate eyes and
sweet smile, holding my hand proprietorially in his) of our old
life: your pictures, my illness, the rat-bite, the night Hector got
lost, climbing the walnut-tree, the Panegyri of St Panteleïmon, the
autumn storm. The *magazí* [shop] is closed, as Spiro can get no
wine, and as it got dark, I reluctantly said goodbye to them till
the morrow, Easter Sunday, and wandered down through the trees
to the Plaka where Mitso was waiting with his βάρκα [boat], and
over the still water to Poros. On the way down under the lemon
leaves, I kept looking back for your long shadow, in blue trousers,
white shirt and *bélisaires*, asking me to sing the Raggle Taggle
Gypsies. Yanni our boatboy was waiting at the quay, and we went
out fish-spearing with a carbide lamp on the front of the boat for
a few hours, across that stretch of water between the Dragoumis
and Tombazi houses. The bottom of the sea looked fascinating in
the bright glare of the lamp – rocks feathered with anemones and
prickly with urchins, octopuses and cuttle-fish coiled in the rock
crevices, silver troops of fish lying silent two fathoms below, or
darting off in alarm at the sudden lunges of Yanni's long, bamboo-
shafted trident. He speared masses of them, and each catch was
greeted with shrieks of delight by the two barefooted boys who
were rowing. I got one *barbouni* [red mullet]. We got back in time
to brush our hair, and join the swarm of Poriots [inhabitants of
Poros] in the church for the Anástasis. There must have been
1,000 people in the square up the hill for the Resurrection, each
eager face lit by its own candle. At the ΧΡΙΣΤΟΣ ΑΝΕΣΤΗ!
['Christ is risen!'] a great jangle of bells broke out, and the
sputter and swish of fireworks, cannons firing at the fort, and all
the candles danced up and down. *Adevărat a înviat!* ['Truly he is

risen!']³ Then to Yanni's house at the end of the village, a giant meal with clashing eggs, and back to bed, a bit drunk and very happy.

Today has been perfect too. I got to the hill early in the morning, having drunk two okes [carafes] of retsina with Yorgo and Stamatina, the shaggy little shepherd couple from the Vonnò, at the Plaka. We talked of our boiling day in that high desert, of all the water we drank as we lay panting under the plane-tree by the spring and the oleander bushes. They are as shaggy and small and brown and sly as ever, Yorgo with awkward hands resting on the shaft of his crook, Stamatina's pretty wrinkled face smiling out of its black headdress. She has a new papoose slung in a sort of leather sling from the saddle of her mule. They are as scorched and penetrated by the sun as a couple of cicadas.

At the mill, we had a huge banquet under the vine-trellis – paschal lamb and retsina and πατάτες φούρνου [baked potatoes] and onions and more retsina, and sang for hours. I made a fresh entry in our big white book (jealously hidden throughout the occupation, now the mill's pride and future heirloom), your health was most feelingly drunk by us all, Marina sang 'Kolokotrones' in her thin, true little voice, blushing like a girl at our applause. We danced terrific Syrtos and Tsamikos [traditional folk dances] (my hands still ache from the foot-slapping!), and all the time, the sun slanted down on us through the young vine-leaves overhead, and through its frame of vine and fig-leaves, our amphitheatre of orange and cypress and olive wavered down to the glittering sea and the island and monastery, and remembered bits of rock – lionlike and smoky as ever – on the blue looking glass that stretched away till it melted hazily with the sky.

I dived overboard and swam for a while in the cold sea on the way back and now sit at the old table, with the caïque masts thick in front, the salt flaking on my new-burnt arms, the sunlight still warm in my relaxed limbs and bones. This is where I wrote that first sonnet when you went to Athens, and I almost feel that tomorrow I will see you walking down the gangway of the Pteroté, in your grey wool Athens suit, silk shirt, blue-and-white tie, and small round white hat. The night is still and warm, friendly figures cross the golden light of the café windows like Karagosi men in their crisp *fustanellas*, and a mandoline and a zither sound their small tinkling cascade of music into the quiet air, answered by a lazy half audible *amané* [an improvised song in the Turkish style] from the steep white arched and staircased labyrinth of houses behind.

This is a kind and happy and simple corner of the world. All the misery and murder and *pumpute* [upheaval?] of the last seven years have shed themselves away like a hateful dream, and I am back for a few precious days in a *glâbre* [innocent], beautiful world inhabited by people like you and Pomme and Constantin⁴ and the two Alexanders⁵ and Guy and Prue [Branch]. I send you, darling, all this. We must continue to hide here sometime, and feel that love and friendship are something separate after all, impregnably so, from the passage of time and its horrors and cruelties and callousnesses. I got your lovely letter, and am answering it when I get back to Athens tomorrow – many pages are already written. This is a parenthesis in it, designed to bring you the smell of the sea and of lemon-trees, and the love and greetings of all your friends in the island and Lemonodassos, and mine.

Hugs and kisses and *gouffis*⁶ to Pomme and Constantin and Ins [their daughter Ina], and quite special *bessonnades* and hugs to Alexander M.; and to Alexander V., and all, all that and more to you, my dearest darling, from

     Paddy

---

¹ The Good Friday custom of priest and congregation processing around the parish carrying a bier upon which is an icon of Christ (often in the form of a cloth) adorned with spring flowers.

² A term of endearment.

³ This is a standard form of Easter greeting and response in the Orthodox Church, except that PLF has provided his response in Rumanian.

⁴ Balasha's younger sister Hélène (1900–83), always known as 'Pomme', and her husband Constantin Donici.

⁵ Balasha's cousin, Alexander Mourouzi, with whom PLF had explored the Danube delta in 1936; unidentified.

⁶ A term of endearment – as is '*bessonnades*'.

This letter was written after Paddy had visited Corfu as part of a lecture tour on behalf of his employers, the British Council. In 1946 Greece was volatile, and would soon ignite into civil war between left and right. Paddy's tour was part of a policy to counter the anti-Western propaganda of the Communists. To the delight of his audience, he had spoken not on cultural subjects, but instead about the wartime operation to kidnap General Kreipe.

Paddy and his companion Joan Rayner had been staying with Marie Aspioti (1909–2000), a writer, poet and publisher who ran the British Council Institute in Corfu, an island with strong British links. (From 1815 it had been a British protectorate, until sovereignty was transferred to Greece in 1864.) According to one of those who knew her, Aspioti 'loved England', and 'gave her whole life to the Institute'. Like Paddy, she would be dismayed by British policy in Cyprus in the mid 1950s.

Almost thirty years later, on 5 August 1973, she wrote to tell him that 'your letter of July 1946 brings me back with a rush those delightful times and is as fresh and alive as when you wrote it. Only the ink has faded.'

To Marie Aspioti   Zante
12 July 1946   British Council
                                                          Corfu

Marie dear,

Here we are still wandering your sleepy seas, malingering in island after island, as if delayed by those spells that always hindered travellers 'round the coasts of Greece; here in Zante, our Circe (or Nausicaa, Ariadne, Calypso) is Miss Crowe, and I am writing from her terrace at (guess what time?) seven in the morning, under a huge mulberry tree, overlooking the bay, and it's surrounded by trees and churches and palazzos, and sprinkled with ships. Miss Crowe is a magnificent old English woman of about seventy, and comes of one of those families that remained behind after the Heptanese was returned to Greece.[1] She looks like a retired British Admiral in an eighteenth-century picture, with high-bridged nose, husky frowning eyebrows and severe blue eyes; an array of telescopes hang among the prints on the walls, and as she paces the terrace – which becomes the quarter-deck of a frigate – stick in

THE BRITISH COUNCIL
Patron: H. M. THE KING.

Represent...
R. D...

27 Capodistriou 3rd floor
CORFU
Telephone : 36

Zante, —
12ᵗʰ July 1946.

Xavier dear, here we are still wandering your sleepy seas, malingering in island after island, as if delayed by those spells that always ... hindered travellers round the coasts of Greece; Here in Zante, our Circe (or Nausicaa, Ariadne, Calypso) is Miss Crowe, and I am writing from her terrace at (guess what time?) 7 in the morning, under a huge ... tree, overlooking the bay and its surrounding ... fatness and churches and ... and sprinkled with ships. ... in a magnificent old English ... at 70 and comes of one ... that ... behind after ... was returned ... Greece. She ... retired ... century picture with her ... wore, husky ... and ... blue eyes; an array of ... hang among the prints on the wall, and as she paces the terrace — which becomes the quarter-deck of a frigate — stick in hand, only slightly stooping, and followed hand, only slightly stooping, and followed by a rippling wake of old and half-blind dogs, you can almost hear the distant booming of broadsides. She sits up late drinking her wine and chain-smoking with a dog on her lap, telling long travel stories in a racy Edwardian idiom. She is a die-hard Tory, and has long arguments every day with Mr Chronopoulos, who lives in Solomos's house next door, a violent Whig who has spent most of his life in England. He is 84 years old, thin and wiry as a hawk, but alert and argumentative and charming, though I believe he is a tyrannical demon to descendants that vaguely surround him in an awed and much less intelligent swarm. He reminisces, and gets angry about, parliamentary debates that he attended in his youth, at which the speakers were Gladstone, Disraeli, Bright, Parnell and Sir Charles Dilke, and Miss Crowe rattles testily on the ground with her walking-stick.

Huddling into the crowded caïque at three in the morning, with you shuddering and waving on the quay in evening dress, and all of us the worse for drink, was the perfect way to leave Corfu after that perfect fortnight. We fell asleep in the bows among coils of rope, waking long after dawn, feeling gloomy at having left Corfu, but excited about Cephalonia.

There was nothing very welcoming about it – No Marie, no Dicky! – but the [Anglo-Hellenic] League is run by a very nice old man called Mr Alevizatos. I gave one lecture, it went fairly well, I think. A very po-faced and irritating old English woman said 'So charming. You must get more lecturers to come in the winter, when we have nothing to do in the evenings. We get so tired of bridge . . . ' Masses of eager boys and girls were crowding in the doorways, too shy to come in, during the lecture, and when Joan suggested they should come and fill the empty places, she said, with a vinegary smile: 'I don't believe in pampering children' . . .

There was quite a rough sea on during the passage here, and a great gale. To the admiration of the caïque captain, Joan and I were the only passengers who didn't get sick. We felt smug and Britannic and could almost feel bulldogs' ears growing . . .

love Paddy

¹ The seven Ionian Islands are traditionally known as the Heptanese. British rule in the Ionian Islands came to an end in 1864.

Towards the end of Paddy's lecture tour, he and Joan were joined by his wartime comrade, Xan (Alexander) Fielding. The three of them visited Lawrence Durrell, then living in Rhodes in a little house with a tangled garden which concealed a Turkish graveyard. 'We sat up in my churchyard until three every morning reading aloud,' Durrell recalled. 'It was an amazing sojourn, spent in talk and music and feasting,' wrote Paddy in a memoir of Durrell. 'Strange things always happened in his company and one afternoon, in the ruins of ancient Camirus, wine-sprung curiosity sent the four of us crawling on hands and knees through the bat-infested warren of underground conduits. We climbed out covered in droppings and dust and cobwebs.' As their clothes were torn and filthy, they decided to continue their exploration naked, while Joan recorded their japes in photographs. Dared to jump on to the top of a twelve-foot column, Xan made a tremendous leap, maintaining his footing though the column rocked alarmingly; he then struck a pose as Eros for a photograph.

In a letter written around this time to his regular correspondent Henry Miller, Durrell referred to Paddy as 'a wonderful mad Irishman [sic]' who 'speaks five languages really well . . . quite the most enchanting maniac I've ever met.' He had spent 'a lovely week' with Paddy and Xan, he told Miller. 'Can't tell you what a wonderful time I had talking books – first time for years.'

To Lawrence Durrell
18 December 1946   Athens

My dear Larry,

    I'm very ashamed of myself and live for the days we spent virtually as your guests in Rhodes. With you, Eve,¹ Joan and Xan altogether, it was [the] perfect ending of a lovely summer. But it was the end, and it has been autumn and winter weather till we got back to Athens last week, except for a week or so of the καλοκαιράκι τοῦ Ἁγίου Δημητρίου [Indian summer] in the islands.

I found Joan a week after leaving you, entwined like a sleeping beauty in the island of Patmos, and stayed there several days, rainy and thunderous ones like those described in your story. I thought very seriously of settling down there this winter. It is one of the most extraordinary places I've ever seen. We left for Samos by caïque, but a storm blew up, and we were forced to put in at a tiny island called Arki. As Joan and I stepped ashore, our bags were grasped in silence by a fisherman, who led us up a winding path through laurels to a large white house, quite alone among vineyards, but with all chimneys smoking. An old gentleman with white whiskers welcomed us gravely on the threshold, as though he had been expecting us, and led us into a great flagged kitchen, where in the shake of a lamb's tail, we were seated with ouzos and mezés. A huge handsome old wife was clanking pots over the fire aided by an army of daughters of outstanding beauty, the son of the house cleaning his fowling-piece with a bunch of partridges beside him. Dogs and cats were everywhere. Any amount of shepherds and fishermen were sitting about talking or eating, and we were soon given a delicious meal – avgolemono [egg yolk and lemon juice] soup, fish, jugged hare, and a splendid wine. All this with scarcely an enquiry as to where we had come from. In fact we were addressed by our names with a gentle, incurious courtesy. It was very strange, and a bit eerie, like the arrival of Odysseus at the palace of Nausicaa's father,[2] or the way-laying and entertainment of travellers by lonely magnificoes in Hungary. It turned out that ships are washed up there so often that their entertainment had become a matter of course. 'One day last year,' Mr Kalantakis said (he's a Cretan) 'the sea brought us seventy-two guests'. We stayed there four days, living in lovely rooms and eating and drinking like heroes, and when the wind changed, said goodbye to our charming and munificent host with real intentions to return another summer. One of our fellow naufragés [castaways] was a Karaghioziman [shadow-puppeteer], unfortunately without his gear, but [he] gave quite a good conjuring display to a kitchen crammed with neighbours and dependants, ending up with the most frightening bit of magic I've ever seen. He made us clench our hands tightly together, saying he would turn them to wood; shouted ONE! TWO! THREE! Up till ἐννέα! [nine!] Τὰ χέρια σας εἶναι ξύλο – δὲν λύονται πιά! . . . ΔΕΚΑ! ['Your hands are stiff as wood! – you can't bend them! . . . TEN!]'[3] And well over half of the company remained with their hands glued palm to palm, tugging and straining till the sweat poured down them, till at last they fell apart when he touched their knuckles with his forefinger. He did it again and again, on my insistence, and once linked a daisy chain of half-frightened, half-giggling peasants helplessly together arm in arm. It had all the excitement, and all the unpleasantness of *Mario and the Magician*.[4] It had to be stopped in the end because the children were screaming.

Our travels took us thence to Samos, Chios, Mytilene, Kavalla, Salonika, and all western Macedonia to the Serbian and Albanian frontiers, where the villages are inhabited by Greeks, Macedonian-Slavs, gypsies, Sephardic Jews, Koutsovlachs, Karakatchamis, Albanians, an occasional Pomak or Turk, and refugees from the Pontus – Trapezuntines and Anatolians, and Caucasians. In the same *kafenion* [coffeehouse] you hear Greek, Lázika [Pontian], Rumanian, Turkish, Bulgarian, Romany, Ladino [Judaeo-Spanish], Russian, Georgian and Gheg [an Albanian dialect]. I hadn't been in those parts since the Albanian war, and long to go again. It is wild, muddy, snowy and Balkanic; and quite unlike anywhere else in Greece. No time now to talk about the *klephtopólemos* [guerrilla war].

I'm leaving in about a fortnight, feeling angry, fed up, and older than the rocks on which I sit. Fucking shits.[5] But I am writing quite a lot, and enjoying it enormously. I have, not very originally, written a long thing about the islands, which I am sending you for criticism.[6] Please do so, could you Larry, if it is not too much of a bore for you. Write here if it will get me before the new year, if later, to the Travellers Club, Pall Mall, London SW1, Xan's and my address. Have had two letters and some sample poetry, very good, from him.

Here are the photos, and very funny they are. Xan as Eros is brilliant. Don't forget copies of the ones you took.

I am writing this from the stove-side in Joan's room. We both think nostalgically of you and Eve among your turbaned monoliths, and send love and kisses and every kind wish for Christmas. Write quickly.

Love Paddy

[1] Yvette (Eve) Cohen, the model for the character of Justine in Durrell's *Alexandria Quartet* novels (1957–60), whom he would marry in 1947 after his divorce from his first wife.

[2] Nausicaa's father is Alcinous, King of the Phaeacians (*Odyssey*, Book VII).

[3] The magician is counting up to ten.

[4] Thomas Mann's *Mario and the Magician* (1929) is an allegory of the rise of fascism. The sorcerer Cipolla uses his hypnotic powers to mesmerise the people into subjugation.

[5] The British Council had decided that it no longer needed PLF's services. Durrell would begin working for the British Council in 1947.

[6] This 'long thing about the islands' may never have been published.

The publisher 'Jock' Murray took an early interest in Paddy's writing. Late in August 1947, Paddy called on him at the firm's offices, No. 50 Albemarle Street, off Piccadilly, to discuss the possibility of a book based on his travels in Greece. 'There is no doubt that he can write though somewhat incoherently,' Murray wrote in an internal memorandum afterwards. 'The main problem will be to get such a book into some shape and give it a sense of purpose.'

First Paddy had another task to complete: he had agreed to write the captions and text for a book of photographs by his friend Costa Achillopoulos. As was often the case with Paddy, he exceeded his brief, captions usurping pictures, so that the work would eventually become a long travel book with accompanying photographs, published in December 1950 under the title The Traveller's Tree: A Journey through the Caribbean Islands. *This letter was written while Paddy was travelling in Central America with Joan Rayner to collect material for the book.*

To Jock Murray   El Vale
4 May 1948   Panama

My dear Jock,

It was a lovely surprise, getting your Christmas greetings, and
thank you so much for them. Owing to our erratic itinerary they
arrived in Tegucigalpa, the capital of Honduras, in Holy Week: a
wonderful baroque capital entirely, while we were there, populated
by the images of saints, moving slowly along the streets on the
shoulders of thousands of Indians, followed by the Doñas de Maria
[devotees of the Virgin Mary], half-Indian, half-Spanish girls in
black mantillas, thousands of them, smelling of camellias and
incense, the young ones all doe-eyed and beautiful, but the older
ones Goya abortionist hags. For a whole week the town was one
enormous wound, and every itch in the palm seemed to herald the
stigmata.

In Nicaragua, we sailed across the enormous lake of the same
name, dotted with volcanic islands, and then for 200 miles down the
Rio San Juan, running through a loathsome forest full of jaguars and
parrots and toucans, to the Mosquito Coast, where, owing to the
Costa Rican civil war,[1] we were marooned in a sodden little village
of the delta called Barro de Colorado. This was beastly, the air was
almost solid with insects, and we felt quite lost in the remote,
desolate, sharky place. Joan and I found two horses, and went for
rides along the reefs between the jungle and the sharks, splashing
through the inlets and longing for the spikes with which the White
Knight equipped his charger's fetlocks,[2] indispensable for horsemen
in these parts. We compared ourselves to Byron and Trelawny
tittupping through the sedge of the Lido in mid-winter, quarrelled
as to who was which, and ended up in furious silent gallops,
speechless with affronts . . . Costa slipped away down the Caribbean
coast while we were on one of these *ausflugs* [excursions], thinking
we would follow next day. But the civil war stopped all sea-traffic,
and his launch was kept out to sea by the revolutionary guns at
Puerto Limon, while we made our way to the capital of Costa Rica
for the last days of the war, and then to Panama, where we

re-agglomerated for a day before he flew home. We leave on an
Australian ship in three days' time, and should be in England within
three weeks.

Alas, I have not written another word of the Greek book since
leaving England, and have had a terrible time keeping up to date
with notes and diaries about the Caribbean and Central America
Balkan[s] and a series of articles. But as soon as I have sloughed the
literary commitments of this journey, I long to resume writing about
Greece, and will certainly do so.

We must meet and dine as soon as we get back. Joan sends her
love, and every kind wish to you both from me and to Peter
upstairs.[3] Hoping to see you soon,

Yours ever

Paddy L. F.

[1] Approximately two thousand people are estimated to have died in this civil war,
which lasted for only six weeks (12 March–24 April 1948).

[2] *Alice in Wonderland*, Chapter 6.

[3] As editor of the *Cornhill* magazine, PLF's friend Peter Quennell had an office in the
John Murray building.

*Paddy had first met Joan Rayner in Cairo during the war. He was not the
first to be struck by her beauty, and impressed by her calm, her good sense,
and her intelligence. 'Like all adorable people Joan Leigh Fermor had something enigmatic about her nature which, together with her wonderful good
looks, made her a very seductive presence,' wrote the artist John Craxton in
an obituary published after her death in 2003 (Independent, 10 June 2003).
'She was also naturally self-effacing. Even in a crowd she maintained a deep
and private inner self.' She did not share Paddy's love of society, often choosing
to stay with her beloved brother Graham rather than join Paddy in house
parties. 'Paradoxically, she loved good company and long and lasting friendships,' continued Craxton. 'It was her elegance, luminous intelligence, curiosity,
understanding and unerring high standards that made her such a perfect muse
to her lifelong companion and husband Patrick Leigh Fermor, as well as
friend and inspiration to a host of distinguished writers, philosophers, painters,
sculptors and musicians.'*

Easily distracted, Paddy found it difficult to write in London, and sought out a succession of retreats where he could work in isolation. The next three letters are written from the monastery of Saint-Wandrille, the first a few days after his arrival there.

To Joan Rayner,   Abbaye de Saint-Wandrille
11 October 1948   Rancy
                                                    Seine Inférieure

My own darling,

Two lovely letters from you, hotfoot on each other's traces! Aren't these absences curious? The agony of waiting for letters, and, when they arrive, the sudden bomb-like detonation of delight. In a heautontimorumenos[1] kind of way, it's almost worth it; but not quite. Darling are you *really* coming soon? Your first letter was awfully depressing, as if you were going to let the Channel have its way forever, but things look better in today's . . . Keep it up, darling! My sweet little bewildered thing, I really could eat you . . .

For some miraculous reason, and without my doing anything to remove its causes or exorcise it, my guilt has been evaporating this last week. I think it must be because I'm doing some work. Anyway, it's put the roar of the chariot-wheels[2] temporarily out of earshot. Also because my nerves have become tremendously quiet, through silence, absence of stimulus and hangovers, and *immediate* causes for guilt. It seems to have cleared my mind, so that it is like the stillness of a room that has suddenly been evacuated by a hideous gang of urchins that, year in year out, do nothing but fight and scream and pull each other's hair and sulk and fall over and blub and break things, so that the solitary grown-up in the corner has been capable of nothing but hiding his eyes and blocking up his ears. Drink and idleness and my bogus dogma of excess are to blame. Now that the surface is temporarily clear, ideas, letters, poems, books, even consecutive trains of thought, float to the top one by one . . . I almost feel at moments, that with an effort, my life need not necessarily be a failure. Then, like a distant, just-audible rumble over the horizon, I remember towns, 'alcoholic my dear',

noctambulism, whorish anxieties about being liked, delights and
disappointments about fifth-rate things, and the sort of general urban
nervous frenzy of excitement and remorse that can, in twenty-six
hours, smash up and bury a mood like my present one for months.
Isn't it *idiotic*? At times like this, I even feel capable of making *you*
really *happy*, my darling, and covering you with sunshine as I always
thought I could. At any rate, whatever happens, I can't do without
you, and I know, absolutely quietly and soberly, that I do love you,
really, deeply and completely. For the last week or so, ever since
passing through the miserable transition period, I have gone to bed,
tired with work, at about midnight, and fallen asleep almost at once
with my mind full of thoughts like these, longing for you to be
here, but in a lovely calm, happy, confident way that I had forgotten
all about; and slept with scarcely a dream crossing my mind; a
miraculous light, innocent kind of sleep, as if my brain were a boat
gliding across the deepest and smoothest of lakes, waking up as
easily and inevitably as the faint touch of the keel on the sand of
the opposite bank. My darling sweet Joan, I send you this quiet
mood as present here and now. Please remember it when you go to
bed, and imagine we're curled up utterly happy and trusting and
quiet, and that you are being kissed and looked after, and that I'm
smoothing out your poor little tormented forehead, my poor angel.
And then sink into sleep, and slide through the Horn Gate of happy
dreams or dreamlessness. You have nothing to be guilty about *me*,
indeed, 1,000 times the reverse. That's a start for you! But don't try
and fight all these night-time tormentors. I'm sure it's what they
want – resistance, torture, turmoil. Lie down and feign dead, and let
the whole loutish procession go storming and brawling over you,
and way into the dark . . .

NON TIMEBIS A TIMORE NOCTURNO
['Do not be frightened by nightmares']

The abbot[3] and I have become great friends. He is about sixty,
and, in a frail way, very handsome. He speaks a little English, but
fortunately very seldom, as his French is the best I've heard for

ages, rather complicated and antique, in what they call a deep
musical voice and scarcely ever a gesture, except, very occasionally,
a slow marking time to his discourse with his right hand, out of
an innocent kind of vanity, I suspect, because of his very long
white fingers and enormous ring. His other hand vaguely toys
with the gold cross round his neck. He is a doctor of philosophy,
and has spent many years in Rome. Occasionally he lapses into
Latin as if it is quite a normal procedure. It is the first time I have
ever heard it spoken as a living language, and while he does this, I
flog my brains to construct a sentence, feverishly trying to get the
syntax right, usually a question that at last I enunciate with as
much nonchalance as I can muster, to keep going the flow of this
silvery monologue about the nature of Divine Grace, or how every
action is ontologically good, and only morally good or bad . . . All
this sounds as if he is an elaborate, perhaps affected creature, but
he is, as a matter of fact, rather diffident and shy until he gets
interested. These conversations take place walking from urn to urn
under the beech-trees, in the library or walking round the
cloisters. His theory about Marie de l'Incarnation[4] is that her
writings look like love-letters because there is no vocabulary to
express the intensity of divine or spiritual love, so all the mystics
have been forced, by the violence of their feelings to resort to this
equivocal kind of language, as there is no other. I suppose that is
true, and may apply to Saint Teresa; but Marie de l'Incarnation!
And if it's true, what an appalling poverty in Christianity, not to
have hacked out a convincing terminology for their most pressing
needs. There is so much in Christianity that is unconvincing for
the same reason. For instance, in its symbolism how vague and
boring and unconvincing heaven, the prize and mainspring of the
whole thing, is! Cities with jewelled streets, clouds, harps, angelic
choirs – it doesn't sound like a place one could tolerate for more
than a week; and 'oneness with God', 'the inexpressible felicity of
the Divine Countenance in Eternity' is not, except for a real
mystic, much of a draw either. How very much better the
Buddhists have managed here. And, to a certain extent, the
wretched Mohammedans. And yet (in spite of the lameness and

insipidity of the terms of reference) for religious people, the monks for instance, heaven *is* a real, infinitely desirable thing, and not just a non-hell. There has certainly been no fumbling about the terminology and the symbolism here; in fact hell is so real and charming that celestial symbolism, and all we can grasp about heaven, is, next to what we feel about hell, as pale and unreal as a toy ship beside a blast furnace. I suppose this is why death is always represented by scythes, skulls, hourglasses, flames, devils and pitchforks. Because the threat of hell carries weight for everybody who believes in the whole set-up, while the promise of heaven, except for an initiate, doesn't. How negative and sloppy a predicament for a religion of love! It is this lame inadequate terminology that has turned so much of Christianity into a sad and forbidding thing.

Does the possibility of spending Eternity in the arms of your Maker excite you? Not particularly, as I understand it. Does burning forever in a lake of brimstone frighten you? Yes, yes, yes!

Saint Teresa and Marie de l'I, and people like that are positive, are on a better track, obviously: anyway, for a more exciting religious life in this world than the overwhelming mass of negative hell-funks. But after death they are swallowed up in the same nebulous 'peace which passeth all understanding' as any bourgeois who manages to skip hell, purgatory or limbo. *Needed*: somebody to make heaven as real as hell.

A thing that strikes me as really new and noble, and, as it were, aristocratic, is Saint Teresa in her absolute refusal to bargain with God. She did good and led a saintly life, not for the boring reason of doing good for good's sake, nor above all, to stake a claim in heaven and avoid hell, but out of *love* for her divine sweetheart because good pleased Him, and [she] simply didn't want to discuss or hear about what the rewards and risks were. Nor is there any of the tacit 'I'll leave it to you, and I'm sure you'll behave handsomely and do the right thing by me when the time comes' – to such an extent, that one almost feels she would feel happier if Hell, or intense suffering, or a sort of long-drawn-out Harikiri, would be the price of her love. *Vivent les âmes bien-nés* ['Long live the noble souls'] . . .

Life in La Grande Trappe [monastery] sounds pretty odd. Their day starts at 1 a.m. and ends at 8 p.m. Only five hours' sleep. They sleep on two planks in minute cubicles with two blankets and pillows stuffed with hay, and are forbidden to undress. They work in the fields all day, and are not allowed to put on extra, or remove a garment, in snow or mid-summer. The rule of silence is absolute. They eat standing up, and never have meat, eggs or fish, but live entirely off roots, salads, potatoes etc. They dig their own graves when they join, and live to tremendous ages. When they are in the infirmary, on the point of death, they are lifted from their beds onto a heap of straw scattered on the ground, as a final gesture of humility. All the monks come to assist at the last rites, and watch over the corpse in chapel all night, lowering it into a nameless grave with ropes round the shoulders and feet; no coffin. Chateaubriand wrote a tremendous description of 'la Mort d'un Trappiste'. I'd rather like to go there for a day or two as an adventure in masochism[5] . . . There's not enough Mortification here!

The library has a mass of stuff about Stylites,[6] which I am devouring. It's too enthralling and insane; all the details of their life, food, sanitary arrangements, fasts, mortifications, hair shirts, flagellations, etc. There were lots of them – St Symeon Stylites the Ancient, S. Sim. Styl. the Younger, St Daniel, St Alypius, St Luke, St Lazarus the Galiziote. Then there were Dendrites that lived in trees, with a chain round their ankle, in case they fell, sometimes for 60 years. The Stylites used to stand nearly all the time, with or without a leaning post, and never left their pillars even in the snowiest winter, with nothing except a goat-skin tunic to protect them, though some built a little shelter, in the Decadence. St Symeon was nearly blind from the Sun. There was one who hung in mid air by a rope under his armpits from the cupola of a church. This is something I *would* like to write an article about – 'The Stylites, and certain extremes of Oriental Christian Monasticism', for instance. I knew a very old woman in Athens whose father had been alive when a Stylite was living on top of one of the pillars of Olympian Zeus.

Darling, I'm afraid you wouldn't be allowed to take photographs here, as no women are allowed actually inside the precincts of the abbey. Only in the chapel, the ruins and a part of the gardens. I would like to write something about this abbey, though, and must try and get some photographs from somewhere. One gets so used to 'life in a monastery' being something conventionally strange, that one files it away in one's mind and leaves it at that. I had very little idea of what it was going to be like, how very individual and odd and disconnected from ordinary life. What I would like to do (but it would take months) would be a short biography of each monk – age, position in secular life, married or single, education, age on taking vows, *reason* for vows etc., for all sixty.[7] I can't do it, because they are so shy and inaccessible, and would close like oysters if I set about it at all briskly. But what interesting material it would be at the end.

All the monks I have dared to touch on the subject with so far are beatifically happy, and their only regret is that they waited so many years in the world. Most of them began as *oblats seculiers* – 'secular offerings', as civilians, meaning that even then they dedicated themselves to God. The next step is joining the monastery as a postulant for a period of months, then becoming a novice for two or three years. A novice is ceremonially invested with a black habit, hood and scapular (a sort of long black oblong with a hole in the middle for the head, reaching the ground at the back and in front). And their hair is cut short but not tonsured. Then they are either accepted as *frères convers* or trained as priests – 'choir monks' able to administer the sacraments. These are all tonsured, leaving a thick band of hair round their shaven crowns to represent the crown of thorns. Two postulants were accepted as novices yesterday, one aged twenty, the other twenty-eight, recently returned from ten years soldiering in Indochina. It was a very striking ceremony, in the seventeenth-century rococo chapter house, a vast room with a painted ceiling, twirly grey panelling, black and white chequered marble floor. The abbot sat on an elaborate throne with a white stole over his flowing black robes, wearing a tall white mitre, and holding a long gold crozier in his left hand, the

ringed one resting on his pectoral cross, and his right foot on a
purple velvet footstool. The monks sat round the walls in their
stalls. The two young men, one in tweeds, the other in pin-stripe,
were led in, and fell flat on their faces on the marble, where they
remained while the abbot delivered a homily over them in Latin.
After a while they were allowed to kneel up. Their coats were
removed (one wore a belt, the other braces) and, in the middle of
an outburst of chanting, black habits were slipped over their heads,
a rope round their middle, then the scapular and at last the hood.
After this the abbot gave another sermon in French, describing the
rigours of monastic life. *Rien ne change dans la vie monastique, mes
chers enfants. Chaque jour est exactement pareil à l'autre chaque année
comme celle qui la précédait, et ainsi jusqu'à la mort* ['Nothing changes
in monastic life, my dear children. Every day is exactly the same as
any other, each year like the one that went before, and so on until
death'] . . . I had a sudden intuition of what the sermons of
Fénelon or Bossuet[8] must have been like, the voice, décor,
atmosphere, mood etc. Then we all processed out into the cloisters,
leaving the two hooded figures still kneeling there. That evening in
chapel, their hair had been cropped level with the scalp. They were
indistinguishable.

* * *

The curé of the village is an impassioned royalist. Signed photographs
of the Duc de Guise and the Comte de Paris[9] everywhere. He never
refers to the latter except as Sa Majesté Henri VI and his son as
Monseigneur le Dauphin. He used to be a frequent contributor to
l'Action Française,[10] and I suspect was a near-collaborator during the
war. His favourite pastime, when not writing erotic poems about
Sicily or composing on the harmonium, is to work out the
quarterings of the Comte de Paris, proving how many times he is
descended from Hugh Capet, Saint Louis, Henri IV, Louis XIV etc.,
and marshalling his arms in their full achievement, on yard after yard
of artistic deckle-edged paper. Ten years too late for me, whatever
you pretend!

The whole of this part of Normandy was very heavily occupied, and collaboration was pretty general. Five women had their heads shaved in Caudebec, by the Maquis, such as it was (two miles away). Apart from the werewolves, the region, it seems, is troubled by Wills o' the Wisp.

Darling, I've suddenly heard the bells ring, it's 4 o'clock! (in the morning!) I'm nearly asleep, in a sort of trance, and if I don't stop now, I'll go on gently raving till dawn. 4 a.m! It's just about now the Inspector[11] might be dropping in. Wish I was there to help lock him out. I've made you out a little charm, which I'm sure ought to work.

Goodnight my darling, darling angel. All my love to you sweet little mite, darling heart, small portable figure and pet,

from Paddy

I'm so sleepy, I can hardly get up out of my chair, let alone get undressed. I won't reread this letter, do forgive me if it is unintelligible.

P

xxxxx

[1] *Heauton Timorumenos* ('The Self-Tormentor'), a play written in 163 BC by the Roman dramatist known as Terence.

[2] 'But at my back I always hear
Time's wingèd chariot hurrying near'
Marvell, 'To his Coy Mistress'

[3] Dom. Gabriel Gontard, the Lord Abbott of Saint-Wandrille.

[4] Marie of the Incarnation (1599–1672), French nun whose passionate visions were described in published letters. She referred to God as her 'divine spouse'.

[5] PLF would spend ten days there in the second half of December 1948.

[6] The Stylites were Christian ascetics. The first of them, St Simeon Stylites (*c.*388–459) lived for thirty-seven years on a small platform on top of a pillar near Aleppo. Several later Stylites followed his example.

[7] Rereading this letter in 2005, PLF added 'a terrible idea!' in the margin.

[8] François Fénelon (1651–1715), Archbishop of Cambrai, theologian, poet and writer; Jacques-Bénigne Bossuet (1627–1704), Bishop of Meaux, preacher and writer.

[9] Jean Pierre Clément Marie d'Orléans, Duc de Guise (1874–1940), and his son Henri d'Orléans, Comte de Paris (1908–99), successive pretenders to the defunct French crown.

[10] An extreme right-wing political party in France which reached its apogee between the wars, despite being condemned by Pope Pius XI.

[11] In a letter to PLF, Joan had referred to a nightmare in which she was visited by 'the Sanity Inspector'.

'My darling Paddaki,' wrote Joan while Paddy was at Saint-Wandrille, 'I find your life very hard to imagine — I try to think of you tucked up in your cell at night or sitting silent & undrinking among the monks, but it is difficult & makes me feel v far away from you.' She had hoped that she might have been pregnant, which might force him to marry her, but 'all hopes ruined this morning. I think perhaps you had better rape me one day when I am all unprepared . . .' In her letter she returned several times to the subject of marriage: 'I do think it would be lovely to get married awfully soon.'

To Joan Rayner
12 October 1948   Abbaye de Saint-Wandrille

Darling Angel,

I've been wondering what can be done about these silent meals in the Refectory, and am just beginning to see daylight. In the library, piled up in a dark corner in a trunk and covered with dust, I've discovered a mass of tenth- to sixteenth-century folios bound in vellum, all dealing with the point where mysticism and necromancy merge. Chaldean magic,[1] the Cabbalah,[2] Hermes Trismegistus,[3] astrology, the Rosy Cross,[4] etc. I think that within a fortnight by dint of reading these books, by fasting and prayer, and resort to the abbey's arsenal of flails and hair shirts, I ought to have mastered certain powers. I shall then initiate some of the likelier monks, beginning with the ones that look like Philip [Toynbee], Brian [Howard], Maurice [Bowra] and Cyril [Connolly] (no doubt more tractable in their monkish shape than I've found them in real life). Then, at a prearranged tap of the abbot's mallet, we shall all levitate ourselves three yards in the air, and no sharp words will bring us down, in fact nothing will, until we obtain a number of concessions: no more reading aloud from the Doctors of the Church, an end to the rule of silence, half a bottle of wine with each meal and a glass of Benedictine afterwards: all very reasonable demands. It might be the beginning of a reform for the whole order.

I got up at 6 this morning, and went for a long walk in the beech forest above the abbey. The whole valley was full of mist and only the ruined arches and gables and chimneys of the abbey stuck out. There are romantic rides running through the forests, carpeted already with rotten leaves, and something damp and autumnal like your description of the banquet of Haut-Brion. Every now and then, where the rides cross, there is a pillar supporting a grey stone seventeenth-century arch; or there is a rococo archway crowned with a scallop shell containing the lilies of France, or the mitred arms of the abbey. Squirrels are everywhere. I haven't drunk anything for three days and feel wonderfully clear-headed and light, the whites of my eyes are becoming as clear as porcelain, and bones are slowly emerging. I can't quite remem' what a hangover feels like.

My darling pe don't any England forever, and above all, don't run away with anyone, or I'll come and cut yer bloody throat. This is on the road between Rouen and Paris. You might come and pick me up here or we might meet at the Smart's, or in Paris.

All my love, many kisses and hugs, from

Pad

P.S. I brought the back here by mistake, but sent it back to Paris by registered mail before leaving the abbey. If I hadn't, either the suitcase and I would have gone up in a sulphurous cloud, or the abbey would have come down like Jericho.

---

[1] The Chaldeans were a Semitic people, said to possess occult knowledge, who emerged in Mesopotamia in the tenth century BC, and disappeared from history four centuries later.

[2] An esoteric method, discipline, and school of thought originating in Judaism.

[3] Purported author of the *Hermetic Corpus*, a series of sacred texts written in ancient Hellenic times, popular among alchemists.

[4] A symbol associated with Rosicrucianism.

[5] Amy, Lady Smart, the Egyptian wife of the British diplomat Sir Walter ('Smartie') Smart, who had a house at Gadencourt, Normandy.

[6] Possibly *Les 120 journées de Sodome ou l'école du libertinage*, written in 1785 by the Marquis de Sade.

To Joan Rayner
13 October 1948, 10 p.m.   Abbaye de Saint-Wandrille

Darling,

I've just had such a shock. After compline, I went to the library to make some more notes about Stylites, and stayed there till a few minutes ago, all the monastery being in bed and asleep. I put all the lights out, locked it up, felt my way through the dark refectory (full of the noise of rats gnawing and scuttling,) and out into the cloisters, a square pool of icy starlight. At the other side of the cloisters is a dark Gothic doorway opening onto a passage that leads to my part of the abbey. Still thinking about the deserts of Chalcedon and Paphlagonia,[1] I walked through the archway, and happening to look to my left, saw a tall monk standing there, his face invisible in his cowl, his hands folded in his sleeves, quite silent. It was so frightening, I nearly let out a scream, and can still feel my heart thumping. Phew!

Sweet darling, thank you so much for your telegram, about the broadcast. I managed to hear it on the Curé's wireless set – there are none in the Abbey. I would never have recognised my voice, if I hadn't known who it was. Does it really sound like that? I thought it sounded rather affected and la-di-da and frightfully gloomy, as if I were about to collapse in floods of tears. Did you manage to hear it? I don't expect you did in London. You didn't miss a great deal. Oh, darling, in case it came gobbled by telegram, the Cephalonian Saint is St Gerasimos.

Joanaki, about these Stylite saints. I have got the material in the utmost detail for a history of column-dwelling ascetics from St Symeon Stylites the Elder down to modern times (they only came to an end in the last century), with absolutely enthralling racy sidelights on their way of life, deaths, beliefs, biographies, sores, mortifications etc. I would very much like to write an article about them. The only two publications I can think of that are suitable, and that I would like to publish it in, are *Horizon* and *Cornhill.* Now if the H.[2] really wants the Voodoo article, he obviously won't take another, so I think I ought to write to Peter, and suggest it. What do you think, darling? I don't want to write it *blind*, as it were, without knowing where to place it, because it means quite a lot of work and I've got masses already; and one knows far better *how* to write something if you know what it's destined for. If you see Robin Fedden, could you ask him if he knows anything about the *base* of Symeon the Elder's column, still in existence at Quala'at Sema'an in Syria? Does he mention it in his book?[3] Also – I'm sure Cyril has got it – are there any details in E. M. Forster's Guide to Alexandria about *Pompey's Column* in that city? It was apparently a Stylite's perch at one time. An Arab climbed up it in the eighteenth century, by shooting an arrow on a string through a loop in the moulding of the capital, hauling a rope up, and then himself. Some British sailors also managed to get up it by somehow attaching a rope to the top by flying a kite, in 1773. The top is hollowed out, they discovered, and there is room for eight people there with ease, which is enormous . . .

You won't forget the *paper*, my angel, will you? The best place for it is Rymans, in Albemarle Street. If they say they'll take ages to get the holes punched in the right places, don't worry, and I'll do it myself with a machine the librarian has . . .

A curious thing *que je constate* [that I notice] is that the Humanist's devotion to you makes him much more sympathetic to me than before. It's about our only thing in common. But, please, my darling, I think it's absolutely essential – I'm studying *his* interests, as a writer – that it should be an *unrequited* devotion . . . I wonder how it's all going. Any obstacles can be overcome by dogged perseverance. *Parturit ridiculus mus et nascuntur montes.*[4] And if not the Humanist, what about the unknown [illegible] stranger? Eh? Do tell me all about your London life. I'm afraid it's dreadfully exciting . . . Oh, oh, oh! . . . And tell me all about your new clothes. I wish you were in France . . .

I forgot to tell you, my friendship with the abbot bore, about a week ago, the most magnificent fruit: I was changed from my cell to an enormous room across the passage, a really splendid one, about fourteen yards long, with three tall eighteenth-century windows, rounded into gracious cockle-shells at the top; one overlooks the courtyard, the library, the well of the cloisters and the Gothic ruins, the two others the sloping garden and the village, whose beamed cottages I can just see through the leaves of a dozen mammoth chestnut trees; a 'charmille' [an alley formed by hedges] with a Louis XV figure in its green alcove – actually the Virgin, but looking more like Pomona or Ceres;[5] and the abbey wall, pierced by a stately, armorial rococo gateway surmounted by a carved stone Pelican in its Piety, pecking its breast to feed its three craning chickens. The room itself is the sort of thing you would expect a cardinal to inhabit, except for the tin wash-hand stand. The *lit à baldaquin* [four-poster bed] is enormous, curtained with rather threadbare gilt-fringed crimson velvet, and the wall it backs onto is covered by a tapestry, where Actaeon is being devoured by the hounds of Diana. The ceiling is high and moulded with every possible volute, while the white walls, apart from the usual crucifix, are adorned with two sooty oil paintings, one (how nice!) of Saint Teresa, a skull, and a lot of shadows – a bad Murillo, it might almost be – the other (school of Luini) of Christ dripping with blood, crowned with thorns, his head flung back, stripped to the waist, with his hands tied together holding a bullrush; but both so dim and smoky as to be almost effaced and quite un-depressing. The rest of the furniture is a big metal stove with its tin tunnel piercing the plaster, a pontifical looking *prie-dieu* [prayer-stool], and two tables, one of them a giant escritoire on which I am writing now, seated in a high-backed embroidered armchair. And lastly, standing inexplicably in the middle of the pink tiled floor, a wooden fluted Corinthian column, supporting nothing, exploding three yards up in a riot of carved acanthus leaves. It looks as though it were awaiting a minute Stylite. I wonder what on earth it's doing here. It must be part of the canopy of some enormous high altar. No curtains on the windows which is all the better, because it bares the lovely shelving white planes through the thick walls and the elliptical moulding at the top. Occasionally a monk comes in and talks for a bit, a pale waxy figure lost in his black robes and cowl. They are restful company – they have soft voices and beautiful manners, and are as gentle as girls.

The room is an extraordinary mixture of austerity and splendour

– the tiles, the bare white walls, and then the four-poster, the arras, the peculiar column. It has some slight analogy to the disparate elements of some Guatemalan churches. It's a wonderful room to wake up in. The sunlight streams in through all three windows, and from my bed, all I can see through them are layer on ascending layer of chestnut leaves, like millions of spatulate superimposed green hands, and then the pale crystalline October sky, framed by this reflected blue-white, or thick milk-white, or, where the sun strikes, white-gold surfaces of the walls and window arches or embrasures. A miraculous, feather-light, innocent, clear awakening!

My darling angel, I meant this to be a short, brisk letter, I see it's straggled over several pages already. I'm so alone here at night, I can't stop talking to you; it's such a luxury. Darling, don't feel *ever* obliged to write long letters, and put them off, *in my way*, because you haven't got time to settle down to a whopper. You're in a capital city, I'm in an abbey, don't I know what it means! I do enjoy and look forward to your letters so, you've sent some lovely long ones. But do write *often*, even if terribly shortly. I wake up in a dither about the postman. And don't you think these accounts of cenobitic [monastic] splendour mean I'm OK here alone! I miss you the whole time, my dearest angel, and launch armadas of kisses in the direction of Curzon Street, great hugs and feverish clinches, and long angelic tender and gentle ones as if we were on the verge of falling asleep tangled up together.

All my love to you, darling, mignonne sweet Joan, from
    Paddy

---

[1] Regions of northern Asia Minor of significance in the early history of the Christian Church.

[2] 'The Humanist', PLF's nickname for Cyril Connolly.

[3] Robin Fedden was the author of *Syria: An Historical Appreciation* (1946).

[4] Paddy is adapting Horace's *Epistle to the Pisones*, which reads *Parturient montes, nascetur ridiculus mus* (perhaps punning on his nickname for Joan). This means, literally, 'The mountains will go into labour, and give birth to a ridiculous mouse', i.e. that huge efforts may amount to very little.

[5] Pomona was the goddess of fruit and nut trees; Ceres goddess of grain-crops.

From Saint-Wandrille (pictured above), Paddy moved on to the monastery of St Jean de Solesmes, and eventually to La Grande Trappe.

To Joan Rayner   Abbaye de St Jean de Solesmes
undated [November/December 1948]   Sablé sur Sarthe
                                        (J-P) Sarthe[1]

My darling sweet angel,

I'm feeling so gloomy tonight, I don't know why, and long to be with you so that we could just curl up into a ball together and snore our way through the night. It's frightfully cold and lonely here, and I feel absolutely miserable climbing alone between these icy sheets. Boo-hoo.

I hoped there would be a letter from you this morning, and pelted down to the gate-house, but only got a bill from London. I've been monstrously bad about writing darling, and please forgive me. The trouble is the post goes at 3:30 in the afternoon, and as I'm writing like anything, I always think it's earlier and the bloody thing has left by the time I get ready to write, so I put it off till tomorrow thinking 'I'll write the Rodent[2] a really long fruity one tomorrow-morning' etc.

After this, I'll send you something every other day at the very least,
and please, *please* darling, write to me absolutely *constantly* or I'll only
get terribly downcast, and you wouldn't like that!

Darling, what an unmitigatedly happy time we had in Paris.
Scarcely a moment of guilt or saturation or big-town-blues. Once or
twice at the very most, but the rest of it sheer heaven. You were so
sweet my angel. I really could eat you.

I'm not enjoying Solesmes quite as much as I did Saint-Wandrille, I
don't know why. Perhaps it's because it's cold and wintry. But there are
many more monks here, everything is much more organised and
impersonal. And of course Saint-Wandrille was incomparably more
beautiful. Here there are lots of long, cold, echoing, bare, clattery
passages, and swing doors with frosted glass in, that give me a slight
feeling of going back to school the winter term. The country round
about is very pleasant, rather like flat English country, with plenty of
hedges and little villages. The Sarthe flows just under my window, and
falls over a weir, making a slight rushing noise all night. At first I was
in a lovely big cell with an open fire in it that blazed all day; but an
old country abbé came here with Parkinson's disease looking so frail
and shaky that I did a Philip-Sidney-at-Zutphen[3] act of abnegation
and shifted into a smaller one without a fire, and alas the radiator has
stopped working, so it's jolly cold. Apart from all this, it's a delightful
place, with a great atmosphere of scholarship and serious meditation.
The library is enormous, much bigger than the one at Saint-Wandrille,
and wonderfully kept up with card indexes; but it is terribly difficult
to get in, or take books out, it's so efficient. No question of browsing
all night by myself, as I did at St W., then locking it up with my own
key. The great thing here, of course, is the liturgy, ceremonial and
chanting. The church is a thin, high Gothic one, with perfect acoustics,
so that the monks can really let themselves go. The vestments, and the
quality of acolytes, cross-censer-candle-bearers, priests, deacons and
sub-deacons that participate in a single office is unbelievable, and every
detail is so studied and impeccable that a mass here really does look
like a mediaeval illumination . . .

The nineteenth-century refectory is astonishing: stage Gothic-
Norman-Saxon, with huge German-looking chimney pieces, fat granite

pillars, cold in atmosphere and columns of Keats's St Agnes Eve, Old
Vic Macbeth, Rossetti, Burne-Jones, Wm. Morris, Walter Crane and
Corvo. The abbot, unfortunately, is away, presiding at the election of the
Mother Abbess of a Benedictine convent in Holland. Solesmes is the
chief of the Benedictine foundations for all Western Europe, and
immensely powerful. No change can be made in any Gregorian music
throughout the whole of the Church, unless Solesmes OKs it. But I
long for the wonderful buildings of St-W., the less grand atmosphere,
and those enormous damp beech-forests within two minutes of my cell.

Do you remember, darling, Mr Monk talking about an English
Trappist, ex-RAF monk that he saw in Brittany? Well, he's just arrived
here three days ago, an extraordinary man, about my age, very slightly
insane and absolutely enthralling. He got shot down at Danzig,
imprisoned, studied for the Anglican church after his release, went over
to Rome, and finally went to the worst Trappe of the lot, Timaduec in
Brittany. He was there for a year, couldn't stand it, and is on his way
to the Benedictines in the Isle of Wight. It wasn't the dead silence for
twelve months that got him down, so much as the gruelling work in
the fields, digging up carrots, smashing stones, sorting turnips, living
the life of a navvy without a single moment's solitude; and with
monastic discipline from the Dark Ages. No meat, fish, only veg, for
meals, scarcely any sleep. He looks a nervous wreck, wild eyes, chapped
hands, and broken nails, talks the whole time – terribly well – and
can't believe he's out of it. He's a fascinating boy, extremely sensitive
and well educated, an omnivorous reader, a sculptor & musician. He
felt he had to go to the furthest extreme in the Catholic faith, 'to
do penance for the misery of the world'. His reading in Christian
mysticism carries him to all kinds of miseries, and ecstasies. He is at
the moment gobbling up the works of St Dionysius the Areopagite,[4]
his lips mumbling away, and his eyes rolling. He has the most dreadful
doubts every now and then and careers into my cell to ask for advice.
He told me the dream he had last night: 'I was in a stable somewhere,
they were saddling up a horse for me. But the saddle hadn't got any
stirrups! And by God! I noticed the horse was getting smaller and
smaller – shrinking and shrinking till it was the size of the dog that
pulled the little milk-cart at the Trappe. I got on the thing, we set off

at a gallop. No stirrups and the horse shrinking all the time. Hell of a
job to stay on. Faster and faster! Then I noticed we were heading for a
small hole, about the size of a mouse's. I was still hanging on somehow,
and we were going like the wind. The horse shoots through the
hole and disappears, and BANG! I crash into the wall, knock myself
silly, and wake up. What do you make of *that*?' What do you? Has it
got a psychiatrical or a mystical exegesis? Good old womb stuff, or
heading for the mystic's inner chamber of oneness with the Godhead,
supported by a diminishing spark of faith?'

I am working like anything at the moment, and in spite of
Benzers,[5] feel absolutely exhausted. The books I read in the intervals
are a Flemish mediaeval mystic called Ruysbroeck, and St Angela of
Foligno,[6] who even surpasses Marie de l'Incarnation. I would like to
have a year doing nothing except read in an enormous library with
you somewhere. I feel I might use it properly at last, instead of
mucking about in the manner I have done all my life so far. The time
I have wasted makes me shudder with horror. No hope, I'm afraid!
Anyway, one would need five years.

I finished the Maya article before I left Paris. Only 300 words beyond
the right length for once. The typescript hasn't arrived yet, but when it
does, I'll send you a copy, and darling, I want them to reproduce a
photo of the Young Corn God and a really good Copán Stela,[7] and the
best and most representative modern Maya faces. *Contact*[8] probably won't

know which is which. Could you bear to go to Nicholson & Watsons (the publishers) and help choose the photographs which may not be labelled? I'm afraid they'll make mistakes otherwise. I'll tell Nigel Nicolson I don't think the article is as bad as it might be (seeing how little I know!) I don't know. It was a terrible sweat.

Darling, I'll leave here at the end of the week, and go to the Norman Grande Trappe at Mortagne, but will wire you dates and addresses. I long to be with you, my own smooth little darling, and send you lots of hugs and stroke your ears and put a bow on your tail for you, my tiny muskin.

All my love to you my sweet darling from
Paddy

---

1 PLF plays on the similarity between the place name and that of the philosopher Jean-Paul Sartre.

2 i.e. Joan.

3 Sir Philip Sidney (1554–86), Elizabethan poet, courtier, scholar and soldier, was fatally wounded in the Battle of Zutphen, fighting for the Protestant cause against the Spanish. While lying wounded he is supposed to have given his water to another wounded soldier, saying, 'Thy necessity is yet greater than mine.'

4 St Dionysius, who lived in the first century AD, author of a series of writings of a mystical nature.

5 Benzedrine tablets PLF used to sustain his concentration.

6 John of Ruusbroec (1293/4–1381), Flemish mystic; and St Angela of Foligno, Italian mystic, founder of a religious order.

7 Mayan monuments consisting of tall shafts of sculpted stone.

8 The magazine that was publishing the Mayan article, started by George Weidenfeld, who employed Nigel Nicolson as assistant editor. *Contact* had no connection with the book publishers Nicholson & Watson, referred to in the next sentence.

Paddy and Joan discussed getting married, but they were very short of money, and for much of the time reliant on her small private income. This was an extra spur to his writing. 'Darling we are absolutely broke,' Joan wrote to him while both were in Italy trying to earn some extra money, 'so do try to live for ages on what you have.'

Paddy was used to living on air. He was adept at borrowing friends' houses, often for long periods of time. This letter was written from a house in Italy lent by 'Mondi' Howard.

To Joan Rayner   Sant'Antonio
undated [February/March 1949]   Tivoli
                                               Provincia di Roma

My darling little pet,

Ζήτω! Ντὰν-ντὰν-ντὰν-ντὰν-ντάν! [Hurrah! Ding-dong-ding-dong-ding!] Your letter to Pienza and your telegram arrived within half an hour of each other, causing the postman two bicycle trips. My angel, I'm so relieved, as I was getting lonelier and more Ariadne-ish[1] every hour. I've missed you so frightfully all these days, thinking that you'd got nothing from me, didn't know my address, and that we might lose each other for ages, as we almost did at Patmos. Δόξα τῷ Θεῷ! [Thanks be to God!]

What fun your Sicilian journey must be! I wish to hell I hadn't got this appalling grind to get through, I can't imagine anything better (quite apart from ourselves, my darling sweet) than doing it with you & Hamish[2] & Peter.[3] Do tell me all about it. Does Peter sit in the back? Any quarrels? None, I bet. I'm longing to hear every single detail. This is bound to be an absolutely idiotic letter, as I'm quite *gaga* with writing at the moment, and have reached a sort of saturation point where no further sense can come out. Darling, look out for some hospitable Duca or Marchesa with a vast castle, and try and get off with him, so that he could have us both to stay. I wish you could come and stay here, *I wonder if you could?* It's so lovely. When you get to Rome, do go and see the Howards[4] with Hamish. He might, very tactfully explain the form, – you know, that we are good as married, and will be soon anyway, etc. I wish I knew him – Mondy – better. On paper he's a pretty devout Catholic, but is certainly far from being a bigot. He has got a strange gentle kind of charm, and a rather unusual mind that obviously thinks things out carefully and deeply, and gives you a considered, often rather unexpected answer to any question. We met and became friends in Bari when I was waiting to be dropped into Crete. I know his brother Henry much better.

Darling, I like the glib way I talk about getting married; but I do hope you'll still have me! I have been such a preoccupied empty bore these last weeks, that perhaps you are thinking better of it.

Darling, please don't! I'll be all right again as soon as it's finished, I promise! (I send yer lots of 'ugs.)

Oh dear. I got a terribly gloomy letter from Lindsay Drummond. It really is serious.[5] I've written to say that I *can't* have the whole book ready by the end of this month, but have promised to let them have it by the first of May, if they can possibly still manage it then. Now, I can just, but only just manage that, I think, if I turn myself into a non-stop writing machine, and do nothing else. Darling, could you bear your Zombi-lover till then? I blame myself, rightly, for this mess, for my slowness, idleness, dilatations [*sic*], dilatoriness, scatter-brained-ness; the result of all this is that I feel miserable, fraudulent and guilt-haunted whenever I'm not working at the beastly thing. I really could strangle myself with remorse that this bloody business has come to a head while we are in Italy, Moloched,[6] and in spring. Darling angel, I really will be all right when it's all over; please trust me. I was usually so diffident and secretive about the book not because you had broken my spirit by jeering at my early articles, but because there was so little of it, and so bad.

Thank heavens, I'm catching up here a bit – a lot in fact. There is nobody to talk to, and I haven't got a single book to read, except my tedious old reference books – how I'm longing to put them all away forever! This is my day: I am called at 8 with coffee and bread, and am up by about 8.45. Then I walk along the edge of the Sabine hills till about 9.15, and work till 1. Lunch finishes about 1.30; then work till about 5, when I go for another half-hour walk, and work till 8. Then writing from 8.30, after dinner, till the small hours, 1 or 2 a.m. Alas, this bloody programme is what I've let myself in for now, every day till it's over. Actually, once one has slipped into this rhythm, it is, in some curious way, terrifically stimulating, and at least, as one sees the sheets mounting up, guilt is at bay.

Darling little thing, don't think that this is the sort of thing I'm condemned to for life! Living a settled life, a few hours a day – as long as it's every day – will finish a book in two or three months easily. These shock-tactics are purely and simply the DAY OF RECKONING. I'm longing to organise my life so that there never are any: so far it has always been aimed purely and simply, one would say, at incurring them, though occasionally wars or luck have avoided or postponed them – and then living at breakneck speed to try and forget their existence.

Darling Joanàki, goodnight, and hundreds of tons of love to you, my sweet, kind, adorable little love. Please don't hate me, and write as much as you possibly can. I only get gloomy ideas if you don't!

xxxxx JEMY[7]

P.S. Lots of love to Peter and Hamish. Don't tell them about my problems!

[1] Ariadne, daughter of King Minos of Crete, was abandoned by her lover Theseus.

[2] James Alexander Wedderburn 'Hamish' St Clair-Erskine (1909–73), second son of the 5th Earl of Rosslyn, Nancy Mitford's first love.

[3] Peter Quennell. PLF and Joan had driven down through France and Italy with St Clair-Erskine before parting: while he worked on the text of *The Traveller's Tree*, she accompanied Quennell and St Clair-Erskine to Sicily, where she was to take photographs for an article Quennell was writing.

[4] Edmund Bernard Carlo 'Mondi' Howard (1909–2005), writer, soldier and consular official, married to Cécile, née Cécile Geoffroy-Dechaume.

[5] Lindsay Drummond's publishing firm, which had commissioned *The Traveller's Tree*, was in financial difficulty. The book was eventually published by John Murray.

[6] PLF means that they have their car; he and Joan called the car 'Moloch' because of its thirst for fuel.

[7] PLF often signed his letters to Joan 'JEM' or 'JEMY', obviously an acronym.

Paddy would often stay at Gadencourt, the Normandy manor-house owned by Sir Walter and Lady Smart, friends from wartime Cairo days.

To Joan Rayner   Gadencourt
'Thursday' [May 1949?]   Pacy-sur-Eure
                                                                    Eure

My darling pet,

Thanks for your lovely Greek postcard (there's a pretty picture for you at the end of this letter) and telegram. You write Greek *beautifully*! Darling Amy [Smart] has got other people coming here for the weekend, so Patrick [Kinross] and I have got to leave. Shall I really come and find you at Bordeaux? At the Chapon Fin?[1] I might do that, or I might, if that was difficult, manage to stay with somebody in Paris. L. de Vilmorin[2] vaguely asked me to stay; she sounded as if she meant it then, but she might have just been being charming. But I can always go to La Petite Boucherie! But I'd much rather come and find you than anything. Do telegraph *at once*!

I love this life, and hate the idea of leaving it. I've discovered that I can write absolutely the whole day long with the utmost enjoyment, settled quietly in the country. I only move from my desk – a heavenly *malampia* [cornucopia?] of books and papers now – from 9 a.m. till 9 p.m., for mealtimes, which *I* never thought, seriously, I could do. How different writing a book is from articles! If ever the Muse flags, I nip into the dining room and swallow a *coup de rouge*, and pause for a moment in the sitting room on the way back, where one's morale is finally restored by the huge Narcissist's looking glass there. The shutters are closed in the daytime, and all one can see is a dim figure, vague, noble and contemplative, against a background of enormous volumes of Molière, Tacitus, Racine and Corneille, exactly, in fact, what one would like to be! It's tremendously invigorating. All writers should be equipped with these auxiliaries. This retirement for writing purposes makes me feel a bit like Saint Jerome in the desert finishing the Vulgate, with Amy as one's major feline[3] . . . Smartie is better again, and he, Amy, Patrick and I spend hours talking after dinner. He (Smartie) is such a beauty, I never get tired of looking at him. He's half Holbein's Erasmus and half Voltaire at Ferney, with a curious dash of Peter Q[uennell], somewhere, an older and more distinguished one. Last night he talked for hours about life at the Persian Court at the beginning of the century at Teheran and Shiraz, the clothes, the mammoth turbans, the imperial receptions in colonnaded courtyards in the evening, tanks full of water-lilies and the emperor on a peacock throne smoking a *narghiléh* while the court-poets competed . . . He wrote an essay on existentialism last month that he sent to Cyril [Connolly], but C. must have been in France by then.

We went to a village fête on Sunday in a barn. There were

wonderfully bad ballets by the schoolchildren, some of the best clowns
I've ever seen, and a one-act-play acted by the grocer and his wife. The
Pacy string band played, without rehearsal, with the Gadencourt brass
band, the latter completely drowning the former with deafening
sequences of farts down huge battered lumps of plumbing, while the
former twanged bravely but furiously at their absolutely inaudible
pizzicato . . . Fon-fon, the bistro-keeper's wife, had a buvette on a trestle
table outside, and everybody was rolling by the end. A lovely afternoon.

There is one of those enormous Norman cart-horses opposite,
quite alone in a meadow and looking ten times the normal size. If it
didn't move about now and then, you would take it for the Trojan
Horse, or part of a colossal equestrian group by Verrocchio or Della
Robbia (!) mysteriously abandoned there riderless in the long grass.
It positively screams for a vast *condottiere*[4] in plate-armour.

I have reread (in bed, in the day) *Paludes* and *Les Caves du Vatican*.[5]
I wonder how many times I've read them now and how many times
I will again? [illegible] How good they are! When I have finished
writing these two books [*The Traveller's Tree* and another, never-
published travel book about Central America], I think I'll translate
them into English, if it hasn't been done already. I can't think of
anything easier and more pleasant. In 'Les Caves du V', there is
another glâbre–hirsute, eugène–mortimer group antithesis I had
forgotten about: *les subtils et les crustacés*.

I say, I *hate* the idea of going back to jail, don't you? I wish we
hadn't got to ever again! I must finish this now, darling, to catch the
post. Write – or rather *wire* – at once about the Chapon Fin.

A million hugs & kisses and love from
    Paddy

Love to Cyril.

---

[1] One of Bordeaux's oldest and most highly regarded restaurants.

[2] Marie Louise Lévêque de Vilmorin (1902–69), novelist, poet and journalist, and
heiress to a great family fortune. She had a slight limp that became her trademark. As
a young woman she had been engaged to Antoine de Saint-Exupéry, but the engagement had been called off. She was a notorious *femme fatale*, with many lovers, and was
for some years one of Duff Cooper's mistresses.

3 St Jerome (*c.*347–420), author of the translation known as the Vulgate Bible, was supposed to have tamed a lion in the wilderness by healing its paw.

4 Leader of a band of mercenaries engaged to fight for the Italian city-states in the fourteenth to sixteenth centuries.

5 *Paludes* (1895) and *Les Caves du Vatican* (1914), by André Gide, were favourites of Balasha's before the war. *Les Caves du Vatican* distinguishes between two categories of people: the subtle, who recognise each other, and the 'crustaceans', or normal people, who do not recognise the subtle.

Paddy had discussed his idea for a book based on his Greek travels with Harold Nicolson (1886–1968), who as well as being a fine writer himself was a regular book reviewer. On 8 December 1950 Nicolson wrote to tell Paddy that he had read The Traveller's Tree *'with the greatest interest and pleasure'. He revealed that he was reviewing it for the* Observer, *'so you will see what I feel about it. I think that you have really written a most vivid and human account of those (to me) rather dull islands . . .*

'I think you have a truly excellent style which combines all the architectural qualities of classical French with the exuberance of your Celtic ancestry, together with a little tough touch that is all your own.

'I do hope that when you start upon the Greek book you will not allow yourself to become overburdened by your material, and plan the thing in definite themes and chapters. Your "Traveller's Tree" (why you chose such an absurd title I cannot think) suffers a little from the feeling that it grew too luscious in the tropical air and that you decided to give us only branches of it which were lopped and chopped all anyhow. You really are such an excellent stylist that I feel your planning in the next book should be very careful and that you should be very fussy about the actual shape it takes . . .

'As you drink your resin wine and consume immense quantities of ouzo, murmur to yourself the words, "shape, shape, shape".'

To Harold Nicolson
20 December 1950   Poros

Dear Harold,

Thank you very many times for the magnificent review of my book in *The Observer*, and for the kind and invaluably helpful things you wrote in your letter. I got the letter a week ago, on returning slowly to Athens via Arachova and Hosios Loukas, and, owing to some hitch in the mail, the *Observer* came well over a week after it had appeared. You can imagine my agony and impatience and final delight when a copy turned up at last. I'm certain it's the kindest, friendliest and most encouraging review a first book could possibly receive. And I feel specially grateful that you could have written such a long and wise and valuable letter as well. I've reread it several times, and thought hard about your advice, and feel spurred, sobered and on my mettle about the Greek book. I would very much like to ask you more about the shape and planning of a book when I get back. Your final words have burned their way into my brain, and not a drop of ouzo or retsina now passes my lips without a silent invocation of 'μορφή! μορφή! μορφή!' ['shape! shape! shape!']

I'm delighted to have got those wretched [Caribbean] islands out of my system and to be in the right archipelago once more. I'm spending ten days in the first Greek Island I ever came to, fifteen years ago, to do some work. Nothing seems to have changed except a few more wrinkles on the islanders' faces, one or two deaths and a rather older reflection of my own face in the barber's looking glass when I went to get my hair cut. The rest I can remember off by heart. The forest of caïque masts, the departure of the sponge-fishing boats, the miraculous smoothness of the air and the sea, the lemon forests that surround my watermill, the olive and cypress trees and the clear outline of the Argive mountains. I wish I could send these all to you as a present for Christmas.

I'm deep in the Claudel–Gide correspondence.[1] Phew! It's a real mill-stone book all right. I'm three-quarters of the way through, and it looks so far as though Gide will win easily. I like *je préfère être vomi que vomir* . . . ['I prefer to be rejected than to be the one rejecting'].

This will miss you for Christmas, so every kind wish for New Year and to Ben and Nigel,[2] and 1,000 thanks again, dear Harold, for help and kindness and counsel. *Je tâcherai de les mériter* [I shall strive to deserve them].

Yours ever
Paddy

The storms threatening last fortnight have blown away. There is not a cloud in the sky, and it's warmer than spring. Bright sunlight. I'm writing this under a plane tree in shirtsleeves.

[1] Letters between the diplomat Paul Claudel and the writer André Gide written between 1899 and 1926, edited by Robert Mallet and first published in Paris in 1949.
[2] Nicolson's two sons.

Jock Murray's decision to take on the publication of The Traveller's Tree *was the beginning of a lasting association with Paddy. Murray's forbearance would be tested by Paddy's habitual procrastination, his perfectionism, and his requests, which went far beyond those usually asked of a publisher. After Murray's death in 1993, Paddy would add a personal tribute to Nicolas Barker's obituary in* The Times *(24 July 1993), and gave the address at the service of thanksgiving held at St James's Piccadilly on 26 October 1993. 'The kindness, the comic sense, the wisdom, the thoughtful response to life, the enthusiasms, and the good repair in which he kept his friendships can never be replaced,' wrote Paddy. 'He was the ideal, the quintessential publisher, and his success was rooted in his total and passionate devotion to literature in general and to books in particular, and hence, to the people who wrote them. "I don't mind tuppence about the overshot deadlines," he said to an author long overdue with the last volume of a sequence, "I just want to see how it ends before I die." 'The unnamed author was Paddy himself.*

To Jock Murray   Monastery of Panagia Faneromeni
February–March 1951   Salamis

My dear Jock,

Many apologies for any slowness in answering your two letters. I've been on the move in Attica and Boeotia lately, and scribbling away hard, and feel very remiss as a correspondent.

Lovely news about the reprint coming through so soon (any chance of the Voodoo picture? It's becoming a slight obsession!) How many are you doing? Good news, too, about the Americans, but I wish the cautious wretches would start manufacturing on their own account.[1]

I knew it would take some time before I actually got any royalties, what with advances, Costa's advance, the 50–50 split and so on. Actually, I'm getting awfully low [illegible] about pennies. I was wondering if you could manage to scrape together £100 for me, as I really do need it. It will only be a matter of time before we cover that by sales, and well beyond, won't it? Do see what you can do, Jock. I wouldn't have suggested it if it wasn't a bit of an SOS. If it could be arranged, I'm sure my bank (Hambros, Pall Mall) could arrange for it to be released as future bait for dollars, which the arrangement with Harper's apart from anything else would bear out![2]

I'm so glad you liked Joan's photographs and the Cappadocian articles. I'm preparing some more, as well as preparing the book, here in Salamis, where I'm staying in a sort of Hermitage belonging to Sikelianos, the great poet of Modern Greece.[3] The book on Greece (I keep racking my brains for a title. It's got to be a really good one) is steadily taking shape in my mind. Lack of shape was the only serious criticism that Harold made about the Tree in a letter sent at the time of his review, and I think of scarcely anything else now.

It was lovely seeing Peter [Quennell] the other day. I went to meet him with Louis MacNeice[4] at the airport, and saw a lot of him. We had luncheon in the old quarter on the day of his lecture, then wandered about the Acropolis, then down through a maze of tavernas, having a swig in each, almost till zero hour. The lecture was excellent.

A tremendous film tycoon called Michael Powell[5] came out here a month ago, on his way to explore Crete with a view to making a film of the capture of General Kreipe.[6] I sent him to all my old mountain friends, who dragged him all over the mountains, filling him with wine and playing the lyre and firing off rifles. He came back after three weeks foot-slogging wild with excitement, and determined to start 'shooting' in May. It's going to be a sort of superfilm, apparently!

When I came here three or four days ago, on the advice of a friend who hasn't been since the War, I was astonished to find the monastery inhabited not by monks, but *nuns*. There's been a changeover after the liberation. Dear little mousy black-clad things.

Anyway, they violated their rule by letting me stay for two days, then I telephoned to Sikelianos in Athens, who let me stay here, under the abbey walls. A nun trots along three times a day with bread, rice, cheese etc. They're sweet. This vast paper belongs to Sikelianos – reams of it, covered with pentameters, litter the house. It must be a sort of decoy for the Muse! No more now.

Write soon & all the best, yrs ever

Paddy

¹ Books manufactured were usually sold to American publishers royalty-inclusive, resulting in a lower earning per copy for the author.

² Murray obliged with a further advance of £100, which Joan brought out to Greece in late March.

³ Angelos Sikelianos (1884–1951), lyric poet and playwright. This refuge would not long be available to PLF because Sikelianos would be dead within a few months, after drinking a proprietary disinfectant, mistaking it for medicine.

⁴ The poet Louis MacNeice had just been appointed British Council representative in Athens.

⁵ Michael Latham Powell (1905–90), film director, celebrated for his partnership with Emeric Pressburger.

⁶ Based on the book by W. Stanley ('Billy') Moss, *Ill Met by Moonlight* (1950).

To Jock Murray   Zitza
18 March 1951   near Yannina
                                                        Epirus

Dear Jock,

Thank you so much for your letter, and forgive my long speechlessness, due to wandering about Thessaly for the past two weeks, too tired to do anything except keep my diary up to date. The arrangement with Joan sounds fine, and thank you for fixing it up. I'm sure we'll manage. Also, I forgot to thank you for letting me collect your bookseller's debts in Athens. It was wonderfully handy, and I almost bought a bowler before calling on him. He says, could you let him have half a dozen copies of *The Tree* on approval. They will be sold at once.

I'm writing from rather a momentous place, the terrace in front

of Zitza monastery, where Byron and Hobhouse stayed twice in Oct.
1808 (see *Childe Harold*).[1] It's a very beautiful, derelict thing, on top
of a hill north of Yannina near the Albanian border, surrounded by
the snow-capped peaks of the Pindus. The region teems with
memories of Byron, some rather disconcerting. I came here from
Yannina this afternoon, after having come across the Metsovo pass,
staying with Vlach villagers and exploring Thessaly. Yannina looks
wonderful at the moment – brilliant spring weather, with Ali Pasha's
domes and minarets reflected in a bright blue lake. I leave here for
Souli and Parga, then south to Lidoriki & Missolonghi, and back to
Athens to meet Joan. No more now! Write soon.

    Yours ever
      Paddy

[1] 'Monastic Zitza! from thy shady brow,
    Thou small, but favour'd spot of holy ground!'
        Canto II, Stanza 48

To Jock Murray
5 August 1951   Skopelos

My dear Jock,

    Thanks for the letter. Both Joan and I are delighted with the
appearance of the Meteora[1] article – I'm so glad the corrections
weren't too late.

    Well, the notes for the Greek work are assembled at last! I will
be heading for home at the end of this month, after getting back to
Athens and spending a few days winding things up and a day or
two in the National and Gennadius[2] Libraries. I've got a formidable
amount of material, and all of it fascinating. I hope to be able to
borrow Amy & Walter Smart's cottage in Normandy to do the
writing in – it's only a few hours from Victoria – but, in case that
falls through, you couldn't ask all your pals about a pleasant and
cheap cottage for the winter, suitable for a hermit embarked on a
major literary enterprise, could you? I send the same request in all
letters home!

Important. Could you ask your bookkeepers to forward as soon as poss. the Meteora fee (£30, he said) to Messrs Hambros, Pall Mall, for me (as all odd monies that may crop up in future). Thanks very much, Jock for deputising for me at the R.S.L., and sending the dough to the right place.[3] Eddie Marsh,[4] the Secretary of the Soc., and Rab Butler[5] (who wrote me a friendly note) said you did it 'charmingly'! Will there be any pennies for me from *The Tree* when I get back? I'll be rather low. I've hopes of a flash article being printed about the Cyclades with Joan's photos, which will be a great help. Otherwise, bar Ian Fleming's[6] thing, there'll be nothing much in the kitty.

I've forgotten where I last wrote to you from, but I think Kardamyli, in the Mani, after trudging over the Taygetus mountains. Well, it proved (the Mani) better and better as we went on. Blood feuds everywhere, and the only music, rather beautiful strange poetical dirges, a number of which I collected, and will translate. It's absolutely barren mountain country and every village is a conglomeration of sky-scraper towers (never written about or photographed as far as I know), far stranger than San Gimignano, where the feud-haunted clan chiefs would immure themselves, secretly importing cannon and mounting them after dark, to bash away at their adversaries across the street for decades on end, who were similarly armed. (It gives one a hallucinating impression of village life.) Thence we struck north to Sparta and Tripoli again, then through Arcadia, and along peculiar gorges, past the monasteries of Kalavryta and Magaspilio (burnt by the Germans, now restored like blocked-concrete Park Lane luxury flats on dizzy crags). So, along the Gulf of Corinth to Athens again. I've retired to these queer little islands (Skiathos, Skopelos, Skyros (where Brooke[7] is buried) – 'The Sporades') to attack the book proper, and am actually embarked. I'll be more detailed about movements when I get back to Athens next week.

Love from Joan, and all the best –

Yours ever

Paddy

[1] 'The Monasteries of the Air', published in the *Cornhill* magazine, summer 1951.

[2] The Gennadius Library in Athens, owned by the American School of Classical Studies.

[3] On PLF's behalf, Jock Murray received the Heinemann Foundation Prize for *The Traveller's Tree* at the Royal Society of Literature on 26 June 1951.

[4] Sir Edward Howard Marsh (1872–1953), poet, translator, patron of the arts and senior civil servant.

[5] Richard Austen 'Rab' Butler (1902–82), politician and President of the Royal Society of Literature. He would be appointed Chancellor of the Exchequer when the Conservatives were returned to power in October 1951.

[6] Ian Fleming, then working for the Kemsley newspaper group, had proposed a limited-edition volume containing two articles PLF had written about life in the monasteries.

[7] The poet Rupert Brooke died on active service in 1915, on his way to the landings in Gallipoli, after developing sepsis from an infected mosquito bite. He is buried on Skyros.

To Joan Rayner   c/o Mrs Batt
undated [January 1952]   Britcher Farm
                                 Egerton
                                   Kent[1]

My darling pet,

Thank you so much for your heavenly letter from Dublin. It was absolutely maddening, I had to go to London in the middle of the week to do another recording of my Maya talk, and stayed on next day to hear Pallis's lecture about the Greek War of Independence.[2] Your letter, meanwhile, had been forwarded to Kent, where the idiotic Batts[3] sent it to London, where I got it, thank heavens, the second I was leaving, but too late to catch you at the Shelbourne[4] before you set off for London or Paris . . .

I dashed back to Chesham Place by taxi, and collected the guidebook, but of course, your bus had just left when I got back! Wasn't that bad luck? When I got back again, I lay down on the bed and finished the last page of Patrick's book,[5] and as I shut it, the telephone went, and a female voice asked for you. It turned out to be Angela ex-K.,[6] asking you and me to a party that evening. I went, of course, and wish you'd been there, because there were Patrick and Angela laughing away in front of the fire with their arms interlocked like the most inseparable friends. It was a problem to know whether to press her hand in silent commiseration or to wring Patrick's in congratulation.[7] I also had a drink at Diane's[8] who sends her love. Peter Rodd[9] was there, extremely drunk and boring, so I retreated to the Travellers where Harold Nicolson was dining alone, so we went to Pratt's together, and sat drinking port and talking till it closed. Very agreeable.

The day I came to London for the recording (they had scratched the disc or something), I dined with a posh friend of Georgia's & Sachie's[10] called Dottie Beatty,[11] for Georgia's last evening before sailing for Canada. Company half sympathetic, half hirsute: Alan Hare's sister called More O'Ferrall, Seymour Berry, Joan Aly Khan, Georgia, Sachie, Lizzie[12] etc. I do believe my snobbish days are over, and about time. Drinking afterwards at Joan's vast new house, and a lot of talk with Sachie, who suggests I take some work to Weston for a few days sometime, as he'll be alone. Nothing I'd love more, but I doubt if anything will come of it, as he's so shy and dilatory about independent decisions. Lunch next day with Daphne & Xan,[13] then to the French pictures again with D., where I again saw Patrick, with his Mum, who (P) wants to see us both. Then here. I saw Ronald Storrs[14] in the Travellers who told me he's sent you an invitation to a tremendous Handel concert in St Paul's. I think he's in love with you. He always asks after that beautiful, splendid girl, and pumps away at my hand with vicarious ardour. Roger Senhouse[15] has asked me to translate *Julie de Carneilhan* by Colette, for Secker's. It's apparently Raymond's responsibility.[16] So I'm doing that, which is rather boring but absolutely potty,[17] and as the book is only about 40,000 words, it will be over in no time, – two weeks? and will produce £80 or so (£2 per thou. words).

My dear little thing, I'm longing to hear all your adventures. Do wire me the *moment* you get to London. Are you taking Barbara's house.[18] Tell me when I can telephone you.

Lots and lots of love, my darling sweet, and lots of hugs and kisses from

Old Mole

x x x x

P.S. I've got a new pen.

¹ Written on Travellers Club notepaper.

² Given at King's College London by A. A. Pallis, Anglo-Greek author and head of the Greek Office of Information in London, 1945–52.

³ PLF was a paying guest of a couple called Batt at their farm in Kent.

⁴ A well-known Dublin hotel.

⁵ Patrick Kinross's *The Orphaned Realm: Journeys in Cyprus*, which PLF reviewed in the *Observer* on 13 January 1952. 'The light and readable manner of this excellent book proves an apt instrument for tackling the more serious, as well as the light-hearted, aspects of Cyprus.' The book was published under the name Patrick Balfour, though the author had inherited the title Lord Kinross on his father's death in 1939.

⁶ Angela Culme-Seymour (1912–2012), Kinross's ex-wife, described in a *Daily Telegraph* obituary as 'a dazzling feature of smart society before and after the Second World War, changing husbands and lovers with bewildering regularity; they included, but were not limited to, Churchill's nephew, an English peer, a French count, an Army major and a professor of atomic physics who was married to her half-sister.'

⁷ Kinross was homosexual.

⁸ Lady Diane Abdy (1907–67), daughter of 5th Earl of Bradford, who married Sir Robert Abdy, Bt.

⁹ Peter Rodd (1904–68), the estranged husband of Nancy Mitford. He is said to

have been the model for Evelyn Waugh's character Basil Seal in his novel *Black Mischief* (1932).

10 Sacheverell ('Sachie') and Georgia Sitwell.

11 Lady Dorothy Beatty, the American ex-wife of the 2nd Earl Beatty.

12 Elizabeth Cecilia More O'Ferrall (1914–90), daughter of the 5th Earl of Listowel and older sister of Alan Hare, an officer in SOE who had been a frequent visitor to Tara during the war; John Seymour Berry (1909–95), politician and newspaper proprietor, who would succeed his father as 2nd Viscount Camrose in 1954; his mistress the Hon. Joan Aly Khan, ex-wife of Loel Guinness and Prince Aly Khan, son and heir apparent of the Aga Khan; the Sitwells; unidentified.

13 Xan Fielding and his first wife Daphne (née Vivian), who had previously been married to the Marquess of Bath.

14 Sir Ronald Storrs (1881–1955), a retired Foreign and Colonial official.

15 Roger Senhouse (1899–1970) was himself a translator, and co-owner of the publishing house Secker & Warburg.

16 Knowing PLF to be short of money, Raymond Mortimer had suggested him for this task.

17 PLF apparently means that the work will be easy for him.

18 Joan's friend Barbara Warner had given Joan the use of a flat in Charlotte Street belonging to her mother.

Paddy first met the writer Patrick Balfour in the 1930s, at the Gargoyle Club in London. The two men shared an interest in Islamic history and culture, and became close friends. Kinross stayed several times with Paddy at Gadencourt, and later at his house in Greece.

To Patrick Kinross   Gadencourt
17 February 1952   Pacy-sur-Eure

My dear Patrick,

Thank you so much for your letter. I'm so glad you liked the review – I enjoyed *The Orphaned Realm* immensely, and do hope the one on Turkey is going strong. I'm struggling with an opus on Greece, and hope to have it finished by early summer.

I don't think Percival Marshall[1] are doing all that they should about shoving *The Orphaned Realm* about. The *Observer* never got a copy sent to them, and I had to show it to the editor and ask to review it. Surely a paper like that ought to have received it automatically? I imagine they have made the same omission elsewhere, which is really scandalous. I think you ought to write quite a stiff letter to them.

What do you think about the Egyptian goings on? Thank heavens Amy, Smartie, Eddie etc. were OK.[2] They frightfully kindly let me live here for the whole winter. Why don't you come and move in on your way home? It's been raining and snowing like mad for the last week or so. I listened in most of yesterday to the Royal Funeral,[3] and for someone like me, who reacts to these things exactly like a scullery-maid, it was almost too much – a knot in the throat for six hours on end, bosuns' pipes, cannon booming, the sound of horses' hoofs, clink of bits, muffled drums and distant pibrochs[4] . . . Phew! The mention of the emerald Henry V had worn at Agincourt glittering on the crown on the bier was a dangerous moment. You'll have to be shaking the moths out of your ermine soon, if, as I hope, you are taking part in the Coronation. *You really mustn't miss it.* Xan is in Crete preparing a vast book.[5] Daphne went to stay with him for two months before Christmas, and is going back next month. I'd love to see her trudging over the rocks with an escort of lovesick brigands. Joan alternates between here and London, and will be back in a couple of weeks. Do let me know how you are getting on. I think you're very brave living in Kyrenia after roasting the inhabitants so! Rose Macaulay[6] is going to Cyprus soon, writing a book on ruins. Do you know her? I think she's a heavenly person. No more now, as the *facteur* [postman] is at the gate,

> love
>
> Paddy

[1] A publisher specialising in technical books and magazines, many about locomotives, with a sideline in country sports.

[2] There had been widespread rioting in Egypt in protest against corruption and the general belief that King Farouk was a puppet of the British.

[3] The funeral of King George VI had taken place on 15 February 1952, and was broadcast on the BBC World Service.

[4] A form of music played on the Highland bagpipes only, by a solo piper.

[5] *The Stronghold: An Account of the Four Seasons in the White Mountains of Crete* (1953) is 316 pages long.

[6] Rose Macaulay (1881–1958), novelist, biographer and travel writer.

Paddy had agreed with the publisher Derek Verschoyle to write a chapter for a book with the arresting title Memorable Balls; *but as was often the case with him, this task outgrew its original function and became a full-length book, Paddy's only work of fiction. The following letter was written while he was still working on the book, and was staying with his new friends, the writer, politician and diplomat Sir Alfred Duff Cooper and his wife Lady Diana at the Château de Saint-Firmin, the exquisite eighteenth-century house that they rented in the grounds of the Château de Chantilly.*

To Joan Rayner
undated [Spring 1952?]   Chantilly

My own darling little Muskin,

   Here's a fine thing, my not writing for all this time, and please forgive me, darling. I simply don't know how it happened – specially after your lovely long and juicy letter. Well this is what has been happening to me roughly. I stayed on in the forest of Compiègne almost a fortnight, indeed until the place shut up for the end of the winter season. I was the only person staying there in the end, and I gradually, by bits of conversation overheard from the kitchen, gathered that the ancient old girl who kept the place was an ex-semi-tart of the Paris music hall stage. She was Belgian and slightly deaf and conversing eternally with two other contemporaries that had formerly been colleagues on the boards round about 1900. They were always talking about the tremendous offers they had had from South American admirers in the good old days – *des messieurs vraiment bien* ['true gentlemen'], possessing ten or twenty thousand, or once, two hundred thousand heads of cattle on the pampas! The last day I was there it rained cats and dogs without stopping, and these old girls played an endless game of belote[1] over the kitchen fire, all croaking with laughter like witches; and, when I left next day, the proprietress told me, that as I was the only man in the house, they had been playing for me! *L'enjeu, était vous, Monsieur!* ['The stake was you, Monsieur!'] I think it very delicate and considerate of her only to have told me the day after . . .

I got to Paris, and found a room in the Louisiane,[2] that gloomy little one next to our old circular one, where you have to have the light on even in the daytime. I met Desmond Ryan and Mary Rose Pulham[3] (she had my coat, and I felt rather a pig taking it off them, as it had obviously been a godsend to the whole family. But I had to as I was absolutely shuddering by then). I had one or two nice meals with them.

I've forgotten to tell you that, except for two paragraphs, I have at last finished the story of the Antillean ball, and feel terribly excited about it. It's twenty thousand words long, I'm afraid, instead of four, and I would like it to be printed as a small book. I don't know what it's like, really, but I think it is exciting and alive and rather odd. Did I tell you that it is called *The Violins of Saint-Jacques* – do you like that as a title? A day or two after, I got letters from Annie and from Ian,[4] who had got the address from you, saying they were arriving and bringing the proofs of the monastery book to be corrected and (bugger it) added to. So I waited on in Paris, wandering about by myself, drinking too much and getting into a fearful state of depression. It will be a great day when I realise when I'm being bored . . .

I rang Annie up the day she arrived and appointed a rendezvous at the Deux Magots, but when I got there, found Pierino, the Coopers' chauffeur, waiting for me, who drove me off to that house in the Rue de Lille (Tanis Dietz's) where the Coopers live[5] and where Annie was staying. The Coopers were there too – tremendously friendly greetings, and a lot of mock scolding of you and me for going through/being in France without going to Chantilly. Annie I thought nicer & friendlier than ever before, but pretty ill. I had supper with her while Duff and Diana[6] wandered about dressing for a first night, to which I accompanied them & John Foster,[7] of Henry Bernstein's[8] [play] called *Evangeline*. Horribly boring. Afterwards to Maxim's and a lovely supper with lots of champagne and talk, getting pleasantly tipsier, till very late, and laughing a great deal. I was planning to go and stay with Amy [Smart], but Diana persuaded me to go to Chantilly, saying Rowley and Laurian[9] were coming through on their way back. So went on

Friday, party consisting of Coopers, me, and to my sinking heart, Ed Stanley,[10] who I've always disliked. But he was so funny over dinner and so much more intelligent than I had thought and so much friendlier (always difficult to resist) that I ended by liking him. He is hoping to get a job as Speaker of the House of Representatives in Lagos, capital of Nigeria, which I think is rather funny. Next day the Flemings turned up, also Liz v. Hofmannsthal[11] for a long stay. Odd people turned up. I managed to do a lot of work (finished *The Violins!*), correcting & adding to *Monasteries* etc., in my room and under the big tree at that round stone table, where I am writing at the moment. The first day I felt rather awful and shaky, slinking about like False Sextus who wrought the deed of shame;[12] but soon recovered and felt regenerated and reborn by this heavenly place.

On Saturday, over luncheon, the conversation was almost entirely about Cyril's 'Missing Diplomat' articles,[13] and was a regular tempest of anger and indignation, led (naturally) by E. Stanley, and seconded by Duff, who, though he likes Cyril very much, grew red in the face till the veins stood out about C's exposing his friends as drunkards, traitors, sadists, buggers, bolsheviks etc. etc., cashing in on friends' failings etc. I may say that I was the only one to take the opposite view, which I did with some vehemence, till there was practically a free fight and danger of being knocked down with a decanter. I actually meant it too, as I thought the articles very good, though they told us nothing new − but they did establish, and in a way, I thought, rehabilitated them both as human beings, fallible etc., but not the shifty and guilty shadows that have emerged in the press so far. What do you think about all this? It was a real shindy. For heaven's sake don't mention it to Cyril (unnecessary injunction).

Apparently Ian had heard how much longer I'd made my memorable ball than was planned (via Peter Q. [Quennell] from you) and suggested printing it as an illustrated special book like the monasteries. If Derek Verschoyle doesn't want it, I suppose one might. The ideal would be to have it done as a £4 book with a limited circulation and a cheap one for general circulation, if both publishers would agree, and get paid for both. I'll put this to Derek & Graham when I hand it over, as it all depends on them. *American*

Vogue are reprinting the Jamaica article on the fifteenth of this month, which seems odd. I hope it means extra pennies. I wish they'd do the Greek one with your snaps.

There has been great fun here planting narcissus and daffodil bulbs, in which pursuit Diana presses anyone who comes near the house. You punch holes with a tubular instrument like a spade, and I have usually been allowed charge of this, and have laid them out in all sorts of sentimental messages, transfixed hearts, great bears, Pleiades, Orion's belts[14] etc., which will look very odd when spring comes round, and perhaps awful. Lovely walks in the woods and trips into Chantilly to buy *moules* and chestnuts and things. The trees are a wonderful mixture of autumn tints, and there is a constant rustle of falling acorns. I do wish you were here, my darling love, and so does everybody else, especially Duff, several times a day. They really seem (and other people have told me so 'quite unsolicited!') very fond of us both indeed, so we can come absolutely any time. I propose to go back this afternoon to Paris with the Coopers, Liz & their maid, stay a night in J. de Bendern's flat[15] (which may be rash), then go to Amy's for three to four days, and either come back to England or to St W. for a bit. I'm longing to see you again, Muskin darling, and miss you quite horribly. I also feel rather guilty hanging about like this, and being so slow in writing, but please don't be cross, I don't know how I've contrived to indulge so . . . Well there it is, and no draggle-eared rabbit nonsense either. My capacity for solitude is dwindling fast and gloom and loneliness and homesickness for being with you sets in almost at once, coupled with sleeplessness and bloody dreams. It's raining now, late afternoon, the autumnal park outside, the plunging ducks, the statue of the Constable de Montmorency,[16] and the sheet of water looking romantic, *solitaire et glacé*, and I'm scribbling in the room near the bar – lovely and warm in here, fire blazing. I wonder how Cape Palinuro is looking now under the autumn rain, and Tarquinia, the *pale* waves of Nar, San and the Volsinian mere?[17] I think so much of our last two months (Cimbrone[18] has quite disappeared, strangely enough) and what an unusual and oddly enriching (not financially) and rewarding time it has been, and how happy, in spite of my ghastly procrastination over writing. I've had two charming & funny cards from Peter [Quennell], and think of him with great fondness. Do let's wander about the Basilicata[19] sometime in search of Greek stragglers, it would be a wonderful quest. *I must learn to drive.*

Gadencourt, Tuesday (eight days later)
It looks as if this letter will never depart! I scribbled you a letter, which I sent off yesterday, roughly telling you what plans were, unless you thought I'd fallen under a bus or lost the use of my right hand.

Of course, everything turned out differently from what I'd expected. Drove to Paris with Diana and Liz, left my luggage at the Travellers where I was to meet J. de Bendern later to be given the keys of his flat, and went with Liz to Dessès [the fashion designer, Jean Dessès] and saw Lilia Ralli[20] for a moment. Then to the Travellers, where I found John de B. & Ed Stanley in an advanced state of intoxication, and positively reeling. John's life is extremely complicated. You remember that tale about the gypsy flower-girl he picked up on the Champs Elysées? Well, she was now established in John's flat in the Rue Surcouf, just off the Invalides. There she was, a tremendously attractive creature with a husky voice and an unbelievably *gavroche* accent. The thing is, she wasn't *sleeping* with John (though I think they actually curled up in the same bed), at least, so they both explained to me at length; he was in love with her but not she with him. Meanwhile he was busy getting engaged to a Catalan girl – 'a lady' – called Mercedes who was terribly in love with him. This and John's drunkenness and absences with flash tarts all night finally had become too much for Thérèse the gypsy, who did a bunk while I was there, and Mercedes came in to clear up the mess. All very complicated. I telephoned Amy, who couldn't have me till Sunday as the house and bistro were full. Also Xan and Daph., on their way to Capri, had announced their passage through Paris, calling at Chantilly on the way. Another wait. On Thursday I went to a first night, with the Coopers, of a film called *Sound Barrier,*[21] presented by Alexander Korda, who took us to a horrid nightclub afterwards, from which Duff, Diana & I escaped and went and drank several bottles of Alsace wine at the Brasserie Lipp till it closed, and I went down to Chantilly again next day, till Amy could have me – a lovely quiet time of the sort we had this spring, including a heavenly walk to that deserted Cistercian monastery by the green trout stream, where we sat and drank wine under a willow tree. I came here to Gadencourt on Sunday night – just Amy & Smarty, both very sweet and friendly, not, I believe, quite as ruined by the Naguib reforms in Egypt[22] as I had feared, but still hard hit. No suggestions so far about letting us have Gadencourt for the winter! I'm getting a free lift back to England in D's car the day after tomorrow, being picked up at Pontoise[23] on the way, which will be fun. So darling, I'll probably arrive hotfoot on the tracks of this, so, unless there is something wonderful you've planned, please keep Friday free!

My darling little Muskin, many many hugs and kisses
from your old Mole

[1] A popular card game in France.

[2] An hotel in Saint-Germain-des-Prés which PLF had used before as a place to write. 'From my bed I looked out onto the tossing manes of three gilded metal horses' heads above the shop front of a horse butcher; it was like waking up holding the reins of a troika. The Deux Magots, the Flore, and a half-dozen other existentialist gathering places were just round the corner.'

[3] Desmond Francis Ryan (1910–76), soldier, and his wife Mary Rose Pulham (?–1991).

[4] Ann Fleming and her husband Ian.

[5] No. 69 rue de Lille was owned by Loel Guinness, who lent Duff Cooper and his wife Diana the first-floor flat on the front. His sister Tanis and her husband Howard Dietz lived in another part of the building.

[6] Duff and Diana Cooper.

7 John Galway Foster (1904–82), barrister, Conservative MP and Under Secretary of State for Commonwealth Relations,1951–4.

8 Henri-Léon-Gustave-Charles Bernstein (1876–1953), French playwright. *Evangeline* was his thirtieth and final play.

9 Rowland Denys Guy Winn MC (1916–84), soldier and Conservative politician, eldest son and heir of the 3rd Baron St Oswald, had been one of the *habitués* of Tara during the war. He married Laurian, daughter of Sir Roderick Jones, in 1952. PLF was best man.

10 Edward John Stanley MC (1907–71), 6th Baron Sheffield.

11 Diana Cooper's niece.

12 PLF is quoting from Macaulay's *Lays of Ancient Rome* (1842):

> 'By the right wheel rode Mamilius, prince of the Latian name,
> And by the left false Sextus, who wrought the deed of shame.'

Sextus Tarquinius was the third and youngest son of the last King of Rome. His rape of Lucretia precipitated the overthrow of the monarchy and the establishment of the Roman Republic.

13 The diplomats Guy Burgess and Donald Maclean had disappeared the previous year, and there would be much public speculation about what had become of them until they surfaced in Moscow in 1956. Cyril Connolly's *Sunday Times* articles, which revealed some of the personal qualities of the missing men, were thought by some to be in poor taste; they were subsequently re-published as a booklet by Ian Fleming's Queen Anne Press.

14 These are all constellations of stars.

15 Count John Gerard de Bendern (1908–97), private secretary to Duff Cooper 1946–7, who had recently divorced his wife, Lady Patricia Sybil Douglas, daughter of the 11th Marquess of Queensberry.

16 Anne, Duc de Montmorency (1493–1567), soldier, statesman and diplomat. As *Connétable* ['Constable'], he was commander-in-chief of the army, outranking all the other nobles and second-in-command only to the King of France.

17 PLF is quoting again from Macaulay's *Lays of Ancient Rome* ('The fortress of Nequinum lowers o'er the pale waves of Nar'; 'Best of all pools the fowler loves the great Volsinian mere').

18 The Villa Cimbrone in Ravello, owned by Lord Grimthorpe, whose nephew Martyn was a friend of Joan and PLF

19 A region of southern Italy, the 'instep' of the Italian boot.

20 Jean (Lilia) Ralli (1901–78), an Alexandrian Greek who worked for a Paris fashion-house and was a close friend of Cecil Beaton.

21 *The Sound Barrier*, directed by David Lean and written by Terence Rattigan, had just been released by Korda's production company, London Films.

22 In July 1952, a group of disaffected army officers led by General Muhammad Naguib and Colonel Gamal Abdel Nasser overthrew the government of King Farouk. Naguib became prime minister, and legislation was passed to enact a land redistribution programme.

23 A Parisian suburb.

*As one of the first Europeans to travel through the southern Arabian deserts,
Freya Stark was already well known as an explorer and travel writer when she
met Paddy in Egypt during the war. She was one of the stars of John Murray's
list; in all, she wrote more than two dozen books on her travels in the Middle
East and Afghanistan, as well as several autobiographical works and essays. In
1950 she spent a day with Paddy and Joan as guests of the British Ambassador,
Clifford Norton, and his wife Noel Evelyn (known to friends as 'Peter'), at
their cottage near Piraeus. 'Yesterday we had a cheerful party down here with
Paddy Leigh Fermor and Joan,' she wrote afterwards to her husband, Stewart
Perowne: 'Paddy looking in this wine-dark sea so like a Hellenistic lesser sea-
god of a rather low period, and I do like him. He is the genuine buccaneer'
(Freya Stark to Stewart Perowne, 27 August 1950).*

To Freya Stark   Castello della Rocca di Port'Ercole
8 June 1953   Orbetello

My dear Freya,

1,000 congratulations on the CBE! I've only just read about it in
a very belated newspaper, and am absolutely delighted, as everyone
else must be. A jolly well-deserved one and about time too!

Thank you very much for your kind postcard which I got weeks
and weeks late, as I was trudging about in Umbria with Peter
Q[uennell]. The 'Violins' story is coming out as a book soon, which
I'm very thrilled about, as it's a first attempt at fiction, which was
something I'd always looked on with superstitious awe. It was
certainly easier than the last phases of the travel book about Greece
that I'm struggling with at the moment.

I'm longing to hear all about your adventures in Asia Minor with
Fn Balfour,[1] and envy you them very much. I wonder what it was
like when there were Greek villages dotted all over Bithynia,
Cappadocia, Pontus[2] etc. – at least one would have been able to
converse. Did you learn Turkish at all? I admire their undoubted
stirling qualities – honesty, courage and so on – but have never
managed to like them, or be amused by them. Reports of the
Turkish celebrations for the quincentenary of the fall of

Constantinople[3] make very irritating reading, though I suppose one can't blame them. I had a plan to go to Constantinople and, for as long as the mafficking went on, drive round and round the city in a hearse, with six black horses in sable housings and feathers, and with a long crape round my stove-pipe hat, in mourning for the death of Constantine XI Dragatses Palaiologos,[4] who fell on the battlements on that horrible Tuesday . . .

I am established in a damp and ruined Aragonese fortress on the edge of the Tuscan Maremma, a sort of Zenda, really. I don't know how Joan, who appears in a few days, will like it; but it's wonderfully cheap − 1,000 lire a day for two rooms and an immense mileage of *pasta* twice daily. This is supplied by the owner, an ex-schoolmistress dwarf from Pesaro who acquired the huge ruin in payment of a debt fifteen years ago. It's triumphantly gloomy, like something out of Mrs Radcliffe or Sheridan Le Fanu − especially at the moment, with a downpour and ear-splitting thunderstorm raging all round it − but fairly good for work.

Will you be coming to this part of Italy at all? If not, we must try and make a *sprung* [leap] in your direction on the way back if you are still there! I long to hear all your news. How has drawing been going?

Many, many congratulations again, dear Freya, and love from

    Paddy

---

[1] The Arabist and former political officer Frank Balfour, a friend of FS's since the 1930s.

[2] Provinces of Asia Minor.

[3] Constantinople fell to an Ottoman army on 29 May 1453, following a seven-week siege.

[4] PLF is referring to the last emperor of Byzantium, Constantine XI Palaiologos (1405−53).

Paddy's next refuge was a mansion − a 'fine family ziggurat' − belonging to the artist Niko Ghika on the island of Hydra. 'He was seldom there, and, with boundless generosity, he lent it to Joan and me for two years,' recalled Paddy. 'It was an inviolate island, as empty of wheels as pre-Columbian America. Many of our friends came to stay − Nancy Mitford, Diana Cooper, Cyril Connolly, Dadie Rylands, Maurice Bowra, Freya Stark, and others.'

To Jock Murray   c/o Niko Ghika
30 July 1953   Island of Hydra

My dear Jock,

Many apologies for my remissness in writing. I got yours of the
30th of June about ten days ago, but have been on the move
constantly since, and procrastination, I'm ashamed to say, set in.

First of all, thank you so much for sending £50 to Hambros. It's a
real stitch in time, and v. kind. Secondly, I'm sure you're right about
films, birds in hand etc. I wonder how your chat with Ivan Moffat[1]
went. These glowing suggestions, when it comes down to it, are
often very like the bit out of the Pied Piper of Hamelin . . .

> 'A thousand guilders?' the Mayor looked blue;
> (So did the Corporation, too)'

. . . ending up with 'Come! Take fifty!' Anyway, I'm sure you'll
manage everything for the best.

So glad the galleys turned up all right, and a duplicate set sent off
to America. I've had another very nice letter from Canfield,[2] who
really does seem keen on the 'Violins' project. What is the projected
publishing date?

I've just got a rather sad letter from George Psychoundakis,[3]
saying how hard up everyone is in his village, and notably his own
family. He says, inter alia, 'I wonder if the remainder of the £75 of
which Mr Murray sent 40 could be sent, if it were not too difficult,
if some friend were coming out who could bring them . . . Forgive
me for asking, but things are pretty bad.' I see authors' letters don't
vary much! I enclose the original, for the records. It ends up 'with
love to you (P.L.F.) and all our friends Mr Murray, Aleko (Xan),
Ioanna (Joan), Daphne (Mrs Xan) etc.'

What are your views on his book? I think with cutting and
polishing and our trimmings & pictures, it could be first rate. I wish
now, I'd brought the typescript with me, instead of leaving it at Taffy
Rodd's[4] flat in Rome, as I am static again for a few weeks. But
Greece soars forwards.

The Greek venture[5] has been a tremendous success. We went by road to Brindisi (across Apulia, via Lucera, Bari and those queer domed villages, Casa Rotonda and Alberobello), shipped the jeep from Brundisium to Corfu, and from there over to the Epirote coast at Igoumenitsa, and along the Kalamas valley to Yannina. Did a certain amount of Ali Pasha research, had a good look at the remains of Byron's house, and went to the Monastery at Zitza ('Romantic Zitza, on the shady brow . . . ' etc. see *Childe Harold*) where Byron and Hobhouse stayed twice, on way to and from Tepelen.[6] Then up into the Pindus, to revisit the Vlachs of Metsovo. Then south to Preveza and from Preveza over the mountains and the Acheron & Cocytus rivers to Parga, which I'd never seen before: wonderful, surrounded by steep, Albanian-speaking villages. Then over the Thesprotian mountains to Paramythia, up into the Cassiopeian range to Souli, where I left the others and trudged for two days over the mountains to the rock of Zalóngo, where the Souliot women leapt dancing into the void, in flight from the Arnauts of Ali Pasha.[7] Collected lots of splendid material from old kilted and whiskered chaps, whose grandparents can almost remember these great events. So, on to Arta, round the Ambracian gulf, through Vonitza to the island of Levkas (Santa Maura), then south through the Acarnanian mountains to Astakos and Ætolikon, & so to Missolonghi by sea. (Nearly all these places come into *Childe H.* & the Notes, which is fun.)

Here the great search for Byron's shoes began. I hadn't got Lady Wentworth's[8] letter with me, containing the address, and of course, she had lost it, she writes. I asked all over the town − mayors, local bigwigs etc. − for an old man who had a pair of Byron's shoes. They all said they'd never heard of them or him, and he must be an impostor. But I tracked him down in the end, a very decent wall-eyed old man called Charalambi Baïgeórgas or Kotsákaris, descendant of a family that played a considerable part in the siege. Along with a lot of scimitars, yataghans [short Ottoman sabres], pistols, powder horns etc., he produced a parcel, already addressed, on the strength of my letters last year, to 'the Baroness Wentworth, Crabbet Park, Sussex'. Since then, though, he seems to have fallen in love with them, and (rather understandably) wants to leave them to his

children. (Lady W. would probably have had them turned into
nosebags for Arab colts.) Before opening the parcel he told me the
following tale.

Byron, when he was in Missolonghi, often went out duck-
shooting in the lagoon in the boat of a fisherman called Yanni Kazìs.
(It was, Baïgeórgas states, on one of these outings that the fatal
'pneumonia' was caught. Mavrocordatos,[9] on the enclosed 'mourning
order', calls it a 'flaming rheumatic fever' – 'φλογιστικὸς ῥευματικὸς
πυρετός'.) Byron died, and, in due course, Kazìs, leaving three
daughters. Two of them married, but the youngest went away to
Jerusalem, and became a nun. She returned to Missolonghi, a very
old woman – eighty or ninety – in 1921. As she was penniless and
had nowhere to stay, Baïgeórgas gave her a little room in his house
where she lived a few years, and then died, handing over an old box
to Baïgeórgas, containing a few mouldy religious books, some odds
and ends, Mavrocordatos' 'Mourning Order' (enclosed – they are
quite common), and – Ld Byron's slippers, which, she said, he used
often to wear about the house when he returned from riding or
from these duck-shooting trips. He gave them to her father, who
kept them previously, leaving them to her when she died.

Old Baïgeórgas then undid the parcel, and produced a pair of
slippers that looked more Turkish or Moroccan or Algerian (or
Burlington Arcade oriental) than Greek, to my surprise, as I had
expected an ordinary pair of pom-pommed Evzone *tsarouchia*
[wooden clogs worn by palace guards]. I enclose a sketch and a
description of the colours. They are leather-soled, turned up at the tip,
and with uppers of cotton and embroidered silk, rather faded. The age
looks just about right. I made a tracing of both of them, also of the
parts of the soles where the criss-cross tooling is worn smooth, in
case it should corroborate, or conflict with, known facts about Byron's
malformation. Also, the size might be a help. I made enquiries about
Kazìs – everyone knows about him. Also it is true that his daughter
died in Baïgeórgas's house. Baï himself makes the impression of an
absolutely straight man. Personally, I'm inclined to think they really
are Byron's shoes. There was something wonderfully convincing about
them. Could you ask Harold [Nicolson] & Peter [Quennell], showing

the tracing? They are boat-shaped and roughly symmetrical, but one must bear in mind that they were traced *sole downwards* on the paper, and the worn parts copied down by holding them *sole upwards*, if you follow me. The worn parts are notably different on each – but so, quite often, are the shoes of normal people . . . Please don't mistake all this for ghoulish Trelawny-like inquisitiveness – I'd just like to know if there is any possible chance of corroborating the old boy's story. Joan took a photograph of them, also enclosed.

Well, after that, on to Nafpaktos (Lepanto), where I again left the others, and went for three days up into the Aetolian mountains, to the Kravara – the remotest villages in Greece, where all the villagers used to be trained from childhood to feign lameness and distortion, in order to go begging all over the world. I collected some amazing stories, also a vast glossary of their very peculiar thieves' cant. Then to Athens. All this was a revisiting of places I had been to two years ago, but about which I had lost the notes. I got very much more this time, and it was well worth it. After a few days in Athens, I came out here, to the painter Niko Ghika's house – quite empty, very romantic and beautiful, on a headland of the island of Hydra opposite the Argolid peninsula of the Peloponnese.

No more now. I'm working hard on this new stuff, and will be here certainly, for three weeks: so would you write me any news ℅ Poste Restante, Hydra, Greece, and, if in any doubt about time, duplicate to the British Consulate, Athens.

Γειά σου, γειά σου, καὶ ἡ Παναγία μαζί μας! [Goodbye! Goodbye! And may the Virgin be with us!]

Yours ever

Paddy

---

1 Ivan Moffat (1918–2002), screenwriter and film producer. It seems likely that he had expressed interest in making a film of one of PLF's books.

2 Publishing executive Cass Canfield (1897–1986), president and publisher of Harper's.

3 George Psychoundakis (1920–2006), shepherd, writer and war hero. During the Second World War he served as a dispatch runner between resistance groups and SOE units in occupied Crete. Afterwards he wrote his memoirs, which PLF translated into English and helped to arrange their publication by John Murray under the title *The Cretan Runner* (1955).

4 The Hon. Gustaf 'Taffy' Rodd (1905–74).

5 PLF was collecting material for his book on Greece.

6 PLF misquotes *Childe Harold*. He had apparently forgotten that he had already described a visit to Zitza in another letter to JM written more than two years before, in March 1951.

7 In 1803, the women of Souliot climbed the bluff above the convent, performed their national dance, and then leapt with their children into the void in order to escape capture by 'the red-shawled Arnauts', the Albanian followers of the notoriously cruel Albanian brigand, Ali Pasha.

8 Judith Anne Dorothea Blunt-Lytton (1873–1957), who was known as Lady Wentworth, lived at Crabbet Park in Sussex. She was the only surviving child of the poet Wilfrid Scawen Blunt (1840–1922) and his wife Lady Anne King, the daughter of the 1st Earl of Lovelace and granddaughter of Lord Byron.

9 Alexandros Mavrocordatos (1791–1865), statesman and diplomat involved with Byron at Missolonghi.

To Freya Stark
August 1953   c/o Niko Ghika
Island of Hydra

Dear Freya,

Thank you so much for your nice letter & invitation. As La Mortola[1] is bang on the way home, I think I'd love to stay one or two nights there when my parole away from England expires. How ungracious that sounds! But what I meant was, even if dead broke & crippled one would be able to do it so easily, while Asolo[2] would need a bit more planning: though, I must say, not much!

I'm longing to hear more about Ionia. What is the best book about the Greeks of Asia Minor? Old Prof. Dawkins[3] knows a lot about them – I go and stay with him sometimes at Oxford, he's eighty-two and quite tireless. I long to know more too, about the modern (up till 1922) Greeks of Turkey – especially the Lazi of Pontus & Caucasus and the Turkish-speaking (but Greek and Orthodox) Karamanlis of the interior.

Tom Dunbabin,[4] my old Cretan colleague, has written a first-rate book *The Western Greeks* on the Greek colonies – up till *circa* 500 BC – of Sicily, Campania, Apulia & Calabria.[5] But I long for a book about the Byzantine and post-Byzantine Greeks of southern Italy, from when Robert Guiscard[6] overthrew the Katapan of Bari till today. Do you know of any? They still speak a kind of Greek, I believe, in villages near Taranto and Lecce, and I would like to go there – also to Cargèse in Corsica, where there is an eighteenth-century Greek refugee colony from the Mani.

I very much want to hear more of your theory of Byzantine tradition among the Turks – it was obviously enormous, and I've been touching on it from time to time in the book I'm on at the moment, but rather nebulously, as I don't really know much about it. I wonder where to look. Von Hammer?[7] Yes, the honest Turks *are* heavy and dour, aren't they, as though the leaven had been forgotten when the dough was being kneaded in central Asia. But I do resent their presence in Byzantium!

Joan – who is here, & sends love – leaves in a few days to drive about in Italy (central) with Maurice Bowra & a friend, while I stay on here two to three weeks or so, perhaps reuniting with her, perhaps both returning separately. But it would be lovely to halt at La Mortola on the way back. I've just been trudging through Epirus, Acarnania & Aetolia, – *trois fois vainqueur j'ai traversé l'Achéron*,[8] swimming in it each time!

Hoping to see you in about a month, & love from

Paddy

---

[1] FS's family home at La Mortola, on the Italian coast not far from Ventimiglia and five minutes from the French border.

[2] FS recovered from the exertions of her travels at her villa in the hamlet of Asolo, in the Veneto.

[3] Richard MacGillivray Dawkins (1871–1955), Fellow of Exeter College, Oxford; Director of the British School at Athens, 1906–14; Bywater and Sotheby Professor of Byzantine and Modern Greek Language and Literature, 1920–39.

[4] Thomas (Tom) James Dunbabin (1911–55), Australian classicist and archaeologist. During the war he held the rank of lieutenant colonel and served as an SOE field commander on Crete, where he played a key role in organising the local resistance and earned his DSO. He used the Greek codename *Yanni* and was also known to locals as *O Tom*. He died in his mid forties from pancreatic cancer.

[5] *The Western Greeks: The History of Sicily and South Italy from the Foundation of the Greek Colonies to 480 BC* (1948).

[6] Robert Guiscard (*c*.1015–85), Norman adventurer, captured the city of Bari in 1071, after a three-year siege. For the previous century the city, on the Italian Adriatic coast,

had been ruled by the Byzantines and administered by a *katapan* (governor).

7 Joseph Freiherr von Hammer-Purgstall (1774–1856), author of *Geschichte des osman-ischen Reiches* (10 vols., 1827–1935).

8 'I have overcome death three times.' The Acheron is a river in Epirus, believed by the Greeks to be a branch of the underground River Styx, across which Charon trans-ported by boat the souls of the dead to the underworld.

> '*Et j'ai deux fois vainqueur traversé l'Achéron;*
> *Modulant tour à tour sur la lyre d'Orphée*
> *Les soupirs de la Sainte et les cris de la fée*'
> Gérard de Nerval, *The Chimera* (1854)

The vivacious society hostess Ann Fleming would become one of Paddy's close friends and most regular correspondents.

To Ann Fleming   c/o British Consulate
undated [October/November 1953]   Athens

Darling Annie,

I *say*, what a lovely and cheering letter! Very many thanks for it, coupled with apologies for delay in answering. I got it just on the brink of leaving for Crete fresh from quake-struck Cyprus.[1] Joan suddenly appeared, just in time to nip a fearful *cafard* [bout of melancholia] in the bud, and off we went to Crete, trudging over rocks like scimitars or jolting about in mule-saddles, drenched to the skin half the time, eating a dozen meals a day, lest Cretan village hospitality should be offended, and putting down raki and wine by the hogshead – expanding, as you might guess, like dirigibles, our breath deteriorating and our eyes dwindling and turning scarlet, and finally vanishing. Phew! But there were lots of compensations, lovely dances by booted mountain thugs bristling with daggers, every one blazing off *feu de joie*[2] and some tremendous singing. On the last night we sat up till eight in the morning, to the tunes of a Cretan lyre, a lute, a fiddle, and a zither, and were loaded on board with egos boosted a mile high, several stone heavier, and completely drunk. For a day or two, our hangovers will be so real and positive, it will seem almost as though we were four people instead of two . . . But they will gradually fade away, leaving nothing but a fragrant memory. We only got back to Athens this morning, so our footsteps are still dogged by our ashen, accusing and malodorous doubles . . .

Clarissa was quite invisible here, shrouded in dazzling ministerial convalescence;[3] but I saw lots of Bridget[4] who thought Greece was really tremendous. Another white ladyship, Baba Metcalfe,[5] came later, vying in marble blankness with Pallas Athene herself. It's been a lovely summer, full of movement, excitement & fun, and justifying a minimum of work as a guilt-remover . . . Joan is planning a wonderful party when we are back, in about three weeks, which will be nice for all of us. I've got to stop in Rome to collect my luggage there (I'm shivering in tattered and filthy summer drill, having come here for three weeks and stayed nearly four months), then I hope, in about ten days' time, Chantilly for two to three days, & London. I do hope you won't have vanished to Goldeneye?[6] Love to Ian – we'll all be meeting almost at once; and thanks again for writing that nice letter!

Love from

Paddy

(also from Joan)

1 In September 1953 the Paphos district of Cyprus suffered a destructive double earthquake.

2 A rifle salute fired by soldiers on a ceremonial occasion.

3 Clarissa Eden, wife of the British Foreign Secretary, Sir Anthony Eden.

4 Lady Mary Bridget Parsons (1907–72), daughter of the 5th Earl of Rosse.

5 Lady Alexandra 'Baba' Metcalfe (1904–95), daughter of the Marquess of Curzon. Her husband 'Fruity' Metcalfe had been best man when the former King, Edward VIII, married Wallis Simpson.

6 The Flemings' house in Jamaica.

Paddy came to know Lady Diana Cooper in 1951, and would maintain a correspondence with her until her death almost four decades later. According to her granddaughter, 'each discovered that the other was the sort of person they liked best'. His letters were written to amuse and entertain her; they were affectionate and not a little flirtatious, despite the twenty-three-year difference in age between them. 'Being alone with you is what I like best, a delight of which I can never tire,' he had written to her in March 1953. Paddy usually addressed her as 'darling'; she addressed him as 'Paddles'.

The letter reprinted below was written after Duff Cooper's death on 1 January 1954.

To Diana Cooper
11 January 1954

Birr Castle
Co. Offaly
Ireland

My darling Diana,

I'm so phenomenally and abnormally bad at writing letters at times like this – and the greater the loss and the fonder I am of the people involved, the more hopelessly pen-tied I become – that I rather cravenly put off doing so until it was almost too late, hoping to replace it with cables and the telephone. But, darling Diana, you have been in my mind, quite literally, practically every minute of the last eight days, and I can still think of little else. Vain regrets, but I wish I'd managed to fly to Vigo[1] – poor Diana, I hate to think of you coping all alone, and still more dread the loneliness you must be feeling, but was also a bit afraid of intruding. I wonder how much of a help it is to know how much you are adored, by people who also want to share in this and help and console, however clumsily? I keep on thinking of Duff talking away by candlelight dinner, and having to stop reading *Vile Bodies* out loud by the fire afterwards, to mop away the helpless tears of laughter that were streaming down his face. None of the obituaries I've seen quite get the point – all the vigour and fun and enjoyment and wit and irascibility and kindness. *The Times* I thought hopeless: priggish and lame and not very well disposed. It was lucky having Daph and Xan near at the time as fellow mutes to hold hands and send off massed waves of love and sympathy to you through the air.

They left Luggala[2] (where we all stayed for Christmas & New Year) four days ago, and I came on here. Christmas was quite extraordinary there: a mixture of nightclub, the Hons' Cupboard[3] and the Charge of the Light Brigade, so tremendous was the pace, even for me, all day and night – hell for leather, with many a riderless chair at luncheon each day, but everyone miraculously in the saddle by sunset and streaming across the country once more, along the bottle-strewn valleys of the night . . . Here, staying with Michael and Anne Rosse,[4] all seems astonishingly quiet and mild, though all the nobs of western Ireland are assembled and blazing away, while the pyramids of dead pheasants mount up. Do you know it? Lovely rushing streams under one's window and pretty willow-pattern trees under a rainy Irian sky; and pleasant evenings drinking round peat fires, with Bridget's brow growing blacker with each succeeding flutter and pout from Anne . . . (mine too, a bit, I must say . . .)

Diana, I'm so glad you've gone to stay with David[5] in Tangier. Far, far best. Do, *please* write as detailed a programme as you can of your plans, in case I might make a getaway and come and see you somewhere for a few days.[6] (I'll be at Travellers again at the end of this week.) No more now, but *do write* as soon as you possibly can; and remember, dearest Diana, that you are being thought of with love absolutely every instant.

With devotion, hugs, etc. from

Paddy

P.S. *Bien des choses* ['best wishes'], as they say, to David.

---

1 Duff Cooper had died aboard a French liner bound for the Caribbean, which put in to the Spanish port of Vigo.

2 The house of Oonagh Oranmore and Browne, née Guinness, then romantically involved with Robert Kee.

3 PLF refers to the linen cupboard where the Mitford sisters – all 'Hons.' because daughters of a peer – would gather to gossip, plot and keep warm.

4 Lawrence Michael Harvey Parsons (1906–79), 6th Earl of Rosse, Irish peer whose family seat was Birr Castle, brother of Lady Bridget Parsons; and his wife Anne, née Messel, mother from her first marriage of Antony Armstrong-Jones (Lord Snowdon), who in 1960 married Princess Margaret.

5 The Hon. David Alexander Reginald Herbert (1908–95), referred to by Ian Fleming as 'the Queen of Tangier'.

6 PLF joined DC in Rome for a fortnight.

*From Rome, Diana Cooper went on to Greece, while Paddy returned to England
to write, bearing an envelope filled with her letters of thanks to those who had
sent her messages of condolence. This letter was written while he was staying
with John and Penelope Betjeman in Berkshire. Penelope's recent conversion to
Catholicism had put their marriage under strain.*

To Diana Cooper
'Sunday' [February/March 1954]   c/o John Betjeman

My darling Diana,

I wonder if you are in Athens yet? Anyway, here goes, a provisional
letter just in case you are. Before I start, darling, there is a shaming
disaster to report. When, on getting to Charlotte Street on Wednesday,
I made a dive into my ragged bag for that envelope with your letters
in – nothing there! I didn't *by any chance* give them back to you or
anything, did I? I'm convinced not, I would have remembered. Could
they have fallen out, I wondered, in the aeroplane or customs, or 'bus'
when I dug out a book? I've made a thousand enquiries, all with no
result so far, which is the cause of my delay in writing till now, as
some needed a day or two's delay, the air people said. I can't think
how they vanished, unless someone pinched them through the torn
top of my bag (in lieu of traveller's cheques) . . . They may appear,
but I'm not sanguine. I should have had them in my pocket. This is
simply ghastly and I feel very ashamed, especially after your disaster
over letters with Norah,[1] the Augean stables of correspondence you
have to cope with, and in view of the sacredness of letters etc. *I do
hope* there was nothing tremendously vital and irreplaceable in any
of them . . . Can I, if you send me the names of the addressees, ring
them up and explain why they have not heard from you? Take (quite
rightly!) the blame? Most abject apologies again. It's totally mysterious
and profoundly humbling . . .

It started snowing last night, and there is a North Pole landscape
outside the window this morning. It's still snowing slightly, and the
cold goes straight to the bone if you stick your nose outside. But it's
rather a nice vicaragy frowst indoors: vast log fire, millions of books,

strong drink appearing any moment. We had great fun last night looking up obscure poets – South Africans, Australians, Canadians, etc. – and reading them aloud in turn in the appropriate accents. We also drank a great deal of whisky, until everything we read seemed uproarious. I had to read, in an Australian voice, the following line:

'And lo! The sward was pocked with wombats' holes!'

We found drunken tears streaming down our cheeks, and had to chuck it for the night . . .

Penelope's Catholicism has obviously split the household.[2] There is a certain amount of doctrinal bickering and smart rejoinders, surreptitious reading of the *Catholic Herald* (quickly stuffed under a cushion if John comes into the room), and sudden withdrawals by Penelope into her bedroom, of which I caught a glimpse – a grotto of images, rosaries, crucifixes, and sacred hearts. It's a sort of microcosm of Reformation England inside out.

London, next day . . .

The fortnight in Rome was one of my happiest for ages. You are more fun to be with, travelling about, exploring etc., than you can possibly imagine, and turn everything to magic. Do let's do it again . . . Darling Diana, try not to be so desperately lonely and miserable, and, if you find yourself becoming so, remember how passionately adored you are by so many people, and think of happy times to come. You seem a miracle of guts & stoicism to me, and one could weep at the idea of you being unhappy and lonely. I really do adore you, and you are far too precious to everyone for the idea to be at all bearable . . .

Many, many thanks now again, Diana darling, for being such a heavenly companion in Rome and Florence, and please take tremendous care of yourself, for all our sakes! Also, if poss., do write almost at once.

Fondest love, hugs, devotion, etc.

Paddy

---

[1] Norah Fahie, Lady Diana Cooper's 'secretary-gardener'.

[2] Betjeman became attached to Lady Elizabeth Cavendish, sister of the Duke of Devonshire, whom Betjeman's daughter Candida Lycett Green would describe as her father's 'other wife'.

The visit to Betjeman inspired Paddy to write this parody of his style, first published in the Cornhill *magazine in the summer of 1954.*

'In Honour of Mr John Betjeman'
by Patrick Leigh Fermor

Eagle-borne spread of the Authorised Version!
Beadles and bell ropes! Pulpits and pews!
Sandwiches spread for a new excursion
And *patum peperium*[1] under the yews!

Erastian peal of Established church bells
(Cuckoo-chimes in Cistercian towers!)
Bugloss and briony border our search. Bells
Toll the quarters and toll the hours.

Unscrew the thermos! Some village Hampden
Swells the sward. Fill the plastic cup
For a toast to Brandon, to Scott and to Camden,
To dripstone and dogtooth, with bottoms up!

Herringbone-tweed (one more? Shall we risk it?)
Mimics the moulding from neck to knee.
(Ginger beer, and a Peek Frean biscuit?)
Then here's to Pugin with three times three!

Basketed bikes on the lych-gate leaning
(Headlamp and rearlamp, pump and mac!)
Bask in the sunshine, the privet screening
Raleigh and Rudge[2] till we both get back;

Back from the church where the rood screen false is
Bogus both squint and architrave.
Lord! Let an Old Marlburian's Dolcis[3]
Quicken the echoes of the nave!

Let an Old Marlburian Veldstchoen[4] waken
Ghostly incumbents along the gloom,
And the rattle of anthracite long since shaken
Out with the slag in the boiler-room.

Raven-black sway the phantom cassocks,
Ruby the silk of an M. A. hood;
Sweet is the incense of fragrant hassocks
And tiger-lilies and Ronuk'd[5] wood . . .

Sarum-chants of celestial cities,
Rustic anthems in harmony
Quavering rune of the *Nunc dimittis*,
Gaslit groan of *Abide with me!*

Back to the lamplight, back to the crumpets
Under the cliff by the seaside path
An Old Marlburian treads through the limpets
Home through the sunset's aftermath.

The 7.10 whistles, and helter-skelter
Wild foam flies by the wayward sea;
Bladderwrack pops under Lotus and Delta[6] . . .
Holy Saint Pancras, pray for me!

[1] Anchovy paste, traditionally spread on toast, marketed as 'The Gentleman's Relish'.
[2] Bicycle manufacturers.
[3] Shoe retailers. Betjeman had been educated at Marlborough.
[4] A form of welt used to make shoes weather-resistant.
[5] Brand of wax used on floors.
[6] More shoe retailers.

While Diana Cooper was in Athens, Paddy based himself in her house by the sea near Bognor Regis. The letter that follows describes a visit to Lady Wentworth, the eccentric châtelaine of Crabbet Park (see note 8 on page 77). An account of this visit appears in his book Roumeli, *though there it is conflated with an earlier visit.*

To Diana Cooper   West House
22 March 1954   Aldwick
                                                   Bognor Regis

Darling Diana,

   I bought 200 of these titanic sheets of paper at Lechertier Barbe[1]
in Jermyn Street last week, as nib-coaxers when pen paralysis seems
imminent, and I must say it seems to work like magic – you just
glide along like a figure-skater on a perfect rink, leaving a wonderful
track of conceits, tropes, paradoxes, thrusts, sallies and
apophthegms . . . It's a pity most of it has to be pruned away next
morning.

   Your catalogue of places in Greece turns me green with envy,
nostalgia, and feelings of frustration at not being there too, trudging
along among the rocks and asphodel (which must be smothering
everything by now – marvellous in the mass, a sort of pale haze over
the country, but so disappointing individually), and knocking off after
culture for delicious *retsina* under plane trees. I think that, after olives
& cypresses & vines, which are more symbols than plants, plane trees
come next on my list of favourites. It always means there's water near
– emblems of salvation in August! – and, in a village they are the
heart of everything, sheltering those little colonies of rush-bottomed
chairs and round, tin tables where all the old boys wile their days
away over coffee and amber beads. Often, several yards of their
circumference, right up to the first branches, are whitewashed, which
looks marvellous. Then, a labyrinth of huge peeling branches patched
and mottled like pythons, and millions of those complicated leaves
producing a Marvellian[2] penumbra, and all on such thin and flexible
threads of stem that the faintest suspicion of a wind sets up a liquid
mysterious whispering. You ought to be there in mid summer to see
them really come into their own as public benefactors. Do you know
the first thing the old boys under them ask you when you've arrived
in a muck-sweat, had a drink, lit a cigarette and come to after some
appalling climb? It's: 'What do you think of our water?' They go on
about it like Connolly or Waugh over Cheval Blanc.[3] I had a French
guidebook once which said in the preface – '*C'est surtout l'eau qui*

excite la gourmandise des Grecs.[4] It's the same throughout the Levant. I believe that the Turks used to have tremendously grand *water-parties* in the past. They would settle on carpets and cushions in the cool of the evening in the garden of some palace on the banks of the Bosphorous with hookahs and tchibooks – those cherry wood pipes with straight stems six or eight feet long – and a Circassian or Caucasian girl playing the baglama (a sort of dulcimer suitable for damsels) while beautiful youths of equivocal status carried round trays laden with blood-red and gilt cut-glass carafes from Prague filled with different waters, which the Vizir would offer in turn to the beys and pashas beside him on the grass: 'Try this one, Selim – it's from the snows of Bithynian Olympus!' or 'One of the Sweet Waters of Asia . . . ' 'And this one, Cadi Effendim, is a rather rare one from the Taurus mountains.' 'This little fellow arrived by caravan last week from Azerbaijan.' 'That's just an ordinary Armenian.' 'What do you make of this, gentlemen? It's one of the Bulgarian tributaries of the Danube, a spring called Studena Voda . . .' Just think of all the water snobbery that must have gone on, the *expertise* and beard-stroking and rumblings and kissed fingertips and cries of Bismillah! ['In the name of Allah!'] and gurks of approbation! The gatherings would go on till moonrise, when the guests would be helped to their little private caïques by turbaned negroes and rowed reeling home, lulled by the sound of flutes, to the Golden Horn . . .

Last weekend I went to stay with an old friend called Antony Holland,[5] who lives between Brighton and London, in a very agreeable tumble-down, vicaragy kind of house full of books. (He's a great-great nephew of Sydney Smith's,[6] a fact which sets all my historico-snobbish fibres a-tingle.) Do you remember I told you all about the adventure with Lady Wentworth & Byron's slippers in Missolonghi last year? Well, we drove over again to Crabbet for luncheon on Sunday; the Hollands are the only people who are allowed to go there – she's quarrelled with everybody else in the world except her squash-partner (ex. All-England champ), now head groom and putative ex. conc[ubine]. Antony H. tells me that another of Wilfrid Blunt's mistresses, a Mrs Carleton, still lives in a cottage, not far away; always referred to by Lady Wentworth as 'that woman'; do you know anything about her?[7] We first bowled past the Catholic convent[8] where Wilfrid Blunt had 'Skittles'[9] buried, then past sleek cavalcades of Arab steeds galloping under the chestnuts, with KEEP OUT! NO TRESPASSING! notices everywhere, suggesting mantraps and spring-guns; then the burnt-out royal (real?) tennis court where the Souls' tournaments were said to occur,[10] and up to the house, where she is looked after by two nonagenarian female twins – 'my twins'. The house is untidy as a barn – trunks trussed, and excitingly labelled 'LD BYRON'S papers – LDY BYRON'S papers' in chalk, pictures stacked, piled furniture, wallpaper, curtains etc. exactly the colour and shape of coloured Phiz or Leech: illustrations to *Ask Mamma, Hawbuck Grange*, or *Mr Sponge*[11] – gilt, faded plum and canary; v. grand and dusty. We had rather a mouldy luncheon, ending up with spotted-dog, in a room as full of papers, pictures, horsey accoutrements and favours as a jackdaw's nest. Lady Wentworth was wearing, as usual, gym-shoes from playing squash, a Badminton skirt to the ground, a woollen shawl, a gigantic and very dishevelled auburn wig that looked as though made of strands from her stallions' tails gathered off brambles, and on top of this a mushroom-like, real Sairey-Gamp mob-cap,[12] but made of lace and caught in with a Nile-green satin ribbon. Rather a fine, hawky Byronic face under all this, but scarlet patches on the cheeks as from a child's paint-box; I think she's eighty-two or eighty-three[13] – and a very thin, aristocratic, bleak voice – *'have some more spotted-dog?'* sounding like a knell. The house is full of pre-Raphaelitish pictures of her by Neville Lytton,[14] many of them in elaborate Arabian clothes. She must have been a knockout except for those alarmingly suspicious eyes: a real vixen or Medusa glint. We had another look at Byron's Greek costume & sword (which the British Council are asking for, to send to Sr. Chas. Peake's Philhellene exhibition.[15] We exhorted her a lot about this) and managed to find, after a long search among draped furniture, a fascinating portrait of Byron which has never, to my knowledge, been reproduced.[16] It's rather amateurish (unsigned), but he is so young and charming-looking in it – eighteen at the most, and full face, I do think the Peakes ought to ask her for it for the exhibition. I'll write to them, but do mention it, if this gets you while you are still there.

After luncheon she led us, all three grasping a whiskey and soda, up some stairs to a long billiard room, where she drew the curtains, and switched on the lamps over the table, poked up a vast log fire, began chalking a cue and said, with no preamble, *'Would you like spot or plain?'* So we began playing, and she beat us hollow, one after the other, again and again, scoring breaks of 50, 70, 90, and once, 108. It began raining and blowing hard, the wind making strange noises among the elms outside and down the chimney. No other sounds except, occasionally, a falling log or the hiss of the syphon, the click of the balls or the plop! into the pocket, with Lady Wentworth working away in silence except, now and then, *'Put the red in its place, would you?'* or *'Hand me the rest please . . .'* On and on it went, like something in a terrifying Norse legend, gambling for one's life with a man-eating witch in a dim, shadowy cave at the bottom of a fjord. As the hours passed, the illusion grew. I could see Antony was thoroughly rattled too. We were losing by larger and larger margins with each successive game, and still the grim work went on, our whole life centring on the bright rectangle of green: *click! . . . click-click! . . .* and the wind outside blowing up to a gale. Lady Wentworth's eyes under the lace fringes of her cap were kindling with ever more alarming sparks of triumph. It was ghoulish. At last, after twenty defeats, at 7 o'clock, Antony managed to say, in a strangled voice, 'Lady Wentworth, I think we ought to be leaving . . .' It must have been the counter-charm. The spell was broken! She just said, 'Oh, I'm so sorry . . .' and all the glint died from her eyes. But if she'd said, *'Oh, but you're staying to dinner!'* I know one of us would have screamed, for it would have been all up. The double doors would have leapt open and *'The Twins'*[17] magnified and reproduced a hundredfold – centuplets! would have come galloping in howling with choppers and skewers and cauldrons and faggots . . . We drove off through the blizzard with pounding hearts.

It's a successful sunny spring day, but pretty cold. I'm writing at that pillared writing table with the let-down flap by the fire. Two crows, looking enormous, one poking about for worms on the lawn. On the other side of the house Artemis peers over the edge of her pram like a Ribston Pippin.[18] Work soars ahead. Mrs Wakefield[19] came over two days ago, and we sat over the fire drinking sherry. She was awfully nice, and I enjoyed this irruption into my bachelor solitude. She said there was some idea of you collecting and publishing old letters. Diana darling, why on earth don't you? I'm red-hot for this! I guard your vast and wonderful coronation letter as though it were the *Codex Sinaiticus*,[20] and there must be masses more knocking about the place. Surely it would be enormous fun to do? If you did, and needed any kind of a fag to help, do ask me to unless you've got someone else . . .

I'm wildly intrigued by the extraordinary building estate that rears its portals opposite your humble wicket. The houses are incredible, John Betjeman rampant – Stratford-upon-Avon, Sandringham, Arundel, South Carolina, Uppark,[21] West Wycombe;[22] what can go on inside? Surely not just TV, for which they are all whiskered? Overcoming my natural diffidence, I had a drink in an unbelievably depressing place called the Tithe Barn Club there – it's not a real club, you just wander in. The denizens looked boring and usual enough – retired overdraft-refusers [i.e. bank managers] for the most part I should say – but still waters run deep. I'm terribly tempted to do some anthropological fieldwork there, if only I weren't so busy with other things. Do you think there's a vice-ring? or smuggling? And what about all that bungalow-life at Pagham?[23] What goes on in those converted railway-carriages? I'm afraid we'll never know.

A thrush has just started singing like mad from the direction of those beehives. He really does do it twice over, too.[24] Do come back soon, but not before having filled eyes, ears, lungs, heart with Greece, as I think it has a therapeutic quality which is close to magic, more than anywhere else in the world. I long to hear every detail of places, people etc., impressions. Even if long accounts must wait (owing to the pending pyramids of answers, whose height I've done so signally little to reduce!) Don't let me languish without news of movements etc. Must stop now. God Bless you, my dearest Diana, and fondest

love from
Paddy
xxx

P.S. Two people came to look at the house yesterday, with a view to renting it. I could tell Miss W.[25] hated this by the rather skittish grimaces of collusion she made me from behind their backs. They didn't want it though, 'too cold', they said, the idiots. It's *warm* as toast in here. They looked frightful. Miss W. & I decided afterwards that they were 'a couple of real miseries'. Would it be all right if I hang in here two weeks more – that is, if nobody turns up? I'm having luncheon with JJ[26] at Joan's on Friday.

[1] An artists' suppliers founded in 1851 and located at No. 95 Jermyn Street, SW1. The paper itself was A3, soft and creamy.

[2] A reference to 'The Garden', by the metaphysical poet Andrew Marvell (1621–78).

[3] One of the finest Saint-Émilion wines.

[4] 'It's water above all which excites the taste-buds of the Greeks.'

[5] Antony James Holland (1913–82), who lived at Old Lullings, Balcombe, in West Sussex. Paddy had known Holland since they were officer cadets together at the beginning of the war. He and Antony's father, Michael James Holland, had visited Lady Wentworth at Crabbet the year before.

[6] The Reverend Sydney Smith (1771–1845), celebrated wit, about whom Hesketh Pearson wrote his classic biography, *The Smith of Smiths* (1934). His eldest daughter married the physician and travel writer, Sir Henry Holland.

[7] The Scottish artist Dorothy Carleton had in fact been dead twenty years at the time of this letter. Though younger than Blunt's daughter Judith, she had become his mistress. When Blunt moved her into Crabbet Park, supposedly as his 'niece', his long-suffering wife asked for a legal separation.

[8] Actually a Franciscan monastery.

[9] Catherine Walters (1839–1920), courtesan. Her nickname 'Skittles' is thought to have originated from her employment at a bowling alley near Park Lane. Her classical beauty was matched by her skill as a horsewoman: the sight of Catherine riding along Rotten Row in Hyde Park drew huge crowds of sightseers. She counted among her many lovers the Marquess of Hartington (later the 8th Duke of Devonshire); Napoleon III; and the Prince of Wales (later King Edward VIII). She was also Blunt's first love, and he remained infatuated with her for the rest of his life.

[10] 'The Souls', a loosely knit but nonetheless distinctive salon that flourished in the late nineteenth century. Its members included many of the most distinguished English politicians and intellectuals. They enjoyed playing stické, a form of real tennis. Diana and Duff Cooper were members of 'The Coterie', many of whom were children of the original 'Souls'.

[11] Three novels by R. S. Surtees (1805–64): *Ask Mamma* (1858), *Hawbuck Grange* (1847), and *Mr Sponge's Sporting Tour* (1853). Many of Surtees's novels were illustrated by John Leech.

[12] Sarah or Sairey Gamp, the sloppy, dissolute, and usually drunk nurse in Dickens's *Martin Chuzzlewit*. 'She wore a very rusty black gown, rather the worse for snuff, and a shawl and bonnet to correspond.'

13 She was eighty-one.

14 Lady Wentworth's former husband, Neville Bulwer-Lytton, 3rd Earl of Lytton (1879–1951), soldier and artist. They had divorced in 1923.

15 Sir Charles Peake was British Ambassador to Greece, 1951–7.

16 Probably one of the miniature portraits by George Sanders known to have been in the possession of Lady Wentworth, at least one of which has never been reproduced. There is some evidence that Lady Wentworth may have overpainted one of these portraits, not necessarily to its advantage. See Annette Peach, *Portraits of Byron*.

17 Two Irishwomen, identical twins, domestic servants at Crabbet Hall, who earlier had served tea.

18 Diana Cooper's granddaughter Artemis, who would eventually write Paddy's biography. PLF compares her to a variety of apple with a distinctive orange and russet red colouring.

19 Lady Diana's secretary.

20 The oldest substantial book to survive antiquity, a manuscript containing the Christian Bible in Greek, including the oldest complete copy of the New Testament.

21 A seventeenth-century house, now owned by the National Trust, set high on the Sussex Downs.

22 A Palladian house, built in the Georgian period, also now owned by the National Trust.

23 A village on the West Sussex coast, now effectively a suburb of Bognor Regis.

24 'That's the wise thrush; he sings each song twice over,
   Lest you should think he never could recapture
   The first fine careless rapture!'
                    Robert Browning, *Home-Thoughts, from Abroad*, 1845

25 Miss Wade, Lady Diana's maid.

26 Diana's son, John Julius. He had inherited the title Viscount Norwich on the death of his father.

To Ann Fleming   Poste Restante
22 June 1954   Hydra
                                                    Greece

Darling Annie,

It's very exciting to think you may be here in about a month. Joan got a letter a few days ago from Eroica Rawbum,[1] and he seems very keen. Joan wrote to Eroica, painting rather a primitive picture, not to discourage him, but as a sort of insurance policy against disappointment. But the truth is it's getting better and better every day, and I'm sure you'll love it. It's a large house on a steep slope with descending terraces like a Babylonian ziggurat, a thick-walled, whitewashed empty thing surrounded by arid reddish rocks and olive and almond and fig trees, and the mountainside goes cascading down in a series of tiled roofs and a church cupola or two to the sea, which juts inland in a small combe ten minutes' walk below (quarter of an hour up!). About three miles of the Aegean sea separate Hydra from the Argive coast of the Peloponnese – succeeding stage wings of mountain on the skyline, each one a paler blue than the one in front. The sun sets in the most spectacular way over these mountains and the sea, and every night Joan and I watch it from the top terrace drinking ouzo, then eating late – about 9, when it is dark – by lamplight at the other end of the terrace. There has been a full, then a waning, moon the last few nights, making everything look insanely beautiful. A great scraping of cicadas all day. So do come! I know we'll have the greatest possible fun.

I spent three days at Chantilly on the way out: Diana was more adorable than ever, a saint in helping to organise tickets, visas etc. in Paris like a tremendously responsible sister. I do worship her, I must say. She's got a heavenly broad-brimmed hat with a huge black satin bow hanging down the back. My train's pace was slower than a slug's, creeping across North Italy and then through Yugoslavia (which seems inhabited by a gloomy lot of brutes) and at last into Macedonia and Greece. I found Joan in Athens, hotfoot from Beirut, Damascus and Cyprus, and brown as a berry, as the saying goes. We are both turning mahogany at a great rate; but I suppose it'll all peel off, leaving one pink as a baby's bum once more . . . There's lots of lovely swimming and goggling (the fish, I must admit, are the size of tiddlers compared to Goldeneye) and lying about in the sun; also sitting about in the harbour drinking retsina at night. I've got a marvellous empty studio to work in, where I write away all day like a fire hydrant. Cyril and Baby[2] may come next week – I wonder how Hydra will stand up to the Skelton blight?

Do make serious plans about coming here. Meanwhile,

heaps of love from

Paddy

Best love to Ian, also to both from Joan.

[1] PLF's anagram for Maurice Bowra.
[2] Barbara Skelton (1916–96), novelist and socialite, married to Cyril Connolly. They divorced in 1956.

To Ann Fleming   c/o Niko Ghika
18 September 1954   Hydra

Darling Annie,

Very many apologies indeed from both of us (1) for neither having answered your lovely long letter, full of exactly the sort of thing one wants to hear – it was a masterpiece, and by far the best of any ex-Hydriot[1] so far; and (2) for being such laggards in saying 'thank you' for *The Dynasts*.[2] It really *was* kind of you to remember it. Joan is now in the thick of the first vol. – the second, which is reprinting, will follow soon, your bookseller says. It arrived just as we were about to run out of books. That green detective one, *The Gilded Fly*,[3] which vanished so mysteriously, miraculously materialised on the hall table yesterday!

You were missed a great deal by everyone, including the servants, who still talk affectionately of Kyria Anna. Soon after you went, I got a letter from Kisty Hesketh,[4] introducing her brother called Rory McEwen[5] and a pal called Mr Vyner.[6] You probably know the former, v. good looking, and a champion guitar player it seems, and probably very nice. They both seemed wet beyond words to us, without a spark of life or curiosity, and such a total lack of conversation that each subject died after a minute's existence. We had sixty subjects killed under us in an hour, till at last even Maurice and I were reduced to silence. Joan did her best, but most understandably subsided into a bored scowl after the first few hours.

We heaved a sigh when they vanished after two days that had seemed like a fortnight . . . Your fortnight, I must say, passed with the speed of a weekend. Joan saw Maurice off in Athens, another sad wrench.

Diana, JJ and Anne[7] finally turned up on the 2nd September. The last two left four days ago and D. is still here. They were not nearly such a handful as we feared, in fact very nice and easy and resourceful, Anne painting away industriously, or wandering off independently with JJ, who gave us lots of splendid guitar playing – always stopping in time & not boring at all. I think they enjoyed it very much. Diana, who is in your old room, seems as happy as she is anywhere now, and is very easy and unfussy, enjoying everything, loos, odd food, garlic, ouzo, retsina, etc., mooching about in the port, darting off to Athens, once to see Susan Mary Patten[8] off a caïque (but she wasn't there), once to see the Norwiches off, returning both times laden with Embassy whisky and so on, which was gratefully lapped up. We had a very entertaining old Greek friend for last weekend, Tanty Rodocanachi,[9] which was a great success, lots of funny stories and old world gallantry . . . But Diana's presence proved a magnet for other yachts, first of all Arturo Lopez[10] in a very sodomitical-looking craft, done up inside like the Brighton Pavilion, a mandarin's opium den and the alcove of Madame de Pompadour. Chips[11] was on board, le Baron Redé, a horrible French count called Castéja [Lopez-Willshaw's son-in-law] and a few other people who looked unmitigated hell, but I didn't quite manage to take them in during our two hours on board. We all felt a bit bumpkin-ish as we clutched our weighty cut-glass whisky goblets and perched on the edge of satin sofas. We were put down at the little restaurant down the hill, to the wonder of the assembled crowds; and the Balkan dark swallowed us up. They were off for the Cyclades and Beirut.

But this was nothing compared to five days ago, when a giant steam yacht (with an aeroplane poised for flight on the stern) belonging to Onassis[12] came throbbing alongside. It was followed by an immense three-masted wonder ship with silk sails, miles of corridor, dozens of Impressionist paintings, baths to every cabin and regiments of stewards, belonging to his brother-in-law, Niarchos.[13] They have made 400 million quid between the two of them, and own, after England, USA and Sweden, the largest merchant fleet in the world, all under Panamanian flags; and all, it seems, acquired in fifteen years. We only saw Niarchos, who is young,[14] rather good looking, very drunk and tousled, not bad really. On board were Lilia Ralli, several blondes, a few of the zombie-men that always surround the immensely rich, Pam Churchill & Winston Jr.[15] Sailing beside it was another three-masted yacht, gigantic by ordinary standards, but by comparison the sort of thing one sees inside bottles in seaside pubs. This was also Niarchos's, a sort of annexe for overflow, *soi-disant*, lent to Lord Warwick, though he is plainly some kind of stooge.[16] He looked like a Neapolitan hairdresser run to fat. We did a certain amount of drinking and social chat on the big one (spurning Lord Warwick's cockleshell) and wandered through labyrinthine corridors gaping at the fittings. I gathered from Pam C. next morning – the focus of all eyes on the quay in pink shorts, gilt sandals and a-clank with gems – that it's pretty good hell aboard: no sort of connecting link between all the guests, disjointed conversation, heavy banter, sumptuous but straggling meals at all hours, nobody knowing what is a test. Diana, Tanty, and the Norwiches got a lift in this to Athens (D. returning next day), and Joan and I trudged up to fried salt cod and lentils and garlic. We learnt on Diana's return that the massed blast of our five breaths nearly blew the whole party overboard. There is something colossally depressing about contact with the very rich. What I want to know is: *why the hell don't they have more fun with their money?*

Modiano's Cyprus article was the best I have seen so far.[17] After you left Athens, I accompanied the whole of the demonstration: oaths in front of the Unknown Warrior's tomb, the burning of the Cyprus sedition proclamation, also of bundles of Union Jacks, cries of 'Down with the English! Down with the Barbarians!', then, from the steps of the University, an awful incendiary speech from the Rector that overstated the case so much (he ended with an undying curse and anathema to the English!) that nearly all the sensible Greeks feel ashamed. What a bore it is, and so foolishly unnecessary.

Niko G[hika] comes back next week, but may not be able to stay on, as he is a lecturer in Athens. Joan returns sooner than me, so I'm going to keep my teeth into Hydra till the last possible moment. In spite of all the goings on, I've managed to keep on scribbling. I hate the idea of another uprooting and would like to stay till winter starts.

Thanks again, dearest Annie, for *The Dynasts*, and *do please* write another London newsletter! Lots of love from Joan and Diana, also to Ian, and from me. All wish you were here.

Love

Paddy

[1] i.e. their guests in Hydra.

[2] An ambitious verse-drama in three parts (1904, 1906 and 1908) by Thomas Hardy, set in the Napoleonic Wars.

[3] Edmund Crispin, *The Case of the Gilded Fly* (1944).

[4] Christian Mary 'Kisty' McEwen, Lady Hesketh (1929–2006), politician, journalist and educationalist. After the early death of her husband, she was left a widow with three young sons at the age of only twenty-five. In the 1950s she organised the annual charitable fancy dress ball of the Royal College of Art, where PLF was a regular guest. Among her remarkably varied activities was a stint as rugby correspondent of *The Spectator*.

[5] Rory McEwen (1932–82), Scottish artist and musician.

[6] Henry Vyner (1932–96), a neighbour of the McEwens in the Borders.

[7] Diana Cooper and her son John Julius, with his wife Anne.

[8] Susan Mary Patten (1918–2004), one of Duff Cooper's mistresses and later a leading political hostess in Washington. She had her hair done daily on the chance of a sudden invitation to the White House.

[9] Constantine Pandia 'Tanty' Rodocanachi (1877–1956). Before the war PLF translated his novel *Ulysse, fils d'Ulysse* into English. It was while visiting Tanty and his wife in the spring of 1935 that PLF had met Balasha Cantacuzène.

[10] Arturo Lopez-Willshaw (1900–62), homosexual Chilean millionaire, who lived with his lover Oskar Dieter Alex von Rosenberg-Redé, aka Alexis, Baron de Redé (1922–2004). Lopez settled $1 million on Redé shortly after they became a couple in 1941, when the latter was nineteen years old. Their parties were famous; the world of Lopez and Redé has been described as like a small eighteenth-century court. Nevertheless, Lopez continued to maintain a formal residence with his wife, Patricia, in Neuilly.

[11] Henry 'Chips' Channon (1897–1958), homosexual, American-born Conservative MP and diarist.

[12] Aristotle Socrates Onassis (1906–75), billionaire Greek shipping magnate and businessman, who amassed the world's largest privately owned shipping fleet.

[13] Stavros Spyros Niarchos (1909–96), another Greek shipping tycoon.

[14] He was then forty-five.

[15] Niarchos's mistress, Pamela Churchill (1920–97) (later Harriman), ex-wife of Randolph Churchill and mother of Winston Churchill, Jr.

[16] Charles Guy Fulke 'Fulkie' Greville (1911–84), 7th Earl of Warwick, lived abroad for much of his adult life. He became the first British aristocrat to star in a Hollywood movie, and was nicknamed 'the Duke of Hollywood' by the local press.

[17] 'A Quarrel between Friends', *The Times*, 19 August 1954, written by Mario Modiano,

Athens correspondent. Nationalist agitation for an end to British rule in Cyprus and union with Greece had led to an upsurge in anti-British sentiment. See page 111.

To Freya Stark   c/o Niko Ghika
25 October 1954   Hydra

Dearest Freya,

Very many thanks indeed for having 'Ionia'[1] sent to us. It arrived yesterday, after what must have been a delayed journey. I have only darted about in it, and the bits I have alighted on have been entrancing, and make me long to follow your and Herodotus's tracks. The quotations from the Greek anthology are beautifully chosen, and seem to turn up so fortuitously and casually, as a delightfully uninsistent proof of all you are saying. It's going to be a great treat, I can see.

I think Jock has made a fine job of it. It's beautifully printed and bound, and your photographs are jolly good. There is one that I turn back to often, as it seems to symbolise the situation (to me, that is, who hasn't been there) in the former Greek parts of Asia Minor: the one of your guide, a heavy, rather oafish, empty-handed lout planted as inertly as a sack of potatoes on the capsized capital of a broken Greek column. An agreeable bumpkin, I feel, with quite a nice smile; but he oughtn't to be there . . . The picture is almost heraldic in the simplicity and directness of its message, like the Red Heart of the Douglas[2] or the Bloody Hand of Ulster.[3]

It seems very quiet here now, with just Joan and me in the place, and all the summer visitors have migrated elsewhere. Diana, with John Julius and Anne, stayed about three and a half weeks. She seemed very happy, as much as she is capable of, that is, and one has never seen less of a fusspot about the comparatively ungracious living of the place. The rains have begun intermittently, and all is quiet and perfect for work, and the pile of MSs grows like a ziggurat. I wonder how you are getting on at Asolo. I'm going to keep my teeth into Hydra as long as possible, all winter if Niko Ghika will let me, as it is the perfect workshop.

Thank you again, dear Freya, for your lovely present, which will provide many happy hours. I'm longing to see the next volume!
With love from
    Paddy

(also from Joan)

¹ Freya Stark's *Ionia, A Quest* (1954) was followed by several more books on Turkey: *The Lycian Shore* (1956), *Alexander's Path: From Caria to Cilicia* (1958) and *Riding to the Tigris* (1959).

² As he was dying, the Scottish King Robert I ('Robert the Bruce'), is said to have asked his ally and friend Sir James Douglas (c.1286–1330) to carry his embalmed heart to Jerusalem, where it would be presented to the Church of the Holy Sepulchre. Douglas set out for the Holy Land, but was killed fighting the Moors in Spain, and the embalmed heart was returned to Scotland. Later Douglas lords attached the image of Bruce's heart to their coat of arms, to strike fear into the hearts of their enemies and to exhibit the prowess of their race.

³ The Red Hand of Ulster, originally a Gaelic symbol with its roots in ancient Fenian culture, has been appropriated by Northern Ireland's unionists and loyalists.

Since 1953 Lawrence Durrell had been living on British-controlled Cyprus, working as an information officer and editing the government-funded Cyprus Review. *For Durrell, this was an increasingly testing time, given his philhellenic sympathies and the deteriorating situation on the island.*

To Lawrence Durrell   Οἰκία Χατζηκυριάκου-Γκίκα
24 November 1954   ἐν Ὕδρᾳ
                              [c/o Hadjikyriakos-Ghika, Hydra]

My dear Larry,
    . . . I felt very jealous of Joan's adventures with you and Maurice [Bowra] early this summer, and long to see you both. Joan left last week alas, but I'm sticking on in Niko's house as long as he'll let me – it's the best bit of high-level cadging I've done for years, a real haul. I wish you'd come over and stay for a bit. It's a perfect Shangri-la for work, and at last I'm getting a move on, and feeling excited. How are

you getting on? I imagine the *Cyprus Review* takes one hell of a lot
of work – do send a copy or two. I'm so glad they got you to do it
– I first learnt by that nice bit about it in *The Spectator*. It must be a
very delicate business. I do wish the whole thing was settled. It makes
both the English and the Greeks conduct themselves like complete
lunatics, and grotesque caricatures of themselves.

I've just got Xan's new book *Hide and Seek*, a very lively and
dashing account of wartime adventures in Crete; also Daphne's
autobiography *Mercury Presides* (good title!)[1] which is rattling, splendid
stuff, not a bit the niminy-priminy society memoir you would think,
but hell for leather, a mixture of lyrical charm and touchingness with
a clumsy, rustic tough edge to it which is most engaging and terribly
funny. Rather like the letters of Lady Bessborough or Caroline
Lamb,[2] half-sylph, half-stablehand.

I'm so glad you met Xan and my old friend Arthur Reade.[3] I'm
terribly attached to him, though I haven't seen him for years. The book
which I translated from the Greek of our shepherd-guide in Crete[4] will
be coming out soon (*The Cretan Runner*, Murrays). I think it's tip-top, a
real primitive, [illegible] Douanier Rousseau[5] kind of war-book.

No more now, but I'll write again as soon as the stuff arrives. Lots
of love to Eve and Sappho.[6] [George] Katsimbalis is due back any
moment from phenomenal adventures in America, France and
England that I burn to hear. They should be *quelque chose*!

love

   Paddy

---

[1] Her memoir of life as one of the 'Bright Young Things', reviewed by Evelyn Waugh:
'The childhood is admirable. The adult part is rather as though Lord Montgomery
were to write his life and not to mention that he ever served in the army.'

[2] Henrietta Ponsonby (1761–1821), Countess of Bessborough, had numerous lovers. Among
her admirers was William Lamb, later Viscount Melbourne, who married her daughter
Caroline (1785–1828). Lady Caroline Lamb conducted a scandalous affair with Lord Byron.

[3] The SOE officer Arthur Reade, who served with PLF and Xan Fielding behind the
German lines in occupied Crete. His son Patrick was PLF's godson.

[4] George Psychoundakis.

[5] The naive French artist Henri Rousseau (1844–1910) was known as Le Douanier
Rousseau, a reference to his job as a customs officer.

[6] Durrell's daughter by his wife Eve.

To Diana Cooper
3 January 1955   Hydra

ΧΡΟΝΙΑ ΠΟΛΛΑ ΚΑΙ ΑΓΑΠΗ ΚΑΙ
ΧΙΛΙΕΣ ΕΥΧΕΣ ΔΙΑ ΤΟ ΝΕΟΝ ΕΤΟΣ 1955
['Many happy returns (as they say here), love and 1000 wishes
for the New Year 1955']

Diana darling,

It was lovely to find your Betjeman booklet[1] when I got back
here from the Peake fleshpots of Athens, and thank you so much for
them. One or two are rather hell, I think – have you read them yet?
– rather embarrassing jaunty high Anglican stuff (. . . it gives a
chance to me, To praise our dear old C. of E. etc.), one or two of
them charming. Very pretty Piper drawings. But there's a terrible
note of the headmaster beginning a confirmation class with the
words 'Now do remember, God is such FUN!' (I say, talk about gift
horses in the mouth. Especially when I haven't sent you one yet,
because of being out of touch with contemporary literature! I've
been cudgelling my brain for a month and feel inspiration will
come soon.)

I'm terribly distressed by one thing in your letter – that you seem
to have dropped the Persian Gulf Plan. I'd got so used to the idea of
your stopping off in Athens on the way, and was already looking
forward like anything to jaunts in Attica together, – even to a wintry
descent to this now verdant isle – as if they were certainties. Because
alas, I don't quite see how I *can* get to Italy in the middle of this
month. It's a terribly tempting thought, though, and I haven't
absolutely chucked it. I won't bore you with enumerating what the
difficulties are, they're too tedious to go into, but pretty prohibitive
none the less. Thank heavens, dough for once is not one of them, as
I'm wildly solvent for once (for me that is) except Italian currency.
But, Diana darling, is Athens *absolutely* ruled out for you? Do please
write again as soon as poss. and tell how plans have matured.

I got back from Athens on Christmas Eve, after staying with the
Peakes[2] for a week, which, I must say I simply loved, though I

seemed to be out of the building and on the tiles most of the time.
(The point of my stay was arranging about the unveiling by the
King of a monument all the English-who-were-in-Crete are putting
up, and, Cyprus willing, it is to take place some time in May.) They
really are the most wonderful kind and hospitable couple –
tremendous fans of yours (which I think is really why they asked
me) as you know. We had lots of sitting up talking about poetry,
scanned by the soft hiss of the soda syphon (my favourite noise, I'm
beginning to realise, and one that has been silent in ouzo-ridden
Hydra for many a long month). And the baths, – I turned on those
resplendent taps with some of the rustic wonder of a Red Army
corporal in the Imperial quarters of Peterhof – *meat*; delicious, almost
Chantilly standard breakfasts in bed; ironed clothes; glittering shoes.
They asked me to stay for Christmas, but I thought it would be
overdoing it, so crept back to Hydra with an alibi, but even so, a day
later than I meant to, as on the last night, I went to a party which
ended at 6. The butler came to wake me up at 7 for the 8 o'clock
Nereid,[3] shook me and put a sponge on my brow – all no go.
Stalwart young maids were called in to shake [me] but apparently it
was like trying to raise a fallen dolmen. One of them managed to
prise open a single bloodshot eye, and fled in terror . . . So I went
to a dinner party of Niko Ghika's with the tolerant Peakes, which
was absolutely delicious, based on some marvellous quenelles made of
thousands of mussels, and got off safely next morning, though the
time of the boat had been put off to 2.00 p.m. because of fêtes. I
spent happy hours wandering round that hideous but absorbing port
[Piraeus], where there are not only quarters inhabited by Cretans,
Maniots, Epirots, Thessalians and Macedonians, but by refugees from
all the biblical region of Asia Minor – Pisidia, Paphlagonia (as in *The
Rose & the Ring*)[4] Cappadocia, Pontus & Bithynia & from the borders
of Kurdistan, all with their customs & dialects intact. You only have
to *march* into the right café to be spiritually in the heart of Caesarea,
Iconium or Trebizond. The place was looking very queer that day,
because all the children were holding balloons twice their size shaped
like colossal space cats with jutting whiskers and eyes like round
towers. Other children – the equivalent of 'waifs' – were prowling

from shop to shop holding antediluvian gramophones with petunia horns the size of a man-eating convolvulus and playing eardrum-splitting and cacophonous carols on records scratched beyond recognisability. They would take up positions with this apparatus outside cafés and shops till they had tortured the owners into giving them danegeld.

I got to Hydra grasping a wonderful turkey (a dead one) under my arm, like a golden goose, a present from Catherine Peake. Yanni roasted this on the great day, and I had a banquet in the drawing room, the big dining room table with lots of candles and a star-shaped pattern of uprooted sea-squills and pink geraniums in the middle, which looked nicer than it sounds. Gladys[5] and Tanty had originally been coming for Christmas, but both had cried off at the last moment (the cold? Actually it's as warm as anything with both stoves roaring). So I had Russian Lil Heidsièck (who you never met) with her Lost Boys, an English couple called the Goschens,[6] and two people from the Art School. Over New Year the island filled up with Young Intellectuals from Athens, some of whom stayed with me, and we had a great party of about twenty-seven, starting at 9, going on till about 5 also up here. They were very nice indeed, and the thing was really kept together by a very talented art student with a guitar which he played and sang to with an almost JJ virtuosity. A girl, eating a stewed mussel (which had actually come out of a tin) found a minute pearl. Isn't that strange? I had a great success with all the songs I cribbed off JJ this summer. They've all vanished now, the island seems rather bleak and deserted and life goes on with the faint gloom of an anti-climax.

I have been very much cheered up by something I have discovered today. It's rather elaborate. From the Middle Ages till the beginning of the last century, Piraeus was known as Porto Leone, after a large, ancient, marble lion standing at the entrance to the harbour. (It had some Nordic runes carved on its shoulder by Harald Hardrada,[7] when he was in the Mediterranean.) The lion was looted and carried off to Venice by Doge Francesco Morosini in *1687* and placed outside the Arsenale where it still stands. In *1750*, an Englishman from Bristol called Bill Falconer, second-mate of the brig

Britannia, was wrecked off Cape Sunium. When he got back to England, he wrote a splendid long poem about his adventures and impressions of Greece called *The Shipwreck*. About Piraeus he says:

> The wandering traveller sees before his eyes
> *A milk-white lion of stupendous size!*

Now of course, the traveller does nothing of the kind, and what's more, *neither did he*, the old fibber – the lion had been in Venice for sixty-three years! Talk about piling it on! I am positively haunted by this robust couplet, and have been repeating it aloud to myself all the morning. Do try it – in a deep voice, if possible in a West Country accent, if not, cockney, and very loud. It grows on you.

Next Day, Epiphany (written outside The Poseidon, waiting for the letter to catch the slow Pindus*, which has now taken over from the* Nereid*)*
Thank heavens, it's a lovely sunny spring day, as this is one of the great feasts of the Orthodox Church. All the shops are shut, and everyone in their Sunday best. The hideous Hydriot girls wear plastic high-heeled shoes and blinding satin dresses of apple green, scarlet, royal blue and petunia (often a combination of all four), and reek of attar of roses. They look exactly like boiled sweets. The old men, with their wicked old Albanian faces, look magnificent. Nearly all of them limp from sponge fishing mishaps: a shark bite in the thigh off the Libyan reefs in 1896, a leg carried off at Mersa Matruh in 1904, an arm at Benghazi in 1911 . . . There was a huge procession, headed by dozens of boys carrying candles and lanterns in red silk dalmatics from which socks and gym-shoes projected, and little black skull caps, their cheeks downy with the sort of moss that reindeer graze on all through the winter in Lapland. (One of them, oddly enough, was a man of seventy with a piratical black patch over one eye.) Then sailors carrying ikons of Our Lord's Epiphany before the Wise Men of the East, and also of the Baptism (as today is also the Vigil of the Feast of the Baptism). Then a swarm of cantors groaning Byzantine anthems in quarter tones, grass-green deacons with censors, a swarm of priests in vestments every colour

of the rainbow, black veils on their cylinder hats, a court of prelates,
and finally the Archbishop of Spetsai & Hydra, a wicked old man of
stupendous size (odd that such a tiny see should have an archbishop),
a pillar of gleaming cloth of gold and chains & plaques and pectoral
crosses, beard a yard long, flowing white hair down his back,
wearing a colossal, onion-shaped mitre of gold and silver studded
with enormous jewels and diamonds, his gold crozier topped, like
the caduceus of Hermes, with two gold and twirling serpents. He's
got an appalling reputation.* (But one must remember that
preferment in the Eastern Church goes entirely by height.) The
procession wound up the hill to bless and asperge the island's only
freshwater spring, then back to the quay and along to the end of
that mole that runs out across the harbour, where the Archbish
settled on a throne at the heart of a dazzling galaxy. The liturgy
went on, His Beatitude leaning back like a figure from [El] Greco,
exchanging heavy banter, quite loud, with the other prelates. One
almost expected him to take out a double Corona and slowly light
it . . . Then his eyes kindled with approbation as a caïque-load of
naked boys, all shuddering with cold, sailed up and dropped anchor
a few yards away. The chanting soared and His Beatitude stood up
and threw a cross into the sea. A huge splash, and all the boys
plunged into the icy main and started swimming like tadpoles.
Meanwhile all the bells began pealing, the sirens honked, and the
old War of Independence cannon fired salvos. A terrific tussle in the
water, till at last one of the boys splashed ashore, put the cross in
the Archbishop's lap, and drenched everyone by shaking himself like
an otter-hound. His Beatitude, with eyes ablaze, kept patting his wet
shoulder with a large, horny and mottled hand, repeating 'Bravo! . . .
bravo, my boy!' again and again. The procession returned to the
church, the ceremony was over, and everyone made a dash for the
unshuttering tavernas and ouzo.

---

* The Archbishop of Spetsai & Hydra
  Condemned bestial vice ex-cathedra.
  (But he rogered a bay-horse
  Outside the pronaos
  And a skewbald inside the exedra).

I must stop now, Diana dearest, and get this off. Please write at once with full plans and please try and make them include Greece! with love and hugs from

Paddy

xxxxx

---

1 *Poems in the Porch* (1954), an anthology of verse originally written for broadcast on a weekly BBC radio programme. Betjeman himself had misgivings about whether the poems were worth publishing.

2 The British Ambassador Sir Charles Peake and his wife Catherine.

3 The ferry to Hydra.

4 William Makepeace Thackeray's *The Rose and the Ring* (1854) is set in the fictional countries of Paflagonia and Crim Tartary.

5 Gladys Stewart-Richardson, who kept a shop in Athens.

6 John Alexander Goschen (1906–77), 3rd Viscount Goschen, and his wife Alvin.

7 Harald Sigurdson, known as Harald Hardrada (c.1015–66) spent fifteen years in exile as a mercenary before becoming King of Norway in 1046.

Paddy first spotted Deborah ('Debo') Mitford — as she then was — at a regimental ball in the 1940s, though she did not notice him at the time. They came to know each other as acquaintances at London parties in the early 1950s; but their friendship took off in the mid 1950s, when they began to correspond regularly. By this time she was married to Andrew Cavendish, the 11th Duke of Devonshire, with a family of young children. Their correspondence would continue until Paddy's death, more than half a century later. Over the years Paddy was often a guest at one of the Devonshire houses, Chatsworth in Derbyshire or Lismore Castle in Ireland.

Paddy sent inscribed copies of each of his books to Debo. 'Look here, honestly, it's awfully good, frightfully good,' he would say; and she would reply, 'All right, Pad, I will try one day,' but she never did.

There was speculation that 'Debo' and Paddy had once been lovers, but those who knew them best doubted this. Their relationship has been described as 'a deep, platonic attraction between two people who shared youthful high spirits, warmth, generosity, and an unstinting enjoyment of life' (Charlotte Mosley (ed.), In Tearing Haste: Letters between Deborah Devonshire and Patrick Leigh Fermor, *2008).*

As their correspondence has been published separately, only a few introductory letters have been included in this volume, with a couple of late, previously unpublished letters towards the end.

To Debo Devonshire   c/o Niko Ghika
26 April 1955   Kamini
                                                          Hydra

Dear Debo,

    I've just heard from Daphne on the point of departure to stay
with you. Why does everyone go to that castle[1] except me?

    My plan is this: there is a brilliant young witch on this island
(aged sixteen and very pretty), sovereign at thwarting the evil
eye, casting out devils and foiling spells by incantation. It
shouldn't be beyond her powers to turn me into a fish for a
month and slip me into the harbour. I reckon I could get
through the Mediterranean, across the Bay of Biscay, round
Land's End and over the Irish Sea in about twenty-eight days (if
the weather holds) and on into the Blackwater. I'm told there's a
stream that flows under your window, up which I propose to
swim and, with a final effort, clear the sill and land on the
carpet, where I insist on being treated like the frog prince for a
couple of days of rest and recovery. (You could have a tank
brought up – or lend me your bath if this is not inconvenient
– till I'm ready to come downstairs. Also some flannel trousers,
sensible walking shoes and a Donegal tweed Norfolk jacket with
a belt across the small of the back and leather buttons.) But
please be there. Otherwise there is all the risk of filleting,
meunière etc., and, worst of all, *au bleu* . . .

Please give my love to Daphne if she's with you. You can let her in on this plan, if you think it is suitable, but nobody else for the time being. These things always leak out.

Love
Paddy

P.S. Please write & say if this arrangement fits in with your plans.

¹ Lismore Castle, County Waterford, overlooking the Blackwater River, has been the Irish home of the Dukes of Devonshire since 1753.

Among the Greek friends Paddy made while working for the British Council in Athens after the war was the poet George Seferis, whose work would be recognised in 1963, when he was awarded the Nobel Prize for Literature. The citation noted 'his eminent lyrical writing, inspired by a deep feeling for the Hellenic world of culture'.

To George Seferis
22 June 1955

Οἰκία Χατζηκυριάκου-Γκίκα
ἐν Ὕδρα
[c/o Hadjikyriakos–Ghika, Hydra]

Dear George,

Niko [Ghika] has just been here for a few days, the first time for ages. It was great fun. He and Joan played endless games of chess, out of which Joan came slightly the winner, in the end, and we went on a hilarious pleasure journey to Spetsai with Nancy Mitford, who was also staying.[1]

The *meltemi*[2] has started. Also a small plague of horseflies. As there are no horses in Hydra, they console themselves on us, riddling us like colanders, as we emerge defenceless from the waves, each armed with a proboscis sharper than a bradawl for puncturing the withers of a carthorse (I'm afraid it's softening them). There are also, at the moment, large numbers of centipedes about, and always in trouble: falling off walls they are attempting to scale, getting trodden on and being washed down drains. One would have thought that, with all their advantages, they would have got further. It makes one proud of being a biped.

Not only are there no horses in Hydra, but it is as empty of wheels as America before the conquistadores arrived. The islanders boast rather loosely about the presence of a barrow somewhere. But nobody has set eyes on it . . .

Many thanks again, dear George, and best love to you both from
    Paddy

(also from Joan)

A butterfly has just flown in through the window. You will not be surprised to hear that it is a Red Admiral.[3]

---

[1] 'I made great friends with Paddy Leigh Fermor,' Nancy Mitford wrote to Christopher Sykes after this holiday. 'He is a shrieker and how rare they get.' Charlotte Mosley (ed.), *Love from Nancy: The Letters of Nancy Mitford* (1993), pages 342–3.

[2] The strong, dry north winds of the Aegean, which blow from about mid May to mid September.

3 A pun (PLF's father was a lepidopterist). Several of the ships used in the Greek War of Independence and their admirals came from Hydra.

Paddy left Hydra for France in the autumn of 1955. He felt he was becoming stale there; as perhaps he was, because his book based on his Greek travels was still unfinished. 'I'm afraid he is too much Penelope-ising with that book,' George Seferis confided to Joan.

Moreover, the ill feeling engendered by the situation in Cyprus was poisoning relations between Britons and Greeks. Greek opinion had long regarded the island of Cyprus, a British colony, as rightfully theirs. A nationalist popular movement named EOKA agitated for unification with Greece ('Enosis'). The situation was complicated by the presence of a substantial Turkish Cypriot minority on the island. Impatient with the lack of progress, EOKA had declared an armed struggle against British rule. In response, the new governor of the island, Sir John Harding, formerly Chief of the Imperial General Staff, adopted stringent measures to improve the security situation.

An official at the Greek Aliens Office on Hydra attempted to have Paddy and several other British nationals deported; and though this attempt came to nothing, it unsettled him. There was a heated exchange between Paddy and his old friend George Katsimbalis on the subject of Cyprus. 'I am in such despair about it all,' Joan wrote to Seferis. 'George Katsimbalis refused to dine with Paddy and me on my last night in Athens, which upset me dreadfully,' she continued. 'What are we to do? I can't think about it any more without bursting into tears.'

After leaving Hydra Paddy wrote from France to Ghika and his wife Antigone.

To Antigone ('Tiggie') and Niko Ghika   c/o Diana Cooper
1 November 1955   Château de Saint-Firmin
                                                        Vineuil
                                                          Oise

Darling Tiggie and Niko,
    Everything, to my eyes adjusted for Hydra, looks very peculiar in France. All this green gives one the sensation of living in the heart of a giant lettuce. It's a lovely autumn evening, with bonfires burning

under trees in the park, a constant flutter of falling leaves, dew, a thin
mist over the lake, and, the other side, in front of the big chateau, the
dim silhouette of the Connétable Anne de Montmorency equestrian,
in full armour, stirring up the evening air with a huge sword . . .

I found Joan in Normandy, staying with the Smarts — I don't know
whether you know them — who live there in summer, Egypt in winter.
I'm going to camp in the house for three months (c/o Lady Smart,
Gadencourt, Pacy-sur-Eure, Eure. Tel: Gadencourt 6) — I send these
details hoping that you will write or telephone when you get to France
and stay a weekend or something . . . Niko, would you ask Boukas[1]
to get in touch with me about the photographs as I will have a great
conference with Stephen[2] about the timing and layout of the article, etc.

I think with immense nostalgia & gratitude of Hydra, where most
of my book will have been written — in fact 1954–5 is a great *étape
dans ma vie* [stage of my life]. I didn't need to tell you both how we
loved it and how valuable and important it was, because I think you
know. I really felt I had to vanish from the raw material of my work
for a few months, like Niko into a cellar with his sketches. But I am
certain that without Hydra, the book would never have been written,
and can never thank enough! Do, please, make a sign when you come
here.

Meanwhile, fond love to you both from
        Paddy

[1] Philip Boukas, photographer.

[2] Stephen Spender, poet and critic, co-editor of *Horizon* and *Encounter*. Earlier in the
year Spender and his wife Natasha had come to stay on Hydra with PLF and Joan.
PLF was writing a piece for *Encounter*, as he explained in an undated letter to Diana
Cooper. 'I've written a long thing in my book (which Stephen Spender is printing in
one of the next two months' 'Encounter' — the new *Horizon*) evoking all the different
parts of Greece — mountains, towns, rivers, islands etc.' PLF's article 'Sounds of the
Greek World' would appear in *Encounter* in June 1956.

*George Katsimbalis was the central figure in the group of Greek writers and
intellectuals whom Paddy came to know in Athens after the war. The two men
had met briefly in 1940, in an Athens nightclub. Paddy's head was wrapped*

*romantically in a bandage, and this deceptively heroic appearance had earned
him several free drinks. To Katsimbalis, who happened to be there, he admitted
that the wound had been the result of nothing worse than a car accident.
Katsimbalis laughed and advised him not to tell anyone else.*

*Katsimbalis was a tremendous talker, whom Paddy nicknamed 'the Gas-Bag
of Attica' – though of course he was quite a talker himself. In the spring of
1955 the two men travelled together round the Peleponnese by bus; afterwards Paddy remarked on 'George's unstaunchable and, I must say, wonderful
storytelling'.*

*This letter was written after Paddy and Katsimbalis had been reconciled,
following their heated quarrel over Cyprus.*

To George Katsimbalis
5 November 1955   Château de Saint-Firmin

My dear George,

I tried to ring you up before leaving (the day of Papagos's
funeral)[1] but couldn't get through, alas; so set off in the pouring rain
with a mound of luggage, and that bloody crate with the Μεγάλη
Ἑλληνικὴ Ἐγκυκλοπαίδεια,[2] which turned out to be a terrible
nuisance. Half a ton of untapped knowledge! I felt like Sisyphus.
What a job it was getting it across the frontier at Gevgeli, into
Serbia, and trundling it up the Vardar valley. Thank God, I lost it
temporarily at Belgrade, but the Embassy have found it, and it
follows me by goods train to Paris.

Belgrade is awful. I got a sleeper fortunately, and there was an
uncouth Serbian airman in the lower bunk whose hand appeared
beside my pillow every quarter of an hour with a bottle of slivovitz
followed by his only word in a Western language '*Disinfectant*'. We
crossed Croatia and Slovenia in a trance . . . Returning to my
compartment at Milan after a kilometre of macaroni in the Wagon-
restaurant, I found his place had been taken by a Japanese
businessman with teeth twice the normal length, each alternately
edged with gold and lead and revealed in a perennial smile. Between
these old ivory gnashers all night a succession of double-Coronas

were stuck, which embowered me, in my top bunk, in a buoyant cloud of apotheosis, and wafted me, shrouded thus across the Lombard plain, under the Alps, through the Simplon and, next day into the smiling plains of France and along the Valley of the Yonne. Who could have thought that those fragrant leaves, rolled on dusky thighs in Cuba, would one day, in contact with those Nippon tusks and Fujiyama nostrils, achieve a combustion that would float me, enclouded like Zeus when visiting Semele,[3] westwards across Transalpine Gaul? Inscrutable destiny . . .

Lovely weather in Paris! I met Joan for a drink at the Brasserie Lipp, and then we went and had a formidable meal at the Roi Gourmet, in the Place des Victoires, out of doors under the front hoofs of Louis XIV's rearing mount: foie gras, chateaubriand with béarnaise, perfect brie, a bottle of Château Margaux followed by several Marc de Bourgogne; then reeled around the Etruscan exhibition at the Louvre. After this we went to Normandy to stay with the Smarts (friends of George S[eferis]'s), till Joan went to England and I came here for a few days (Diana Cooper's house). Do write the address down as – usual style! – I've managed to [illegible] for the winter: c/o Lady Smart, Gadencourt, Pacy-sur-Eure, Eure. It's very comfortable, half cottage, half farmhouse, & full of books. The Smarts, my benefactors, spend the winter in Egypt. If you come to France, do come and stay. There are several important *relais gastronomiques*[4] in the neighbourhood – Conches, La Roche Guyon and Vernon, where I ate a remarkable *poularde* with a cream sauce and morels – those little black mushrooms – the other day. The meals are so copious they can only be managed by burning holes with a swig of calvados between the courses; the *trou normand* as they call it.

I came across a small book called *Recits Byzantins* by Pierre Almanachos at Gadencourt, rather fun. Is it the same chap who got into trouble for you-know-what . . . ? There are nice tales of Nik. Choniates, Michael Akominatos, the Fall of Constantinople etc. George, *please* see if you can possibly find a decent, authoritative book or pamphlet on the Sarakatsans,[5] as it's an awful gap. I've got sheafs of notes on them, but nothing really solid on their background. I lie awake for hours at night, conceiving what exactly

I ought to write about Cyprus and for whom, and think I am onto
the right track at last.[6] It's not at all easy.

The villagers are enormous blond brutes, obvious kinsmen of
William the Conqueror & of Tancred, Bohemond etc. who destroyed
the Empire. If you come and stay, we might lay on a little massacre;
you as a Byzantine, me as a Saxon . . . I return there tomorrow, then
to England (Travellers) for two to three weeks, and back to
Normandy.

It's lovely here at Chantilly, with lawns sloping down to the big
park and the lake of the Condé castle, vistas of trees leading to an
equestrian statue of the Connétable Anne de Montmorency waving a
huge sword in the evening mist.[7] Crimson leaves falling everywhere,
silver frost on the grass, a tissue-paper-thin pane of ice on the lake.
Dew! Lovely-smelling smoke of bonfires everywhere.

Write and tell me your news, and kiss Spatch,[8] & give her my
love. Καὶ ὁ Θεὸς νὰ μᾶς ποντικοδυναμώνει! [And may God
strengthen our muscles!]

    love from
      Paddy

[1] Marshal Alexander Papagos (1883–1955), commander of the Greek Army in the
Second World War and in the latter stages of the Greek Civil War (1946–9). On retiring
from the army he founded a new political party, which he led to victory in two
elections, becoming prime minister from 1952 until his death.

[2] The *Great Greek Encyclopaedia*, published in twenty-four quarto volumes. PLF had a
special crate made to transport it across Europe.

[3] Semele, princess of Thebes, who burst into flames when Zeus appeared before her
in his full glory.

[4] An association of hotels and restaurants formed in 1954, setting high standards
in cuisine and luxury.

[5] Ethnic Greek shepherds, who move with their flocks between higher pastures in
summer and lower valleys in winter. Historically centred on the Pindus mountains
of northern Greece, they are also present in the neighbouring countries of Bulgaria,
Macedonia and Albania.

[6] In a two-part article for *The Spectator* ('Friends Apart' and 'Friends Wide Apart',
9 and 16 December 1955), PLF condemned both the incendiary broadcasts from
Athens and the British government's refusal to hold talks on the future of Cyprus,
which he criticised as 'evasive, graceless and insulting'.

[7] Born in Chantilly, de Montmorency resurrected the medieval castle there.

[8] Katsimbalis's wife Aspasia, known as 'Spatch'.

To Jock Murray   c/o Lady Smart
undated [November 1955?]   Gadencourt
                                                        Pacy-sur-Eure

Dear Jock,

Thank you so much for your two letters, and 1,000 apologies for
my delinquency as a correspondent. I've been meaning to write daily.

Our stay in Greece ended in a glorious hol on a yacht[1] skilfully
borrowed by Diana Cooper, on which I was allowed to have almost
entire charge of the itinerary (Mykonos – Delos – Amorgos – Ios
– Rhodes – Symi – Kos – Kalymnos – Chios – Psara – Skyros –
Skopelos – Skiathos), and to fill in my chaplet of the archipelago
with several missing beads. Everyone vanished when we got back to
Athens. I stayed on a week to fix everything up, buying books etc. I
finally ruined myself by buying the *Great Greek Encyclopaedia* for £45;
a wonderful thing which I've longed for for twenty years – twenty-
four colossal quarto volumes. Crated, it weighed half a ton, I should
think; several hundred weight, anyway, of compact ratiocination,
which proved like the Stone of Sisyphus to trundle across the Balkan
frontiers. I finally left it in Belgrade to follow me in its own time,
trusting love and knowledge to find a way.

I was quite glad to leave Greece – though I hated quitting Niko's
lovely house – for two reasons: (1) New stuff kept piling up every
day so that it was impossible not to notice and absorb, and if I stayed
on, it would have been like trying to pay off the interest on a debt
which kept mounting up at compound interest; and (2) The political
situation in Greece, the mess we have both[2] (but mostly we) have
made of it began to develop into a kind of obsessive and paralysing
compound of anger and gloom that departure may exorcise. Now,
(luck of luck!) our old friends the Smarts have lent me this house!
I shall stay here these winter months and finish all. I came to stay
skulking this side of the Channel, I hoped, to have something
complete to cover the shame of delay with you on my return. Since
arriving, I find myself struggling with a long article (I don't know
who for) about Cyprus – roughly, a plea that we should change our
entire policy there. I don't think I'll be able to do anything before

it's off my chest. My plan is to return sometime next week (%
Travellers). I'll get in touch with you at once.

Thank you so much for news of Freya. I'll try and get in touch
with her (a) for the fun of seeing her and (b) to bully her a bit
about her famous Turks.

Must dash to post!

Yours ever

Paddy

So pleased about George [Psychoundakis]'s dough.

P.S. You must come and stay here.

1 *Eros II*, a yacht belonging to Stavros Niarchos.

2 i.e. Britain and Greece. The British authorities in Cyprus declared a state of emergency on the island in November 1955, following the assassination of five soldiers.

To Ann Fleming   c/o Lady Smart
7 January 1956   Gadencourt

Darling Annie,

It's too late for Christmas greetings, and New Year and even
Epiphany & probably premature for Sexagesima, but anyway; Happy
1956! I tried to telephone you several times (in vain, alas; all
occupied, and then you were gone) to say thank you 1,000 times for
that lovely dinner and classical ball.[1] I wish you hadn't left so early. I
stayed for ages and ages, enjoyed it at a steadily increasing ratio, and
swallowing immeasurable amounts of all kinds of delicious drinks. In
fact, I'm not quite clear about the end of the evening. The mists of
the Dark Ages set in, mimicking in a lesser degree the talk of Rome
when the hoofs of Alaric splintered the Capitoline marbles . . .
When the mists of Oblivion parted, I found myself, at high noon
next day, light-headed and unshaven in the middle of Knightsbridge,
a lady's overcoat over my tarnished armour, still trailing that bloody
trident and waving for a taxi in vain.

It's all very different here, and heaven in its way: no sound but the industrious scratching of nibs, long-playing records in the evenings and the patter of Norman rains. Lovely and warm, thank God. If you come to France, please for heaven's sake telephone (Gadencourt 6, 'près de Pacy-sur-Eure'. Please write down). It's only an hour from Paris. Joan's brother Graham[2] was here for Christmas & New Year, and we made many a gastronomic pilgrimage to the starred restaurants of Normandy, & left not a truffle unturned. Joan returns sometime towards the end of the month, and I think we go to Chantilly *next* weekend on Diana's way to Switzerland.

Do please write a short *chronique scandaleuse* of metropolitan life, and bear France in mind. I feel very excited at the thought of one vol. of my Greek rigmarole appearing in late spring,[3] and am busy clipping, brushing & polishing. V. many thanks again, Annie darling, and best love

from

Paddy

P.S. I must record a curious phenomenon. I am writing this letter in bed, & the garden outside is white with frost. The only two occupants of it are a large tabby cat belonging to the house and a robin fidgeting about on the branches of an apple tree, and it's so cold and frosty that their breath streams into the air in great clouds of vapour. It looks most odd. They survey each other from a safe distance like two chain-smokers . . .

Beyond, in an indistinct field, a number of surly looking black and white cows (many of them with crumpled horns, I'm sorry to say) float about in the mist. I often single one out on my afternoon walks and try to hypnotise her by gazing into those great idiot eyes and willing her to (1) lie down, (2) shake her head three times and (3) moo. So far, alas, with no success at all.

---

[1] At the Royal College of Art, organised to raise money for a charity supported by the Earl of Arran ('Boofy's beastly East End children'). See Mark Amory (ed.), *Letters of Ann Fleming* (1985), page 164.

[2] Graham Eyres Monsell (1905–94), later 2nd Viscount Monsell.

[3] This was optimistic. The book was eventually published in December 1958.

The most prominent of those calling for Enosis was Archbishop Makarios, head of the Greek Orthodox Church in Cyprus and de facto leader of the Greek Cypriot majority on the island. On 9 March 1956 Makarios was taken into custody and exiled to an island in the Seychelles.

In the Sunday Times of 8 April 1956, PLF challenged the definition of Enosis advanced by Sir Richmond Palmer, a former Governor of Cyprus, in a letter published two weeks before, and repudiated the idea that the term implied the restoration of the Byzantine Empire, including Constantinople. The claim to the lands of Asia Minor inhabited by Greeks since ancient times had been discarded in the early 1920s, he wrote. 'The fact that as high a former official of the Colonial Office can be in a muddle about so crucial a point as to the implications of "Enosis" will dishearten those who look forward to the clearing up of the Cyprus tangle and the re-establishment of Anglo-Greek friendship.'

Facing growing criticism in the United Kingdom about the methods he used and their lack of effectiveness, Sir John Harding would resign as Governor of Cyprus on 22 October 1957.

To Lawrence Durrell
14 March [1956]

c/o Amy
Gadencourt
Pacy-sur-Eure

Dear Larry, παιδάκι μου [my dear boy],

I *say*, what *is* going on? I can quite imagine Gen. Harding, Maurice,[1] you (or me if I were there long enough) maddened by duplicity, blackmail, bullying, bombs, deceit, suddenly saying 'to hell with it!' and packing Makarios off to the Antipodes. But what I *can't* understand is the Cabinet accepting such a cracked idea, knowing full well the damage it was going to do outside Cyprus, considerations which, after all, are nothing to do with Harding's brief. The whole thing should have been fixed up years ago. Now the only hope is straightjackets all round for the Cabinet and a resumption of talks – but with who? – while – ideally – an exiled Eden works his way through Meredith and Trollope among the mangroves of Tristan da Cunha.

I wonder what feelings prevail in Cyprus. Away the British, I imagine, jubilation followed by a sort of *post-coitum-triste* – deflation and doubts beginning to creep.

I must say, there is something horrifyingly grandiose about it all, like setting light to a really large bonfire. What about Niko Kranidiotis[2] and Rhodis Rouphos?[3]

Did you read a wonderful book by Ommanney which appeared a few years ago, called *The Shoals of Capricorn*, about the Seychelles?[4] I've always longed to go there. (Should I send it to the Archbishop?) There is one island in the archipelago wholly populated by giant land-tortoises over a yard in height by two yards long. The entire atoll is covered with these bumps, like Byzantine cupolas or the roofs of an Arabian madrassah, the vast majority of them empty, containing nothing but complicated cobwebs and the delicate little skeletons of incumbents that died centuries ago. About one out of ten of these concavities is alive. They trot up to the rare travellers who land there, in hopes of company. There are also quantities of sea-turtles which are caught *en masse*, rendered down, and poured into tankers which set sail for Tower Bridge, where the stuff is hosed ashore into municipal water carts and off to the Mansion House for city banquets.

I had news of you and Maurice from Ed Stanley,[5] who I like in spite of the shocking balls he writes about Cyprus. How is Eve?[6] Also Maurice & Leonora? Do give them lots of love from me, also to Sappho. Do please, write and tell about Cyprus. I loved your recent short poem in the *TLS*, *Spectator* or *Statesman*. *Important!* You never sent me a copy of the *Cyprus Review* with my bit in, though I got the dough. Joan is here and sends her love; also lots, from

    Paddy

Xan and Daphne arrive here in two weeks, on the way back to their Casbah. Wish you were too. We stay on in Smarties house[7] till May. The first vol. of my Greek book comes out in late summer.

P.S. Here is a sonnet I wrote for Roger Hinks,[8] who I like in spite of Geo. K's dislike. It needs some explanation. He told me of a

dream last year when, looking out of his window, he saw a steam
roller driving up to the front door in which sat four black-faced,
sinister, bolt upright Edwardian gamekeepers, gazing at him with
dead eyes. Panic-stricken he made a dash for the back of the house,
but there they were . . . He awoke in acute anguish. The Bergomask
at the end of the octave is Caravaggio, who was born near Bergamo.
Hinks has written a book on him, as well as on several other Italian
painters: he's a v. elaborate aesthetic figure.

'Wall me with banquets, Titian; Tiepolo,
'Roof me with rapes! The enemy's at the door.
'Minims and semibreves defend us! Floor,
'Hide under Aubusson. Stop gaps, Palladio,
'With trompe l'oeil vistas . . . Candlelight connives
'To gild my golden eclogues by the fire . . .
'Paint out the frontiers, Bergomask, with lyre
'And luteplayers, dormitions and still lifes.'

But, e'er the *fine* can warm inside the glass,
Or spacecat fly a league, four baleful shapes
Glide up the drive, borne by a steamroller's
Slow steam roll. *The back door, quick! The grass!*
Too late! The roller's there, four Raglan capes,
And four deerstalkers on four gamekeepers.

---

[1] Maurice Cardiff (1915–2006), writer and cultural attaché, then working for the British
Council in Cyprus; married Leonora Freeman in 1939.

[2] The diplomat, poet and writer Nikos Kranidiotis (1911–97) was Makarios's right-hand
man.

[3] Rodis Kanakaris-Roufos (1924–72), diplomat and writer.

[4] Francis Downes Ommanney, *The Shoals of Capricorn* (1952).

[5] See page 66 (letter to Joan Rayner, spring 1952).

[6] Durrell and his wife had separated in 1955 and would be divorced two years later.

[7] Gadencourt, owned by Lady Smart.

[8] Roger Hinks (1903–63), art historian with a particular interest in Caravaggio; director
of the British Council in Athens, 1954–9.

To George Katsimbalis   Gadencourt
Monday [? March 1956]   Pacy-sur-Eure

IN HASTE

Dear George,

Did you get my long letter, & the book, which I sent you two
months ago? V. many thanks for the beautiful France-Grèce books,
which arrived safe: also for Geo. Seferis's collection[1] of [all] too
prophetic poems.

The point of this hasty letter is to commiserate and let off steam
about the dangerous lunacy of the British Government. I think the
whole lot ought to be put in straightjackets before they can do any
more damage. What possible good do they think is going to come
of all this?

As I explained in my letter, I am 100% pro Enosis, and – I can't
help being – 100% anti the methods used by EOKA, as also the
lunatics of Athens radio. But this last stuff beats anything. I wrote a
very long answer – same length as an article really, which is probably
why it wasn't printed – in answer to critics of my *Spectator* articles
and I will send you a typescript when I can get one. When I see
more clearly what is going on about Makarios, I'll write something
else.

Things look black indeed. I have not seen or heard from anyone
who approves of the exile of Makarios, and I think the reaction will
be very violent in England, which may be to the good.

Anyway, dear George, all my love to you and Spatch, as always,
and from Joan, καὶ καλὸ ξεμπέρδεμα. Νά τὰ χάλια μας! [and let's
hope we get out of this quickly. Such is our sorry state!]

    love

     Paddy

P.S. I heard from Philip yesterday that his book on Greek poets[2] is
about to appear, and I hope to review it for the *Sunday Times*.

¹ Seferis's collection of poems inspired by Cyprus, entitled . . . *Cyprus, Where it was Decreed for Me* . . . (1955), later retitled as *Logbook III*; the title is a quotation from Euripides' *Helen.*

² Philip Sherrard's *The Marble Threshing Floor: Studies in Modern Greek Poetry* (1956), reviewed by PLF on 22 April.

To Jock Murray   Gadencourt
16 April 1956   Pacy-sur-Eure

My dear Jock,

No *please* don't come here yet, because I simply can't face you till I hand over the completed vol., for shame, confusion etc. I am working away very hard at the moment, and things have taken on a spurt which I hope is the home stretch, in bed with a minor un-painful come-back of lumbago (owing to a long bicycle ride in pouring rain) which is very conducive to writing. In about seven days' time I fly to the corner tower of a castle in Ireland (Co. Waterford), and hope to present you with the whole thing when I get to London eight days later. Do come to Gadencourt then and we'll talk about Vol. II and drink to a more propitious delivery.

I'm only too aware that my hopeless dilatoriness about the final stage of this vol. seems inexcusable and infuriating. I think I got rather jammed up by constant gloom about the Greek–Cyprus business in the back of my mind, a feeling that my book, in these circumstances, may appear unhelpful and trivial, wondering what I ought to do to change it (which would, of course, change the whole nature of the book!) etc., etc. Quite futile, of course. I wish I'd had the sense to finish the whole thing a year ago – or that the English & Greeks had postponed their deadlock for a year. Streams of letters and cuttings from Greece aren't much help.

Here comes the postman. No more now, but many apologies and I really am working!

Yours ever
Paddy

Love from Joan

The following was Paddy's response to a sad and angry letter from Seferis (20 March 1956: translated from the original Greek), which reveals the depth of feeling over the British handling of the Cyprus emergency. Seferis berated 'Panty' for his 'infinite admiration for Mr Macmillan and Mr Eden', and his 'blind loyalty to English diplomacy'. He deplored the 'gangster-like' treatment of Makarios. 'I know that you are pure and that you really love Greece,' continued Seferis, 'but this is not enough. You must be convinced that the English policy is criminal and sworn to ruin us.' Seferis fulminated against the 'lies and calumnies' of the British government: 'To hell with the Anglo-Saxon treachery and hypocrisy . . .' Later in the letter he apologised for losing his temper. 'Forgive me, Panty, my dear. My sorrow is great. An incurable sorrow. We all feel like deceived lovers, because we loved nothing more than England and the English people . . . Even after fifty or a hundred years the bitterness will always remain in the depth of our soul. And grandfathers will be telling their grandchildren how much we suffered because of our insidious and disloyal friend whom we had, once, so much loved.'

To George Seferis   Gadencourt
25 May 1956   Pacy-sur-Eure

My dear George,

Very many apologies for not answering your card before.[1] I was away in Ireland, having got badly stuck here in Normandy, where I have been scribbling away, *tant bien que mal* ['with difficulty'] all winter. Things are going a bit better now. George K. had sent me . . . Κύπρον, οὗ μ' ἐθέσπισεν . . . [. . . *Cyprus, Where it was Decreed for Me* . . .] a few weeks before. I had been meaning to write to you about them. I like them immensely and have read them all several times. Some of them I knew. Did you have Φιλεντέμ [Filedem][2] in mind in the Πραματευτὴς ἀπὸ τὴ Σιδῶνα ['Peddlar from Sidon']? (Τουρκοπούλα . . . ρόδα στὸ μαντύλι)? ['A young Turkish girl . . . Roses in a kerchief'] I hadn't seen Στὰ περίχωρα τῆς Κερύνειας ['In the outskirts of Kyreneia'][3] before; it's terribly good and quite pathetic. The English world there has exactly the stale and faded atmosphere of a nightclub in the morning, as in John

Betjeman's poem. Σαλαμίνα τῆς Κύπρος ['Salamis in Cyprus'][4] is still my favourite. I'm keeping it for you to sign.

My book has swollen to such proportions that John Murray is going to publish in thirds, coming out at intervals, the first to appear being the one on the Mani. Although it is an extremely pro-Greek book as you can imagine, I tremble to think of the sneers and jeering and hatred that lie in wait for me in the columns of the Ἑστία, the Ἀκρόπολις and the Ἀπογευματινή[5] – 'αὐτὸς ὁ δῆθεν "Φίλος" τῆς χώρας μας' . . . 'Προτιμοῦμεν τοὺς ἐχθροὺς', κ.τ.λ., κ.τ.λ. ['That so-called "friend" of our country' . . . 'we prefer our enemies', etc., etc.] – I could write them myself. I know it so well. 'It is obviously the intention of this agent of the Intelligence Service (a true representation of perfidious Albion masquerading as a friend) to discredit Greece in the eyes of the so-called "civilized" world by representing our fatherland as a race of poverty-stricken and illiterate peasants living by sheeptheft and the vendetta, believing in nereids, gorgons, werewolves, and vampire bats. May we, perhaps, remind this gentleman that when his own "civilised" country – a "civilisation" of which we can appreciate a shining example in Cyprus today! – were still barbarian savages dressed in wolf-skins and painted blue, the ancestors of the humble "peasants" he describes so patronisingly were . . . etc. etc.' *Oh God!*

Not that the cheap English press is much better, and perhaps worse, *mutatis mutandis.* One of the many gloomy aspects of the present bloody situation is that it seems to have turned both Greece and England into enlarged caricatures of everything that their worst enemies have always pretended they were and both seem at the moment odious. Φουκαράδες! [Poor bastards!] The only hope lies with liberal opinion on both sides; but this, in moments of stress, as we know from Yeats, is the first thing to go.[6] What could be less reconcilable than the present situation – a just cause injudiciously applied, and an unjust cause applied with all the punctilio of legality? It might have made things more soluble in the end if the British government really *did* have a bit more of the Macchiavellicism [*sic*] attributed to it by the Athenian press. I'm certain *Il Principe* would have known better than to create a hagiography by exiling the

ArchB [Makarios], and martyrology by hanging two Cypriots, however many poor devils get bumped off or killed by bombs. I absolutely disapprove of, and hate, the official British policy over Cyprus and am deeply convinced of the justice of Enosis; but I can't think anything but ill of EOKA. None of us liked Gen. Grivas[7] – do you remember? when he commanded X, or approved either of his politics or his methods, and the latter seem to me no better now, when disguised by a heroic name and a noble cause. It seems to me that values have got dreadfully mixed up for newspapers to compare his activities to those of Greek resistance to Nazi occupation, at any rate, as I saw it in Crete. For one thing, the assassination of isolated Germans was strictly forbidden by a joint decision of the Cretans and the few Englishmen working with them because (a) the penalties were the lining up and machine-gunning of several hundreds of men, women and children, and the dynamiting of entire villages and (b) quite literally, because, though extremely easy, such assassinations seemed both pointless and cowardly. As, in Cyprus (a) (thank God!) doesn't apply, (b) seems to me to apply with double force EOKA's activities up till now would have resulted in the execution, not of two men, but of two or three thousand and razed a score of villages to the ground. Also, during the whole occupation, the Cretans bumped off very many less Cretan traitors *than* EOKA have so far killed among the Cypriots. The Germans in Crete were just as courageous, probably more efficient, four times more numerous and a hundred times more ruthless than the British in Cyprus – and yet we all managed to survive quite easily, having the entire population on our side, as, one must assume, EOKA has; and yet, nobody thought it phenomenally heroic or wonderful (quite rightly, because it wasn't): also, it was rather fun. All this being so, it leaves one rather puzzled to read of the intrepid exploits of the second Digenis Akritas[8] against the ruthless and blood-thirsty tyranny of the blood-soaked butcher Gauleiter von Harding, whose μεσαιωνικὰ βασανιστήρια [medieval torture chambers] – βασανιστήρια [torture chambers] are always μεσαιωνικά [medieval] – outdo the Nazis a thousand-fold . . . All this bragging and exaggeration seems a terrible abuse of language and shows a great ignorance of what the German

occupation really meant. I have never met him, but apparently all
who know him think very highly of Harding as a just, well-
intentioned and humane man – including (according to Francis
Noel-Baker,[9] who was here the other day) Makarios himself and
Niko Kranidiotis and quite a number of pro Enosis Greeks in
Cyprus. After all, handing over Cyprus does not depend on *his*
decision, but the government's, and the job of keeping order is a
ghastly one. I wonder how any other general of another nationality
would have managed – supposing the whole situation were reversed.
Would a Greek general have done better? (I don't mean Grivas!)

Dear George, I hope you don't mind me asking all these
questions. The thing is that I spend my time putting the Greek side
of the thing to any Englishmen I can get to listen, and in any
periodical that will publish it, and all this is a sort of devil's
advocate's argument. Things which I carefully omit and have rather
on my conscience. I have become fairly expert at expanding the
opposite of all I have just written, and have accumulated a
considerable dialectical arsenal for the demolition of anti-Enosis
arguments!

To go on with these private perplexities – all this is largely
prompted by a constant avalanche of lurid newspaper cuttings sent
[to] me by the Colossus [Katsimbalis], all headed with the ironical
comment Ζήτω ἡ Ἀγγλοελληνικὴ Φιλία! [Long live Anglo-Hellenic
friendship!] in red chalk! – Let us admit – indeed, proclaim – that
the initial fault lies with the British, in their unjustifiable (in view of
Greece's offers of bases etc.) retention of Cyprus, and proclaim still
louder the blame due to Eden and the British Government for their
insulting and destructive policy over the whole question, louder still
their willingness to let non-existent Turkish claims strengthen their
case (though I do not believe – it is part of my anti-Machiavelli
theory – as all Greeks do, that this was actually engineered by the
British; I think it was merely welcomed by the Government, with
crocodile tears of regret, to bolster up a weak and unjustifiable line
of argument). We must also admit that there have been faults on the
Greek side, which seem to me to be the timing of the whole thing
(in view of their old friend England's difficulties and embarrassments

all over the world and especially in the Levant), the campaign of
hatred in the newspapers, incendiary broadcasts to Cyprus and the
activities of EOKA. Of this, far the gravest seems to me to be the
irresponsible and hydrophobic behaviour of the newspapers; the last
two – broadcasts and EOKA – must be largely by-products of this. It
seems to have cowed all voice of protest into silence. What I mean
is, that at least half of the stuff appearing on Cyprus in the English
press is opposed to Government policy, and most of this is not
partisan journalism of the opposition, but private protest dictated by
liberal sentiments. But any trace of self-criticism seems to have
vanished from the Athenian press, leaving the field open for all the
evils we've been talking about. Nothing but extremes remain, an
hysterical world of fantasy only populated by saints, martyrs, heroes,
tyrants, butchers and traitors. If I were a Greek peasant in Epirus,
Acarnania, Mani or Crete (say), brought up with patriotism as a
religion, my mind unencumbered by any reading except the
newspaper, the kapheneion wireless my only link with Athens, and
the priest, the *proedros* and the *daskalos* telling me every second
of the day that England means the destruction of Greece and the
massacre of Greek heroes – spiritual descendants of Lambros
Katsionis, Athanasios Diakos, Archbishop Germanos, Kolokotronis and
Pavlos Melas[10] – in enslaved Cyprus, I am convinced I would be a
violent fanatic – there would be no opposition view to prevent me
being so; and supposing you in Athens had written an article
suggesting a different and milder policy towards the Cyprus question
and hinting that all Englishmen were not the treacherous and blood-
thirsty ogres the newspapers say, and supposing some paper had the
guts to print it – I would probably be in the front of an indignant
mob in ὁδὸς Ὑπερείδου [Iperidou Street], throwing sticks and
stones at your window and shouting "Ἔξω ὁ Σεφεριάδης! Πράκτωρ
τοῦ Δήμου Φὸν Χάρντινκ! Προδότης! Χαφιὲς τῶν Ἀγγλων!
Πουλημένος!' ['Out with Seferiadis! Agent of the executioner von
Harding! Traitor! Stool-pigeon of the English!'], etc. That is exactly
what the newspapers seem to have done to nearly all of Greece.
How on earth will it ever unwind again? Because, presumably, it will
have to, if the Greeks and the English are to settle anything about

poor old Cyprus. I keep hoping and praying for a sudden change of policy in England that would make the unwinding process possible in Greece. But at the moment the English and the Greeks seem to have gritted their teeth in resolution to prove that the English are not to be cowed by gunmen, nor the Greeks by hangmen, a sterile competition that can only lead us all further into the dark . . . The real tragedy is that it is all so easy to solve, as we all know! According to the Colossus, it will take 100 years for Anglo-Greek friendship to be re-established. I wonder if he is right.

In arguing with anti-Enosis people, I always say, at this point, that *without* the activities of EOKA, nothing would have happened at all. 'Never' would never have become 'sometime'. Alas, perhaps it's the truth. The Turkish threat I regard as absolutely chimerical – as if they would attack the island if there was a British or NATO base on it! If only EOKA had behaved differently during the talks with Makarios, I really believe something at last [might] have come of it. I don't know.

I rather regret having gone into all this. Poor George! Don't bother to answer the Cyprus part, it's too shattering, and I suppose, rather boring too. But this winter has been a nightmare & has practically stopped me writing. Most of the above, I think, must have been prompted by the Colossus's letters & cuttings. He writes like a lunatic! I have tried to get him to come and stay here, so that we could have a gargantuan gastronomic tour of all the splendid Norman restaurants, but he's been unable to get away. Joan is in Paris, & returns tomorrow, but asks me to send all love, to which I add mine!

Yours ever
Paddy

---

1 Seferis had complained that PLF had not answered an earlier card.

2 The title of a popular Cretan song: apparently such a favourite of PLF's while he was in Crete that he was sometimes known to his Cretan comrades as 'Filedem'.

3 Another poem in the same book by Seferis, which takes the form of a dialogue between two British expatriate women living in Cyprus; one of the two epigraphs is from Betjeman's poem 'Sun and Fun: The Song of a Nightclub Proprietress', published in *A Few Late Chrysanthemums* (1954).

'But I'm dying now and done for
What on earth was all the fun for?
For God's sake keep that sunlight out of sight.'

Seferis's purpose was to show how alien the British are to the Cypriot landscape.

4 Another poem from the same collection, critical of the British for denying Cypriots their right to be reunited with their fellow Greeks.

5 *Hestia, Akropolis* and *Apogevmatini*, all Athens newspapers.

6 Seferis underlined these last few words in pencil. PLF refers to Yeats's 'The Second Coming' (1921):

'Things fall apart; the center cannot hold
Mere anarchy is loosed upon the world,
The blood-dimmed tide is loosed, and everywhere
The ceremony of innocence is drowned;
The best lack all conviction, while the worst
Are full of passionate intensity.'

7 Georgios Grivas (1897–1974), a Cyprus-born general in the Greek Army, leader of the EOKA guerrilla organisation.

8 A legendary Byzantine hero.

9 The Labour MP Francis Edward Noel-Baker (1920–2009).

10 All heroes of the Greek national liberation movement against Turkish rule, except the last, who was commander of the Greek forces in the struggle for Macedonia.

To Debo Devonshire
26 August 1956   Aix-en-Provence

Darling Debo,

I'm terribly sorry not having written half a century ago, after telephoning you on the eve of leaving to join Xan and Daph in the South of France. Things there were such turmoil that I don't think any of the hundred-odd people engaged on making that film wrote so much as a postcard the whole time. D, X & I talked it over and decided you would have hated it. I did, rather, and buggered off after about a week.

It was all pretty queer. First things first: Dirk Bogarde, the actor who is doing one in the film,[1] is absolutely charming – slim, handsome, nice speaking voice and manner, a super-gent, the ghost of oneself twelve years ago. He and Daph & Xan had become bosom friends by the time I got there, and he and his equally nice manager (rather a grand thing to have?) are going to stay with them for Christmas in Tangiers. We all lived – us, the other actors, directors, cameramen etc. – in a vast chalet, miles above the clouds in the French Alps, leagues away from anywhere and at the end of an immeasurable tangle of hairpin bends. The film itself, what I saw of it, is tremendously exciting – tremendous pace, action galore, staggering scenery, with the guns of whiskered and turbaned Cretan guerrillas jutting down from every rock and miles of peaceful French roads choked with truckloads of steel-helmeted Germans bawling 'Lili Marlene'. It'll certainly be a thumping success, and when it finally appears at the Odeon or elsewhere, I propose to sneak in and see it in a false beard night after night. Some bits – not yet filmed, fortunately – turn Bogarde–Fermor into a mixture of Garth[2] & Superman, shooting Germans clean through the breast from a dentist's chair,[3] strangling sentries in an offhand manner – all totally fictitious! I'm having a terrific tussle getting them to change these bits in the film, not because I really mind, but because anyone who knows anything about the operation knows that it's all rot. There are scores of small things dead wrong, & Xan and I are having a death struggle to get them put right, mostly for the sake of Greek and Cretan friends. It's all v. rum. The main trouble is that once a filmscript is written, the authors themselves bow down and worship it as though it were Holy Writ. *IT* becomes the truth and anyone trying to change it (like X or me) incurs the horror of heretics trying to tamper with the text of the Gospel.

Well, I baled out of this mountain madhouse after seven days and retreated to a minute Provençal village called Auribeau, where I stayed in the pub and scribbled all day (against time) in the priest's leafy garden overlooking a forested valley along which flowed a swift and icy river with deep green pools dappled with the shadows of leaves where I splashed and floated between paragraphs for hours among the dragonflies. There was never anyone there except occasionally a solitary fisherman with a straw hat and never a bite (perhaps because of the splashing I mentioned).

Then everything changed 100%, when Annie Fleming went to stay with Somerset Maugham[4] (not Willy to me) at Cap Ferrat, where he inhabits a gorgeous villa. It was a concerted plan that she should try and wangle my staying there for fun, for a few days. She duly got me asked there to luncheon,[5] and afterwards, as if by clockwork, Mr Maugham asked me to stay several days and everything looked like a triumph of Annie's engineering and plain sailing. *But there were rocks ahead.* (Do you know Somerset Maugham? He is eighty-four, and his face is the wickedest tangle of cruel wrinkles I have ever seen and so discoloured and green that it looks as though he has been rotting in the Bastille, or chained to the bench of a galley or inside an iron mask for half a century. Alligator's eyes peer from folds of pleated hide and below them an agonising snarl is beset with discoloured and truncated fangs, but the thing to remember is that he has a very pronounced and noticeable stutter that can seize up a sentence for thirty seconds on end.)

All went better and better — a sort of honeymoon — as the day progressed. But at dinner things began to go wrong.[6] Two horrible and boring guests arrived (publishers) called Mr & Mrs Frere.[7] Mr Frere made some sweeping generalisation and

ME: 'I love generalisations — for instance, that all Quakers are colour-blind (you know the line) — or that all heralds stutter!'

MRS FRERE: 'Stutter?'

ME: 'Yes.'

MRS FRERE: 'How do you mean, stutter?'

ME: 'Stutter . . . you know, stammer . . .'

Later on, after that fatal eighth glass of whisky, I was in trouble again: —

SOMERSET MAUGHAM: 'It's a c–c–confounded nuisance t–t–today b–b-being the F–feast of the As–as–as–assumption. N–none of the g–gardeners have d–done a s–s–stroke . . .'

ME: 'Ah yes! The Feast of the Assumption of the Blessed Virgin! Just after the Pope gave out the dogma a few years ago, I was going round the Louvre with a friend of mine called Robin Fedden (who, by ill luck, has a terrible stutter)[8] and we paused in front of a huge picture of the Assumption by (I think) Correggio (*ah, oui*) & Robin turned to me and said "Th-th-that's what I c-c-call an un-w-w-warrantable as-s-s-sumption".'

There was a moment's silence, the time needed for biting one's tongue out. When bedtime came my host approached me with a reptile's fixity, offering me a hand as cold as a toad, with the words: 'W-w-well I'll s-s-say g-good-b-b-bye now in c-case I'm not up b-by the t-time y-you l-l-leave . . .'[9]

Annie helped me pack next morning, and as I strode, suitcase in hand, to the door, there was a sound like an ogre's sneeze. The lock of the suitcase had caught in the sheet, leaving a jagged yard-long rent across the snow-white expanse of heavily embroidered gossamer. I broke into a run and Annie into fits of suppressed laughter. As a result of bullying by Annie & Diana Cooper (who turned up in the area, where I had settled in a horrible millionaires' hotel, soon after) I was asked by W. S. M. to a meal of reconciliation and amends, where we met as affable strangers. It was really a gasbag's penance and I, having learnt the hard way, vouchsafed little more than a few safe monosyllables.

The rest of my short stay in that area was spent with D. Cooper, Annie, Robin & Mary [Campbell],[10] & Hamish [St Clair-Erskine] (who were all staying with Mrs Fellowes).[11] *I hate it* – the Côte d'Azur I mean – and will never set foot there again.

I've taken rooms here for a week – ending tomorrow – in a pretty, retired midwife's house, in whose garden I write. This ravishing town, full of chimes of bells, fountains, peasants playing *boules* in the shadow of lime trees and splendid decaying palaces and churches, is a wonderful disinfectant after that revolting coast. All is splendid or dilapidated, nothing smart.

In two days' time I set off on the great yacht Diana has borrowed,[12] with D[iana], Joan, Alan Pryce-Jones and a couple called Frank & Kitty Giles:[13] Corsica, Sardinia, Sicily. It really would be a kind act were you to write c/o British Consul, Cagliari, Sardinia.

Meanwhile, please give my love to Andrew, to Emma & Stoker[14] (angels in human form) & to your Wife.[15]

Lots of love from

Paddy

[1] Dirk Bogarde (1921–99) was playing PLF in the film of *Ill Met by Moonlight* (1957), which was being shot in the French Alps.

[2] Muscle-bound hero of a strip cartoon which ran in the *Daily Mirror* from 1943 to 1997.

[3] In one scene, the PLF character pretends to be a patient in a dentist's chair when two German military policemen come into the dentist's surgery. One of them is suspicious: he pulls back the sheet covering PLF, revealing that PLF is holding a pistol. PLF pushes the German against a wall and shoots him in the gut.

[4] The novelist and playwright W. Somerset Maugham (1874–1965), who had lived at the Villa Mauresque on Cap Ferrat since his divorce from his wife, Syrie, in 1927.

[5] 'Paddy was invited for lunch and arrived with five cabin trunks, parcels of books and the manuscript of his unfinished work on Greece strapped in a bursting attaché case.' Ann Fleming to Evelyn Waugh, 27 August 1956: Amory (ed.), *The Letters of Ann Fleming*, pages 184–6.

[6] 'Paddy who never travels without a bottle of calvados appeared more exuberant than one small martini could explain' (ibid.).

[7] Alexander Frere-Reeves (1892–1984), for many years head of William Heinemann, Maugham's publisher. He was married to Patricia Wallace, daughter of the thriller writer Edgar Wallace. 'The conversation turned to tropical diseases and Paddy shouted at length on the stuttering that typified the College of Heralds. I intervened with a swift change of topic and thought the situation saved, but Frere (nasty man) made us all angry by saying that no author wrote for anything but profit; this put my voice up several octaves as well as Paddy's' (ibid.).

[8] Some small excisions Paddy made when this letter was published in *In Tearing Haste* have been reinstated.

[9] 'He then vanished like a primeval crab leaving a slime of silence; it was broken by Paddy who cried, "Oh what have I done, Oh Christ what a fool I am" and slammed his whisky glass on the table, it broke to pieces cutting his hand and showering the valuable carpet with blood and splinters' (ibid.).

[10] Robin Francis Campbell (1912–85), soldier and painter, and his second wife Lady Mary Sybil, née St Clair Erskine (1912–93), daughter of the 5th Earl of Rosslyn (and sister of Hamish).

[11] Marguerite (Daisy) Decazes (1890–1962), the well-dressed, sharp-tongued daughter of the 3rd Duc Decazes, and heiress through her mother to the Singer sewing machine fortune. She owned the luxurious villa Les Zoraïdes on Cap Martin, near Monaco, and had married Reginald Fellowes, her second husband, in 1919.

[12] Diana Cooper had again been lent the *Eros II* by Stavros Niarchos.

[13] Frank Giles (b. 1919), foreign correspondent, married to Lady Katherine 'Kitty' Sackville.

Corfu, 1946: Paddy spent two weeks there as part of a British Council-sponsored lecture tour. 'Huddling into the crowded caïque at three in the morning, with you shuddering and waving on the quay in evening dress, and all of us the worse for drink, was the perfect way to leave Corfu after that perfect fortnight,' he wrote afterwards to his hostess on the island.

Paddy's pre-war lover,
Balasha Cantacuzène.

Paddy in his early twenties, during the time when he and
Balasha were together in Rumania.

Paddy in moustache and civilian clothes, southern Crete, May 1943.

Major Leigh Fermor gives a post-war lecture on the
operation to abduct General Kreipe.

Brothers-in-arms in Crete and friends ever after: Paddy and Alexander 'Xan' Fielding.

A rare shot of Paddy's lover Joan Rayner, who disliked having her photograph taken (late 1940s).

Astride a mule in the Caribbean, during the winter of 1947–8.

Eye to eye with a
Greek goat, aboard
a caïque, *c*.1946.

In the late 1940s and early 1950s Paddy retreated to Normandy, for several spells, to concentrate on his writing. His letters to Joan from the monasteries in which he stayed were adapted into a short book, *A Time to Keep Silence* (1957), beginning a lifelong relationship with the publisher 'Jock' Murray. This picture shows Jock in the mid-1970s, at work on the chaotic manuscript of *A Time of Gifts*.

In bandana and sunhat.

With the painter Niko Ghika,
in the studio at Ghika's house
on Hydra, early 1950s.

In the village of Samaria in western Crete, 1951. The 'Cretan runner' George Psychoundakis and the artist John Craxton are at the centre of the group.

With Eleni, daughter of Paddy's wartime comrade Manoli Paterakis, at his village, Koustogerako in western Crete, c.1951. During the war the village was burned by the Germans in reprisal for partisan activities.

14 Debo's husband, Andrew, and their two oldest children, Emma (b. 1943), and Peregrine, known as 'Stoker' (b. 1944).

15 Lady Katherine (Kitty) Petty-Fitzmaurice (1912–95), Baroness Nairne: DD's closest friend, whose nickname, 'Wife', originated from an involved family joke which began when a man repeatedly referred to his wife as 'Kitty my wife' in one breath. It was adopted by DD to describe any great friend of either sex. Married 3rd Viscount Mersey in 1933.

'The first problem was, Where to write the book? I began in a little hotel on the edge of Dartmoor, run by Mrs Postlethwaite Cobb, the daughter of the chaplain at West Point, a firm friend; she had retired there after founding a home for superannuated donkeys in Algeria. Work was broken by fox hunting three times a week.'

To Diana Cooper
28 September 1956

Easton Court Hotel
Chagford
Devon

My darling Diana,

Pretty different here from our recent habitat! My muse and I are cloistered here, a gale howls down the chimney, cats and dogs come down on the sodden fields outside in an almost unbroken stream and a wind blows that would unhorn cows. I don't think you've ever been here, but it's a great retiring place for literary purposes, for E. Waugh, & Patrick Kinross and others – I first came here seven years ago with Patrick when we [were] both struggling with books, and have been back several times *in extremis*, as now (Saint-Wandrille was full, alas!). It is owned & run by an odd couple, Mrs Carolyn Postlethwaite Cobb, an elderly American of very improbable shape, now largely bedridden, and her middle-aged ex-lover Norman Webb, a Devonshire chap she met a number of decades ago running a team of donkeys in Biskra or Fez. Their youthful flame has burnt out I think but they remain loving and inseparable and Norman wanders about beaming and bottle-nosed and prone to cider-sprung meandering. Both are very nice, and, miraculously, in spite of the awe-inspiring fourteenth-century beams and inglenooks, fires blaze in hearths, water is piping hot, central heating leads its secret life and the food's not bad at all.

Now for the brief and not very exciting saga that connects goodbye to you on the deck of the *Eros* in Portofino and these dank pastures: dinner on the train with Stuart Hampshire, his/Freddie's son,[1] and Isaiah's stepson,[2] travelled through the night in luxurious *wagon-lit* parcel post, out into a bright but colder Paris, dinner with Nancy, then two days at Gadencourt where the Smarts were Normandy-logged by Nasser,[3] and Russell Page & his wife[4] were staying, back to Paris, & luncheon with Kitty & Frank [Giles] (I am amused and pleased to see how Joan has taken to the former, & to the latter also. I must say, the trip has drawn my fangs, too. I think all this gorgeous matiness may be the cause of much of the defence mechanism of facetiousness melting – or has custom merely equipped one with shock-absorbers?) At the airport we met and flew with Vivien Leigh & Mr Beaumont[5] (she clutching a neatly packed shrub hot-root from Portofino) with happy & cheering news of you installed in the castelletto. How nice she is. A hilarious dinner with Peter Q, Sonia [Orwell] & Cyril Connolly, then to that curious nightclub I took you to for a moment after that dinner at Scott's, where I saw 'Rock 'n Roll' for the first time; it looks exactly like ordinary jiving.

Joan's house,[6] which we went over next morning, looks tip-top, and could be made charming – you must come and see it and advise. Joan thinks aubergine stair carpets. It will be wonderful to have somewhere for both of us to assemble scattered books, clothes, papers etc. and a proper base to be nomadic from. It's rather demoralising, always returning to improvisation.

I set off here the day after arriving in London, and have immersed myself in an Augean accumulation of work, only sneaking out for a couple of hours every day, whenever the rain stops, to tittup round the moors and lanes on an amiable black horse that lives hard by, usually getting soaked by sudden showers or by crashing along overgrown rides where each of the millions of leaves one collides with seems to shed a couple of table-spoonsful of rainwater. There are very steep hills separated by swift tree-arched streams running with water as dark as Guinness, overgrown with red rowan berries, Lords and Ladies run to seed, ragged robin & willow herb dribbling with the spit of cuckoos long flown, and dank woods thick with lichen, so that the branches are like green coral where many a fox could be decadently gloved in magenta.[7] Primitive stone bridges, as uncouth and angular as in early heraldry, span these streams, ringing hollow underhoof, and the dampness, darkness and greenness of the woods give them a submarine and legendary feeling, as though one should be dressed in full armour under shoals of green-haired mermaids drifting through the oak branches on slow and invisible currents to the sound of harps.

Dartmoor, which starts a mile or two away, is dotted with druidical stones – dolmens & cromlechs in gap-toothed rings or slanting monoliths jutting from a sea of red bracken – and above this bracken, like chessmen and T'ang objects, peer the heads of wild ponies, the size of large dogs, gazing as though mesmerised as one approaches cautiously at a walk. Most of them are bay, but others are black, chestnut & roan, white & grey, dappled, skewbald or piebald, in bold geographical designs, one or two practically striped like zebras, many of them with blond flapperish manes and tails, one raffish grey stallion, obviously of authoritative standing, has a mad eye surrounded by a piratical black patch. Up you creep till, with a sudden mass decision, they are off helter-skelter in a flurry of flying manes & hoofs, the burglarious stallion taking advantage of the disorder by trying to inflict the last outrages on minute mares at the gallop, the foals pounding anxiously after them and so small that only a ripple over the top of the bracken indicates them. At a safe distance, they freeze again, as in grandmother's steps. Most have been apprehended at some time during the last few years, branded and let loose again by various local people with some claim on them, and expeditions are now in progress to round them up for the annual pony-fair that takes place in Chagford later this month. The ones caught are then broken & sold as pets, for children or for circuses, formerly to costermongers, and alas! too awful to think of after this free & dashing life on the moors – dimgloomed in northern coalmines, or worse still, it is rumoured, shanghaied onto tramp

steamers for Belgians to munch. The molars of Madame Lambert and
Father de Grunne and André de Staercke closed on them . . . [8]

I went out on one of these raids yesterday with a local stable-
owner with a Devonshire accent almost as incomprehensible as that of
his Dumnonii ancestors who fought the Romans here; also eight farm
boys on horses of various degrees of culture, a ragged equestrian
troop of the kind one seldom sees out of Ireland. It was a long job,
because, as the leader warned me, these ponies are contrary and artful
buggers. It was a mixture of stealthy encircling advances through the
bracken, long waits in the howling wind stuffing with blackberries,
and sudden gallops, cracking whips like mad while the boys made
shrill noises like dogs barking and owls hooting, till we had about a
hundred of them cornered in a lane at the moor's edge, kicking,
leaping and whinnying and trying to clamber over each other. Thirty
were picked out by their brands and off we set home in a miniature
stampede, along a ten-mile labyrinth of trough-like lanes as the sun
was setting, horsemen going forward to block escape routes at
crossroads. Night had fallen as we drove these artful buggers through
the lamplit streets of Chagford, aborigines emerging glass in hand
from pubs to watch the bewildered pigmies pound by. It was past ten
when we herded them galloping into a field in which three sleek
elderly giants were already grazing. They stopped and raised their
heads in amazement as though a horde of teddy boys stunted with
gin or cigarettes had suddenly rocked and rolled into the Athenaeum.
(What lies ahead of these problem ponies? Will they settle down?) I'm
glad to say that by the time we left them there, in the dark, one of
these fogeys was diffidently rubbing noses with a shaggy newcomer
about the size of a dachshund, which I thought particularly decent.

Darling Diana, I've not said a word so far about the trip, but you
know how I adored it, and a trillion thanks. In its very different way
it was as heavenly as last year, if not more. Every single inch of it
was unknown to me, and I'm still thinking hard and assimilating &
digesting all we saw. I do hope you loved it too – I heard a few
sighs, but perhaps there were so few out of stoicism! I know Joan
loved it, and I think – indeed, I'm sure – everyone else did.

Do write quickly and tell your plans. I've got to stick in the kingdom, mainly because of work but also because this is the critical time for the wretched Crete film, and I want to watch it like a hawk and steer them, as much as I'm allowed to, from disaster. God, the rain!

  Lots of love, darling sweet Diana
    and tremendous hugs
      from
        Paddy
          xxx

P.S. I think the Cap Ferrat chapter of future reminiscences should be called: 'How to win friends and influence people.'

1 The philosopher Stuart Hampshire was married to Renée, ex-wife of his colleague A. J. 'Freddie' Ayer; her son from her first marriage was widely believed to have been fathered by Hampshire, so that he was known jokingly as 'Julian Ayer-shire'.

2 Earlier in the year the philosopher and historian of ideas Isaiah Berlin (1909–97) had married Aline Halban, daughter of the Baron de Gunzburg, and the mother of three sons by her two previous marriages.

3 Nasser's decision to nationalise the Suez Canal had prompted a diplomatic crisis.

4 Montague Russell Page (1906–85), garden designer and landscape architect, married to Vera Milanova Daumal, widow of poet René Daumal and former wife of the poet Hendrick Kramer.

5 Hugh 'Binkie' Beaumont (1908–73), successful and influential theatre manager and producer.

6 JR had bought a small house in Pimlico, No. 13 Chester Row, SW1.

7 A play on the word 'foxglove'.

8 All Belgians: Austrian-born Baronne Joanna 'Hansi' Lambert (1900–60), née Reininghaus, hostess of a literary salon who married into a prominent Belgian banking family; Jean-Dominique de Hemricourt de Grunne (1913–2007), elegant, sophisticated and worldly Roman Catholic priest at Oxford University in the 1950s, who left the priesthood after his mother's death; André de Staercke (1913–2001), former political adviser to the Belgian Prince Regent. PLF is commenting on the Belgian liking for horsemeat.

To Billy Moss   Easton Court Hotel
1 October 1956   Chagford

Dear Billy,

  Back from foreign parts, & have scuttled down here to hide until I dare meet two publishers, one with a book one and a half

years overdue, the other with a preface a mere six months.[1] My
life story could be entitled 'The Case of the Overshot Deadline'.

I missed Powell & Pressburger[2] in London as they are off in
Corsica, shooting the Brian Coleman[3] shots, but Micky [Powell]
assured me by letter that he was 'able to put right nearly all the
things I was afraid about'. I wonder how much that covers. During,
& after, the days I spent watching the shooting, I wrote them three
interim reports containing comments & advice and criticism, some of
it very severe. They sent me typed copies of them – perhaps they did
you too, I hope so. If not, let me know and I'll send you mine &
you can give me them back in London. They are posterior and
additional to going over the script and bringing up all the points we
raised together, in great detail. You and Manoli[4] now leap on the
sentries and truss them hand & foot, but my fucking dentist's chair,
alas, remains. They seem to be in love with the scene, and it is
impossible to either bully or shame them out of it. With this glaring
exception, I somehow feel it won't be too bad. By some miracle, you
and I work out all right. Xan says that it's Marius Goring[5] (who I
liked v. much) who hams it up by being a sort of caricature Prussian.
I tremble to think what it might have turned into without
interference.

In spite of all this, I can't help liking this curious couple. I really
do think they want to make us and the Cretans happy about it as
much as in them, & the awful conventions of the film-world, lies;
and others might have been far more ruthless and unscrupulous.
They will get in touch with me on return & I will keep you posted
on everything. Micky has a very bad-mannered little son called
Columba, who was crawling all over the location – he never
answers anyone who speaks to him. One morning Emmerich
[Emeric Pressburger] said 'Good morning Columba' and Columba
spat at him full in the face. Very wittily, I think, Emmerich then
produced his handkerchief and said 'You are the spitting image of
your father.'

With lots of love for Sofe & love from
Paddy

¹ The first is PLF's Greek book, published by John Murray as *Mani* in 1958; the second is probably *The World Mine Oyster* by Matila Ghyka (trans. from the French by the author), which was published by Heinemann in 1961, with an introduction by PLF.

² Emeric ('Imre') Pressburger (1902–88), Hungarian-born screenwriter, who collaborated with Michael Powell on thirteen major films made between 1943 and 1955.

³ Lieutenant Brian Coleman was captain of the motor-launch which spirited General Kreipe off Crete.

⁴ Manoli Paterakis. 'He was my guide and closest Cretan friend in the island,' PLF wrote to Debo Devonshire after Paterakis's death, 'hand in glove in all sorts of risky ventures, a man in a million, two years older than me, v. funny with a hawk nose, piercing eyes, and vast knowledge of the mountains' (*In Tearing Haste*, page 235).

⁵ The English actor Marius Goring (1912–98) played General Kreipe.

To Jock Murray	Chaggers
9 October 1956	[Easton Court Hotel
	Chagford]

Dear Jock,

Many thanks for your nice letter. I'm delighted about *A Time to Keep Silence*.¹ The only change I would like to put in is in the Acknowledgements and thanks bit – after thanking you for permission to reprint (or perhaps this is redundant in this case) I would like to insert a bit thanking 'the Hon. Graham Eyres Monsell² for suggesting the title'. I haven't a copy here, but I'm sure it will fit in easily.

Heaven be praised, the neurotic literary paralysis of months has broken up at last, & dissolved into a spate of prose and I feel confident & optimistic for the first time for ages. The only thing that will wrench me from here until the *Mani* is finished will be that there is a chance of seeing the Bolshoi Ballet, in which case I'd come straight back next day. But there is not much hope, thank God.

Carolyn & Norman³ have gone to Denmark for two weeks, & the hotel is comparatively empty, which is nice. I've rather high-handedly grabbed the small sitting room and entrenched myself there behind an inexpungeable palisade of books which frightens away all invaders. I break off for two hours' rural ride every afternoon, back to a vast tea and the waiting foolscap.

Joan is getting a small house in Pimlico, mainly as a place for both to keep our scattered books & papers, a base for departures & caravanserai for returns, so I ought to be assembling my dispersed chattels. Would it be possible to get hold of the ones I have inflicted on you, in about a week? I'm afraid it has been a bit of a nuisance – see you soon,

yrs ever

Paddy

[1] John Murray had agreed to issue a new edition of this small book, originally published in a limited edition in 1953 by Ian Fleming's Queen Anne Press.
[2] Joan's brother.
[3] The proprietors of the hotel.

To Ann Fleming   Easton Court Hotel
November 1956   Chagford

Darling Annie,

I ought to have written days ago to say that, after delivering you safe home, I had another terrific hunt through the taxi and all over the floor and in and out of the upholstery of that nightclub, and *not a sign* of the truant earring, alas! I do hope it has turned up, or not been too grave or irreparable a loss.

How nice Cecil[1] was, cool and bland with his lemon-drop smile. Robin & Mary [Campbell] too, but a bit overcast I thought.

The trees are turning extraordinary colours, and riding along these lanes is like penetrating a cool furnace; until one gets onto the moor, where all is bleak, stricken & damned, it can be very sombre & forbidding at dusk. I almost expect, as I trot along, to be addressed by a hideous and toothless crone bent double under a load of sticks, who, if I befriended her, would be able to grant me three wishes not yet formulated. But such an event presupposes that two churlish elder brothers should have already ridden that way, and not only refused help, but derided her age and infirmity. My mind's eye depicts two members of the Berry family,[2] so perhaps I'm well out of it.

The horse I rode ('Flash') stopped dead at a gate on the way home this evening and a cart-horse the size of a mastodon came pounding over the grass to rub muzzles. They then placed their nostrils end to end and blew – it was no kind of a fit, owing to the newcomer's size – filling the frosty air with clouds of steam; but they obviously liked this so much that I'm thinking of taking it up.

MORE EQUINE INTELLIGENCE

I was woken up at 2 a.m. this morning by the hoof-beats of a cavalcade under my window sounding as eerie as smugglers, highwaymen or a troop of hired assassins making for an ambush with dark lanterns. I leapt out of bed and craned out like Old Mother Slipper-Slopper,[3] but there was nothing but darkness, wind and rain. I told all this to Barbara the housemaid this morning, who said it must be ghosts or (rather wittily) night-mares. But she came back in a minute or two, and said others had heard it – it was merely a pack of wild ponies driven off the moor by the weather. ('It must be terrible cold up there for them, poor mites.') It seems that in really cold weather they range through the villages in gangs, and have even been known to clatter through the streets of Exeter and whinny in the cathedral close, making many a citizen and many a minor-canon sit bolt upright and gaze into the darkness with wild surmise . . . But it really wasn't cold enough last night for these doings to be attributed to anything but instability –

   lots of love
   Paddy

---

[1] Cecil Beaton (1904–80), fashion, portrait and war photographer, interior designer and stage and costume designer. He kept diaries. 'In the published diaries, opinions are softened, celebrated figures are hailed as wonders and triumphs, whereas in the originals, Cecil can be as venomous as anyone I have ever read or heard in the most shocking of conversations,' wrote his biographer, Hugo Vickers.

[2] The Kemsley Newspaper Group, owned by the Berry family, owned the *Sunday Times*, which employed Ian Fleming as Foreign Manager. PLF wrote regular book reviews for the *Sunday Times*.

[3] 'Then Old Mother Slipper-Slopper jumped out of bed
   And out of the window she pop't her head.'
      From the folk-song 'The Fox'

*In the spring of 1957 Paddy returned to the Abbaye Saint-Wandrille to work
on his still-unfinished Greek book.*

To Joan Rayner   Abbaye Saint-Wandrille
undated [April 1957]   Seine Inférieure

Darling,

All goes splendidly. This extraordinary place really does seem to
do the trick. I think it is partly the atmosphere of activity, and
cramming so much into the day, of the monks that shames one out
of one's selfish and brooding sloth. They get up at 5 and go to
church, for longer or shorter periods, about seven times a day. Yet
a moment before each office, and immediately after, the whole
monastery is dotted with toiling figures in boiler-suit habits covered
in dirt, oil, earth, flour or shavings. But all of a sudden, there they all
are, tooling up the aisle in spotless black habits with the precision of
slow marching guardsmen, followed by splendidly arranged figures in
gleaming vestments, carrying candles, censers etc. – as if their only
plot was the perfection of ritual & gregorian chant. The second it's
over, off they scutter. So it is from 5 a.m. to 8.30. I got off to a
whizz-bang start, and have done more in three days than any ten in
London. I really am sanguine about finishing soon. I'll stay on over
this weekend, then make my way back *via* Dieppe. It was a false
alarm about having to find rooms in the village. The guest house is
full of *lyceéns* [schoolboys] from Le Havre, but the Père Hôtelier has
put me into a colossal room, usually kept for the Archbishop of
Rouen, half as large again as the drawing room at Tumbledown
[Dumbleton Hall], full of *dix-huitième* furniture, with a washing place
in one curtained alcove, the bed in another, and, above the vast desk,
a cloudy oil painting of Clement XIV, the Pope who dissolved the
Jesuits – a charming sign of their feud with the Benedictines (they
hate each other). They really are kindness itself here, and have been so
warm & welcoming. Everyone remembers Eddy [Sackville-] West
with great affection. I keep on remembering my first visit, and my
almost daily voluminous letters to you on which AT to KS[1] was
based. It really is a case of *Le jardin n'a rien perdu de son charme, ni le*

presbytère de son éclat.[2] It's 8 in the morning, a brilliant day, hundreds
of white chestnut-candles on the great trees outside, and lilac
everywhere, a cuckoo hard at it. It's like writing in some delicious
room in a remote chateau, peopled by figures called Celimène and
Clitandre, instead of le Père Prieur, le Père Hôtelier, l'Hôtelier
Bibliothécaire . . .

No more now, darling Mushy, except heaps and heaps of love
from

JEM

[1] *A Time to Keep Silence*, published on 29 May 1957.
[2] From Gaston Leroux's *Le Mystère de la chambre jaune*, one of the first works of 'locked
room' crime fiction. It was first published in France in periodical form in 1907, then
in novel form the following year.

*The peace of Saint-Wandrille was shattered by an unexpected telephone call
from the American film director John Huston, who asked Paddy to write a
screenplay (though usually he wrote his own). Paddy's task was to adapt a novel
by Romain Gary,* Les Racines du ciel *(1956), which became the film* The
Roots of Heaven *(1958).*

To Debo Devonshire   Hôtel Prince de Galles
5 August [1957]   33 Avenue George V
                                                      Paris

Darling Debo,

Everything's fixed. I only finished reading the book three minutes
before meeting Mr Zanuck,[1] but it didn't matter, because he burst
into his suite at the Savoy like a rifle bullet saying: 'Swell to see you,
Mr Feemor, it's really swell. I'm off to the Belgian Congo in three
days, and I've just taken two yellow pills & three injections and don't
make much sense, so you mustn't be sore at me if I talk a whole lot
of boloney.'

He's tiny, with bright blue minute eyes glinting with mad intensity,
a ragged sandy moustache and his injections had clearly incapacitated

him from judging distances, as the colossal cigar in his mouth – as irremovably there as part of his anatomy – was snapped in the middle, one half hanging at right angles and belching volumes of smoke, like the funnels of one of those Thames steamers going under Chelsea Bridge. He must have charged into a door or a wall or perhaps a mirror.

I can't remember if I told you that the whole of the book is a plea against elephant shooting, in case the species becomes extinct. The villain of the book goes berserk and shoots them by the score in a sort of demon's passion. This is obviously the bit Mr Zanuck likes best, because when I met him next day he said: 'It's a swell book, Mr Feemor, a wonderful book. The best bit is when they bump off all those elephants. But we'll run into difficulties here because of all that goddam humanitarian hooey in England and America. I'd like to do the thing properly, and shoot a whole lot of them, a whole lot . . .' his blue eyes kindled dreamily. 'I doubt if I get permission to shoot more than a dozen.' He looked rather dejected for a second, but then said, cheering up, 'I tell you what we'll do! We'll only shoot a dozen or maybe fifteen, but I'll put lots and lots of cameras about at different angles so it'll look as if it were killing hundreds! But what a book!'

There never seemed to be a second's question of my *not* doing the thing, so now I've got to start work full steam ahead and hope for the best. It's rather an alarming, but v. exciting assignation. I had luncheon with the old French authoress[2] the day before yesterday and with Mark Grant,[3] and there was much loving talk of you, and swapping of Athenian for Irish tales. Otherwise, Paris seems stripped of all my friends and has become one of the major tropical cities of the world. The policemen are in shirtsleeves and khaki solar-topees, as though it were Khartoum. I wandered around by myself till 7 a.m. in Montmartre the first night in countless bars full of negroes, soldiers, sailors, toughs and tarts of all colours and a few noseless pimps, and on the second night till 8 a.m. in Montparnasse and Les Halles. Here, very strangely, I fell in with two Australian nurses who seemed a bit lost, and fed them onion soup as day broke, surrounded by porters and butchers in blood-stained smocks as though they had just been helping at the guillotine. I am writing this in the mosaic courtyard of this luxurious hotel, with a bogus Spanish fountain tinkling in the middle. The Frogs and Americans here look awful, exactly like pigs, with tiny pig's eyes. I have just caught a sobering glimpse of my own reflection, and so, alas, do I. Circe has done a thorough job. How I wish you had been here! Just think of the night prowling and dark dancing, all the fun. I long for you like anything, and *yearn* and gaze towards the dividing Channel with hate.

Meanwhile, a billion tons of love, Debo darling, and promise to write hourly.

Paddy

1 Darryl Francis Zanuck (1902–79), American film producer and studio executive.
2 DD's older sister, Nancy, who lived in France.
3 PLF's wartime comrade Mark Ogilvie-Grant, who lived in Athens.

To Joan Rayner   L'Arche de Noé
31 December 1957   Îles de Porquerolles
                                            Var

My darling Muskin,

Lots of adventures to tell! First of all the Chasse à Courre from Chantilly.[1] I thought I was pretty smartly turned out with my new coat, boots, velvet-cap and all, but I can't tell you how quiet and modest I appeared – like a female *quetzal*[2] as opposed to a male – when I went to have breakfast with M. de Souza Lage (I've got to chuck this horrible Biro) across the road from St-Firmin. (No, here's another that actually writes.) He was dressed in a long-tailed blue coat with enormous gold and silver buttons and masses of pockets, a yellow waistcoat with gold buttons, white buckskin breeches and huge glittering jackboots like the Blues or the Life Guards. When we set out, he put on a belt with a silver-hilted sword about a foot and a half long, and one of those enormous horns over one shoulder and under the other. We had a great breakfast of omelettes and fried mushrooms washed down with a bottle of claret and then set off. The meet was at Royaumont, with Max Fould (Alan's brother-in-law)[3] doing the honours, half in his house, half in the courtyard of the Abbey, now full of other splendidly dressed men and women in tricornes trimmed with gold lace, while haughty steeds led by smart grooms & second horsemen neighed and stamped under coronetted blankets and huge black and white hounds, leashed together by the half dozen and flogged and held back by glittering and bottle-nosed hunt-servants, slavered and bayed. It was a bright, slightly frosty morning and it looked glorious. The Master was a splendid old boy called le Marquis de Roüalle. Lots of handshaking and flourishing of doffed caps, assembling and mounting, then a terrific fanfare. All the male members of the hunt blow these, not only the hunt servants. How they manage to ride with these orchestral instruments and above all, continue to learn and remember the 200-odd most complex tunes that mark the different stages of the chase is a mystery.

Off we tooled into the woods opposite, escorted by fanfares, and were hanging about in a field covered with haycocks when the hounds started kicking up a great fuss in the undergrowth, and out of the wood, with enormous leaps, came two stags, one of them a 'royal' with twelve points like an enormous scaffolding, the other with six: intelligence which was at once blown down the horns. They were just the opposite side of a stream, leaping along in great parabolas through the haycocks against a background of forest – it was just the kind of tapestry-vision I was longing for. We jumped over the stream (not a big one) – de Souza Lage and I, that is; I stuck to him like a limpet all the time, on a lovely mare called *Herodiade* – and we set off full tilt through the woods after the stags (the hounds and everyone else taking a different route) and followed them through a sort of *petén*[4] for about two miles, tormented by brambles & roots and ducking under low branches – I see the point of those caps now – till we lost them. All this sounds odd, but de S. L. is considered one of the crack chaps in this queer society, so I was in good hands. We were soon quite lost, and made our way back to the nest by listening for horns, and found everyone again in a built-up area like Welwyn Garden City, our horses thick in sweat as though preparing for a shave in a barber's shop. The *'royal'* was lost, but we pounded about for another hour after the six-pointer, by no means always sticking to the rides as I had imagined, but through the underbrush half the time, till we came to some swampy country with enormous tufted reeds ten feet high like the upper reaches of the Amazon, with the hounds making a great noise somewhere. De S. L. and I were alone again. We gave our horses to a girl to hold, dismounted, and plunged into the middle of this. Most of it was several inches deep in swamp, and trotting through in boots and spurs was no joke. It became less of one when S. L. gave me his crop as well as his horn, scabbard & belt to carry, and advanced brandishing the naked blade in order to plunge it into the stag's breast if it broke in our direction. It nearly did for me! After half an hour of this hell, we came on the stag *aux abois* ['at bay'], surrounded by hounds. It broke through them at our approach, galloped off, and was shot (as it was in the outskirts of a village) a mile off by one of the hunt servants with a special gun, as there were lots of people and children about, and, if they attempt to despatch it with their long daggers in such circumstances, there is danger of the stag goring a bystander (A *piqueur* [whipper-in] was killed last year – more than you can say of fox hunters!). The poor quarry was put in a truck and taken back to Royaumont. We followed it, and, while it was being cut up and the venison distributed to the innumerable peasants who help in the hunt, we drank whisky & white wine and ate smoked salmon & caviar sandwiches, then gathered round the remainder of the stag, – all the innards, etc., which were wrapped in its skin – for the *curée* as it is called: i.e. a grizzly banquet when the hounds eat up all this: three-quarters of an hour of antiphonal hornblowing, recounting all the different – phases? – of the day, the members of the hunt divided into two orchestras, as it were, the hunt servants into a third, each playing in turn, sometimes all together, in elaborate obsequies. The impression of something ancient and mediaeval – almost Merovingian – was overpowering. All was over by 3.30, rather early, as it often goes on long after dusk. D. S. L. – a jolly, hirsute, good-looking, half-Brazilian – then suggested that we should sneak off and drive over to another forest, send for two more of his horses,

and follow another hunt, a much rougher one, belonging to a
Comte de la Béraudière; so off we set, only to discover that they
hadn't even found; so we went back to this house and drank maté[5]
– it's rather good – then lots of gin & tonic. Patrick [Kinross]
turned up that evening, Alan & André
de Staercke next day; a huge lunch, then dinner at Cécile de
Rothschild.[6] It was a nice weekend, except that poor Diana had a
dreadful cold, which she seemed to master towards the end. The
hunt was the highlight for me. I managed to come out without
disgrace, thank God, & Souza Lage is very eager that we should do
lots more of it – horses any time! – and promises to take me to a
boar hunt, which is fast and furious. Here the quarry is killed with
a spear, often wreaking havoc first with its tusks. Their speed and
fierceness is apparently quite something. Last year a boar was marked
in north-east Poland and killed in the Camargue a fortnight later!
Think of all the countries, frontiers, forests and rivers it must have
crossed! The Vistula, the Elbe, the Oder, the Rhine, or the Danube,
the Saône, the Rhone delta, with all its tributaries, perhaps the
Etang de Vaccaris and the moat of Aigues Mortes!

I caught the night train to St Raphael on Monday, catching the
bus thence to St Tropez next morning. And it was raining! Miles of
vineyards under water, long detours caused by overflowing rivers
– one bridge washed away! – and St Tropez, when I got there, a
steep labyrinth of cascading streets and a wicked criss-cross of
gushing gutters overhead. Françoise [Germaine Tailleferre's daughter]
and Jean-Luc were waiting in ground-sheets, Wellingtons &
Sou'Westers. For some reason, we were not staying in the villa 3
miles from the town, but in a large gloomy palazzo-like building in
the middle of the town; huge, but not big enough for the quantity
of people staying there – my two, three children, two crop-headed
lesbians smoking cigars and a shifting troop of friends and
hangers-on and an enormous and very funny Provençal femme de
ménage who sat down to table with us. All this revolves round
Germaine Tailleferre.[7] She's not at all brilliant, as Freddie G. said, but
funny, charming, friendly, kind and nice. Philippe Soupault[8] caught
influenza at the last moment and couldn't come, alas! I think it

would have killed you, the noise and the lack of privacy, and I
thought I would expire too – for the first day; then I seemed to slip
into the general lunatic atmosphere and enjoyed it a great deal. It's
the most bohemian thing I've had anything to do with for ages.
Nobody seemed to have a bean, & lived like Elijah fed by ravens, but
it was all very gay and happy. G. Tailleferre is a wonderful mimic and
raconteuse, full of funny & scandalous tales of Cocteau, Morand,
Radiguet, Charlie Chaplin, Les Six, etc., Boeuf sur le Toit,[9] Ernst,
Jacob etc. She played us the first two acts of the opera she is writing
to P. Soupault's libretto, of Hans Andersen's *Little Mermaid*. It seemed
awfully good. She kept forgetting the words, and when this
happened, improvised ones of such startling and inventive indecency
that all were very soon in tears. But after three days I baled out, as it
was quite impossible to do any work, and escaped here, where I set
to like a madman, and I'm already two-thirds of the way through the
proofs, and feeling much happier.

It is simply heavenly here, rather like the forested part of Spetsai,
rocks and pine-needle-covered pathways, jagged cliffs, calanques and
inlets, and ilex, arbutus, thyme, marjoram, bay, μαλοτήρα [mountain
tea] and φασκομηλιά [sage] everywhere, smelling exactly like Greece.
I bathed this afternoon, and my word it was cold! But there has not
been a cloud or a drop of rain since I arrived: long walks in
shirtsleeves and two glorious sleeps in the sun under an ilex. This
hotel is delightful – Odette P. R.[10] told me about it – and I have a
lovely room down three steps with a red-tiled floor and a window
overlooking a tiled roof, reeds, bamboo, trees, masts and the sea. The
food is lovely – urchins, lobsters, brandades, rouille, bouillabaisse,
calamares, all washed down with a terribly good vin-rosé from the
island, or a red wine from opposite called Pradet. My room and full
pension costs 2,200 francs a day.[11] I was going to end this letter by
begging you (reinforced by a telegram) to fly out at once to
Marseilles or Toulon, where I could have met you and then, after a
few days here, go and see Larry [Durrell] and then Amy [Smart].[12]
But, alas! this morning (New Year's Day) I got a telegram saying
(a) John Huston absolutely delighted with script and (b) that I'm
urgently needed in Paris on the 3rd; so, alas, I'm catching the night

train tomorrow, back to St James & Albany.[13] I hope it is only a meeting or something. If so, I'll come straight over to London afterwards. I've got some surprises that I do hope you'll like.

Darling, you were a saint when I left, and I do feel guilty leaving you with all these things unreturned. I'm sending some pennies towards the telephone bill, as most of it must have been mine, and it'll be coming in soon. Do let me know (St J & A) if I can do or get anything in Paris.

I am reading, and am absolutely fascinated by, Valery Larbaud[14] – don't get him, as I've got his complete works. I long to know what you think of him. No more now, my own darling Musk, except a happy New Year and heaps and heaps of love from
          Paddy

We *must* come here together some time. Between New Year and Easter is best. From Easter to October, it seems, is infernal. This hotel, I've just discovered, has one star, and no wonder.

[1] PLF gave a more worked-up version of this episode in a letter written to Debo Devonshire the next day (*In Tearing Haste*, pages 39–41).

[2] A species of bird found in tropical forests; the males are strikingly coloured, while the female plumage is brown or grey.

[3] Baron Max Fould-Springer, whose sister Thérèse ('Poppy') married Alan Pryce-Jones, lived at Royaumont, a Palladian abbot's palace near Paris.

[4] A heavily forested region of Guatemala, visited by PLF and JR in 1948.

[5] A traditional South American caffeine-infused drink.

[6] Baroness Cécile de Rothschild (1913–95), expert golfer and friend of Cecil Beaton and Greta Garbo. Her country house was nearby at Noisy-sur-Oise.

[7] Germaine Tailleferre (1892–1983), composer: the only female member of the group of composers known as 'Les Six'.

[8] Philippe Soupault (1897–1990), poet, novelist, critic, and co-founder of the Surrealist movement.

[9] A celebrated Parisian cabaret bar.

[10] Odette Pol Roger, *Grande Dame* of the champagne family; a friend of Winston Churchill's.

[11] The equivalent of about 50 euros in 2016.

[12] The Smarts were now living in south-eastern France.

[13] The St James and Albany hotel in the rue de Rivoli, opposite the Jardin des Tuileries.

[14] Valery Larbaud (1881–1957), French writer, translator and critic.

To Xan Fielding   Marona
1 April 1958   Cameroon

Ξάν, χρυσό μου [Xan, dear boy],

I'm so sorry being such a sluggard. I ought to have written to you
and Daph ages ago. But, like poor Tom Dunbabin, I just didn't . . .

I say, what's all this about settling in Portugal? It does sound
exciting, and I'd got a very faint impression that Tangier was
beginning to get you down. I loved Portugal when I crossed it by
bus a few years ago and liked the Portuguese. Do write more details,
especially about the farming.

I like Corsair Country,[1] and many thanks for sending it. I've got
several criticisms, all constructive ones I think, and long to see you
to go into it. My Greek book is due out soon and I'm very anxious.

My life has taken a queer temporary turn. John Huston got hold
of me soon after we broke up at Lismore last year, to do the script
of Romain Gary's Prix Goncourt book, Les Racines du Ciel [The
Roots of Heaven], a queer, diffuse, bulky, rather brilliant book about
a sort of Jean-Gabin-esque ἀντάρτης [partisan] who leaps to the
defence of elephants in French Equatorial Africa. I was put up in an
hotel in Paris – St James and Albany – for most of the winter, and
scribbled away like a wild cat, conferring every two days, sometimes
more, with Darryl Zanuck, who is the owner & producer of the
film. A very strange man with a pepper & salt moustache, bright blue
eyes and a colossal cigar, which he mashes to a pulp between
irregular teeth, a barrier for a loud and rasping voice. We got on very
well, and eventually out I flew to F.E. Africa[2] with him & J. Huston,
arriving at Fort Archambault,[3] on the banks of a winding crocodile-
haunted river, the savannah around being full of elephants, lions,
panthers, jaguars, giraffes & buffalo. We lived here in a huge stockade
containing scores of huts inhabited by the 100-odd members of the
unit & there was a stone bungalow in the middle in which dwelt
Zanuck, Huston, Juliette Gréco (leading lady), Trevor Howard, Errol
Flynn[4] and me . . . All pretty odd. The camp is a seething mass of
cliques, largely based on nationalities, and I compatriotically belong
to the French one – Juliette, a girl called Anne Marie Cazalis, a

pansy actor called Marc Doelnitz, a journalist called Hedny and me. It is by far the most fun, full of secret languages and jokes and, I fear, cordially hated by all and sundry, who – like last year – hate to see one group having such a good time. Juliette is the most interesting by far – oddly beautiful, utterly bohemian, erratic, very well read and brilliant, and with a tremendous sense of humour. We became great pals at once. The life of this clique is not plain sailing by any means, as Juliette is supposed to be living with Zanuck, but gives the impression of shuddering with horror at his touch. He is blinded with violent and pathetic jealousy, and two days ago knocked her out clean, and then sobbed for two hours. I know she must be an infuriating girl for a rejected lover; but God, God spare us all this.

We are now in the Cameroon. Marona is a labyrinth of conical huts inhabited by jet-black Moslem horsemen with sabres and spears, sometimes chain mail, vast turbans wound round their heads so that only their fierce eyes peer forth. Their horses are caparisoned to the fetlocks in bold black and white checked housings. The surrounding mountains and savannah are inhabited by fetish-worshipping animists who live in caves, wear *not one stitch* of clothing and never sally forth without an assegai, a bow and a quiver full of long arrows.

John Huston is very amusing and very odd – as you know – and needs to be watched like a hawk. The only way of dealing with him is to diagnose his weak points and hit very hard and again and again. This establishes a humorous and rather friendly *modus vivendi*. We both know from the glint in each other's eyes what we are up to and it's rather stimulating. Thin ice work.

To my astonishment, Errol Flynn and I have become great buddies. He is a tremendous shit but a very funny one and we sally forth into dark lanes of the town together on guilty excursions that remind me rather of old Greek days with you. In fact, Juliette and he are my real standbys. Otherwise I loathe the whole atmosphere of the film world. Everything in it seems counterfeit except the money, of which, fortunately, there is a lot. I think, nevertheless, that the film stands a chance of being terrific.

What are your and Daph's plans? Do write at once, giving full details. I have none – can't have any, because of the film – in the immediate future, except going to one of the Greek islands – Paros, perhaps – with Joan & Maurice Bowra in June. I long to *feel* those waters washing away the last traces of all this rubbish. Will you write to The Rock Hotel, Bangui, Oubangui Chari, French Equatorial Africa, whither we move in a few days? It's close to the Equator, on the edge of the great rain forest that follows the basin of the Congo.

I long to see you both again soon. Give Daph lots of hugs from me, and lots of love to you.

Γειά σου, γειά σου! [Goodbye! Good health to you!]

Paddy

1 *Corsair Country: The Diary of a Journey along the Barbary Coast* (1958).

2 French Equatorial Africa, a federation of French colonial possessions which included Cameroon, Gabon, Chad, Central African Republic and Congo-Brazzaville.

3 The French colonial name of the city now known as Sarh.

4 Juliette Gréco (b. 1927), bohemian French actress and singer; Trevor Howard (1913–88), English actor who became a star after appearing in *Brief Encounter* (1945); Errol Flynn (1909–59), Australian-American actor known for his swashbuckling roles.

To Joan Rayner   Marona
Easter Monday [7 April] 1958   Cameroon

Darling,

Χριστὸς ἀνέστη! Χρόνια πολλά! [Christ is risen! Long life and happiness!] I gave a lovely Easter party last night, about twenty people, outside the little house I've taken here. It was terribly pretty, with lamps shaded by carved Fulbé[1] half-calabashes, all on straw mats, sitting and lying under the lamplit leaves of two enormous mango trees. Zanuck was ill, thank God – poor chap! – so couldn't come and ruin it. I had two stark naked animists turning a lamb on a spit – a '*meshoui*' such an occasion is called here – and a vast cauldron of very strong iced sangria. Gréco and two other Frogs came early and we cut and spread lots of caviar sandwiches. Most of us, for fun, wore the thin flowing embroidered baggy trousers that the local grandees wear, and we lolled happily talking away under the leaves till the small hours – Gréco, Flynn, Huston, Trevor Howard, Friedrich

Ledebur,[2] Grégoire Aslan[3] and the local governor, who is a charming lonely white Russian called Sarkisoff, and a few more. I do wish you had been here. It was lovely and strange and gloriously different from the usual awful film atmosphere, which I grow to detest more and more.

The day before yesterday the French High Commission[er] flew from the capital in the south – Yaoundé – to decorate half a dozen powerful Fulbé Lamidos[4] of this area, 'our' Lamido – 'Marona' – and the Lamidos of Bogo, Mirdif and Foumban. Each Lamido was enthroned under a vast coloured umbrella which gyrated and hovered up and down by his court, with vast retinues of draped horsemen behind them with spears, rifles and scimitars. Each had a storyteller and jester and a swarm of splendidly clad swaggering minor potentates and his team of drummers and trumpeters. The noise was deafening – hundreds of drums hammering away, across which cut the sound of ear-splitting fanfares every now and then, as the trumpeters put their long thin instruments to their lips. They are of brass, *four or five yards long*, exactly like the ones displayed on Egyptian bas-reliefs. When each *légion d'honneur* was pinned on, there was a pandemonium of firing, drumming & trumpeting, and the whole thing ended up by swarms of horsemen galloping and caracoling[5] past in a whirl of dust, brandishing their sabres and spears. The best of all was the queer and beautiful young Lamido of Bogo – jet black, distinguished and nourished on all that is rarest and most decadent in French literature, lolling in sober and grand robes at the heart of the most glittering and martial court of all and escorted by a fluttering troop of fan-bearers.

We push off to Rock Hotel, Bangui, Oubangui-Chari, French Equatorial Africa, in three days' time.

All my love, darling

JEMY

---

[1] The Fulbé of Central Africa (also known as the Fula or Fulani) are a pastoral, nomadic people.

[2] Friedrich von Ledebur (1900–86), Austrian-born character actor who gained international recognition after playing the role of the South Sea islander Queequeg in John Huston's film *Moby Dick* (1956).

3 Grégoire Aslan (1908–82), known as 'Coco Aslan', was an ethnic Armenian actor and musician.
4 Local ruler, the African equivalent of the Arab title 'Emir'.
5 A caracole is a half-turn executed by a horse and rider.

To Joan Rayner   Rock Hotel
25 April 1958   Bangui
                                        Oubangui-Chari[1]
                                  French Equatorial Africa

My darling Musk,
      What a long delay, caused by our deracination from the
Cameroons and the shift to the Oubangui-Chari, and by various
misadventures and the grind of script writing. I'm so sorry, darling.
      Marona became an inferno of heat and anger and anguish before
we left it. Ice became more precious than diamonds, as a glass of
water left standing for half an hour practically reached boiling point.
Great dust-devils a mile high whirled over the plains and the
dried-up riverbeds. But there were lovely moments, and perhaps the
best of these were early morning and evening rides, with Friedrich
Ledebur – who rides like a saint – or alone. The horses all have
saddles rather like Guatemala and Nicaragua, and no doubt they are
of identical Moorish origin. They try to canter all the time and the
Fulbé never seem to move at any other gait. Some of these rides
were wonderful. One sometimes got mixed up in a whole troop of
Fulbé tittupping along in clouds of dust. It was specially nice in the
evening, with wonderful red sunsets behind mountains like groves of
thunderbolts and long streams of ibises and crested cranes homing
overhead with sad cries. I went on one of these evening rides on a
black half-broken Arab that behaved more and more queerly and, the
moment the sun set and it began to get dark – you know how
quick it is – broke into an unhaltable gallop across the plain.
Terrifying! No stopping him. On and on he went for half an hour
till he suddenly stopped dead outside the walls of a Fulbé village,
banging me against a tree with terrific force. I only stayed on by
grasping the pommel like mad; and somehow managed to get home

without disaster, aching like hell. My left elbow was scratched and bloody, so I put some iodine on, but a week after getting here it swelled up double the size and went an awful shiny dark red, so I was stuffed with antibiotics and put to bed. After two days of hell they cut it open in the hospital and let out the flags of all the nations – it was almost as if they had removed an alarm-clock, it throbbed so. All's well now, but it was awful while it lasted. Everything seems to go septic here.

We flew here by relays over endless tracts of semi-desert and then over endless tracts of *petén*-like forest. Bangui is rather a gay little town – a bit like Scarborough in Grenada – on the banks of the Oubangui river, which is the same sort of thing as the Rio San Juan, except that it has great rocks and islands jutting from it. The other bank is the Belgian Congo. There are pygmies in the forest, and, it is hoped, elephants. I have got a lovely studio here, over a restaurant, a huge L-shaped room which I have curtained and hung with glorious lengths of cloth which the women wear here – all from Manchester, France or Japan, but specially made for the African market, and very odd and strange (I'm bringing lots back, which you can have made into washing dresses or cushions or something).

My French chums were saints while I was laid up, arriving with loads of pawpaw, flowers, soursops, mangoes etc. Also, I must say, John Huston & Zanuck. John H. has been joined by Suzanne Flon, the French actress he is in love with, who is charming, unspectacular, funny and quiet.[2] I've got to like him a great deal better. It's all much better when he realises that one is fully aware of what a wicked old scoundrel he is. He is in no doubt about this now, and all is fine.

Two lovely letters of yours – one to Marona and a much older one to Fort Archambault – arrived just as I was getting better from the arm, but still bedridden. What a lovely account of your French trip, it did sound fun. I felt like crying at the news of all our friends, they seemed so far away and remote and so utterly different from the fifth-rate world I'm surrounded by here – there are only about three people I would ever like to see again – and as inaccessible as Olympians. I realised how outstanding and what exceptions they all were from ordinary life, how spoiled one is. Starting with you, they all seem more rare than black pearls.

I don't know how the film will be. But I think very good. It's exciting work and maddening at the same time – John H. is such a last-minute changer, utterly empirical on the surface, but perhaps with a dash of underlying genius which will make the whole thing cohere. The changes in the script can be either an exciting challenge to one's talents and skill in marquetry; or deadening, heart-breaking mortician's work, rouging and curling a corpse, when one goes over a scene for the fifth or sixth time. Apart from the pennies, I think it's an utter waste of time, or almost. There may be some lessons about concision and dexterity in manipulating plots which might conceivably be of use.

There are terrific tornadoes here, whirling El Greco skies that turn black and break to smithereens with forked lightning and thunderclaps, all the branches thrashing together and splitting and the pouring clouds and the seething Oubangui joining in a palisade of water. They make the town seem cowering and fragile and pathetic and the forest appears to make a threatening leap forward, with its disturbing content of fierce fauna and strangling vegetation and arrows and drums and pygmies and fetishes and ritual murders. The Rock Hotel is a ghastly modernistic Corbusier smart building. I went into it after one of these tornadoes, and found it cloudy with flying termites and moths & bats, the floor two inches deep in drifts of termites' wings and hundreds of frogs leaping hither and thither, with Juliette Gréco's mongoose running wild among them, killing frog after frog, and, when he could take no more, vomiting frogs' feet and heads onto this eerie carpet of broken-off wings. It was like the last gasp of Babylon or Nineveh.

I wandered off into the forest some nights ago and slept under a tree, rather like the Negress in D. Rousseau's picture[3] hoping a lion might come and rub muzzles and move on. When I woke up I was soaking wet and lashed to the ground by thousands of strands of gossamer, like Gulliver waking up in Lilliput.

I've had a case of local butterflies made for you by a woman who became expert in such matters in Indo-China, they look very pretty & strange and I hope you like them.

I've no idea what's to become of me. We may go to the Belgian Congo – or we may go back to Paris for the studio shots in a week or so. So alas! no good writing. I'll keep you in touch. I *do* miss you darling, and long to be in Chester Row planning more sensible journeys than this!

lots and lots of love from

JEMY

xxx

oxo

---

¹ Known since 1958 as the Central African Republic.
² Huston described Flon as 'the most extraordinary woman I have ever known'.
³ A reference to Henri Rousseau's painting *The Sleeping Gypsy*.

Joan allowed Paddy to pursue other women, secure in the knowledge that he would never leave her. In October 1958 he went to stay in Rome with his friend and former lover, Judy Montagu. There he met Lyndall Birch, who was working as a proofreader for the Food and Agriculture Association (FAO), while she tried to write a novel in the tiny flat in the Via del Gesù she shared with the photographer Josephine Powell. Still in her mid-twenties, she was beautiful but shy and unconfident. Earlier in the year she had played a small part in the film The Nun's Story, *directed by Fred Zinnemann and starring Audrey Hepburn. When she met Paddy she was secretly engaged to the bisexual Lord Montagu of Beaulieu, though both were experiencing doubts and this engagement was broken off soon after. Her liaison with Paddy was the first of what she would later describe as 'a chain of disastrous affairs'. This letter was written after Paddy had returned to London for the publication of the first volume of his long-awaited book on Greece, entitled* Mani; *he enclosed a photograph of himself in the same envelope.*

To Lyndall Birch
23 November 1958   13 Chester Row, SW1

Darling Lyndall,

I packed off a whole bundle of deathless prose [i.e. *Mani* and earlier books] to you a few days ago, something to get your teeth into! But it probably takes ages for parcels to reach the Via del Gesù, and up all those stairs. But at least they won't have to sneak in on tiptoe, like their author! I did love that. It gave everything a wonderful feeling of conspiracy and romance – not that the latter was lacking anyway. I loved those coffees and rolls, too, in different cafés, in a lovely, early morning unbreathed Rome, and walking on air back to the Tiber island along a labyrinth of palaces. I played through the whole of Don Giovanni last night, and felt very homesick for your pretty room and heavenly hours.

I saw Ivan[1] several times in Paris, and he seemed pretty keen on the Zurich idea. I cracked you up like anything to David O. Selznick,[2] backed by Ivan, pointing out that you had a jolly good, steady and well-paid job in Rome, so it would have to be a pretty good offer to prise you out of it. Could you leave your Rome job for say, six months, make a vast quantity of money, and return again? That would be the ideal.

You are clever to live in Rome. It's cold and foggy here, but quite pretty in a misty, lamplit, muffin-man kind of way. A seagull flew up the street, from the Thames I suppose, this morning, probably bent on an island holiday: anything for a change.

I've got Josephine [Powell]'s lovely enlargement of the mosaic of the Marriage at Cana[3] pinned on the wall by my desk, and I like it more and more. Please give her my love and could you ask her, if she ever makes any enlargements of the kneeling figure of the Logothete Theodore Metochites[4] with his enormous headdress, also from the Kariyé Djami in Constantinople, please to put me at the top of the list of *buyers*. It really is a beauty.

I'm tremendously excited at the moment, as *Mani*, my new book, comes out in three days' time, and I await the first reviews with my heart in my mouth.

Please write and tell me what you are up to. Also, how things are faring for Judy.[5] Between you and me, everyone is a bit anxious about her in London, her present imbroglio, and how well or ill she will take it if things go wrong. It's hard to know what to wish for – that it should go well, and for Judy to be happy, for a while at any rate, or for it to go ill and for Judy to be well out of it, if she weathered the shock. It's in this last clause that all the danger lies.

I adored my time in Rome and adored you, and greatly miss our secret conclaves. I keep on finding myself humming about the holly and the ivy and the running of the deer! So please write, darling Lyndall.

With lots of love from

Paddy

xxx

¹ Ivan Moffat (see note 1 on page 76). LB had become friendly with his mother, Iris Tree.

² David O. Selznick (1902–65), Hollywood film producer and film studio executive. LB was offered a job working for him.

³ One of the mosaics at the Church of the Holy Saviour in Chora, in the north-west of Istanbul.

⁴ Theodore Metochites (1270–1332), Byzantine statesman, author, gentleman philosopher, and patron of the arts. His political career culminated in 1321, when he was invested as Grand Logothete ('grand chancellor'). He used his wealth to subsidise the church's restoration after it had been damaged during the period of Crusader rule. This included not only repairing the building but commissioning mosaics and frescoes, many of which survived even though the church had been made into a mosque after the Islamic Conquest. Metochites's portrait can still be seen in a famous mosaic in the narthex, above the entrance to the nave.

⁵ Judith Venetia 'Judy' Montagu (1923–72), daughter of the Hon. Edwin Montagu and Venetia Stanley, with whom PLF had been involved a few years earlier. She had given up her London life and moved to Rome after falling for the American photographer and art historian Milton Gendel (b. 1919), whom she eventually married in 1962. PLF had been staying in her Rome flat on the Isola Tiburtina when he began his affair with Lyndall Birch.

After spending the winter in England, Paddy returned to Italy in the spring of 1959. 'Back in Rome, I met a man who owned a castle in the Alban Hills, not far from Palestrina,' he later recalled. 'It had been fought over by the Colonna and the Orsini for centuries, then abandoned for a further hundred years. I had developed a passion for places like this and I asked him if I could rent a couple of rooms there. He laughed and said, "You must be mad! You can have the whole place free." '

To Jock Murray   Castello di Passerano
10 [?] May 1959   Gallicano nel Lazio
                                        Provincia di Roma

Dear Jock,

I hope you are impressed by this new departure.[1] It's not for
serious writing but for doing a fair copy at the end of the day in
order not to be too depressed as the weeks go by at the spectacle
of the mounting pile of yellowing and dog-eared and erased and
ballooned pages.

Now, my doings. The drive went off swimmingly. Got out of the
aeroplane at Le Touquet, and reached Chantilly that night, then on
to Avallon at end of next day's driving. Grenoble the next night,
through the Basses Alpes and the passes of the Vercors the next,
sleeping chez the Smarts, on to Savona the next, along the Ligurian
coast, La Spezia, inland to Pisa, slept at Siena, through Tuscany and
Latium next day, reaching Rome at night. Drove straight up to the
Capitol and drove a sort of triumphal dance about fifty times round
the statue of Marcus Aurelius and only stopped when a bewildered-
looking *carabiniere* sauntered onto the empty square; and down at last
to Judy Montagu's flat on an island in the middle of the Tiber.

Of course the option on the house at Anticoli had just elapsed so,
based on the Tiber, I started raking Tuscany, Latium and Umbria and
at last found this stupendous castle and contrived to borrow it. It
stands on a forested hill and dominates a rolling fleece of treetops
and freshly mown hay-fields. Millions of birds with the cuckoo well
in the lead, except at night when scores of nightingales take over as
well as owls, crickets, nightjars, frogs and the like. It looks from afar
like Windsor, Carnarvon or Lismore with its turrets and the long
sweep of its battlements, but it has actually only four rooms and
none of them have been inhabited for five hundred years or so.
There is a Colonna shield on one corner, to which august house it
belonged at one time like most of this part of Lazio. It is girdled on
three sides by the sweep of the Sabine, Praenestine and Alban hills
tailing off to Mount Soracte and on the fourth by the Roman
campagna with the dome of St Peter's and great Rome itself just

discernible on the horizon. I've managed to borrow some odds and ends of furniture from the Orsini palace and got some nuns and seamstresses in nearby Tivoli to sew a vast heraldic banner several yards square which adorns one wall at the end of a large banqueting hall. I'm tempted to fly it from the highest tower; don't quite dare to yet but doubt if I'll be able to resist for long. Then, when the Black Castellan of Passerano displays his gonfalon from the battlements, the peasants of the valley can hide their cattle and douse their lights and bolt up their dear ones!

To correct this slight attack of *folie de grandeur*, there is no sanitation at all. It's all fieldwork under the trees, and the only lighting is by oil-lamp and very splendid it looks. But what I'm leading up to is that the second vol. is under weigh and going well. And about time too, I fancy I can hear you murmur!

All the best

Yours ever

Paddy

[1] This letter was typed.

Paddy had returned to Italy, excited by the prospect of resuming his affair with Lyndall Birch. But he had not considered her feelings. After his letter in November she had not heard from him again: humiliated and hurt, she had begun seeing another man. When she and Paddy were reunited in Assisi, she told him that their affair was over. In this 'mea culpa' letter he reflects ruefully on his mistakes.

To Lyndall Birch   Sibilla
undated [May 1959?]   Tivoli

My darling Lyndall,

I went out to the Castle again on the way to Tivoli and came into the valley in the later afternoon. The country looked less Canaanitish under the grey mackerel sky; more as though it were embedded in a remote, sad, silent dream. That troop of half wild girls helped me up with a few more folding tables I'd brought out in the

back of the car. I made the two beds, put a table by each with an oil
lamp on it as bits of half-corroborative detail in that inchoate
interior, then sent the girls away that dogged my footsteps, all
watchfully and bewilderedly at gaze; and mooched about the rooms
with the sky fading beyond the still glassless windows like an
interlock of grey angels' wings with all the birds falling silent till it
was completely dark; and felt as sinister as Giant Despair in Doubting
Castle in *The Pilgrim's Progress*. I'm not absolutely convinced that it is
the perfect habitat for me in my present ludicrous state: that masonry
is rife with rich potentialities of self-pity; but I'm resolved to live
there for a bit, though I feel rather as though the dwindling obstacles
between me and incumbency are so many mounting bricks of
someone immuring himself. But there's just a chance that its
promises may be a kind of near-homeopathic device, the hair of a
different dog.

Of course, by the time I tore myself away and went spiralling up
into the lights of Tivoli, it was far too late to knock up Miss
Edwardes[1] in case she hadn't got my letter (leaping at her offer),
which I only sent off yesterday. She's awfully old. So I took a neo-
Gothic room in the Hotel Sirene and slouched off, rather
imprudently perhaps in the circumstances to The Sibilla,[2] where you
and Judy and I had luncheon under the Athenian Sybil's rotunda
when you and I had only just met and all that last autumn's and last
winter's and this spring's work was still to be done; munched my way
through a rather tasteless trout and some gorgonzola, and here I am.
Thank God the room's practically empty, except for a group of
Italians that I find myself looking at from time to time with totally
unjustified scorn, wishing they were Greek and finding them, by
comparison, and in spite of their handsome faces and their lively ways,
like food with the salt left out. But I do realise that at the moment
the poor sods couldn't put a foot right as far as I'm concerned.

***

You must be in the heart of the Blunt world,[3] at the moment, with
all our pals, and I hope it goes well.

I do see that there is a sort of comic justice in my present plight.

I'm counting rather sanguinely on reserves of shallowness and resilience that seem, at the moment, quite beyond my grasp; those particular buffoons have gone on strike. The most irking thing of all is that every time that I think of you with anger or a hard-luck-hang-dog grimace – (which I do now and then, though most of the time I think of you with unconditional fondness and love and friendship and a respectable longing to be able to show it and do something about it, which has nothing to do – or very little to do – with ravening desire (I've managed, like Medea, to drag that dragon into a fitful slumber with little more than the occasional flicker of a scaly eyelid . . .), and nothing whatever to do with guilty feelings about past inadequacy – every time such thoughts come raging in, their brave flames are snuffed at once with the thought that, in our joint feat of flinging a pearl away richer than all our tribe,[4] I was well in the lead. Please pity my frustration in this! Think of the baulked scowl . . . It's infuriating to be utterly in the wrong; unlike you, lucky!

I'm off to bed now, as they're shutting up shop. More tomorrow.

Tuesday

I woke up with the sun pouring through the window, and, when I sat up, there was Sant' Antonio,[5] my old Traveller's Tree refuge [on] the other side of the ravine, under the wavering line of the Sabine Hills, and, immediately below, the Sybil's temple and feathery-looking ilexes with the early sunlight appearing to stream horizontally through them and scatter a bright gold dust of lyrical wonder over everything, the tops of cypresses and what looked like young hazels. A waterfall swished down through the Courbet-looking rocks into a deep, blue-green and secret-looking pool. Wood pigeons wheeled under my window, with the light sliding over their wings and vanishing again as they sailed through the shadows. It was like a grove sacred to a benign sylvan god, and all spoke of sunlight and happiness, so unlike the tearful mediaeval beauty of the Black Bastardy [Castello di Passerano].

I found Miss Edwardes pottering about among the irises and snapdragons under her vine trellis beyond Sant' Antonio, much more

shrunken and old and brittle than I had remembered, her pallor and
her wavering voice belied by her cheerful bright blue and rather small
girlish eyes. We went shopping in Tivoli where she waved her
lorgnette – so at variance with her almost peasant clothes and the
handkerchief over her head – in many a hardly haggled bargain for
the castle. I whisked her off there with a young glazier with a tape
measure and we left him at work, so all will soon be well; then to the
Sibilla, for a feast. My word, she was excited! I don't think anyone
can have taken her out for decades. As we were finishing Nathalie
and Graziella[6] turned up and shocked and charmed her with their
brisk metropolitan chat. (Nathalie had made a mistake about a
called-off lunch with the Quennells.) After that, I wandered off in the
car through the Sabine hills, lying for hours under the olive trees,
thinking about the article I'm supposed to be writing and about you.

＊

I do want you to be clear about last winter. We talked about it,
rather unhappily (and why not, for Christ's sake?) at Assisi, and now,
alas, it's probably only of interest for our sentimental archives. You
know – you must know – how I loved our October life. But, in
illogical contrast to my vanity and conceit in other ways, a sort of
deep-rooted ill opinion of myself (linked, as far as I can make it out,
with the almost subconscious knowledge of how little, as far as a
lifetime goes, I have to offer anyone) makes me the most laggard of
mortals in thinking anyone could be in love with me. This produces
a kind of rhinoceros-hide obtuseness which is less a defence for me
– though it can be – than for the extremely rare other ones the
other side of the carapace i.e. a shield for them against my
inadequacies. This sounds (quite wrongly!) almost noble, so I hasten
to say that it is accompanied by a perfectly commonplace, and in no
way estimable (and it seems to me now, very brutal) lack of
sensitiveness and lack of twigging about what happens to others.

Anyway, the thing is this: this subconscious formula didn't work in
this case, if anything so diffuse and obscure can be called a formula. I
trailed clouds of October glory all through the winter and thought
of you constantly with devotion and excitement and the resolve to

be in Rome again, and with you, constantly and far too
overconfidently. I never deliver these feelings in precise words to
myself, except as the memory and the prospect of magical happiness,
and I found myself smiling with idiotic bliss whenever I thought of
you; and your October self was constantly irrupting. I saw ourselves
rushing into our temporarily suspended embrace and showering each
other with rash unquestioning and uncalculating happiness. But
(through the above mentioned obtuseness) I had no idea what harm
and unhappiness I was unconsciously inflicting. Though now, when I
think of your letters – so beautifully written, so kind and loving and
undemanding, my darling Lyndall, I see that anyone but a savage
would have understood the baleful possibilities of silence: silence
caused by the thought that I would be in Rome again almost at
once; and by the vanity of waiting for the inspiration to write a
letter and then more letters, of immense length and loving tenderness
and brilliant wit and imperishable splendour. Speed and more
humility on my part could have saved on both. I know there is no
defence for me here, and it's no good striding about the room and
kicking the furniture. But please believe that it wasn't indifference. I
don't think you do. It is atrocious bad luck that my eleventh-hour
letter (not such a wonder, I hasten to say, in case it turns up, but it
might have changed things if the magic had not been too
irretrievably dismantled by then) should never have got to you.
You know how ashamed and sorry I am about all this; how bitterly
furious with myself, you can't know.

***

Our stars have been cruelly inauspicious since then.
   My last days in London, ever since writing to you, then the
journey to Chantilly and across France went by in a state of ecstatic
excitement that increased as the leagues diminished between me and
Rome. (You and the town had long since merged.) I had a guilty
knowledge – not nearly guilty enough, I'm sorry to say! – that I had
behaved pretty badly. But I had no idea how badly. I foresaw a few
token reproaches which the joy of being together again would have
ridden over roughshod and scattered in smithereens in the first five

minutes. I also knew something about your complications,[7] didn't
blame you at all (I should hope not, indeed!) and felt supremely
confident that I could send any ghastly intervener flying; chuckled at
the prospect and tooled on singing merrily at the wheel through the
French spring. You sounded so excited and breathless on the
telephone at La Spezia, or so I thought, rashly attributing my own
mood to you. There were nothing but golden prospects ahead. Not
an inkling of how soon I would be smiling on the other side of my
face. Admit you are a bit touched by the staggering absurdity of all
this.

Then all started to go tragically awry. The first meeting on that
beastly film set,[8] so disenchanting for you, but not for me. I ought to
have understood the gloomy implications of your turning your head
aside later on. I felt shattered and groggy after our talk in the bar in
Assisi and only then began to understand how much I had so
foolishly and idly thrown away, how much harm I had done and
how desperately attached I was to you, just as you began to slide out
of reach. But I still didn't know how badly things stood for me. I
hoped our enforced physical aloofness was a temporary thing, which
you might recklessly and generously reverse; didn't know whether it
was an instinctive or a pondered veto. I certainly didn't blame you
for a fraction of a second, nor do I. These things are as merciless and
ineluctable as the weather; but of course I hoped it would change.
So, as I said earlier, I managed to lull that particular dragon asleep,
though I knew it was ready to leap to life again with thrashing tail
and jets of fire roaring down either nostril at a kind stroke on his
poor old neglected head.

There were two things after that, which blinded me to what had
really happened – after all, love takes many shapes, and I had to accept
this one (no choice!). The first was your saying 'please don't go to
Greece!', and the other was: when I asked if you had taken a dislike to
me, your answering at once, and with a kind of sad conviction 'You
are the only person in the world I *do* really care about.' Then
everything, all the factors which, from the start, seemed to be
conspiring to lame and obstruct and turn things grey – that bloody
film, troubles of eyes and throat, tiredness, the arrival of your American

pal[9] – not as a competitor but as a further source of harassment and complication for you (another teacup to flounder in!) and of my Anglo-Italian one[10] (so utterly irrelevant and unwanted and untimely!),* money troubles, typewriters, tape machines, the depression of Lord Montagu's marriage[11] – all of this seemed like a maddening procession of idiotic rivals which must come to an end soon. But they crowded in thicker and faster till I never saw you at all and when any invitation from people you said you despised and were ashamed of, any last-minute excuse seemed a valid reason for not seeing me, I began to feel really mystified and duped, miserable, angry, flouted etc. and that I was the last person in the world you cared about, and wished me not in Greece, but in Timbuktoo or Kamchatka. I am glad that my random remark about it being perhaps better not to meet till we had got over all this (of course it wasn't true. You are the only person, unfortunately, that I want to see. It was a sort of thinking aloud, half an opening for a non-forthcoming argument from you against such a course, but I can't blame you for not twigging this), I'm glad that, at long last, it brought out the stern (withheld till then, I suspect, out of kindness) truth that anyone less imperceptive and maladroit in such matters would have understood a month ago. I wish I had! It leaves you utterly free to do what you want to do – whatever that may be – and saddles me with an unwanted and extremely uncongenial liberty that I really don't know what to do with yet. Boo-hoo.

***

The lunatic aspect of all this is that I seem to have taken over your last winter's symptoms in the exact ratio at which you have been losing them – at least, visibly, because they had been incubating for a long time before: an absurd and unenviable predicament. I don't propose to burden you with all this, it's no longer any business of yours, alas. But when it's over, we'll be able to compare scars like Chelsea pensioners. It can't be helped. Lots of splendid chaps have been in the same fix in the past, I stoutly tell myself.

* The day she left, after, I fear, a rather sad stay, she said 'I had such a queer dream last night. I dreamt I was waving goodbye to you in the street. It was nearly dark, you looked round and disappeared down a lane by the church of the Gesù.'

***

Well, there's my sad case history, darling Lyndall, told in my untutored way, and I fear it makes sorry reading. Please don't worry about it; you're in no way to blame. Sometime, when it comes naturally and without constraint and the lack of need for kindness (which you *don't* need to use. It's worse in the end) or self-defence, guarantee absolute truth, do please tell me yours in its entirety. I'm abreast of scattered fragments of it, but you have too much evidence of my hopelessness as a diagnostician to doubt that I'm still largely in the dark.

Again, please don't be anxious about our comic reversal of roles. I do love you and I'm determined not to lose you as a friend as well as in every other way, and one of the things about loving people is, after all, to wish them well and want to help, comfort, befriend. My inherited distemper will pass. Lucky you being out of the wood! (Fine metaphors, I must say.) I long to see you, and I'm sure that we have countless delights of friendship ahead, trust, love and confidence on their thrones again and all tears dry. The whole miserable nightmare of the last month will evaporate. I'm equally determined not to let more recent hell blacken the radiance of last year, a secret and utterly happy time of music and poetry and of hearts and minds at rest. This is what I'm going to salvage and keep for life, and with endless gratitude.

God bless you, my darling Lyndall
with love from
Paddy

Just as I finished writing this, a gust of wind blew all these flimsy sheets down the terrace of the Sirene.[12] Heart in mouth, I managed to save them before they took wing over the balustrade down through the circling wood pigeons to lose themselves below among the ilexes and elderflowers. It would have been just my luck; but I won this time! P.

[1] Several years before PLF had rented rooms in the Casa Sabina in Tivoli from Miss Edwardes, an Englishwoman.

2 The Sibilla restaurant in Tivoli incorporates two Roman temples.

3 Countess Anna Laetitia 'Mimi' Pecci-Blunt (1885–1971), née Pecci, socialite, photographer and patron of the arts, married a wealthy American, Cecil Blumenthal. She was the niece of Pope Leo XIII, who made Blumenthal a Count as a wedding present, and they merged their surnames to Pecci-Blunt. Her son Dino was courting LB at the time.

4 'Like the base Indian, threw a pearl away
   richer than all his tribe . . .'
                    Othello, V, 2

5 A former monastery built over a Roman villa, believed to have belonged to the poet Horace; now owned by the Landmark Trust.

6 Nathalie Perrone (1927–2014), née de Noailles, then married to Sandro Perrone, the owner and editor of Rome's leading newspaper, *Il Messaggero*; and Graziella, one of the four daughters of 'Mimi' Pecci-Blunt, married to Henri de Beaumont.

7 The other man with whom LB was now involved.

8 LB had a small part in Fellini's *La Dolce Vita*, which was lost in the editing.

9 Jeffrey Selznick, who had fallen in love with LB when she was working for his father, David O. Selznick, over Christmas.

10 Carla Thorneycroft (1914–2007), elder daughter of the Italian Count Guido Malagola Cappi, married the Conservative politician Peter Thorneycroft in 1949. She and PLF had been having an affair.

11 Montagu married only months after breaking off his engagement from LB.

12 The Hotel Sirene in Tivoli overlooks a gorge.

Paddy's apology to Lyndall Birch was at least partially successful, as this letter suggests.

To Lyndall Birch
14 [?] June 1959   Ansedonia

Darling Lyndall,

   What a good idea of yours it was leaving after dinner and driving through the night! I pelted along the empty Aurelian Way *like smoke*, and thought of you driving blissfully from Bologna at dead of night with the concert playing till the car dropped to bits; then slowed down for a while, smoking a terrible Tuscan cigar and watching the cross-eyed beam of my headlamps in the dark, the whitewashed tree trunks whizzing by. I felt my eyelids pricking a bit by the time I got to Civita[1] in an open-all-night café drinking coffee after coffee & eating two Crik-Croks [a brand of Italian snacks]; then set off again into the first glimmer of a wonderful dawn beginning with crimson and zinc and crocus colour in rags behind the dark towers of Tarquinia[2] then on through a slow apocalyptic awakening with a lightening sky and colour magically stealing back into the leaves and stone and mountains and a few early lorries appearing till headlamps were pale and useless and put out, and it was a wonderful unbreathed summer morning over the Tyrrhene sea and the Maremma cornfields. Down to the sea at Ansedonia[3] to bathe, then to bed. *Driving into the dawn!* A new experience. Sad one can only do something, for the first time in your life, *once.* I wonder how many exciting and unique maidenheads of experience lie ahead.

Woke up at midday longing for ping-pong[4] and sentimentally stroked the handle of your cast-down bat. I felt too restless for work so set off for Grosseto under a changing sky of gold and grey clouds − some of them raining over the distant mountains like leaking sacks of dark grain − sudden downpours, thunder and lightning, baroque sunbursts, rainbows and coloured puddles and foxes' weddings,[5] the puddles fusillading the exciting shuddering, orgasmic roar. It was winter by the time I sailed in through the barbican of Grosseto. Found a very good trattoria under the arcade opposite what must be the southernmost Tuscan-striped, though restored, cathedral and read some very funny poems of Wyndham Lewis as I worked my way through a large meal, and found myself laughing out loud quite often at the poems under the stolid gaze of Grosseto's grossest, munching all round in a ring. Paid the *conto,* picked my way through these Ghibelline[6] rotters at their meal, out into the downpour and found myself gazing thunderstruck at my own name a foot high (9' to be exact . . .) *Radici del Cielo!*[7] Couldn't resist it, so into a ghastly cinema for the last third of the film. *My word*, it's been rottenly cut and miserably dubbed, *no wonder* you all scorn it so. It was never a good film, but ten times better than this.

It was a lovely summer afternoon when I got out: flashing & prismatic with raindrops; so I took an inland road through rolling

hills, past rivers and bridges and woods, all quite empty, a sort of
gentle Hereford or Shropshire full of wheat and poppies and
mustard seed and hedges covered with white dog-roses and sleepy
oak spinneys and here and there a green watery valley with dark
woods . . . I swooped, sailed, glided, twisted, sank, surfaced, and
spiralled through this soft and labyrinthine paradise for hours,
sometimes looking down on a soft interlock of retreating hills
shiftily islanded with the shadows of clouds, sometimes along the
bottom of glades and dells with water rushing darkly under small
bridges with tilted sunlit rafts of corn and half-shorn hayfields
high above, beyond treetops, striped with windrows and dotted
with haycocks, sometimes Piers Plowman peasants in green
corduroy reaving those conical ricks that they slice away later, till
by the autumn they are as thin as cigars. Some vines, plenty of
flashing and ruffling wheatfields under dark olives that turned
silver when the wind touched their leaves, like a shoal of
minnows changing direction. Nothing on the roads but an
occasional lorry nigh unto death,[8] a mule team, a flock of sheep,
shorn like the hayfields, or a few moth-soft oxen. (This is the
moment when the flocks, like the police, change into their
summer drill . . .) I drifted through this consoling landscape in a
quiet, all-passion-spent mood, not an unhappy one; still heavy
with the happy mood of the day before and dinner and the
strange ecstatic drive. There was an occasional indestructible old
crone on the road picking herbs or gathering sticks and I gave
one of them and her faggots a lift, and thought, suppose she's one
of those old women in fairy-tales – she might grant me three
wishes! I've no idea what 2 and 3 would be. As to 1, propriety
halts my ballpoint.

What a surprise the villages and little towns are! After curves and
swellings and subsidences, and loops and parabolas, nothing but
angles! Plumblines, perpendiculars, juts, jags, battlements, towers and
crenellations, hard as iron though tamed to biscuit by the falling sun
and the shadows; troglodytic palazzi, small piazzas the size of postage
stamps. One above the other, up lanes that tilt into the sky like
springboards, so steeply that when one gets to the top, a chariot

ought to be waiting to whisk one, like Elijah,[9] up into the rainy clouds.

No more now, my darling angel Lyndall
except lots of love from
Paddy

P.S. If you possibly can, try and keep Wednesday night free. Castle business in the morning!

Love to Iris [Tree]. I'm *so pleased* about her car. xxx

[1] Civitavecchia, a sea port on the coastal road running north-west from Rome.
[2] An old city, a few miles inland from the coast, towering above a river valley.
[3] A small town, then consisting of little more than a few villas, on the Tuscan coast.
[4] A euphemism.
[5] Simultaneous rain and sunshine.
[6] In medieval times the Ghibellines and Guelphs were opposing factions in the city-states of central and northern Italy. Grosseto was a centre of Ghibelline support.
[7] *The Roots of Heaven*, for which PLF had written the screenplay.
[8] 'For indeed he was sick unto death.' Philippians 2: 27.
[9] Elijah was carried up to heaven in a chariot of fire: 2 Kings 2: 11.

To Lyndall Birch   'Da Ernesto'
27 July 1959   Ovindoli
                                         Abruzzi

Darling Lyndall,

Here's a thought: imagine that it came about that you, Henrico,[1] and I were having dinner together and that H. fell wildly in love with *me*. We could start a clockwise chase round the table . . . getting faster and faster, like those tigers on the last pages of *Little Black Sambo* that turned into a ring of vapour round the trunk of a palm tree till they melted to butter and were devoured in the shape of vast heaps of pancakes by the hero. Alas, I think my days of gents falling in love with me are over (or jolly nearly. I had some *very equivocal looks* in Athens last year from an elderly American . . . Non-swanks!)

It's lovely here. Cool, Alpine, innocent, [illegible] and un-Roman.
It's still spring, just about the phase Passerano was at two months ago:
fields of standing corn, guileless-looking peasants scything away, huge
mountains in the distance, and on the airy plateau all round, pretty
conical villages perched on tiered stripes of brown, green, orange and
amber meadows; spinneys of beech and hazel full of harebells &
Canterbury bells and wild strawberries, valleys full of slanting evening
shadows and a pure golden-grey light with just a touch of
melancholy till all becomes a jagged blue-grey silhouette and it's time
for another thumping meal. The cattle are a fine body of cows. They
assemble at immutable rendezvous when the Angelus tolls and set off
for Ovindoli a hundred strong with nary a neatherd [cowherd] and
trudge into the marketplace like a wild army of invaders. Here they
break up and fan off in twos and threes down a warren of lanes, a
gentle horn-tap, when a crone or a maiden emerges and lets them
into a comfortable cellar for the night. All smells of hay.

We push off from here to the castle on Friday, to Rome on
Saturday (where Godsend Adriana will have dragooned her plasterers
into putting things to rights) and off, swayed by Iris's rhetoric, to
Ischia on Monday. You'll probably be off bathing most of the
weekend; *if not*, leave a note on the island – dinner Sunday night? If
we find a haven in Ischia, bear it in mind for Ferragosto,[2] if all else
fails.

I hate to think of you in emptying Rome.

Heaps of love, darling Lyndall, from

Paddy

[1] The handsome painter Enrico d'Assia, son of Mafalda of Savoia, sister of the king
of Italy. PLF was mistaken in thinking that LB was in love with him.
[2] An Italian public holiday in mid-August.

*The post-war restrictions on the export of capital from the UK were a repeated
problem for Paddy, and he was always looking for ways to circumvent them.*

To Jock Murray   Presso Ristorante da Filipo
15 August 1959   Forio
                                                     Ischia
                                            Prov. di Napoli

Dear Jock,

Here are between 6 and 7,000 words of the beginning of Vol. II. At least, I think it's about that, reckoning a page of typescript to be about 390 words. They have taken *days* to transcribe from the jungle of the original MS with my snail-pace one-finger typing. But the MS is such an impenetrable thicket that it was impossible to ask anyone else to hack a way through it.

I feel it's a bit rash to send you this raw lump of prose. Please regard it as roughly shaped marble, to be finished, chiselled and polished when the whole book is completed. Better so than to hold up the progress of the book now. About double the typed part, as near as I can judge, has mounted up, and more every day. Well into Greek Thrace & Macedonia, and, I think, it's unusual, odd and exciting. The Monasteries of the air which will come close to the end (10,000 words?) you already have.

Midwinter is what I've got in mind as finishing time.[1] With luck it might be earlier, if it goes on as well as at present.

As you see, I've removed to Ischia. The castle became unbearably hot and rats, owls, ants and scorpions had resumed their interrupted reign. We escaped to the Abruzzo which was perfect, but could only have rooms available for a week; so came here, and discovered a cool flat on the edge of Forio with a wide balcony looking out over orange-groves and the sea where I sit (as now) and scribble away under a wickerwork awning, charging down into the sea every few pages. I plan to stay on here for a bit – possibly another month or two – then, after liquidating the castle (it's too sad in the evenings) either return to England or – perhaps – push on to Greece, where there are always havens (perhaps Hydra?), by car via Brindisi, Corfu & Yannina. Anyway, sufficient unto the day is my motto at the moment. Joan, alas, returns [to England] soon.

I wrote and asked my bank to try and get sanction from the

Treasury for the despatch of £200. I thought I wrote to you at the same time, but have a lurking fear that I forgot. The funds, I explained (using a formula that would be more *strictly applicable* to a later occasion . . .), were necessary for travel in those parts of Italy which were formerly Magna Graecia, for research into ancient Greek and Byzantine vestiges in Apulia, Lucania and Calabria, both architectural and linguistic, for a companion volume to *Mani*, which, with any luck would, like its predecessors, bring in dollars in due course. Do, please, back me up in this suppositious excursion into the future!

It only remains to renew the rhetoric of my last letter about a magnificent advance, one that will wreathe Mr Teasdale and me with restful smiles. There *are* ways of getting funds here by cloudier channels than the one depending on the Treasury's whim (where would I have been without them, indeed?) but the great thing is for the pennies to be *there*: safely in Pall Mall, I mean. Discretion halts my pen.

What news of America – or about the Violins?

No more for the present, except good tidings about the book. I hope and really do think that it will do us both credit. I foresee a smiling triumvirate.[2]

Much love from Joan, & all the best.

Yours ever

    Paddy

P.S. I enclose snaps of Passerano.

[1] *Roumeli,* the follow-up to *Mani,* was published in 1966.
[2] i.e. PLF, JM and the bank manager.

To Lyndall Birch   Presso da Filipo
25 October 1959   Forio

Darling Lyndall,

I *say*, what excitements! I long to hear about your trip to England, what happened, who you saw and so on, and the progress of Tom's

lightning courtship.[1] I *wonder* how that would be. He was
outstandingly nice, I thought, – but then, our approach can't be quite
the same, I do see . . . I'm very pleased that you are overcoming
your long phobia about England, not for any creditable patriotic
reasons, but because it's a pity to be cut off from all the pleasure,
stimulus, interest, friendship, fun, affection, oddity, unconventionality
and charm which seem to thrive there in a more abundant crop than
anywhere else I know, including Paris and Athens. (We won't
mention Rome and its delightful denizens.) Whatever happens, I
can't help feeling that your gauzy pinions are about to become
unstuck. I can watch all this now with an affectionate detachment
that will be much more use to all concerned than the obsessive and
gloomy commitment which has dogged my footsteps most of this
year. For, you will be relieved to hear, I appear to be out of the
wood which we both foundered in at different times. The trees got
imperceptibly scarcer, and here I am in the open. Hooray! (or
boo-hoo.) The whole cycle for both of us seems to have been
contained in the first year of the reign of John XXIII,[2] incubating
during the conclave and expiring with the anniversary of the last
fumata.[3] Tiaras and crossed keys have a new significance for me from
now, especially the latter: one should be labelled IN, the other OUT.
But I hasten to say, darling Lyndall, that in spite of this change or
transposition of feelings, *my bosom positively teems with fraternal fondness.*

Henry and Virginia[4] left a couple of days ago, to all our sadness.
He was magnificently in, and true to, form. One evening, dining at
Filipo's with Iris, Joan (she got back a week ago) and me, she and
Henry had a slight tiff. Henry flung his hands in the air and shouted
at the top of his voice 'Aha! No sex for *me* tonight, I can see *that!*'
He's a splendidly reckless conversationalist, stuffed to bursting-point
with what Castiglione in *Il Cortegiano* calls *sprezzatura*, the supreme
dialectic attribute of a man of distinction and dash.[5] Friedrich
[Ledebur] has been here several days, staying with Iris, towering over
everyone on the island like a half-ruined and ivy-mantled Danubian
castle, bat- and owl-haunted, the vaults rumbling every now and
then with pythian, pessimistic and almost inaudible pronouncements.
I've got a new pal here, a sixty-year-old, charming, sad, queer,

tremendously well-read old boy called Neil Little who lives in a
pretty house full of Greek and Latin literature, a great friend of
Norman Douglas's.[6] He has a passion for opera and Joan and I have
had two agreeable musical sessions there, the first listening to Callas
singing Bellini's *I Puritani*, the second listening to the same in *Lucia
di Lammermoor*. I'd never heard her before, and I must say, I was
bowled over. It's a kind of musical rape, leaving one's virginal
faculties in smithereens.

The weather gets more astonishing daily, bright, golden and
glittering, driving away all one's scirocco-borne debility. Half of this
headachy malaise, I've determined, comes from the wine, which is
so heavily doctored that pretty well an entire child's chemistry set
goes down with every gulp; which, with the south wind and the
volcanic fumes that steam up through every cranny in the rocks, is
a regimen designed to lame the sturdiest. But all that is over (back
to Chianti!), one is surrounded by a russet and golden Virgilian
vintage world, ringing blue skies and pure brilliant seas with the
ghost of Ponza[7] hovering on the horizon. (The inhabitants claim it
is the birthplace of Pontius Pilate; an odd boast, like a Cornishman
from Liskeard bragging of Judas Iscariot as a fellow villager).
Yesterday Friedrich, Iris, Joan and I went to the top of Mt Epomeo,
and after stocking up on wine and salami at a hermitage-turned-
bistro there, Friedrich and I came down the steep side to Forio
through wonderful auburn beechwoods and clumps of Spanish
chestnuts, leaping from rock to rock like ibexes – you would have
done your glorious [illegible] horse gallop – then down a tortuous
maze of lanes through layer on layer on layer of vineyard, all ablaze
with autumn colours, till we were in a village full of women with
baskets of grapes on their heads, vast waggon-loads of them, and
that lovely heady reek of must and fermentation from many a
wine-press.

No more now. Write and tell me all your adventures. Come here
whenever you want, (if you can) and lots of fond love, darling
Lyndall from
        Paddy

P.S. Larry Durrell is staying in my room in London at the moment. I've just finished your *Balthazar*,[8] and find it astonishing.

P.P.S. Iris, Friedrich, J. & I are off to Capri for two nights. Whoopee!

[1] LB was being pursued by Thomas Egerton (1918–98), racehorse breeder, a friend of Princess Margaret.

[2] John XXIII was elected Pope on 28 October 1958.

[3] The puff of smoke from the chimney of the Sistine Chapel that indicates the end of a round of voting during the conclave to elect a new Pope. Black smoke indicates an inconclusive vote; white smoke, successful.

[4] Henry Frederick Thynne (1905–92), 6th Marquess of Bath, and his second wife, Virginia (1917–2003). His first wife Daphne had married Xan Fielding in 1953.

[5] *Il Cortegiano* (*The Book of the Courtier*) was written by Baldassare Castiglione over the course of many years, beginning in 1508, and published in 1528 in Venice just before his death. It addresses the constitution of a perfect courtier, and in its last instalment, a perfect lady. *Sprezzatura* ('nonchalance', 'careful negligence', or 'effortless and ease') is described as one of the most important, if not the most important, attributes of the courtier.

[6] George Norman Douglas (1868–1952), novelist and travel writer, lived on Capri from 1946 until his death.

[7] The largest of the Italian Pontine Islands archipelago, about thirty miles west of Ischia.

[8] Lawrence Durrell's novel *Balthazar* (1958), the second novel in his *Alexandria Quartet*. LB had lent PLF her copy.

Lawrence Durrell loved Ischia and had spent some time there in 1950.

To Lawrence Durrell   Presso 'da Filipo'
28 October 1959   Forio
                                                    d'Ischia
                                              Prov. di Napoli.

Larry, παιδάκι μου [dear boy],

What a shame, our not overlapping in London! I do hope you wrote something in the *Justine* series[1] when you were staying in Chester Row. It's very exciting that they may make a film of it – mind you get a tidy sum out of 20th Century Fox if they do, as they are as rich as Croesus. Ivan Moffat, whom they will use for the script writing (*why not you?*) if the option is taken up, is in a trance about it; quite rightly. I wish you had contrived to meet. He's an old pal of ours and brilliant on the job. When he left here, I gave him a few Cairo addresses: Georges Henein, Magdi Wahba, Samira W., Marie Rìaz etc. Samira was the only one he saw. I expect she talked about Addison's essays or the poems of Christina Rossetti.

We've just been on a pilgrimage to Punta del Imperatore.[2] It was a grey autumn afternoon looking like a faded watercolour or a mezzotint, the leaves of the stripped vines all golden and infirm on their stalks, a shy wet wind blowing and huge Tennysonian waves[3] breaking in fans of spray on the rocks of Citara.[4] A long sooty loop of migrating birds was flickering southward about a mile out, geese I expect. We found your house at last – Don Vito was down in Forio – and it looked wonderfully Grimm-like among its tiers of dead vines, with that flying buttress of a staircase at the end of the yard, the very place, indeed, for a Stendhal–Lamartine encounter[5] over a cauldron of simmering broth. We trod reverently round the precincts, pondering where they will put the plaque in the fullness of time, then back through the dark, meeting nothing but a crone or two carrying sticks, and a rather good looking vineyard idiot hopping down the steps astride a very elaborate brushwood hobby horse he must have just made . . .

Where will you be later on?

Best love from

    Paddy (also Joan)

---

[1] *Justine* (1957) was the first novel in Durrell's *Alexandria Quartet*.
[2] A bay in Ischia, not far from the Bay of San Montano.
[3] PLF is referring to Tennyson's poem 'Break, break, break', written in 1835.
[4] A beach near Forio.
[5] Both Stendhal and Lamartine visited Ischia several times in the first quarter of the nineteenth century.

After her mother died on Christmas Day 1959, Joan was in a position to give Paddy a large cheque, which he gratefully acknowledged.

To Joan Rayner
undated [February 1960]   Chagford

Darling,

I've been thinking so much about that tremendous sum of
money. It really was an act of superhuman kindness and generosity
and anything I could say about the extent of gratitude would be
putting it mildly, especially now I know all the implications. I can't
tell you what a difference it makes, and will make, blowing away
dozens and dozens of guilty, nagging and haunting worries, all
utterly my fault through neglect, postponement, idleness and
oblomóvshchina[1] (That's the word. I asked Isaiah Berlin). It has
coincided wonderfully with getting this well-omened sitting room
back and to myself to make all seem hopeful, possible & promising;
and, with luck and hard work – which I long for, now that the
Greek incubus has been exorcised – I hope that I'll be able to be
someone. At least, I'll know how not to be such a perfect fool as
that time, over the 'Roots of Heaven'. Anyway, thank you many,
many times, my darling. I won't go on for fear of embarrassing.

It's a day of brilliant, cold, blue sunshine today. I'm hunting on
Saturday on a lovely horse, and I do hope it holds on. I've decided
to chuck hunting on 'in-country' days, only the Moor. Those awful
waits in fields and lanes not only bore one but fill one with guilt:
why am I not at my desk, I keep thinking, instead of hanging about
here? Also, I keep thinking of marvellous ideas & sentences, all of
which evaporate by the time one gets home.

I forgot to tell you on the telephone a snatch of Henry Bath's
conversation on Saturday. (Don't tell it to Janetta [Woolley], as I've
just told her after giving her Iris's address in Spain.) H. was talking
about a conversation he'd had with his butler Donald, after reading
about some awful crime in the papers, urging him to be sure to lock
up all the doors tight at night.

"'It's not because of the *burglars*,' I told him, "because there's *bugger
all* in the house to pinch. *Unfortunately!* It's just that I don't want
any of those blinking *sex-maniacs* to get in." And do you know,

the blighter looked me straight in the eye, in the most *meaning way*, and said, "I shouldn't worry, my Lord. We've got one of those in the house already." *Well* I mean to *say* . . . '

No more now, except lots & lots of love from P

P.S. I did my S.T. [*Sunday Times*] review in a flash the first day I was here, and telephoned it through (reversed charges).

---

¹ Slothfulness, a term derived from Goncharov's novel *Oblomov* (1859).

Paddy had spent Christmas with the Devonshires at Chatsworth, beginning a habit that would last decades. Joan, who had less need of company, preferred to spend Christmas at Dumbleton with her beloved brother, Graham.

To Ann Fleming
1 February 1960   Chagford

Darling Annie,
     You're well out of this sodden kingdom today, it's coming down in buckets. *Here's a riddle*: Why is English country life in Britain as bad indoors as outdoors? [Answer written on inside of envelope.¹ You're done for if you've thrown it into the fire; but of course, lucky you, you can't have.²] I long to see this printed on the back of a matchbox, anonymously.
     You are sadly missed, so don't stay away too long. The capital seems oddly filleted when Victoria Square is empty.
     Christmas was glorious, and went on for ages, consisting of Andrew, Debo and children, Andrew's mother, Nancy, and Mrs Hammersley,³ for whom I developed a reciprocated passion. She strikes a wonderful note of bilious gloom about anything. The sight of Sophia's new rocking horse made her positively cavernous: 'It's one of those new plastic ones – not like the old wooden dappled kind we used to have. If you notice, it's made in two *halves* and stuck together length-ways; and *not* very *securely*, I suspect. It fills me with a sense of impending

disaster . . .' As a matter of fact, it *was* rather a forbidding thing, pinkish, with false eyelashes and tempestuous mane and tail of moulded, hollow rubber, which gives under one's hand like a motor horn; bearing the same sort of relationship to a real horse as Lady Lewisham[4] does to an ordinary human being. The house [Chatsworth] looked lovely, I thought, with steep bare woods outside and rainy mermen, a golden blaze indoors and the feeling that there had been no break in habitation. It's wonderful what forgotten knitting and a couple of seed catalogues will do for a bust of Diocletian. After this, a quietly tight New Year at Bruern[5] (I think Michael's in love with me); then down here to my old literary break-down-haunt, and to work ever since. Thank heavens, all goes well.

Joan's mother died over Christmas, alas, which meant endless gloomy tasks for her and Graham at Dumbleton.[6] They were oddly shattered, mostly I think, through feelings of filial duties left undone in the past; completely baselessly. If you didn't see, do write two lines to Joan, as I overheard a conversation between them saying they wished they had always written to people in the past in like circumstances, because − against all their principles − it gives tremendous pleasure.

I adore this place, and write every waking second, alone nearly all the time, except a couple of visits by Joan, once with Janetta, who has buzzed off to Spain. My resurrected passion for hunting − if one can dignify these shaggy, almost prehistoric helter-skelters over Dartmoor by the name − has revived again, starting with the Master, Chas Hooley, a tremendous shit with carrot-coloured hair and sidewhiskers and a cast of countenance so vulpine that his winters are one long act of fratricide, down to the terrier man, an ex-burglar who has actually done time in Dartmoor, and feels quite queer when the gaunt shape of the jail heaves through the mist. Quite a pretty thin field on weekdays, if it's raining. A fortnight ago I was the only grown-up male follower − not even 'Bunny' Spiller, of Spiller's Dog-Biscuits, was there, and he seldom fails. The country is so moss-covered and primordial − either [illegible] with deep ravines, bracken and boulders and fast brooks foaming with Guinness (five million Guinnesses are enjoyed daily: five million and three, if you include Maureen, Aileen and Oonagh[7]), or a rolling wilderness of moor beset with bogs and tors and druidical stones. We might almost be out after dinosaurs. Last Saturday we met at a minute village called Spreyton. While they were drawing the first cover, I sneaked off 200 yards to have a look at a lovely late Plantagenet church. Maddeningly, I was followed by the entire field (you know what sheep people are) – about forty for once – who looked duped and angry when I dismounted and slunk through the lych-gate. But I'm glad I did, because there was a beautiful Perpendicular painted rood-screen inside and in the church-yard the grave of – guess who? 'T. Cobley, gent of this parish, o.b. 1792'![8] The actual one; Widecombe-in-the-Moor is only 15 miles away, well within grey-mare-range. Bill Brewer's resting place is the next on my list.

I ended the day lost in mist, rain, rocks and swamp in the middle of the moor, miles from anywhere, and dusk falling, joining forces after a bit with another drenched, elderly, chubby and equally lost horseman. He was an odd-looking kind, with a round face as scarlet as his coat, heavy horn-rimmed spectacles and unruly corkscrews of silver hair sticking out under his hat, a sort of Lord Scamperdale.[9] As we hobnobbed towards Postbridge through the downpour, he reminisced happily about Embassy life in St Petersburg, Constantinople, the Atlas Mountains and the absurd prices that Fabergé cigarette cases fetch nowadays. At a dolmen where our two paths forked in opposite directions, we said goodnight with gravely doffed headgear, and the mist and the dusk swallowed us up. I learnt afterwards that he was Harold's elder brother,[10] who lives over towards Tiverton. An odd encounter.

Do send your news. I do envy you. Give my love to Ian and lots of love to you from
    Paddy

1 'Outdoors it rains cats and dogs while indoors dogs and cats reign.'
2 Presumably because there was no need for fires at Goldeneye.
3 The Duke and Duchess of Devonshire; the Dowager Duchess; the Duchess's sister, Nancy Mitford; and Violet Mary Hammersley (née Williams-Freeman), known as 'Mrs Ham', then eighty-three years old.
4 Raine, Lady Lewisham (b. 1929), née McCorquodale, daughter of the novelist Barbara

Cartland. She later divorced her husband and married the 8th Earl Spencer, thus becoming stepmother to Diana, Princess of Wales.

5 Bruern Abbey, the Oxfordshire house of the Hon. Michael Astor, fourth son of Waldorf Astor, 2nd Viscount Astor, and formerly a Conservative MP.

6 Dumbleton Hall, Worcestershire. The house was sold to the Post Office as a convalescent home for sick employees, and Joan's brother Graham moved to a smaller house on the estate.

7 The three vivacious daughters of the brewing heir Ernest Guinness, all 'Bright Young Things' in the inter-war years.

8 As in the song 'Widecombe Fair', in which each verse ends in the refrain,

> 'With Bill Brewer, Jan Stewer, Peter Gurney,
> Peter Davy, Dan'l Whiddon, Harry Hawke,
> Old Uncle Tom Cobley and all,
> Old Uncle Tom Cobley and all.'

With only a little encouragement, PLF would sing this in Italian.

9 Master of 'The Flat Hat Hunt', in R. S. Surtees's *Mr Sponge's Sporting Tour* (1853).

10 Frederick Archibald Nicolson (1883–1952), 2nd Baron Carnock, eldest brother to Harold Nicolson.

Pamela Wyndham, later Pamela Egremont, was another of PLF's long-standing female friends. He wrote the following letter of thanks after staying with her and her husband at Petworth House in West Sussex. He was writing from Lismore Castle, where he and Joan were once again guests of the Duke and Duchess of Devonshire.

To Pamela Wyndham
20 May 1960

Lismore Castle
County Waterford
Eire

Darling Pamela,

What hell it was getting back to London. 'Leave me among the stags and the bluebells' was my inward cry, and jealous meditations about the Bakhtiari.[1] I *did* love it, and many, many thanks for letting me come and wallow in the wonder of it all.

It was a grey and gloomy day in London when we set off yesterday but turned into midsummer halfway across the Irish channel, and, when we landed, all was ablaze. I'm scribbling away in a tower with lots of treetops under the window, and under them, the Blackwater, with occasional salmon glittering as they go about their morning business. Debo is running across a lawn in another direction, followed by a rogue's gallery of ill-matched dogs, all barking fit to bust; Joan roams under some flowery trees beyond, redundantly poring over *Greek Self Taught*: and, every hour or so, a donkey cart clip-clops sleepily over the bridge. All is so soft and relaxing that, if we go on this way, we'll all seize up in a green trance.

A thousand thanks again, dear Pamela, to you and John,[2] and much love from

Paddy

[1] A tribe in south-west Iran, which perfoms an immense annual migration. PW had been on it.

[2] Pamela's husband, John Edward Reginald Wyndham (1920–72), long-serving Private Secretary to Harold Macmillan.

Soon after his affair with Lyndall Birch petered out, Paddy became involved with Enrica 'Ricki' Huston, the fourth and much younger wife of the film director John Huston. The couple lived at St Clerans, an eighteenth-century mansion in the west of Ireland. Their marriage was troubled, not least because Huston was so often absent from home making movies.

To Ricki Huston
undated but postmarked 20 July 1960   13 Chester Row, SW1

Darling Ricki,

1. Don't be surprised if my writing, which is normally elegant but illegible, is now beset by a Neanderthal uncouthness. Tooling across Oxfordshire two days ago in Andrew Devonshire's enormous motor car (a sharp lesson not to motor above one's station) I got my right index finger stuck between the automatically rising upside down guillotine of a window-pane and the frame work, and it is now nail-less and mangled and cobbled with many a

stitch and scabbarded in plaster of Paris, and penmanship has
become as exacting and fatiguing as tossing the caber must be. It
is almost like incising one's thoughts on marble or granite with
a chisel.

The Tourist Hotel in Thasos sent me a copy of the letter they
sent you. Is that any good? Would you like me to do anything
about the smaller hotel at Arkouda, the sparkling beach at the
other side of the island?

2. Was it you who sent me that wonderful gramophone of imaginary
conversations?[1] Boss & typist, Dylan Thomas, etc.? It's amazing,
one of the most exciting and strange things I've ever heard,
certainly the only true dialogue reproduced. I've played it thirty
times or more with ever growing wonder. If it was you, and I feel
sure it is, 100,000 thanks.

I *did* enjoy your brief sojourn in London and felt downcast and
deprived when I had to leave the metropolis. You seemed marvellous
to me, blindingly beautiful and funny and adorned with every
possible grace, charm intelligence and fun, and I do wish you lived
in London, instead of lurking in those western mists like Deirdre of
the Sorrows.[2] I do hope we meet soon.

I'm planning my great Germano-Austro-Jugoslav pilgrimage to
Greece, and leave about the 4th of August. I got a card from
Magouche[3] today, setting off with her nymphet brood on mules
across the wilds of Arcadia on a rash *hijra* [journey] which I managed
to talk her into. Perhaps we'll all meet in Hydra at the end of next
month, or the beginning of the one after.

Anyway, bless you dearest Ricki, and fond love
    from Paddy

[1] Rayner Heppenstall's *Imaginary Conversations: Eight Radio Scripts* (1948).
[2] In J. M. Synge's play *Deirdre of the Sorrows*, first performed at the Abbey Theatre in
1910, Deirdre lives happily on a remote island.
[3] Agnes Phillips, widow of the Armenian-American artist, Arshile Gorky, who bestowed
on her the name 'Mougouch', an Armenian term of endearment. (She was known
variously as 'Magouche' or 'Magoosh'.) At the time of this letter she was the girlfriend
of Michael Astor, having separated from her second husband.

To Joan Rayner
13 January 1961   Athens

My darling Joan,

Now comes a sad tale, but one which could have been far worse.
Last week I set off to Delphi on Saturday, taking Coote[1] (Mark
[Ogilvie-Grant] couldn't come), and settled into the little rooms
next to the Kastalia. We had a very lively and funny evening in
Amphissa and wandered about the rainy ruins all next morning.
Then, in the afternoon I drove Coote into Arachova to catch a bus
for Athens, and returned to Delphi in the rain. About a mile outside
the village, when I was approaching a curve, a white car with two
women in it suddenly shot round the corner right over on my,
right, side of the road. I braked and turned as close in towards the
right edge of the road as I could, the other car streaking towards
its proper side of the road. I just missed it but skidded into the
ditch at the roadside, banging hard against the rock face, damaging
the right front of the car badly, and the windscreen breaking in
a shower of crystals, also a hard bang on the right shoulder, but
nothing serious or bust. The other car stopped. The two women
got out and looked at my damage, then I pointed to the tell-tale
evidence, very politely (all this in French, which they spoke well.
They were Greek) of the tracks on the wet road, showing clearly
our relative positions, and a very wary look came into their eyes.
At that moment a charabanc pulled up and everyone got out to see
if they could help. In the chat and movement of all this, the two
women sneaked back to their car and drove away, with no exchange
of numbers, names, insurance companies or anything. One of the
charabanc people spotted them just as they were haring round
the next bend, let out a shout and, fortunately, took their number.
Everyone was outraged, and stopped the next car, two minutes later,
coming from the Arachova direction, telling the driver to dash into
Delphi and report the number to the police. The driver, a very nice
man, said he would, and all the more willingly as the two women
had barred his way by driving on the wrong side, and nearly sent
him into the rocks like me. The Delphi police turned up five

minutes later, after having telephoned to Delphi and Levadia, to stop
the other car. The police, and everyone else, were 100% on my side,
and the very nice young police chief vowed he'd summons them for
dangerous driving and for making off without the usual exchanges
of details. Lots of names were taken – the charabanc people, all
crowding in with their telephone numbers, and the driver of the
second car. Then we hauled the poor Sunbeam out of its rocky
ditch, hammering the crumpled wing out to free the front right
wheel, and I drove it sadly and slowly into Delphi. Fortunately the
steering and the engine were untouched, but the buckled mudguard
and door and the broken windscreen made it a heart-breaking sight.
Next morning we learnt that the other car had been stopped by
the police in Levadia, and the women held till 10.30, and all details
taken. She is a Mrs Despoina Anagnostou, a bacteriologist in Athens,
who had been week-ending at the Tourist hotel . . . I decided that
it would be best to put the whole car on a lorry and take it back
to Athens like that, rather than drive with a broken windscreen, and,
perhaps, something wrong with the engine that would be increased
by driving; so went miserably back to Athens that afternoon with
the car roped and tarpaulined at the back, delivering it at the BP
Garage to have it examined and the damage assessed. I had also
rung Coote, and got her to put it into Tony Massourides's[2] hands.
He has contacted her insurance company; also, very politely, Mrs A.
Apparently, it would have been much better if I had banged into
the other car (which, of course, has not got a scratch) instead of
avoiding it, and mashing up yours . . . The summonses have gone
out, and Tony hopes that this will eventuate in the thing being
settled out of court, when she sees the way things shape. The great
things on my side are (1) her furtive disappearance and (2) her near
collision immediately afterwards. The BP Garage say they can have
the car as good as new within twenty days. There is nothing organic
damaged, and it's all coachwork. Fortunately the Athens agency has
got some Sunbeam windscreens. BP assess the coachwork repairs at
the appalling sum of 15,000. Tony, when he heard this, was appalled,
and has found a coachwork genius who fixed his car up last year
after an awful crash so that it looks now, as I have seen, straight out

of the factory, and he is undertaking it for 8,000, and is already at
work on it. He is, Tony assures me, absolutely sound and a brilliant
technician . . .

I want to spare you a maudlin wallow in all the distress, shame
and misery I felt and feel that this should have happened when your
lovely car was in my hands. I am sorrier than I can possibly express.
I know I'm in no position, as a rule, to cast stones about driving; but
I have been tremendously careful of the car and the other one was
irretrievably in the wrong. I was well on my side of the road and
driving at an extremely reasonable speed, because of the rain and the
road – there's not much temptation, anyway, to hug the appalling
precipice on the wrong side of that particular one! . . . The case,
when it comes up, will be in Amphissa. The fact that one of the
Delphi gendarmes is Geo. Hrissakis, in whose parents' house at
Kastamonitza, the whole party hid for a week on the way to
capturing Gen. Kreipe, has done no harm.

No more for the moment, darling. I do hope the car will be
glittering and perfect by the time you return. Again, I'm dreadfully
sorry about this calamity, and could tear my hair out in handfuls!

Lots and lots of love from
your very woebegone
    Paddy

[1] Lady Dorothy Lygon, otherwise known as 'Coote'.
[2] PLF's Greek lawyer.

To Ricki Huston   12 Kallirhoë Street[1]
18 January 1961   Makriyannis
                                                Athens

Darling Ricki,

It's too unfair, it looks as if someone has put an evil spell on our
correspondence, because your lovely letter got idiotically sent on to
Nauplia *the very day I left it*, and has reached me *only today*. Can you
beat it for callousness and idiocy on the part of the hotel people

there? What makes it doubly vexing is that I have been wandering about Greece alone by car, on solitary and slightly desolate pilgrimages to places I am writing about, and you would have been the perfect companion & company and cheer and fresh-eyed commentator and fellow guzzler and swigger in dozens of remote and smoky taverns. Can you *think* of greater fun? I feel so maddened with retrospective frustration and disappointment that I would like to blow off steam in some rash and violent act – but how, when, and on whom? It really is too sad. Now, alas, alas, conditions are far less ideal. (1) I've got to remain static somewhere and write like a fiend for all waking hours out of the twenty-four; (2) Joan returning here from England within the next fortnight, possibly a bit less, which is no hindrance to anything, as I'm sure you'd like her and she you, but it makes things a bit more unwieldy for plans, movements, decisions; and (3) the car's out of action for three weeks. (4) All this would interfere with my monopolising you, which I would rather (indeed, v. much) like to have done. I hasten to say, dear Ricki, that if you *did* come out here, I'd do everything I could to help and make it a happy time, and modify plans to do so as much as I could, and I'm sure you would love it (I certainly would); it's only that the circumstances are so much less perfect than they would have been if I'd got your letter in the normal time. Could you dash here for a bit the moment you get this? Otherwise, alas, the ideal would be to postpone it for a month or so. Do write back at once about all this, and, if you can manage any bold and precipitable action, wire.

How sad the first part of your Paris letter was. I'm so sorry about LOVE (your caps) going wrong. I do hope it's gone right since, or some other anodyne has turned up. I wish it were a more reliable apparatus, it's like some ill-starred bit of machinery always breaking down, and one doesn't know what plumber, mechanic, joiner or electrician to summon. Have you read Stendhal on the theme, the crystallisation process as he calls it,[2] and the Spaniard, Thingummy y Gasset?[3] You probably have, but if not, they're well worth tackling. I had a lot of trouble from the same source in Rome last year, a lunatic tangle, and I'm still pulling out thorns.

I do envy you seeing Ivan and the evening at Rosy's Red Banjo.

Iris too? Do give me more news. I wish he'd come to Europe more. Janetta came out here in December and she and Joan and I went on slow and glorious travels in the Peloponnese, and when Joan, miserably, had to return to England, we were about to depart to Delphi and Olympia on a lovely platonic ramble, when a telegraph boy rolled up on a bike just as the car was switched on, announcing Ralph Partridge's death (Frances P. is her greatest friend, as was Ralph), so we had to head for Athens airport instead of Mount Parnassus. It doesn't seem a very lucky winter for me. Yes, I do wish she and Ivan could somehow cleave, as I dearly love them both, and can't help feeling they would both be wasted on any alternative choices.

As I write, it's suddenly begun to snow, eddying down in great gusts of wind. The high mountains have been covered with it for some time. I do hope it stays. I've only seen the Acropolis once under snow, and it was amazing, and as unnatural somehow as a sandstorm in Lapland. Did you know that reindeer graze off moss all the year round, in the arctic tundras? I thought, once, that their antlers were also covered with moss, like those of other deer at certain times: it always looks like it in photographs. But I'm told it's not so; only that they will fidget so when being snapped . . . When Diana came through Athens before we got there last summer, she somehow managed to break in, and deposit on the mantelpiece, as a house-warming present, two stuffed hoopoes with pearl necklaces round their necks and a huge dove-grey and snow-white seagull, a glorious bird. The trouble is, the smoke from the fire has covered the poor bird with soot and now it's not fit to be seen, a very dirty gull indeed. How should I clean it, I wonder? A lot of my seaside childhood was spent sponging oil off the wings of protesting guillemots gummed up by passing steamers; but this isn't quite the same.

So write or wire at once, darling Ricki, depending on whether it's in a month or so, or immediate action. Of course, in spite of all my seeming discouragements, I secretly hope it's the latter. But if it is, let it be today!

fond love

from

Paddy

If you do manage to come, I won't alas, be able to put you up here because of the smallth[4] – Joan and I are continually troubling over each other with objurgations – but I would get a terribly nice room with a terrace for you in the little hotel where Janetta stayed, only about eight minutes' walk away.

[1] Joan had bought this small house in Athens with her inheritance.

[2] Stendhal's *On Love* (1822) describes or compares the 'birth of love', in which the love object is 'crystallised' in the mind, as being a process similar or analogous to a trip to Rome.

[3] José Ortega y Gasset, *On Love: Aspects of a Single Theme* (1957).

[4] The Athens house was tiny, barely more than two rooms.

To Ricki Huston   The Mill House[1]
undated but postmarked 28 May 1961   Dumbleton
                                                   Evesham

My darling Ricki,

I peered through the window of that aeroplane to see if I could spot a red and black blazer anywhere, but nothing but alien tweed was to be seen; then sleep felled me like a lurking malefactor with a mallet. I opened a bleary eye at London airport, closed it again in the bus, opened it once more as the taxi drew up in Chester Row, closed it again for a couple of hours behind drawn curtains in my bedroom, thinking of the curtained alcove across St George's Channel cooling down now, with both its denizens fled; buoyed contentedly into semi-oblivion with remembering all that had been done, and by happy thoughts of all that remained still to be done. There is a sort of duality about these *post-facto* reflections; one re-lives the encounters half as protagonist, half from the ringside, going over knockouts and fouls and scissor strokes and blows below the belt, and yearns for a return match, to be over the ropes again in a jungle of straight lefts, upper cuts, right hooks and clinches that there's no umpire to break up . . . strange contests in which, when all's over, each acts as the other's second, mopping each other's wounds and exchanging glasses of water, smoothing out battered and slithery

limbs, now sleeping intertwining as gently as nurses, heartbeats and
eyelids sinking in a twin cataleptic-trance until a faraway gong-note
sets them sleepily turning and feinting once more and fumbling for
an opening . . . Enough of this pugilistic rot for the moment. Except
that such, gentle reader, were the Dublin-sick thoughts that hovered
round my couch till it was time to dress & pick up Debo and Anne
Tree[2] and head for D. Jackson's[3] banquet at the Ritz. I was between
Magouche (I said I'd seen you at St C.'s [St Clerans] with a stern
friendliness that quelled all eye-rolling) and Lettice Ashley-Cooper,[4]
who gassed away all through dinner about Nigeria, from which she
had just returned. I was bored by the entire meal and listened with
languid fork and day-dreamed − as who will not? − of a different
kind of supper . . .

I went for a long walk in the woods this afternoon on the edge
of the Cotswolds with cloud shadows moving across the Vale of
Evesham below, dotted with tall and pinnacled Plantagenet belfries,
one of them the scene of a bell-ringing marathon, to judge by the
permutations of chimes that followed each other across the fields
non-stop. The woods are rather sinister, choked with brambles,
bugloss, willow-herb and ragged robin. At the bottom of a rather
gloomy dell I came across a young fox with one pad caught in a
trap. I tried to let it out but it snapped and glared so that in the end
I caught and pulled it by the brush with one hand and opened the
trap with the other. Free at last, it paused for a moment and fixed
me with a glance of implacable hatred and limped off, wisely
enough, into a clump of foxgloves . . . If it had been a lion, far from
saving my life years later in the Colosseum, it would have swallowed
me on the spot.[5]

Now, Ricki darling, my plans are these: back to London on
Monday, staying there till Friday night, when I go alone to Michael
Astor's for the weekend (% Hon. M. Astor, Bruern Priory, Churchill,
Oxon. tel: Shipton-under-Wychwood 327). These details are in case
you come to this island. If you did, I was wondering whether I might
suggest to Michael your making a dash there too. If there's any hope,
do wire me % Travellers Club (Whitehall 8688), and I'll see if I can
wangle it. It's a lovely HQ, and he's an old friend and a discreet one.

No more now, my dearest darling Ricki, except 1,000 hugs & love from

Paddy

xxxx

Write at once!

Lots more to talk about . . .

---

[1] After Dumbleton Hall had been sold, Joan shared The Mill House at Dumbleton with her brother Graham; she became its sole owner after his death in 1993.

[2] The Duchess's sister-in-law, Lady Anne Evelyn Beatrice Tree (1927–2010), later a prison reformer.

[3] Professor Derek Ainslie Jackson (1906–82), nuclear physicist and a jockey who rode in the Grand National three times. Among his six wives were Pamela Mitford, Janetta Woolley and Barbara Skelton. He left Janetta for her half-sister, Angela Culme-Seymour.

[4] Lady Lettice Mildred Mary Ashley-Cooper (1911–90), daughter of the 9th Earl of Shaftesbury.

[5] PLF refers to the story of Androcles and the Lion.

To Ricki Huston   Chatsworth
17 June 1961   Bakewell
                                                   Derbyshire

Ricki darling,

Here's the first letter with my lovely grey stolen pen.

This *is* an extraordinary place. I've settled to write in a huge room magnified and reflected into infinity by vast acreages of looking glass. Every now and then I get up and stroll round the room for an Aubusson-muffled furlong or two. Nobody ever seems to come here but me; nevertheless, two giant amphorae, big enough to hide an Arabian thief apiece, are stuffed with freak white roses.[1] A Rembrandt, 3 Titians, 5 Tintorettos, 2 Canalettos, 4 Holbeins, a Ruysdael, a Poussin and a Claude are doing their best for me, glad of the company, I like to feel. A Bronzino peers down, frowning slightly, scenting rivalry; no Mars and Venus, thank God, to reproach me with a mis-spent morning: '*Why aren't you up and doing?*' A twin cherub-borne clock tinkles the wasted quarters away, with nary a

helmet to try on or a breastplate to crawl through, poor little
buggers, *tampocos* both. Sealed away and muted by a series of closed
double doors, I can just hear Joan Drogheda² tinkling away at some
cheerful barcarolle. Outside, a circular lake is followed by an oblong
one about half a mile long, with plenty of jovial fish-tailed stone
horses living it up in the middle of the first one, and burly Tritons
blowing fountains out of their conches. In the middle of the
second an immense plume of water soars high above the
surrounding treetops, placed there in the nick of time, several dukes
ago, for Tsar Alexander II's visit.³ The others here, bar hosts, Joan
and self, are Garrett & Joan Drogheda, Maurice Bowra, Annie
Fleming & Ian (recovering from a stroke, poor chap, and rather
un-James Bond-ish at the moment), and Ronnie & Marietta Tree.⁴
I sat next to Marietta last night, and we hobnobbed matily about
John, among other themes, and I made her laugh with a spirited
imitation of the death of the croc,⁵ which was adroitly capped by
several others from her.

*LAP DISSOLVE to Cliff Cottage, Fforest Farm, Dynas, Newport,
Pembrokeshire, Wales. June 22nd.*
This letter got unaccountably held up by all sorts of things and,
on returning to London two days before yesterday and setting off
on the next for here, your lovely letter from the Coopers arrived,
or rather, was waiting. How I wish I'd finished this one, and got it
off days ago! I'm sorry. It's ghastly to have been off the air all
these days; but everything seems to have conspired to intervene,
mostly changes of plan and rapid movement. What happened was
this: wracked with guilt about how little work I'd been doing, I
managed to borrow Barbara Warner's cottage here for two or three
weeks, and set off with Joan (in a two-car convoy as she will be
going and coming) pausing for a meal with Philip Toynbee near
Gloucester, then on into the wild heart of Wales, to this odd little
cottage on the edge of a cliff overlooking a deep coombe full of
gulls and guillemots and puffins, and, they say, though I have not
seen any so far, seals. The place hadn't been lived in for a year and
smelt like a deed-box as we stole in at dead of night and cows

mooed dejectedly all round among the thistles, with gulls Ibsening[6]
about in the dark overhead. Rather forbidding at first. Everything
seems better now. We have to feign wedlock here, on Barbara's
request, for the benefit of the puritan Welsh, and of B's old daily
woman. A bit of [a] bore. But how nice they seem, the Welsh I
mean; I'm fascinated by their Eurasian accent in English, and wish
I knew some of their language, which they all talk among
themselves here.

I do hope this reaches you, Ricki darling, before your wicked
assignment in London . . . This seems such miles from anywhere.
The only thing is, this village is only four miles from Fishguard, the
sea route to Ireland, and presumably there are airports (Fishguard
to swim, boids got to fly);[7] and, this cottage, an ideal habitat, is
impracticable as an H.Q. The rest of the Welsh coast isn't. It would
be glorious if we could contrive a secret summit conference
somewhere in this Welsh void, should the omens on both sides prove
propitious. There *is* a telephone here, Dinas Cross 244, nr/ Newport,
Pembroke, but best only used at the right moments. The thing is, to
keep in close touch about movements. I think I'll be alone here
quite a lot, salving my literary conscience.

How odd about Magouche and Bruern! I wonder how that leak
occurred. I sat up later after dinner with her last week and, on
purpose, only mentioned you in the vaguest, if very affectionate,
terms. Perhaps that's pretty fishy in itself. Anyway, to hell with it. I
think she was pining to ask questions, and felt rather frustrated by
my studied vagueness . . .

This is a rotten, disjointed letter. Please don't follow my bad
example, but write at once. I think back constantly on all the aspects
of recent encounters and long to be planning future fixtures; and
send heaps of love and hugs, my dearest darling beautiful one. The
Irish steamer from Fishguard is heading for the Irish horizon at this
very moment.

> Frisch weht der Wind der Heimat Zu
> Mein Irisch Kind, wo weilest Du?[8]

as Tristan said, and T. S. Eliot in 'The Waste Land' after him.

All love

   Paddy

   xxxx

1 PLF alludes to the folk-tale 'Ali Baba and the Forty Thieves'.

2 Joan Drogheda (1903–89), a concert pianist, married to Charles Garrett Ponsonby Moore, 11th Earl of Drogheda (1910–89).

3 PLF is mistaken. It is true that the fountain was installed in anticipation of a visit by Tsar Nicholas I (not Alexander) in 1844, but as it turned out he never came to Chatsworth.

4 Arthur Ronald Lambert Field Tree (1897–76), a Conservative MP from 1933 to 1945. He met his second wife, American co-worker Marietta Peabody Fitzgerald, while both were working at the Ministry of Information during the Second World War. Marietta had been the lover of John Huston, who had given her a role in his 1960 movie *The Misfits*.

5 Shot by John Huston while on location for *The Roots of Heaven*.

6 Possibly a slip for Chekhov?

7 PLF refers to a line from the musical *Show Boat* (1927), 'Fish got to swim, birds got to fly'.

8 'The wind blows fresh
  To the Homeland
  My Irish Girl
  Where are you lingering?'
                Wagner's *Tristan und Isolde*, act 1, lines 5–8;
                T. S. Eliot's *The Waste Land,* 'The Burial of the Dead'.

To Ricki Huston	The Mill House
undated but postmarked 11 August 1961	Dumbleton

My darling Ricki,

1,000 thanks for your Paris letter, and apologies for delay. Barbara & Niko[1] came for the weekend, and I had to go to London when they left, with the result that now – Tuesday evening! – just back, I can only get this off express to Paris tomorrow morning. Damn, damn, damn.

Triple damn indeed, and sixfold & 100-fold because alas! I've committed myself, only yesterday, too, to devoting myself to my *mama* in the country this weekend, and I'm such a neglectful and intermittent son that I can't put it off now. Bless you for trying though, Ricki dear, and hell and blast at my inadequacy. I'm longing to see you and hate the thought of your vanishing out of reach for what seems such an age, all unembraced! Bugger (cubed).

I say, what gloomy tidings about the CRABS! *Could* it be me? I'll tell you why this odd doubt exists, instead of robust certainty one way or the other: just after arriving back in London from Athens, I was suddenly alerted by what *felt* like the beginnings of troop-movements in the fork, but on scrutiny, expecting an aerial view of general mobilisation, there was nothing to be seen, not even a scout, a spy, or a despatch rider. Puzzled, I watched and waited and soon even the preliminary tramplings died away, so I assumed, as the happy summer days of peace followed each other, that the incident, or the delusive shudder through the chancelleries, was over. While this faint scare was on, knowing that, thanks to lunar tyranny, it couldn't be from you, I assumed (and please spare my blushes here!) that the handover bid must have occurred by dint of a meeting with an old pal in Paris,[2] which, I'm sorry to announce, ended in brief carnal knowledge, more for *auld lang syne* than any more pressing reason. On getting your letter, I made a dash for privacy and thrashed through the undergrowth, but found everything almost eerily calm: fragrant and silent glades that might never have known the invaders' tread. The whole thing makes me scratch my head, if I may so put it. But I bet your trouble *does* come from me, because the crabs of the world seem to fly to me, like the children of Israel to Abraham's bosom, a sort of ambulant Canaan. I've been a real martyr to them. What must have happened is this. A tiny, picked, cunning and well-camouflaged commando must have landed while I was in Paris and then *lain up*, seeing me merely as a stepping stone or a springboard to better things, and, when you came within striking distance, knowing the highest when they saw it, they struck (as who wouldn't?) and then deployed in force, leaving their first beachhead empty. Or so I think! (Security will be tightened up. They may have left an agent with a radio who is playing a waiting game . . .)

I wonder if I have reconstructed the facts all right. I do hope so; I couldn't bear it to be anyone but me. But at the same time, if it *is*

me, v. v. many apologies. There's some wonderful Italian powder you
can get in France called MOM, – another indication of a matriarchal
society, – which is worth its weight in gold dust. It is rather sad to
think that their revels now are ended,[3] that the happy woods (where
I would fain be, wandering in pensive mood)[4] where they held high
holiday will soon be a silent grove. Where are all their quips and
quiddities?[5] The pattering of tiny feet will be stilled. Bare, ruin'd
choirs[6] . . . Don't tell anyone about this private fauna. Mom's the
word, gentle reader.

I've got to write a full-page article for the *Sunday Times* on
Gluttony. The other six of the Deadly Sins have been allotted to
Edith Sitwell, Wystan Auden, Cyril Connolly, Angus Wilson, Evelyn
Waugh and Eliot. I was given the choice between Gluttony and Lust,
and chose the former, because Lust is too serious a matter. I'm rather
looking forward to writing it. Have you any inspirations? Apart from
this, I have been, thank heavens, in the throes of creative frenzy, and
the pages are mounting up as thick as leaves in Vallombrosa.[7] This is
a great relief, as I was beginning to suffer from faint unavowed
despair about this book; I'd left it too long and it was beginning to
go cold on me; but I seem to have breathed it back again to life
at last.

I got a terribly nice letter from Tony [Massourides] at the same
time as yours, thanking me for *Encounter*,[8] and saying he has
translated 'Sounds of the Greek World' into Greek, and will be
sending it. I'm very pleased about this, and I know you will be too,
being the angelic person you are, fortunately.

No more now, my darling Ricki, as I must leap into my faithful
Standard Companion and dash to the post with this, hoping and
praying it gets you in time. No need to say how much I'm going to
miss you; you know I will. Not only the moon's a rival now, but the
sun and Greece as well, and I know what potent allies they are. But
no moping! We'll make some glowing plan when you get back, and
see what magic the mysterious north can offer. Anyway, bless you a
billion times, my dearest darling Ricki, and lots of love hugs and
kisses

from Paddy

¹ Barbara Warner and Niko Ghika had fallen in love, and would soon marry.
² Unidentified.
³ 'Our revels are now ended': *The Tempest*, IV, i.
⁴ An allusion to Wordsworth's 'I Wandered Lonely as a Cloud'.
⁵ In Act 1, scene 2 of *Henry IV, Part 1*, Falstaff and the Prince enjoy a punning exchange. 'How now, how now, mad wag! what, in thy quips and thy quiddities? what a plague have I to do with a buff jerkin?' asks Falstaff; and the Prince replies 'Why, what a pox have I to do with my hostess of the tavern?'
⁶ Sonnet 73 (see pages 246–8).
⁷ *Paradise Lost*, lines 302–4:

> 'Thick as autumnal leaves that strew the brooks
> In Vallombrosa where Etrurian shades
> High over-arch'd embower.'

⁸ See note 2 on page 112.

To Ricki Huston
26 August 1961   13 Chester Row, SW1

My darling Ricki,

Don't be horrified by this red ink – it doesn't mean murder or a death pact or anything, it's just a lovely new pen I've bought for correcting typescript with in red, and it writes so beautifully I must go on with it for the moment. However, no chance of it usurping your lovely grey one.

I began Sei Shōnagon's pillow-book¹ last night, with my head, appropriately, on the pillow, and have been transported ever since, and feel I'm the inhabitant of a tenth-century Fujiwara palace with snow on the ground outside, or returning from an expedition to listen to the cuckoos in a carriage covered with blossom, trying to think of a poem for the Empress when I get back. It's a marvellous book, and many, many thanks for it.

The trip to Cardiff was very odd, really. It's rather a dreadful town, except for the docks, which go on for miles, endless sad streets along which turbaned sikhs and pakistanis shuffle, and lascars and a few Greeks, also quantities of negroes sit shooting craps for hours on end among the old fag ends and fish and chip-smirched *Daily Mirrors* on the pavements of Tiger Bay. But, inside a dingy and flyblown hotel called The Windsor, in this stricken area, is hidden the best restaurant in the West of England, run by a secretive Frenchman who toils away in some smoky vault, unseen, at wonderful scarlet steaks and soles awash with fragrant liquid beige through which chopped mushrooms peep, rather sadly munched by the sad leading citizens of Cardiff. At the end of dinner here we were astonished to see the three plump jolly and middle-aged waitresses, in their caps and aprons, doing a highly trained tap dance to the tune of a portable wireless, and purely for their own amusement. We made friends with two of these, called Joanna and Rhoda, who took us to an after hours drinking and dancing hell in the bowels of a jet black warehouse on the waterfront, where we sat up till three in the morning, hobnobbing with their various coloured friends, and particularly a young burglar living almost entirely on Preludin tablets,[2] to the detriment of his stern calling. Next day we spent the morning in the Museum where there is an astonishing collection of French Impressionist and Post-Impressionist paintings, then motored to a pretty village called Usk, to have lunch there in a pub with Philip Toynbee,[3] who lives not far off, and his wife, *who has greatly improved*. Then to a wonderful late mediaeval castle at Raglan shooting straight out of a green field and surrounded by oak trees. It is an absolute marvel, and I would have liked to move in and hoist my banner at once. It seemed so wasted on the jackdaws. A not too bad Chinese meal finished that day, followed by the waitresses' nightclub, and then back to London next day, halting for lunch at H. and Virginia Bath's.[4]

My hands are scarlet with leakage from this pen, as though hot from a particularly brutal murder, e.g. Macduff's bedside.[5]

I'd rather planned to treat empty August London like the country; but it's not quite empty enough, and, after a short initial lull, meals are beginning to mount up, the people involved being Niko & Barbara, Stephen Spender & Natasha and a rather nice chap staying with them called Ru Wilson, son to Edmund W. and Mary McCarthy,[6] Annie Fleming & Ian F., P. Kinross and P. Quennell, with C. Connolly looming. But I've managed to get a lot of work done all the same, both on my book and on Gluttony. The awful thing about getting typescript back is one can't leave it alone; I keep pulling it to pieces again, like Penelope at her loom; all this time my suitor – Jock Murray – waits . . . The thing about gluttony is: if it's a mortal sin, entailing hell-fire, it's a case of the condemned man eating thousands of hearty breakfasts.

I say! I ought to have begun this letter with loud cheers for the completed script. How I envy you, and would I could say the same. Darling Ricki, I'm so sorry about the *post coitum triste* feeling. I've got it a bit today, and I've just tried to telephone you at the Saints Pères,[7] but, alas, you were still away in the country. I rather hoped we might pool our melancholies and exorcise them. I'll try tomorrow. How I wish I was at Saints Pères, too, or some other hotel well within bowshot with a bistro and a delicious meal ahead, then the clash of curtain-rings meeting, and lamplit drowning in delight with the towers of St Germain, Notre Dame, St Thomas Aquinas just off the Rue du Bac, Saint Guillaume and the Gare d'Orléans softly tolling the night hours away like bell-buoys.

I've hung a lovely late eighteenth-century French *papier-peint*, bought three years ago at an antiquaire, I think in the Rue des Saints Pères, called *Air de Chasse*, and hung it at the end of the room next to my bedroom. It's about three yards square, and represents a wonderful and mysterious Midsummer Night's Dream forest of oaks and ilexes with a rocky glade full of flowers and creeper and bracken across which the hounds of Hippolyta are pounding, and in the far background, are some bluish mountains with dawn rising beyond them. It's made a magical change to this room, especially after dark, suggesting unicorns and faraway French hunting horns.

This letter never seems to finish.

Friday afternoon! Still here, (the letter I mean). Darling, you did sound sad and upset over the telephone. I do know all those agonies, and exquisite torment they are. I wish I was there to help lick wounds and pull out thorns, and feel all the glummer at being stuck in this metropolis. There's lots to say on this theme; but this much delayed letter *must get off* if it's to catch you; so I'll glue it up and charge down Eccleston St [the Post Office] with it before it's too late, and ring you if I possibly can, on Sunday morning; if I can't, it will not be because I haven't tried, but because I can't. I'll write at

once to the American Express. Meanwhile, preceding this, off across
the Channel go several thousand hugs, embraces, kisses, and fond
love, my darling Ricki,

from Paddy

1 Observations and musings recorded by Sei Shōnagon during her time as 'court lady'
to the Empress Consort during the late tenth and early eleventh century in Japan. The
book was completed in the year 1002. The first of several English translations appeared
in 1889.

2 A form of amphetamine or 'speed'.

3 Toynbee had married his second wife, Sally (1916–2003), an American and, like
Toynbee, an alcoholic, in 1950.

4 i.e. Longleat House.

5 PLF is referring to *Macbeth*; he means Duncan's bedside, where Macduff discovers
that the King has been murdered.

6 Reuel Wilson (b. 1938), son of the novelist Mary McCarthy and her second husband,
Edmund Wilson.

7 The Hôtel des Saint Pères in Paris.

To Ricki Huston
2 September 1961   13 Chester Row, SW1

My darling Ricki,

Mars has had it, I fear, though it beats me how he can sleep a wink
with that little pest winding his conch into his ear; even though the
field-telephone receiver, under the hand of the one crawling through
his breastplate, is off.[1] As for the other brats horsing about with the
lance, it's obviously going to end in tears. And what about Venus? Those
precious morning hours are slipping by, and nothing but snores now. I
think that her left hand, in desperation, is straying inexorably forkwards,
toying indeterminately with the folds of the embroidered muslin, with
which she has prudishly re-draped herself (who would think it was
round her neck five short minutes ago?). And if only that little beast
would stop blowing that conch for a little while. And it's no good Mars
cutting those childish messages on the back of trees . . . '*MARS!*'

Noises off. Sound of scenery being changed. CUT to Faringdon Hall,[2]
a Georgian country house, not far from Oxford, embowered in

gigantic trees. From the terrace, parkland rolls away in green waves.
A lake in the middle distance. In a field, right, some black and
white cows munch resentfully; in a second field, left, two horses
chase each other over the sward in a carefree manner. There is a
whirr of wings, and a flight of multicoloured pigeons, some purple,
some Nile green, some shocking pink, some amethyst blue, take
wing from the terrace and settle along the pediment in open order.
A greyhound, collared with a string of pearls, minces disdainfully
across a croquet lawn, avoiding a peacock. A notice, on the edge
of a flower bed, admonishes the passer-by: BEWARE OF THE
AGAPANTHUS. The trees drink from a recent downpour. From
indoors can be heard the harmony of several clocks striking, one of
them an entire tune on a musical box. A Plantagenet belfry quarter
of a mile away begins to chime for Morning Prayer, scaring the
jackdaws and a number of rooks. Indoors, in many a four-poster,
highborn guests stir indolently; then their eyes close once more. It is
eleven o'clock on the morning of Sunday, 4th (?) of September,
1961. Invisible among the early autumn vapours above the house
hovers Hangover, a baleful spirit . . . *LAP DISSOLVE* to the green
room. Track to a vast safe green rococo bed containing a solitary
figure writing, oddly enough, on sheets of foolscap bought in Larissa
some months ago. Dolly Shot[3] of *P. Leigh Fermor*, agreeably tousled
from slumber. A close-up reveals delicate pink veining in the whites
of his eyes. He lights a cigarette, a faraway look suffusing his
bloodshot orbs. *CUT* . . .

***

As you see, Ricki darling, there's only one thing missing from what
might have been a well-spent Botticelli forenoon . . . How sad that
all these rustling safe green yards [of material] overhead should be
pavilioning solitude; such an unsuitable canopy for austerity; I discern
reproach in its folds . . . I adore this house. It used to be a great
haunt of mine. I wonder if you know who I mean by *Lord Berners*?[4]
He lived here for as long as I can remember, and died alas, leaving
it to a very dotty relation, very good looking and rather wicked, he
was in love with, called Robert Heber-Percy,[5] known as the Mad

Boy, who now lives here, a half-queer, half-debauched, and half-foxhunting squire's life, fortunately still with most of Gerald Berners' old pals as guests. He – Gerald – was a brilliant, charming and eccentric man, a writer, painter, poet & composer of no small merit. He always wore dark glasses in Rome because he said that otherwise he got no peace from the beggars because his eyes were so kind. I think I recited, on our Greek journey, two of the funny poems to you . . . I'm glad that his invention of dyeing the pigeons different colours is still kept up.

The inhabitants of the house for this weekend are the Mad Boy, Hugh Cruddas,[6] his hunting pal and bedfellow, Coote Lygon, a cousin of his called Letty Ashley-Cooper, and a thoroughly cracked, very attractive, very broke and v. young couple who live in a cottage nearby called Victor and Caroline Grosvenor.[7] The drinking before dinner was fast and furious, egged on by John Betjeman, who came for it with his wife Penelope. Then we settled in a decorative orangery, where Coote played all the Mickey Theodorakis 'Epitaphios' records, which made me think of Greece and you. Champagne mixed with brandy and peaches went down at lightning speed, also much singing took place and a tremendous *hasapiko* dance [a Greek folk dance] by me, I'm sorry to announce. Then, led by mad Caroline Grosvenor, the Mad Boy, Hugh, Victor and I charged down the lake, clothes were torn off, and in we plunged, Caroline, who is very pretty, doing a great deal of naked nymph-like showing off, charging about among the trees and reeds, and, I think, longing for either the Mad Boy or me to initiate some adulterous goings on – we both thought the other was the chosen one, and what with that and her husband being there, the woods remained unpolluted by any irregular congress, I'm happy to say . . . It was warm and starry with a half moon, and so many trees round it, all identically reflected, except when our ripples broke it all up, that we might have been in an impenetrable forest. There was a great deal of shouting, singing, splashing and poetry shouted at the top of our voices. When the fishermen arrived at dawn, I fear they must have found the pike, gudgeon, tench etc. so many bags of nerves. We trooped home stark [naked] through the dewy grass with a glimmer

of dawn breaking, Caroline cartwheeling indefatigably over the
sward, still thirsting for love and wine. The house seemed shadowy
& mysterious and full of the smell of flowers and pot-pourri and
the many clocks announcing daybreak. So to bed. I forgot to
mention that, at the end of an alley of hornbeam outside my
window, is an allegorical group of statuary. I can't see what it
represents, but would like to think that it is Alka-Seltzer trampling
Headache underfoot.

I woke up to the sound of a terrible thunderstorm, with real
forked lightning rocketing across the sky, immediately followed by
thunderclaps like the whole of Trafalgar and Waterloo on the roof.
It was a comfort to realise it was an outside job . . .

I don't know what today holds in store. Dawn tomorrow is the
first cubbing of the season – the meet is here! – perhaps, if tonight is
like last night, it would be more sensible not to go to bed at all and
tittup wild eyed through the drizzling spinneys. Perhaps we will still
be locked in bacchic slumber, as deaf to the horn as Mars to that
little wretch's conch in the picture, and for less good a reason.

After that, back to London, and to work. Please forgive my awful
slowness in writing, and, repaying evil with good, write to me at
once. Forgive, too, this rather unedifying letter. I do envy you
Greece, and long to hear all about it. I wish you could leave it this
very second and whizz through the window here and under these
heroic hangings and into a loving and endless embrace. In lieu of
that, my dearest darling Ricki, billions of love, hugs & kisses to you,
and a few sighs,

    from Paddy

    xxx

---

[1] PLF is alluding to the Botticelli painting *Mars and Venus*, which hangs in the National
Gallery, London.

[2] Faringdon House.

[3] A tracking shot, filmed while the camera is mounted on a 'dolly'.

[4] Gerald Hugh Tyrwhitt-Wilson (1883–1950), 14th Baron Berners, composer, novelist,
painter, aesthete and eccentric. His pigeons were dyed in bright colours, and he drove
around his estate wearing a pig's-head mask to frighten the locals. PLF recalled notices
at Faringdon House:

'No dogs admitted' at the top of the stairs and 'Prepare to meet thy God' painted inside a wardrobe. When people complimented him on his delicious peaches he would say, 'Yes, they are ham-fed.' And he used to put Woolworth pearl necklaces round his dogs' necks and when a guest, rather perturbed, ran up saying 'Fido has lost his necklace', G said, 'Oh dear, I'll have to get another out of the safe.'

A notice at the entrance to the tower near his house read 'Members of the Public committing suicide from this tower do so at their own risk'.

5 Robert Vernon Heber-Percy (1911–87), 'a wild and pugnacious character'. He had married Jennifer Fry for a time and their union produced a daughter, Victoria, whose own daughter Sofka would eventually inherit the estate. Before meeting Gerald Berners he had a brief but hectic career in the Cavalry, acted as an extra in Hollywood, worked in a Lyons' Corner House (until spilling soup over a customer), and helped run a nightclub.

6 Known as 'The Captain'. His arrival at Faringdon prompted Evelyn Waugh's comment to Diana Mosley: 'The Mad Boy has installed a Mad Boy of his own. Has there ever been a property in history that has devolved from catamite to catamite for any length of time?'

7 The Hon. Robert Victor Grosvenor (1936–93), son of the 5th Baron Ebury, and his wife Caroline, née Higham (1936–2003).

To Lawrence Durrell   Poste Restante
30 October 1961   Loeronau
                                                                    Finistère

DE PROFUNDIS[1]

Dear Larry,

This is in the nature of an SOS. Do you know of anywhere in your area where there is a huge and sympathetic room, with plenty of striding space, a large worktable, a shaded lamp, a bed, and a view (lasting as long as the sun) lunging away into the distance, and country to walk about in, costing practically nothing? I've *got to finish Mani's* sequel – Thrace, Macedonia, Epirus & Thessaly – within the next three months, before tackling Mexico with Joan in February. Here, alas, is hopeless. Over twenty kilometres from where you are, but under fifty, would seem to me to be the ideal; beyond the nuisance radius for you, and within the one-cheerful-dinner-a-week radius for me. By next to nothing, I had £20 to £30 a month in

mind, with a nice crone to make a bachelor's breakfast and bed
– Joan is in Greece, sniffing round the site of a possible house on the
marches of the Mani, for the evening of life and a haven for all of
us[2] – and a village with a bistro for grub within easy walking or
motoring range. Do think! It's a real emergency. I promise not to be
a pest.

Here, alas, where I've been for the last week or so, is no good.
Brittany just now is too sad, and will get sadder. The end of a long
time-wasting quest all over the duchy is the minute room where I'm
now writing, in a pub called Le Fer à Cheval, with a window
peering into the well of a granite backyard and a funnel of slate
roofs streaming under the downpour. Clogs and Breton chat are
never out of earshot. (I wonder what they are talking about?
Miracles? Shrimp shortages? The danger to traffic of beetroots falling
from farm carts?) Under other circumstances, I might have loved it
here: Arthurian mists, the Forest of Brocéliande and lost Lyonesse
next door, King Mark of Cornwall, Merlin, Viviane,[3] and living on
shrimps, oysters, clams, cockles, mussels and so on, a merman's
regimen. But it's no good now.

Somebody ought to write an essay on the mystical preoccupations
of the Celtic fringe. Amazing granite calvaries prong the entire
peninsula – thieves, virgins, disciples, centurions, soldiers, jews,
horsemen, politicians and piemen jut from the main stalk like several
generations of acrobats in a strong-man-act – and holy wells riddle it.
There's not a village without a miniature Chartres cathedral with a
jungle of flying buttresses, triforia, clerestories, gargoyles, crockets,
finials, executed with an almost Easter Island uncouthness: Gothic
with knobs on. They are nearly all dedicated to Irish saints, most of
whom flew here, or floated in coffins or on mill-stones. My local –
St Roman – came the hard way, on foot the whole distance from
Cork, and worked wonders among the wolves and mad dogs of the
area. I think the elaboration of the churches is an extension in
granite of the prevalent lacemaking tendency. The denizens of these
calvaries – built in the fifteenth and sixteenth centuries – all wear
contemporary clothes, the equivalent Joseph of Arimathea in evening
tails, and Judas Iscariot with a Gladstone bag and a bowler.

No time now, as I do want this to depart and reach you quickly. Do think, dear Larry!

Much love to you and Claude[4]

from Paddy

[1] (Latin: 'from the depths'), a reference to the letter written by Oscar Wilde during his imprisonment in Reading Gaol, to his lover 'Bosie' (Lord Alfred Douglas).

[2] See next letter.

[3] The Lady of the Lake in Arthurian legend.

[4] Claude-Marie Vincendon, whom Durrell had met on Cyprus and married in 1961.

The affair with Ricki Huston petered out around the end of the year. 'I do miss the looming ahead of some dead-secret joint plan, which has played such a part in the last ten months,' he wrote to her in February. 'We'll dissect all this sometime, and I fear I won't come out of it too well. You do, impeccably.'

Paddy and Joan had decided to settle in Greece, using money she had inherited from her mother. When this letter was written Joan was in the Mani, then a completely unspoilt region of the Peloponnese, investigating the possibility that they might convert one or more of the numerous towers around the coastal village of Kardamyli into a house.

To Joan Rayner   Nîmes
26 November 1961   Gard

Darling Joan,

It's *absolutely maddening* my getting your letter and telegrams that fatal day too late. *Of course* I ought to have been there to help with those momentous decisions; the only thing is, I'm certain I would have agreed with you. It sounds absolutely marvellous. I have studied your plan for ages, and think I remember exactly where it is. Quite apart from the towers themselves, what sounds so wonderful is the space and the view – all the looking and striding room in the world, things which, in Western Europe, I'm beginning to realise, are becoming rarer than platinum. It seems to exist no longer, except perhaps for a few clever millionaires; most millionaires, however, aren't happy unless there are at least another twenty millionaires'

houses in sight, and no one else's. I really can't quite believe it. Think
of the hundreds of sunsets ahead, walks through olive groves, meals
under trees, sleeping writing drinking reading with branches
overhead. I do agree about the appalling time, labour and money
involved in starting from scratch, and it seems to me that there's
endless elbow room for inspiration in what there is. I'm sure it's
right, too, to get hold of as many towers near to each other, and,
within reason, as much ground as we possibly can. What a near thing
about the Swiss![1] and I bet, as you say, it was all because of *Mani*. I
feel sure you've sworn in all our families about not talking about it.
(We must contrive, somewhere, a Yannina[2]-Hardwick[3]-more-glass-
than-wall-bit.) I'm dreadfully sorry you've had to struggle with it all
alone; and I feel a bit sad and jealous that I wasn't in on all these
initial labours. I do think you've been brilliant, darling. Of *course*, I'd
have flown there, like a shot. But when we talked on the telephone,
and you were off that second, it seemed hopeless. *If* there's anything
I can possibly be useful about at this late stage, out I'll whizz, even if
only for two or three days. But when we were talking over the
telephone, it didn't sound as if I could be. But only a word is
needed! . . .

What happened at Locronan was, I got more and more lonely and
depressed and rain-sodden, a poste restante haunter, but no letters
from *anyone*, not only you, till I began to feel that no letters ever
could get there, an ill-fated, barren bureau. (Of course, the moment
my back was turned, they must have come in like Niagara Falls, to
judge by the crop waiting here.) If only I'd delayed there, I now
realise, *one more day*, I'd almost certainly have been in Greece now.
I began to feel rather like we both did in Athens last year, just after
arriving. So I packed up and set off, coming the most direct way, I
think, except for the first day, making a longer loop in eastern
Brittany than was strictly necessary in order to see the castle of
Fougères (*mis-en-scène* of Balzac's *Chouans*)[4] and Madame de Sévigné's
Château des Rochers. The first day was intermittent rain and
sunshine, a wonderful sequence of foxes' weddings, driving towards
rainbow after rainbow, like a series of hoops, curving over rolling and
beautiful forests. Then down to the Loire estuary, through

Chateaubriand, having a one star-lunch in Nantes, which is a
marvellous town. I trudged round the Ducal Castle here, and round a
lovely Gothic cathedral with a most beautiful tomb of recumbent
last-duke-and-duchess-of-Brittany-but-one before it was merged with
the French crown, at the turning point of the latest Middle Ages and
the early Renaissance even more moving than Bourg-en-Bresse; went
round a wonderful picture-gallery, a very important, huge treasure-
crammed building. My solitary figure seemed to be the *only one* in
any such place, all the way. So off, over the Loire bridge in the late
afternoon, a wonderful pearly light with streaks of blue over this
lovely river, and a dome or two giving it an almost Roman look
– and into the dark Vendée, fetching up at La Rochelle, arcaded like
Zante,[5] full of statues and harbour-scapes. After a bloody dinner,
prowled into two or three bars, and in one of them picked up a
charming and erudite, perfect English-speaking dilettante, who seems
to know everyone in every country (Julian P. R.[6] stays with him
now and then on the way to and from Fons) called M. Eric Dahl.[7]
We finally drank whisky in his vast and beautiful eighteenth-century
house full of books and rather beautiful Fromentins – Fromentin, the
town's glory, is his great grandfather – and one or two Corots and a
Delacroix, till 4 a.m., talking about painting, history, heraldry, Greek
& Latin literature and kindred themes. He is curator of the
wonderful Natural History and Ethnological museum there, which
he took me over next morning, lots of skeletons of whales, dolphins,
porpoises, some Greek, Roman and Etruscan things, a world-famous
shell exhibition. Then a tour of this town, in pouring rain, during
which a 400-year-old cedar-tree came crashing down a few yards
away and the town's electricity fused like a green sky-rocket from a
telegraph pole. A morning of portents. I don't expect you know who
built the fine eighteenth-century arsenal there? It was Choderlos de
Laclos,[8] town military engineer for twenty years! Then a tremendous
lunch with M. Dahl in his house with a terrific bottle of Château
Latour, that made me wish you were there even more. And away,
south through the Saintonge, stopping to look at two amazing
Renaissance churches recommended by M. Dahl, and suddenly found
myself – all this in a downpour, going v. slow for fear of skidding,

and by now after dark – in Blaye, and thought of P. G. Wodehouse: ('You're so chivalrous Bertie. Just like Rudel.' 'Who's Rudel?' 'Rudel, Prince of Blaye-en-Saintonge, crusader and troubadour, who died for love of the lady of Tripoli.' 'Oh, ah . . . '),[9] so whisked up the rainy ramp of a vast castle, which had indeed belonged to him, and from the battlements, gazed down through the deluge at the huge sweep of the Gironde and the twinkling lights of Bordeaux the other side. So on to Bordeaux in a blizzard, and found it virtually an underwater city. Stopped here in an old-fashioned, slightly moth-eaten hotel, worn plush and brass and endless passages. Next morning the rain was even worse – the heaviest rains for many years, a Greek steamer in trouble in the Bay of Biscay and terrific destruction of the Arcachon oyster beds – so decided not to forge ahead that day, but asked the maid – a tall, sad, beautiful, fair girl, smiling so seldom her heir might have been lost in the White Ship[10] – about Montaigne's tower.[11] She turned out to be from Paris, tremendously well read[12] and with *a day off*, so I went under her guidance, had lunch in Saint Émilion, a wonderful mediaeval hill town, then on to Montaigne's tower. (*It would have been perfect for me!*) It's a high ridge, overlooking green gardens, and a park and a comic neo-Gothic chateau, all the beams covered with Latin and Greek inscriptions put there by Montaigne himself. I get a tremendous kick out of places like this. I don't quite know why. (I clean forgot to have a look at Montesquieu's castle next day.) Annie,[13] the waitress, had a rather sad tale to tell, bad luck with men etc. – they only seemed to be after One Thing, so she always felt unsafe with them – 'Not like with you!' she finished with trusting eyes; which of course completely tied one's hands *should* the idea of a Philip [Toynbee]-like lunge have ever drifted through the mind . . . I enjoyed all this, as bar Mr Dahl, it was the first person I'd spoken to, bar ordering a meal, for weeks; since Pont-Aven, indeed. She told me the happiest time she'd ever had was a solitary holiday near Arcachon last autumn. She has a passion for oysters, and about sunset, when everyone had cleared off, she dived into the oyster beds and swam back to the shore, where her basket, containing knife, bread and butter, was waiting on the sands. She also has a greyhound called Dick – '*Deek*' – who is expert at spotting oysters when they are washed loose after storms, bounding across the sands, then pulling up panting over some scaly trove. I rather like to think of this pale, dune-wandering couple.

Darling, I'm going to break off now, without rereading this, and get it off and continue almost at once, rather than hold things up by continuing. . . . No more now, till this evening darling angel Joan, except 1,000 congratulations again about your great Maniot feat. My telephone number is Nîmes 4346.

Love hugs

P. xxx

---

1 Joan's inheritance had been in a Swiss bank account, and was received free of UK taxation.

2 PLF seems to be thinking of a Turkish-style alcove surrounded by low windows and lined with divans, where one can recline and admire the view.

3 The exceptional amount of fenestration in the Elizabethan house Hardwick Hall in Derbyshire gives rise to the expression 'Hardwick Hall, more glass than wall.'

4 Balzac's *Les Chouans* (1829), part of his great sequence of novels *La Comédie humaine*, is set in Brittany.

5 Perhaps a reference to Miss Crowe's house (see pages 18–20).

6 Julian Alfred Lane Fox Pitt-Rivers (1919–2001), anthropologist and ethnographer, then living in a chateau in Fons, near Figeac, in the Lot.

7 Eric Dahl (d. 1986), son of the Norwegian-born fishery owner Oscar Dahl, and cousin of the novelist Roald Dahl.

8 Pierre Ambroise François Choderlos de Laclos (1741–1803), author of the epistolary novel *Les Liaisons dangereuses* (1782).

9 A slightly misquoted passage from *The Code of the Woosters* (1938).

10 The *White Ship* sank off Barfleur on 25 November 1120. Only two of those aboard survived: among those drowned was Henry I's son and heir, leading to a succession crisis and a period of civil war in England. The King was said never to have smiled again.

11 The southern tower of the Château de Montaigne, the only vestige of the original sixteenth-century castle.

12 As she helped him with his luggage, he quoted two lines of Verlaine (from 'Il pleure dans mon couer'):

> 'Ô bruit doux de la pluie
> *Par terre et sur les toits!*'

which she continued,

> '*Pour un cœur qui s'ennuie*
> Ô le chant de la pluie!'

¹³ Annie the waitress and 'the tall, sad, beautiful' maid were the same person. In contemporaneous letters to Debo Devonshire and Ricki Huston, PLF revealed that they had spent the next day together. On leaving the following morning he had found a Bach record slipped into the car, with a letter from Annie saying the time they had spent together had been some of 'the happiest hours of her existence'.

To Jock Murray   The Mill House
9 March 1962   Dumbleton

CATS AT NIGHT

Dear Jock,

1. I write to you with my *left* arm (thank God, *and no excuse pending!*) in plaster of Paris owing to a hunting smash-up ten days ago, on the hardest bit of Dartmoor – possibly the part left by Freya to her little godson. A very odd feeling, concussed blithering for ten mins, then a return to sense streaming with blood from two black eyes and forehead and ribs feeling (but not!) like a broken shopping basket. Long live bowlers, which I have always despised; mine's in smithereens, but not me.

2. I enclose Miss Masvoulás's¹ letter. It seems marvellous to me and my feeling is that we shouldn't take any money from it – it would only be 2d anyway. I've only answered by a congratulatory telegram so far. Can you let her have the plates, or whatever she needs, of the Mani photographs? That's what she means by the word κλισέ (clichés!) in her last paragraph. Do write to her and wish her well.

3. Dear Jock, I've done just what you warned me against, and which I didn't mean to do – five brisk pages is what I had in mind – and that is, getting bogged down in Byron's slippers. The whole thing's got out of control and covers many pages. But I hope it will make an odd and unusual chapter; it's full of things I've been longing to write for years, especially about Lord Byron, and I've enjoyed doing it like mad – far more excited than I've been for a long time, and that's usually a good sign. It's when you

begin to bore yourself that you've probably been boring your neighbour for the last ten pages. I hope to finish this tomorrow. It was *meant* to be a lead-in to the Kravara – i.e. beggar – chapter,[2] which is only about fifty miles further along the N. coast of the Gulf of Corinth; but this business has expanded too much to be anything but a chapter on its own; and Miss Johns[3] should have it within the next three days.

4. Remains the beggar chapter, let's wash out the phallic one at the moment, and use the beggars to complete our revisited interior vol. Now, Joan's and my plan is to push off for Sicily to see all the Greek things there – at last – after getting back to the Metropolis the day after tomorrow, viz. Monday. Work will be cut out, I foresee, preparing the work in hand for Miss J., and preparing for departure. What I plan is to make a halt somewhere quiet and wonderful, and write the missing chapter clean through there. What do you think of this?

I feel in such an optimistic mood at the moment, it's the elation of *forging ahead*, even if it's in the wrong direction, or a deviation from plan. It was that great khaki obstacle of Macedonia that has been holding me up, as I believe bunkers do people who play golf.

After all, one of the things about writing is that one should *enjoy* what one's writing. Otherwise no one else will, and one might as well be down a mine.

5. We'll have to start thinking about titles and covers on different lines now, I suppose.

6. No more that I can think of, except let's communicate next week. *Be of good cheer*, I think all's well!

Yours ever
    Paddy

P.S. What marvellous news from those American agents! Bless them. Money plucked from the sky.

P.P.S. Pity the lame and the halt.

¹ She had translated *Mani* into Greek.
² The Kravara region, on the north coast of the Gulf of Corinth. 'Its fame springs from the prevalence, real or supposed, of professional mendicancy' (*Roumeli*, page 187).
³ PLF's typist.

*The plan to convert a tower in the Mani into a house came to nothing, but another possibility arose, as Paddy explained in a letter to Debo Devonshire (*In Tearing Haste, page 92). 'I've spent the last two months trying to find somewhere to live in S.W. Greece, and, the trouble is, I've found it: trouble, because I don't think we'll be able to get it; owned by too many people, scattered all over the globe, who, though none of them live there, are unlikely to want to sell it; but I live in hopes. It's in the Mani, a peninsula in the middle of a steep deserted bay, pointing S.E., E., S.W. and W., with a great amphitheatre of mountains which turn a hectic red at sunset. The peninsula descends like a giant, shallow staircase of olive groves, plumed with cypress trees, platform after platform dwindling to a low cliff thirty feet above deep blue-green glittering sea, with trees and wild sweet-smelling shrubs to the very brink, full of beehives, olives, woodpigeons, and with a freshwater spring. The cliff is warrened with a great sea cave into which one swims, under stalactites and strange mushroom limestone formations. Not a house in sight, nothing but the two rocky headlands, an island a quarter of a mile out to sea with a ruined chapel, and a vast expanse of glittering water, over which you see the sun setting till its last gasp. Homer's Greece, in fact. But I've not given up hope. It would mean building a rambling peasant house, with huge airy rooms, out of the local limestone, on one of those ledges of olive-trees . . .'*

To Joan Rayner   Kallirhoë 12
30 June 1962   Athens

Darling Joan,

Got back from Kardamyli with Tony [Massourides] and his girl Rania at 1.00 last night and hasten to write. In view of all the difficulties, I was secretly hoping that I would be disappointed in Kalamitsi. Alas, alas, when we got there and looked through the trees at the sea under a third moon, it was worse, or better than ever.

Same next morning, when we bathed off the rocks! Tony and Rania
saw in a flash what all the fuss was about, and why nowhere else,
after seeing K, will quite do.

(a) The day before we set off – on Friday – Tony talked to Phikouras
    by telephone, and suggested 180,000[1] as the outside price –
    including sale tax – 20,000 less than the sum we had thought of,
    as giving us, if necessary, something to retreat to. BUT NO
    FURTHER. He sounded interested. *Will he be able to get hold of
    his wicked uncle?*

(b) Tony and I, the justice of the peace and the town clerk of
    Kardamyli, spent hours in the 'town hall', looking up titles, deeds
    of sale etc., in the town records. It emerges from all this that there
    are *four* people who will have to agree to a sale – uncle Geo.
    Stephanéa, old Angela Phikoura, who lives in the hut, another
    eighty-five-year-old brother who lives in the US, and a seventy-
    to eighty-year-old sister, also for the past forty years in America.
    Any sale without their consent would be invalid (Steph never
    mentioned them!). Tony is going into all this, and it may take time.

(c) On Saturday night we had a long moonlight chat with old Angela
    Phikoura, the hut-dwelling old girl who lives on the spot. She
    repeated that we could build there as much as we liked free but
    she wouldn't sell the land (*not* that it is all hers); she said sadly,
    'money's just bits of paper. It flies away like birds. But if you have
    land and olives and vegetables and chickens, you'll never starve.
    I've been all my childhood here, I live a solitary – ἀσκητική
    [ascetic] – life, away from the village.' She told the nice peasant
    couple, all on our side, who are farming it that, once we bought
    it, we might turn her out in her old age with a handful of
    banknotes, in spite of all my reassurances to the contrary. Next
    day, we approached her with the suggestion that we should buy
    the whole property, but in the contract lay down by law that she
    could not only live there for the rest of her days, but have the
    usufruct of the olive trees and kitchen garden too (which turn out
    to be worth a great deal less than I thought, at the moment, but
    could have a profitable yield when properly tended). She seemed
    favourably impressed by this, and swayed in her resolution. Both

the two peasants and Tony urged the sense of this. If the others
assented, there would be no difficulty here. I like her very much,
and can't help seeing her side of things. Her little hut is far from
where the house would stand, rather a nice little enclave of
chickens, beehives and tethered goats and two strong horses. She is
a sort of [illegible] Mary Herbert-faced old [illegible] in patched
clothes, often barefoot, and in a huge Mani straw hat. On her
death, all the usufruct would fall to us. The two peasants, who are
angels, are dead keen to look after everything for us, and pine for
it. They are one of the major attractions of the place.

(d) I asked Tony how he thought the extent of the property
     compared in size to the garden of Niko's house in Hydra. He
     said ten times as big; I, five times. In spite of only being four
     stremmata,[2] perhaps because of the variety of levels and trees, the
     impression is very large and spacious. It seems vast and airy and
     full of surprises, all nice ones.

(e) Tony is going to tackle the possibilities of plot B., without me,
     as a foreigner always sends the price up alas. Soc. Phaliréa thinks
     there will be little difficulty. *One* old man owns it all, and there is
     no water. He never goes there. The two operations, plot A & plot
     B, will be kept separate.

(f) I can almost certainly get the ready money here from Geo.
     Athenogenis who has large interests in both Athens and London;
     in fact, he said it would come in useful to him in the latter.

(g) As the negotiations (if they proceed at all!) will certainly take
     some time, we ought to give Tony power of attorney to deal
     with it for us when I have left . . .

(h) What do you think about the Athens house? If you wanted to
     dispose of it who should deal with it – Zanis or Tony? Shall I ask
     Tony what the etiquette is?

(i) I keep on having a presentiment we'll get this heavenly place; but
     all seems against it!

(j) It would be a lovely place to live in a large tent and bathe, read
     and walk while the foundations were being laid.

(k) Should one, in such a case, sacrifice a cock? I asked Tony. He
     thought, yes.

(l) Your telegram has just arrived. The first part agrees with all the foregoing. I'm not quite happy about the fifty years' lease idea, rather absurdly, because of the possibility of descendants, unless my absolute idiocy has done for this![3] Too difficult to go into now, but not being married seems steadily more ludicrous – and the very possibility of this paradise brings this out in sharper and sharper relief. No more about this now, darling, except I ought to have my head looked at. Even failing these descendants (how they would bless one in 100 years' time!) it would be lovely for people one adored, to inherit.

This *must* get off! Loving hugs and kisses, darling
    from Paddy

I made Tony take lots of snaps. To be forwarded as soon as developed.

[1] 180,000 drachmas was about £2,150 (the equivalent of more than £30,000 in 2016, adjusted for inflation).
[2] A Greek unit of land, equivalent to 1,000 square metres. Four stremmata is about one acre.
[3] Joan was fifty at the time of this letter.

The purchase of the land in the Mani proceeded slowly and was not completed until March 1964. In the meantime Paddy continued to oscillate between resting-places in England and Greece. This letter was written while he was staying as a guest of Kisty Hesketh, at the Hesketh family seat, a glorious Hawksmoor house, not far from the racecourse at Towcester.

To Nancy Mitford   Easton Neston
undated [April 1963]   Northamptonshire[1]

Darling Nancy,
    V. many thanks indeed for *The Water Beetle*,[2] which arrived, re-forwarded from Lismore, just before I left London. I'm taking it with me to the pub I propose to settle in for the next two weeks in Wales, for my *livre de chevet* [bedtime reading]. It looks lovely.

Towcester races took place here Saturday and I made £7. Better still, after the captains and the kings had departed,[3] Kisty Hesketh, Molly Cranborne[4] & self stole out into the dusk on three magnificent horses and pounded round the entire course, these steeds sailing over the hurdles like swallows. It really was lovely.

The pub I settle in tomorrow is an old steward's house built into the ruins of Llanthony Abbey – an Augustinian Priory – in a wild and very remote valley of the Black Mountains in Monmouthshire, inhabited for a time by Walter Savage Landor, who was the local squire. It is one of the most romantic and odd places I've seen in England, and I expect great things of it.

Thank you so much again for the book, dear Nancy, and tons of love from

Paddy

love to Eddy [Sackville-West]

1. For Kisty Hesketh, see note 4 on page 98.
2 A volume of NM's essays, articles and reviews, published in 1962.
3 A reference to Kipling's 'Recessional' (1897).
4 Marjorie 'Molly' Olein Wyndham-Quin (b. 1922), Lady Cranborne, later Lady Salisbury.

To Xan Fielding   Katounia
10 December 1963   Limni
                                                  Euboea
                                                  Greece

Ἀλέκο παιδί μου [Alex, dear boy],

I've been meaning to write for such ages, but I just haven't, as Tom Dunbabin might have put it, (a) to find out how you both are, though I know a bit from Joan's having seen Daph in London and (b) to put you abreast of what I'm up to, because it concerns you a bit.

A few months ago an American magazine called *Holiday* asked me to write a rather well-paid article on *The Pleasures of Walking*. I

pondered the matter and decided to give a brief potted account of
my youthful trudge across Europe. It was supposed to be 2,000
words. I started at full gallop,[1] and have now reached 60,000 words,
and am still in Bucharest with the whole of the Black Sea Coast
looming, then Turkey, Constantinople and The End. I should be
through in about a month and another 20 or 25,000 words i.e., a
normal length book.[2] I don't know what it's like yet. All of Holland,
Germany, Austria, Czechoslovakia, Hungary, Transylvania, Bulgaria and
Rumania are already done, and I think large hunks of it are all right.
I can't think what to call it. *A Youthful Journey* is my working title,
but I'm not keen. I thought of *Seasons and Castles* after Rimbaud[3]
and as touching on my rustic snobbish goings on in Mitteleuropa.
But am not happy about that either. I wish you and Daph would
think of something. Andrew [Devonshire] suggests *Shanks's*
Europe . . .

But where you really come in is that I'd like, with your
permission, to dedicate it to you and also kick off with a longish
introduction, explaining the previous background etc., rather in the
style of Cyril [Connolly]'s long letter to Peter [Quennell] at the
beginning of *The Rock Pool.* There was so much in common between
the years we both spent between leaving – 'leaving' in my case[4]
– school and finally meeting at Yerakari,[5] that you are obviously the
only person. Also, through interminable case-colloquys, you know so
much of it already. Anyway, it would be appropriate and the greatest
fun. I do hope you'll like it.

Joan and I settled here this summer as a scribbling stop-gap, in a
hellish house belonging to Philip Sherrard.[6] Then I was alone a
month or so in this ravishing house belonging to a nice eccentric
man called Sir Aymer Maxwell – absent – whose brother[7] writes
about otters. Joan came back three days ago (and sends love to both).
All goes swimmingly and with any luck I'll be out of the wood by
Christmas. Maurice came here for a fortnight this summer and
seemed to like it, and Eddy [Sackville-West], also Judy and Milton
[Gendel] for a moment, and Janetta with her girls and Julian Jebb[8]
once, and then again with the addition of Jaime [Parladé]. Since then
it has been a perfect Greek autumn of clear, brilliant days interrupted

every now and then by three-day monsoons. Now it is getting cold and snow is on the way, I think. Parnassus, 50? 100? miles away the other side of the Gulf of Euboea, is already white on top.

No more for the present. I meant to write and suggest all this months ago. Do write, and please try and think of alternative names for this book.

With tons of love to you both,
Paddy

¹ 'Work goes on tremendously,' PLF had written to Joan in November.
² The book eventually expanded into a trilogy, the first volume being *A Time of Gifts*.
³ The refrain '*O saisons, ô châteaux*' occurs several times in Rimbaud's poem *Happiness*.
⁴ PLF means that he was asked to leave King's School, Canterbury, after being discovered holding hands with a greengrocer's daughter.
⁵ In German-occupied Crete, during the summer of 1942.
⁶ Philip Owen Arnould Sherrard (1922–95), author, translator and philosopher, who settled in Greece after the Second World War. He lived in a house he had restored near the small town of Limni on the island of Euboea.
⁷ Gavin Maxwell, author of *Ring of Bright Water* (1960).
⁸ Julian Jebb (1934–84), journalist, then living in Rome and teaching English. In 1967 he joined the BBC, where he co-produced a succession of documentaries, with a mission to put writers on-screen.

To Diana Cooper   Katounia
late December 1963   Limni

My darling Diana,

Here I am, slogging away as usual in island seclusion. Not, thank God, for the last three months in the hell-hole that Judy may have mentioned,¹ but in a ravishing house on a hillside covered with lemon trees and cypresses belonging to a new friend, who has lent it out of pity, called Sir Aymer Maxwell, an eccentric and amusing half-absentee laird that you would like very much. He's very good and inventive about games, and cottoned on to the ancient SS. Gregory and Augustine-at-twilight business² at once, and produced some beauties. Here's one from just before his departure: the two saints are due to inspect the working of democracy in space. But when they join the queue boarding the rocket ship, they are turned back because of their cloth. What does the Pope turn to St Augustine and say? *Answer:* 'This is not astral socialism but social ostracism.'

I've been writing like mad, still on my great youthful trudge, which is nearly turning, though I didn't mean it to, into a year's autobiography. Thank God, I do believe it's working out all right at last. (As a result of this frenzy, this is the first letter to anyone for months, and long overdue.) The only respite from this, and also escape from the horrors of our first habitat, has been odd bits of building, which I hope the inheritors of it like: first, a huge summerhouse out of rush mats and trellis work, supported on a vast tree-trunk-pillar bleached from the sea and hauled from the shore where it was the waves' plaything. In one corner of this building, which is half neolithic temple, half emir's pavilion, I built a lovely moorish fountain with the water gushing or plip-plopping, according to the subtle twist of an invisible tap, from a conch sticking out of an angle of white wall into a whitewashed cube surmounted by spikes, and thence, in two shell-splayed jets, into a bigger, C-shaped and spike-surrounded basin with a stone floor which I painted with the legend of the nereid-gorgon (see *Mani*). Also decorated the white wall above, and the fountain, with bas-reliefs of sea creatures: gorgon, whirlpool, gull, halcyon, sea-urchin, seahorses, octopus, Muraena [Moray] eel and squid, moulded out of gypsum. This has become a slight mania, and a hornblowing Titan now pounds across the wall of A. Maxwell's house. I'll try and find some snaps. If you want a unicorn or similar beast for your garden, I'm your man.

It's been pouring here some of the time, and terribly cold, which gave poor Joan a bit of a surprise when she got back. But today it is winter Greece at its best: the gulf of Euboea sweeping away to the shore of Boeotia bright blue sea covered with white horses, and on the mainland, the soaring and glittering spikes of snow-covered Parnassus. A caïque tosses across these waves, hauling in its net, and a million gulls wheel round it in a private snowstorm; and the fish leap from the narrowing corral of the net only to vanish down these airborne red lanes. Dolphins may surface at any moment.

Joan was told by Robin Ironside[3] that he was invited to the Droghedas' box at Covent Garden, and his heart was in his boots at the gloom and hopelessness of everyone, when you suddenly appeared rather late, and changed everything, as if the Spirit of Spring had suddenly blown into that wilting company. Rather nice?

It is *awful*, not writing such an age. This is really bread upon the waters, to learn all about you: and a happy Christmas darling Diana, and 1,000 fond hugs & love from

Paddy x x x

P.S. Also from Joan.

P.P.S. Where's Iris? Do please send me news about all.

P.P.P.S. Who got the Duff prize?[4] I hate missing the only party I like.

[1] See previous letter.
[2] A play on words, deriving from Gregory's quip to Augustine about the English slave boys: '*Non Angli, sed Angeli.*'
[3] Robin Ironside (1912–65), painter, curator, writer, illustrator and designer.
[4] The Duff Cooper Prize, awarded annually since 1956 for works of non-fiction. PLF had won it for *Mani* in 1959. The winner in 1963 was Aileen Ward, for her biography of John Keats.

Almost a quarter of a century after writing the letter printed below, Paddy paid tribute to Aymer Maxwell in an obituary published in the Daily Telegraph. *'He was a sensitive plant, and the smaller the company, the happier he was.' Though he was shy and formal at first, 'his flair for the comic and the absurd could make tears flow, and with his kindness and hesitation, his cumulative backlog of shared laughter is certainly one of the things his friends will most miss.' His house on the steep shores of Euboea, 'with its pine forest and the ghost of Mt Parnassus beyond a sweep of sea' was 'the background for much reading and late nights and endless talk . . .' Like Paddy, Maxwell liked to surround himself with books, and could recite whole pages by heart. It was he who came up with the line from Louis MacNeice that became the title 'A Time of Gifts' − 'he put me forever in his debt'.*

To Aymer Maxwell   Kardamyli
27 July 1964   Messenia
                                                       Greece

Dear Aymer,

   It was simply maddening to discover at the Olympic Palace,[1]
when I got there on Thursday night, that you had been and gone
the day before. I had been hoping, as the plane left the firmament
from Paris, that I might strike lucky and lure you to a Tourkolimano[2]
banquet. I dashed here in a rush, having heard that the elusive owner
of the neighbouring, coveted plot with the water next door to ours,
was here. Of course he is not, but may loom later; so I could have
helped poor Joan drive out the vast Peugeot 404 station wagon,
loaded with emigrants' gear, tents, entrenching tools etc. She must be
bowling along the Adriatic coast by now, arriving here in a week or
so. I'm making a desperate attempt to decree a rustic pleasure dome[3]
à la Katounia meanwhile, to have somewhere to overflow from our
two Bedouin tents, until we know our fate about where, ultimately,
to build. It will be a great blow if we don't get the Naboth's
vineyard[4] next door, though what we have already got is lovely by
any normal standards. We feel rather like two trappers about to pitch
camp in the Yukon. Nothing but limestone, thistles, bushes and
thorns now run riot under the olive trees where our future mansion
(Doubting Castle? Blandings? Gatherum? Headlong Hall? No. 2, The
Pines?) will one day soar like an emanation. Thank heavens there are
excellent masons, lots of lovely stone as fissile as gorgonzola, old tiles
from ruined houses, slabs etc. All one needs. I plan to assemble a
jackdaw's heap of all this during the next few days: rather fun.

   You *must* try and sail up this gulf in *Dirk Hatterick*[5] sometimes
(even if all the prices go up in this primitive hamlet as a result). Will
you be at Katounia for the next month or so, or away in the
archipelago? It would be lovely to escape from our commitments
here for a day or two, should you be invadeable. Joan and I walked
right along Hadrian's Wall a month ago, with Robin Fedden and
Diana Campbell-Gray.[6] It was wonderful and very impressive, ending
with a swoop south and a luxurious Chatsworth recovery sojourn;

then wild shopping in London and an all too short Paris moment (where I left Joan); and here. I pine for news of developments on all the many fronts in the Katounia sector. Please give my greetings to all in their degree, and to all at the Taverna. No meatballs here, alas, tell Panayiota. How did G's confrontation with his Pyrenean love go?[7] I do hope they hadn't grown out of each other.

No more for the moment, except we must all contrive to meet soon here, in Katounia or in Athens. I wonder how all the slab-laying in your garden went? It's *avga matia* [fried eggs with tomatoes] time.

> Yours ever
> Paddy

SCENE: *A club. A clubman slumbers.*

VOICES (*Pianissimo*): We are the boys that make no noise . . .

CLUBMAN (*Waking abruptly*): Who are?

TWO TALLBOYS AND A DUMB WAITER: We are, sir.

CLUBMAN (*Relieved*): Thank heavens! You did give me a start! (*dozes off again*)

P.S. Would you be impressed if I told you I was elected to Whites[8] last month? No? I feared as much.

---

[1] An Athens hotel.

[2] A small harbour close to the port of Piraeus, known for its seafood tavernas.

[3] Cf. Kubla Khan: 'In Xanadu did Kubla Khan/A stately pleasure-dome decree . . .'

[4] Naboth's vineyard was coveted by Ahab, who was incited by his wife Jezebel to have Naboth executed. Ahab was rebuked by Elijah for his action.

[5] AM's yacht, named after the smuggler Dirk Hatteraick in Scott's novel *Guy Mannering* (1815).

[6] Diana Campbell-Gray (1909–92), née Cavendish, first married to the politician Robert Boothby, later Lord Boothby. Her second husband was Lieutenant Colonel the Hon. Ian Douglas Campbell-Gray. Later she would divorce him and marry Viscount Gage.

[7] Aymer's brother, Gavin; this sentence may refer to his beloved Pyrenean mountain dog.

[8] White's, the oldest and generally considered the most exclusive gentlemen's club in London.

The magazine Holiday *was willing to commission another article from Paddy, apparently undeterred by his failure to produce 'The Pleasures of Walking'. This offered an opportunity to visit Rumania, for the first time since before the war – and, more important, to be reunited with Balasha, whom he had last seen more than a quarter of a century earlier, though they had been in contact by letter. Her life since then had been hard. The Cantacuzène estates had been confiscated by the Communist regime. After trying and failing to escape from Rumania in 1947, Balasha, together with her sister Pomme and her brother-in-law Constantin, had been evicted from Băleni, with only fifteen minutes' notice, and resettled, first in Bucharest, and then in the town of Pucioasa, where they shared an attic studio. Although it was dangerous for them to be seen with a foreigner, they agreed to meet Paddy.*

This letter was written before his visit. Paddy was nervous about what he would find. Five years before, he had plucked up his courage to ask the Greek foreign minister if he might use his influence to help Balasha come to the West, as he explained in a letter to Debo Devonshire. 'She was over ten [sixteen] years older than me when I was twenty – so still must be! – which means over fifty-five (-six since last week). There was a faint chance of her getting out two years ago, but she didn't want to, because, after prison for two years (for trying to escape) and living in utter hardship as a pauper for fifteen years in forced residence & little to eat in a remote village, she said she dreaded seeing anyone again – painfully thin, teeth and hair dropping out fast. It's too awful. Poor Balasha! But I'm sure something could be done about all this, and thank heavens, there are several old friends who will cough up something to begin with. And indeed go on. She's a painter. She always adored Greece, and would probably want to settle here. How wonderful it would be if she did make it! We haven't met for twenty-two years. She used to be so beautiful.' A friend who had succeeded in getting out of Rumania had told Paddy that, 'in spite of all these calamities, she's quite unchanged in character, just as funny and intelligent and charming as ever' (In Tearing Haste, pages 80–3).

To Balasha Cantacuzène
20 April 1965   13 Chester Row, SW1

Darling B,

I'm so *dreadfully sorry* that you haven't heard from me before this. I wrote a very long letter about a month ago, or more, at the same time that I sent the parcel, and I suppose it must have gone astray as the parcel very nearly did, because of my idiotic mistake about the address. It's too sad! I do hope it turns up in the end. But never mind; with any luck I'll be seeing you soon (*if it's not a nuisance, that is!*), and I'll be able to tell you everything by word of mouth. I leave for Germany, the source of the Danube, in three or four days' time, to write a very long article about the history of the river for an American magazine, and will follow its course from Donaueschingen to the Delta, which takes me along a lot of the route of my early journey, and above all, to Rumania! I'm terrifically excited, and above all at the chance of seeing you all. I adored getting your marvellous letters (including Pomme's note) and also one from Ins.[1] What a *pity* about mine. There is no chance of my getting an answer before I leave. The best thing is to write to me in Vienna, % Sachers Hotel. (Why not? I won't stay at that lordly establishment, but they would keep letters if labelled 'to await arrival'.) I'll write to you from there when I'll know when I will be getting to Buc,[2] where I'll write to Ins at once. Do let me know if there is anything I can bring that might be a help; nothing very bulky, as I'm travelling light, and I can send anything larger you need by parcel later − pullovers etc.

Your letters are so gloriously unchanged, morale so high and serenity intact, it's miraculous. I think often and long of those marvellous years before the war and with enormous love and gratitude. It was really the beginning of life for me, and changed everything. How lucky I was! *Now*: bad news briefly. Mamie[3] died last year, having married Robert Mathias and lived very happily. Poor Prue[4] died ten years ago, a frightful loss, through that wretched illness in her back; but not painfully, and just as marvellous as she always had been. She was much beloved by a painter called Robert Beulah; but I don't think she ever quite got over Guy. Bill[5] you know all about (I have tried to ring him once or twice, but he seems to be away). Biddy[6] lives in Scotland, but is down here quite often, and we meet whenever we are both in London, which is not very often. She is as sweet as ever and quite unchanged. I went to Weston to Sachie & Georgia's last year, and know they would send their love, as we always talk about you a lot. I'll be able to tell you

all about Joan (not Jean!) when we meet. She's two years older than
me, fair haired, rather grave and beautiful looking, pretty shy, very
intelligent, devoted to literature, music, painting – not as an executant
– v. funny; *beaucoup de race* ['plenty of pedigree'], as they say, and
much loved by writers, painters, musicians, poets etc. She was called
Joan Eyres Monsell as a girl; rather short-sighted so wears *dark* glasses
a lot of the time, so's not to look it! She knows all about before we
first met – about nineteen years ago, isn't it extraordinary! – and
specially asked me to send her love. She left for Greece two weeks
ago, as I was held up here getting a book ready for press (called
Roumeli, about Greece, due out this autumn.[7] I'll send a copy.) We
are trying to build a small house there, in the S. Peloponnese, by the
sea among olives and I go there when my Danubian job is over.
She became a friend of Eileen and Matila[8] (he's absolutely shattered
by Eileen's death, alas. I will see him before I set off) and liked
Alexander [Mourouzi] very much. What heaven it was seeing him in
Athens! Just as nice and funny and charming as ever. I'm thoroughly
up to date with all your news, thanks to him, also, to a lesser extent,
through Nicky.[9]

I'm sending off all my books to you: 'The Traveller's Tree', 'A
Time to Keep Silence', 'The Violins of St Jacques', 'Mani', and a
book by my Cretan guide during the war (a shepherd) called 'The
Cretan Runner'. *The Traveller's Tree*, my first, which appeared ages ago,
is dedicated to you.

I won't write any more now, my darling B., as I do want this to
get off after all my false starts! Do write to me % Hot. Sacher,
Vienna, and write down the Greek Address, which is 'Kardamyli,
Messenia, Greece'.

Tons of fond love from
    Paddy

Also tremendous *bessonnades* to Pomme, and Ins x x x
    This is such a quick and careless letter. I wish you had got my
other long one!
    How fascinating that excerpt from my youthful diary.[10] It seems
such a short time ago.

1 Ina ('Ins') Catargi, née Donici, daughter of Princess Hélène ('Pomme') and her husband Constantin.

2 Bucharest.

3 Mamie Branch, Guy's mother. For the Branch family, see note 2 on page 6.

4 Prue Branch.

5 William Arthur Henry Cavendish-Bentinck (1893–1977), 7th Duke of Portland. His wife Clothilde, who had eloped with Balasha's husband, later divorced Bentinck on the grounds of adultery with Balasha.

6 Guy Branch's sister Biddy [Hubbard], who had visited PLF and BC at Băleni in the summer of 1938.

7 But not published until the following April.

8 Prince Matila Costiesco Ghyka (1881–1965), Rumanian novelist, mathematician, historian, philosopher and diplomat, married Eileen O'Connor, daughter of a British diplomat. An English-language edition of his memoir *The World Mine Oyster* was published by Heinemann in 1961, with an introduction by PLF.

9 Nicky Chrissoveloni, an old friend of Paddy's who had managed to get out of Communist-controlled Rumania thanks to the good offices of the Greek Foreign Minister.

10 See letter to Jock Murray [undated, winter, 1965], page 237.

'The great news is that I went to see B, Pomme and Constantin in their village (on the back of niece Ina's motorbike) and stayed there (only moving about outside after dark) for 24 hours,' Paddy wrote to Joan afterwards, while he was still in Rumania. 'Time and trouble have left visible marks on all (except Ina, fourteen when I left, now forty) but otherwise they were miraculously intact and there was lots of reminiscing and laughter. I'm so pleased I went; it was a momentous thing for everybody concerned. I haven't quite come round from it yet, half marvellous, half terribly sad and shattering.'

In reality he had been shocked to find Balasha, now in her mid sixties, worn down by hardship, 'a broken ruin' of her former self. Her sad state aroused in him feelings of both pity and gallantry.

To Balasha Cantacuzène   Kardamyli
15 November 1965   Messenia

IN HASTE

Balasha darling,

I've just got your letter of the 21st of Oct. – the one about Ileană
Sturdza [née Ghika]. If she's still there when I go, I'll make a bee-
line for her and do all I can – but it won't be for about a month,
alas. Athens seems about as remote from here as Bucharest did from
Băleni.

Also, by the same post, a marvellous surprise – i.e., a telegram
from A. Argyropoulos[1] saying he has brought a MS from you, written
thirty years ago – which must be those chapters on Greece that I
laboured away at in the octagonal library [at Băleni]. You *were* an
angel to save them. I can't think how you managed under the
circumstances. I long to get at them and see what they are like, but
will have to wait for that, too, until I go to Athens . . .

I've written to a very good bookshop in Chelsea – John Sandoe
Ltd, 10 Blacklands Terrace, Sloane Square, SW3 – and asked them to
send the two Brontë books and Chambers' Dictionary, which I
always use, and a fascinating book called *Brewer's Dictionary of Phrase
& Fable*, a positive treasure-house of amusing oddities. They are also
sending the two vols. of Painter's Life and Study of Proust, of which
the second vol. is just out.[2] I know you were never an admirer,
condemning him, as many people do, on the grounds of snobbery. I
have read clean through all the books twice, and isolated ones many
times since, and each time with greater wonder and admiration. Do
give him another chance as he was so many things beside the fairly
superficial defect of snobbery. The two vols. are simply fascinating;
incidentally, there is a lot about Rumanians in it, also pictures –
Antoine & Emmanuel B[3] (Marthe,[4] too, needless to say!), Anna de
Noailles,[5] Hélène Morand;[6] but the real interest is Proust himself and
the interrelation of his work and life. Do give him another chance!

I've also asked Sandoe's to send you (and of course it means
Pomme too) any books you ask for, in case I'm off in the wilds

somewhere; we'd better wait till I get their answer (I'm sure they will agree) but *please do use them*! It's awful being deprived of books, and I'd be so happy to think I was being a help about this; and rather sad if you don't use him.

Joan's back here, and sends her love. Rain and olive gathering have put a stop to building for a month or two. It has suddenly become very rough, windy and wild here, but it only lasts for a few days; then brilliant autumn days again and blazing starry nights.

Please forgive this untidy scrawl. More later on! Lots of fond love to you all from

    Paddy

---

[1] See next letter, page 237.

[2] George Painter's *Marcel Proust: A Biography* was published in two volumes, in 1959 and 1965. It was awarded the Duff Cooper Prize.

[3] Prince Antoine Bibesco (1878–1951) and his brother Emmanuel (1874–1917). The Bibescos were close friends with Marcel Proust, to the extent that they even shared a secret language of their own devising. PLF knew Princess Priscilla Helen Alexandra Bibesco (1920–2004), the daughter of Prince Antoine and his wife Elizabeth (herself daughter of the British prime minister, H. H. Asquith).

[4] Marthe, Princess Bibesco (1886–1973), née Lahovary, writer and socialite, a Rumanian exile in France.

[5] Anna, Comtesse Mathieu de Noailles (1876–1933), French writer of Rumanian extraction. Proust wrote her sentimental letters.

[6] Hélène Morand (1879–1975), née Chrissoveloni, was Proust's last love. After his death she divorced her husband, Prince Dimitri Soutzo, and married his friend, Paul Morand.

By the winter of 1965 Paddy was in the final stages of work on Roumeli, *the follow-up to* Mani, *which would be published in 1966.*

To Jock Murray   Kardamyli
undated [winter 1965?]   Messenia

Dear Jock,

    Here, at long and terrible last, are the Introduction and the map. I won't describe all the upheavals that have delayed things – sudden loss of our rooms in Kalamata, shifting & storing furniture, rains at Kardamyli, breaking camp, finding rooms in the village etc., with a plague of other minor things connected with hours, workmen, architects, delays, false starts, postponements, etc. I'm dreadfully sorry about this.

This is the fourth Introduction I've written. The others were long, rambling and diffuse, and it occurred to me on reading each in turn, enough to put anyone off reading the book. My reaction to any demand for writing at this moment seems to be to dig an enormous bog and flounder in it for a year. I hope this final version doesn't seem *too* short.

The number of places where the book has been worked on, at the end, is meant to be something of a joke. One might put them in tiny italics in a line running right across the bottom of the page?

At the beginning of the 'South of the Gulf' chapter, could we insert, if it's not too late, the sentence 'Perhaps they were after lobster too,' just before the last sentence, describing a horrible meal in Astakos, which the cats turn up their noses at? Idiotically, I have somehow left my set of proofs with the stored luggage in Kalamata, so I can't quote the actual words.

Now, the *map*. Johnny[1] left me a roughly traced outline and the map he traced it from. On the tracing paper I have put the regional names – provinces, mountain-ranges, islands, seas etc. – which ought to be shown, and on the map I have underlined the place names which ought to come in, and, on a sheet of foolscap, the spellings where the map ones differ from the books. ROUMELI, and also KRAVARA should be shown in a very vague way, I think, and the difference between plain and mountain indicated; but I don't think many details are needed. I've talked a lot about it in Athens and Johnny's ideas seemed very good. I love his cover.

Alas, Abyssinia is out, I'm afraid. I daren't move away from here for long while the house is being built – they have such strange and erratic ideas. My plan is to come home just before Christmas and stay three to four weeks, then back here. My immediate plan is to finish my Danube article now – long overdue, and as you can imagine, much, much too long, and the delay bringing much airmail obloquy across the Atlantic ocean – and then at last, give the death blow to *Shanks's Europe* (*Walking Back? Parallax?*).[2] I wonder if the heroine who was struggling with the MSs has finished it (I'm in a fine position to ask questions like this). I ask with especial sympathy as I'm teaching myself to type and frequently find myself flummoxed by a thicket of indecipherable text, corrections, and balloons. It used to take me an hour per page, it is now down to thirty-five minutes – copying, I mean, I could never do it direct – so she has all my sympathy. However well she has done it, it is bound to be full of mistakes so I implore you not to look at it. I fondly hope that this is going to change everything. In future I will type out each day's work in the evening, and hand over a corrected typescript to a proper pro when each book is finished.

An extraordinary thing happened when I was in Rumania. My old friend Balasha Cantacuzène (dedicatee of T's Tree) managed to salvage, when she was turned out of her house in Moldavia by the communists in the middle of the night at the end of the war, an inch-thick diary[3] I kept on the Great Trudge, covering Bratislava to Bucharest, the Iron Gates to Vidin, all Bulgaria, Bucharest, and the Black Sea Coast as far as Constantinople, including a month in the city. I am surprised how close my reconstruction of it is to this jotted – sometimes very extensively – account, and fascinated by the occasional divergences and lacunae. Nevertheless, I think I'll let the later version stand, though the last bit will be a help for the part that remains unwritten – so have no qualms! Now, suddenly this evening, comes a telegram from Argyropoulos, the retiring Greek ambassador in Bucharest, that Balasha handed over to him an enormous wad of manuscript, which must be chapters of a work I began to write in Rumania about crossing Macedonia and Thrace on horseback during the Venizelist revolution,[4] when I was twenty. I must have written them in 1939, before coming here. I don't think there's much to be done with them, but I long to see them as a curiosity. Strange, these sudden resurrections, and a bit disconcerting.

Well no more for the present, Jock, except great contrition for being such a terrible stumbling block. Do let me know that the enclosed have arrived safely – I had a slightly anxious time about the fate of the proofs, for which the postal strike here was entirely to blame.

We broke camp three weeks ago, owing to the rain, and are now in the little hotel at Kardamyli. It is pouring with rain, the sea pounds away outside, the Milano Sierra butane-gas lamp hisses at my elbow.

Yours ever
    Paddy

Many greetings to your son John.

I can't bear the photo on the back of the cover. I wish we could find something better, and I will have a hunt.

---

1 The neo-romantic artist John Craxton (1922–2009) travelled extensively in Greece after the war, particularly in Crete, where he would eventually settle. He painted the covers and prepared the maps for PLF's books.

2 The book about PLF's 'Great Trudge', eventually published as *A Time of Gifts*.

3 '[I]n Rumania, in a romantic and improbable way too complicated to recount, I recovered a diary I had left in a country-house there in 1939' (*A Time of Gifts*, page 248).

4 An attempted *coup d'état* against the Greek government in March 1935.

Though Paddy's affair with Ricki Huston had ended some years earlier, he would remain in intermittent contact with her until her sudden death in a car accident in 1969.

To Ricki Huston   as from Olympic Palace Hotel
undated [1965?]   Athens

Darling Ricki,

Many thanks for both letters, which arrived two days running, a tremendous treat for Kalamata, a town nobody writes to. I think people are subconsciously repelled by the letter K. It's the reverse of the letter X, which always goes to people's heads. Perhaps if sex were spelt seks or segs there wouldn't be half so much fuss about it: nothing very glamorous about segs kittens or seksual intercourse but write 'sex killer slays six' and you're in business . . .

Here's another *Eh, soul ill, oak we?*[1] I fear there may be one or

two minor differences as I haven't got the original text – tegst –
handy . . .

No more now, as I want this to get off. I leave for Athens in a
few days and then London, within a week or two, so see you and
pretty Allegra[2] then.

Lots of love from
    Paddy

P.S.

The Oracle

When shall I meet her after dark?
When the clothes horse neighs and the fire dogs bark.

When will she love me all her days?
When the fire dogs bark and the clothes horse neighs.

When will my handsome Pete come back?
When the batsman's duck begins to quack.

When shall I know how she really *feels*?
When the fishplates swim and the pig iron squeals.

When shall I know who loves me best?
When the dockside crane constructs its nest.

When shall I see my darling Dick?
When Crompton's mule[3] begins to kick.

When shall I hear from my pretty Jo?
When the dog leg lifts and the ballcocks crow.

When shall I and my true love meet?
When the battering ram begins to bleat.

When shall I make her mend her ways?
The day when the donkey-engine brays.

When shall I be in bed with her?
When the cat o' nine tails starts to purr.

How shall I tell the stroke of Doom?
Bow Bells' bang and Big Ben's boom.

and so on . . . !

¹ A soliloquy.
² Allegra Huston (b. 1964), RH's daughter from her affair with John Julius Norwich.
³ A machine used for spinning cotton.

To Balasha Cantacuzène   Kardamyli
3 July 1966   Messenia

Post leaving! please forgive this uncorrected screed.

Balasha, darling,
    I feel *so awful* not having written for so long – not through not
wanting to (far from it!), but waiting for the right moment to settle
down and write a proper answer to your lovely ones; so do please
forgive and don't think me faithless or callous, because it's exactly the
opposite really – just a *very bad case* of *le mieux étant l'ennemi du bien*
[the perfect being the enemy of the good]. I *must* cure myself of this,
because, judging by me, what one wants is news and a sign, however
brief; lovely long letters if possible, but not silence and neither. I
seem to get fixations about letters – I mean letters to people one
adores – longing for the time, the place and the state of mind all
miraculously to coincide and join forces in producing exactly the
kind of letter one wants to send and thinks would please at the
other end; especially with you. I remember so well how seriously
you read, think about, and enjoy them: all the characteristics, in fact,

that make you such a good and thoughtful letter writer. So *my*
periods of seeming pen-paralysis are perhaps prompted by
subconscious vanity, which is absurd. So to hell with that, and here
goes, sitting under an olive with masons charging up and down
ladders, hammers thumping all round, stones crashing and mortar
sloshing and Niko Kolokotrones, the master mason – and, since three
weeks, Joan's and my *koumbaros* [god-brother] (godson is called
Yorgo-Mihali) – dashing up every now and then with questions. I do
hope the house turns out all right. The stone, chopped out of the
mountainside a quarter of a mile away, and brought here by mule, as
there's only a goat path, is such a lovely colour, that it can't be ugly.
We've managed to find a lot of old and faded tiles, discoloured
russet; so with luck, the whole thing will melt into the surroundings
and almost disappear. We have got two beehives, and Joan disappears
just like Pomme at Băleni with mask – not a fencing one, alas! – and
smoke gun. I don't know when we'll be able to move in. Everything
takes such ages. Meanwhile, we are installed in the tiny hotel in the
village, but have lunch under an archway of the house, bathe, sleep,
then I try to do some work, and when the workmen go, and
everything's quiet, we drink and talk and sometimes play the
gramophone and watch the sun set across the Messenian gulf and
then go back to the village when it's dark, and have an awful dinner
in the local taverna washed down by the worst retsina in all Greece.
But the village and the country are so beautiful that it doesn't matter
a bit. I think the villagers are beginning to like and trust us. After
the first delighted welcome, which one always finds in Greece, a
period of *méfiance* [suspicion] reigned: what on earth were we up to?
Spying? Lunacy? Planning some dreadful scheme? They are very
suspicious of themselves and each other and everything in the Mani,
and the mountain villages are a network of feuds – no longer mortal
ones, thank God, slander, claustrophobia and the feeling of isolation,
changing values and abandonment, as most of the young people
emigrate to Germany, temporarily, to work in factories, or
permanently to Canada and Australia and, if they are allowed in,
America. As all they long to do is to get away, no wonder they are
puzzled by seemingly sophisticated Europeans settling in what seems

to them so wild and God-forsaken a place and all our talk of
beautiful mountains, sea, rocks and light must sound like madness.
But, thank God, the initial distrust is slowly evaporating and we are
beginning to be taken for granted and I hope even liked.

The thing I really dread is that the beauty of the place should
prove its undoing. You've no idea, darling, of what a ghastly plague
tourism is turning out to be; I've touched on it a bit in *Roumeli*, but
it's much worse than that. Athens has become, except in winter, a
slight nightmare, and outside it, and in some of the most beautiful
parts, things are happening which would fill you with horror. I hate
to think of all the Greek rustic virtues being slowly eroded by
creeping Western exploitation. It is still intact here, touch wood, but
danger hovers. Meanwhile, one must give thanks for every day,
month, year of reprieve.

I'm terribly excited by your kind words about *Roumeli*;[1] I thought
of you very often when writing it, and I love to think of you
reading it with such penetration and getting every single point. After
all, one only writes, really, for about half a dozen people, and trusts
to luck that some others might like it and even buy it! . . .

Niko [Ghika] is a heavenly man, tall and Stravinsky-esque in
appearance, and, I think, a brilliant painter, one of the only ones who
has managed to convey Greece, the most unpaintable country in the
world, on canvas. Rather solemn, thoughtful, generous and kind . . .
Barbara is a fascinating person, sister of Jeremy Hutchinson[2] (do you
remember? Guy's great Oxford friend, who Biddy had had a
youthful *schwärmerei* for [crush on]? He came to Earl's Walk once or
twice), daughter of the judge St John Hutchinson and Mary H.,
half-Strachey, very high Bloomsbury, francophile bluestocking, a great
love of Clive Bell's for years, up to her neck in the world of Virginia
Woolf, Duncan Grant, Lytton Strachey, Aldous Huxley etc. She –
Barbara – is beautiful, intuitive, full of flair, with a great gift for
friendship, and side-splittingly funny; first married to Lord
Rothschild, an odd, eccentric, brilliant physicist and Cambridge don;
then to Rex Warner, the novelist, poet and Greek scholar and
translator (a great pal of ours), and finally to Niko; setting, I may say,
many hearts on fire in between whiles. The first marriage produced a

tall and serious son – heir to the famous banking house in England – and two beautiful, unusual and gifted daughters . . .

How wretched about that horrid dream. But here I am! Do tell me what it was; because, oddly I was indirectly involved in a vendetta[3] – all over now – and was nearly shot at from behind a rock in Crete (all part of war-goings-on!). I know how awful such dreams can be.

No more for now, Balasha darling, as I want this interim letter to get off. There are lots of questions to answer, and lots more to say, so I'll do better in a few days' time. Meanwhile, tons of fondest love, and also to Pomme & Constantin.

from Paddy

xxx

---

[1] In a long, undated letter, BC had enthused about 'your beautiful *Roumeli*'.

[2] Jeremy Nicolas Hutchinson (b. 1915), lawyer, worked on the defence team in the Lady Chatterley trial in 1960 and became a QC in 1961. He was married to the actress Peggy Ashcroft (1940–66).

[3] With Yorgo Tsangarakis (see pages 311–14).

To Xan Fielding   Kardamyli
nearly mid July 1966   Messenia

Ξάν, χρυσό μου [My dear Xan],

Κακὸ χρόνο νἄχω ποὺ ἄργησα τόσο πολὺ νὰ σ' ἀπαντήσω! [Curse me for being so late in replying to you!] Things have been in such a flat spin here that I've kept postponing an answer to your marvellous letter, and you know how it is! But I can't tell you how bucked I was by the nice things you said about *Roumeli* and I have been luxuriantly basking in the afterglow ever since. All this was squared or cubed by the thought that you were one of the very few people to read the book who were qualified to grasp scores of things that must have been double-Dutch to many readers. I absolutely agree about the v. constructive criticisms too. It's awful the way one gets certain words or groups of words into one's head and up they come *à chaque bout de change* [at every turn] irrespective of appropriateness or irrelevance!

'Horny hands' – it's too awful! For many a long year I could scarcely write a page that didn't contain the words 'trajectory', 'parabola', and 'ambience'; now 'h.h.' has taken over, but I hope only temporarily. Perhaps one could switch these defaced counters round: 'The cigarette smouldered in his parabola'; 'The shell traversed the battlefield with a wide and horny hand'; 'The arch crossed the back lane with its horny hand'; 'The horny hand in the crowded synagogue was stifling'; 'The rainbow's ambience was taut and multicoloured'; 'His ambience rasped on the axe-helm'; 'Affected by the trajectory, he cupped his parabolas and stopped the ball's horny hand in mid-ambience', etc. Perhaps one should find two words as different as possible in every way, and try the same kind of switch e.g. an anvil and an hour: 'I hammered the hour an anvil ago'; 'Two and a half anvils had passed before Miss Mossop heard the clang of the hour' – nearly all right. 'The heavy anvils dragged past interminably before Harriet heard the negro strike the hour!' OK . . . To hell with all this.

I think I've shot my bolt about Greece for the time being and plan to finish your book – the one Andrew calls 'Shanks's Europe' – and then try to launch out on something completely imaginary but I'm not quite sure what.

Geo K[atsimbalis] – also Janetta, who has just been here – says wonderful things about your new house.[1] It does sound heavenly. I love Uzès and all the country round, and Joan and I, as we settle down to the cold fried potatoes, the almost tasteless mullet of the Messenian Gulf and the ghastly local retsina, munch wistfully, thinking of the marvels that must be sizzling and glowing on your plates, at the same time and only a few meridian of longitude away . . . Larry [Durrell]'s house sounds amazing and enormous (I'm writing to him by the same post equally in answer to a kind *Roumeli* letter.) Building passion seems to have us all by the throat. The *walls* of ours are up, and rafters are beginning to sprout, and tiles to pile up under the olives; but it'll be many a long month before we're in it. Everything here is hard and slow, in spite of a heavenly master-mason called Niko Kolokotrones (!),[2] now Joan's and my god-brother. I think the house will be terribly nice, thanks to the lovely surroundings – on a ledge of olives between a little bay and tall russet-coloured mountains – and, once in, we'll be able to do something about the food and the drink. We long for you both to see it. There's quite a nice little hotel in the village, rather surprisingly, which we live in until we can force an entry. Much better than our former down-at-hell 1925 jazz-Vorticist flat in boiling Kalamata, above the waterfront and an avenue of jujube trees not far from the scene of our semi-submarine feast.[3]

I ought to have written *ages* ago about the marvellous shower of gold[4] suddenly cascading down like Zeus in disguise on the cowering Danaë![5] It's really wonderful news and it has filled anyone who has ever spoken of it with *unalloyed delight* – a high tribute, when one thinks of the undisguisable sorrow that the good luck of others inflicts on most! It's not only marvellous, but a singularly dashing reversal of fortune, far too bold and far-fetched for use in a novel. Amy [Smart] says there are maddening delays; hard to think of more exasperating torment, but never mind. Τοῦτος ὁ ἀνήφορος κατήφορο θὰ φέρει [This uphill will lead to a downhill].

V. v. many thanks again for kind words about *Roumeli*. Do begin to formulate plans about a return to Greece, and a descent here, and encourage Larry to do the same. Meanwhile tons of fond love & hugs to you & Daph

from Paddy

---

[1] After living in Portugal and Tangier (and briefly in the Cévennes), Xan and Daphne Fielding had settled in a farmhouse near Uzès in southern France, not far from Lawrence Durrell.

[2] Kolokotrones was the name of a famous Greek general and leader in the war of independence against Turkish rule.

[3] One very hot day in 1946 Paddy, Joan, Xan and Daphne had carried the restaurant table waist-deep into the sea and eaten there.

[4] XF had launched a court case to recover money owing on a house in Nice where he had been brought up. PLF's congratulations were premature: the case was protracted, and the shower became a trickle at best.

[5] Danaë, a princess of Argos in the Peloponnese, was locked away in a subterranean bronze chamber by her father. Her prison, however, was easily infiltrated by Zeus, who impregnated her in the guise of a golden shower. She conceived and bore him a son, the hero Perseus.

To Jock Murray   Kardamyli
24 September 1966   Messenia

Dear Jock,

   Jane Boulenger[1] sent me two copies of the American *Roumeli*,
asking me what to do with the others in London. The answer is,
burn them. Do please write to Canfield and find out what has
happened, and, above all, sever all connections that may exist between
Harper's and me and make sure that never again do they have
anything to do with me or mine. They have written asking me to
write something – I don't know who or what for – about a new
Mount Athos book they are doing. I'm not writing to them yet, as
my letter would be too intemperate for comprehension; but I will:
when the indignation and fury have simmered down to some
semblance of articulacy.

   Surely the only condition on which we let them publish the
book, after their slovenly exploit with *Mani*, was that they should
manufacture an entirely new book and thus be compelled to take
some trouble about it. Expecting this, and waiting to hear from them,
I had drawn up a long list of all the errors and misprints in an
edition, also a number of deletions and additions and some important
changes. I assumed that we would go through the normal routine of
galley- and page-proofs. But *not a single word* did I get from them,
and the first news of this American book reached me in this
revolting *fait accompli*, replete with all the blemishes and blunders that
contrived to find their way into the English edition: doubly glaring,
and shaming here, because uncorrected; and, above all, *identical*; down
to the off-hand shoving of the dedication to a left-hand page mainly
occupied with small-type information about copyright and other
trade matters. (For me a dedication is like throwing a cloak over
someone's balcony before a bullfight; it's distressing to find it hanging,
as it were, in the staff-lavatory.)

   There were a tremendous number of misprints in the English
edition which were quite non-existent in the final page proofs;
they even invaded the running captions – I was particularly
longing for the ridiculous BAR RUINED CHAIRS[2] to be

redeemed. (Perhaps compositors are not expected to know the Sonnets by heart; but surely they might have thought there was something odd here?) *But here they all are*, all the ludicrous slip-shod errors, punctiliously, slavishly and illiterately reproduced in this repulsive book; *every single one*. I went from page to page with growing dismay and fury and when I got to Bar Ruined Chairs, pitched the book from the top of the cliff as far out to sea as I could throw.

Why didn't they give me a chance to correct all this? Why didn't they rectify some of the obvious howlers themselves? Have they merely photographed the English edition? If so, this is a direct breach of the one condition on which we let them have it. The alignment, pagination, type, etc. look suspiciously similar. *If so, what can we do about it?* The whole thing is a disgrace, and I am delighted to think that this disaster rules out any further connection with these callous, and, it seems to me, underhand people. Cold comfort. I begin to understand why they didn't write.

The whole thing is mysterious and shattering. Do, please, throw some light on it if you can and suggest what we ought to do.

Yours ever, but in bewilderment and disarray,

Paddy

P.S. Perhaps it would be best to send them a copy of this letter to prepare them for the more lucid one which is beginning to take shape in my mind.

P.P.S. George Bonthorpe[3] writes that the income tax people need £50 quickly, and I owe them £20, it seems. He also says you have got about £100 in hand for me − so could you please hand them over to him for these two noble causes . . . Do, please, for heaven's sake let the Bank have anything that comes in as they are kicking up a terrible fuss. It's rather urgent. Forgive haste!

---

[1] Originally John Murray's secretary; then in charge of foreign rights.

[2] The running head on page 93 of *Roumeli* should have read 'Bare ruin'd choirs', a quotation from Shakespeare's Sonnet 73:

> 'That time of year thou mayst in me behold
> When yellow leaves, or none, or few, do hang
> Upon those boughs which shake against the cold,
> Bare ruin'd choirs, where late the sweet birds sang.'

3 Presumably PLF's accountant.

To Ann Fleming   Kardamyli

7 November 1966   Messenia

Darling Annie,

The state of play about this place at the moment is like Dr Johnson & the Giant's Causeway: worth seeing, but not worth coming to see. The house still has not a safe roof and few walls. *If* you were coming to Greece I'd be awfully sad if you didn't come here, but there is too little to offer at the moment, except the heavenly view, to inflict the trip on anyone. There is a nice little hotel with an awful loo, whatever food one can find in the village is pretty hopeless (Joan did some heavenly cooking in a rush hut). Some parts of Greece, and this is one, are so backward they don't know the difference between nice and nasty. I long for you to have another excuse to come to Greece, as I can't wait for you to see this place, however unfinished. The hotel will be empty any moment now, or you could doss down in Joan's tent, and we could live happily like neighbouring sheikhs. So, if you have the *faintest urge* to head for Greece, it would be the *greatest possible treat* for me. If you *did*, the decks will be clear any second now as far as work goes, and we could go for a lovely spin in the Mani or Peloponnese. The weather is lovely, with a hint of autumn after the blaze – and then the unprecedented short deluge, cruel to tent-dwellers – of August . . .

I think the house will be very pretty, in its rough Maniot way, chiefly because of the simple, solid, rather noble local style and the great beauty of the rock out of which it is built – a mixture of light grey, gold, pink and russet, wonderfully harmonious and happy in juxtaposition. So far, there is only a huge cistern 12 feet deep, over

which a loggia with three, I must say, massive and beautiful arches
sheltering the well head, roofed with many beams and reed; a
thick-walled room, and a cool and roomy cellar with an arched vault,
and, outside, an outdoor staircase running across one side, over a
steep arched entry to the cellar – later to be filled with barrels – to
where one wing of the eventually L-shaped house will rest on top of
what is already built, the other wing extending across a rocky olive
terrace. So what we now have is below the ultimate ground level.
Here's a v. rough sketch of what it may look like in the end.

The part filled in in ink is the only part which is actually up; not
much, as you see. It looks big, but will, eventually, have only 3
bedrooms, perhaps 4, a nice kitchen, 1 bath, 2 or 3 showers, 3 loos, a
gallery – & in picture, a nice wide corridor, and a nice big drawing
room (X to X) with a square jutting bay window B. As you see, the
wall has a stone circular window in it, cribbed from those oriels at
Stanway.[1] We'll have to add another room and a studio, if it can be
managed; but a bit later. The ceiling is about to go on the part
already built. The outside walls are about a yard thick, which makes
lovely slanting window embrasures, and, we hope, cool as a tomb in
midsummer, heatable in the mild winters. The masons and workmen
are marvellous chaps, terribly excited about what they are up to, and
enormous fun; all from the nearby hill villages. My regime is Spartan
since Joan left three days ago, but helped out by figs, which I pick

on rising between five and six, marvellously cool; and by cantaloupes which cut like Cuban sunsets.

As you see, there's not much to offer for so ruinous a trip, so I feel I ought not to lure you with too glowing an account; but should you rashly risk it, or succumb to some magnetism more rewarding in comfort and *then* come here – or vice versa to recuperate – it would be the most tremendous treat to me. Every syllable which might sound like discouragement is dictated by the most quixotic altruism.

The wasps and hornets are beginning to vanish, thank heavens; they are terrified of us, but think it's all right if they don't make us angry. Lots of very big, handsome grasshoppers and a small advance guard of mantises; a few cyclamen out, *lots of olives*, some butterflies with queer-shaped wings so that [they] look as if they were flying backwards. A quite large, very old tortoise rustles within earshot, moving through the dead grass as slow as a glacier.

Well, darling Annie, that's about all for the moment. I expect you'll see Joan, who'll tell you more. It's moonlight now, three-quarters, expanding round the little islands and rocks in shiny silver discs, and crickets have taken over from cicadas, a higher but steadier note.

with heaps of love

from Paddy

xxxx

P.S. I've just finished rereading Evelyn's *Men at Arms* trilogy.[2] I hated it when it first appeared; it now seems really wonderful, fearfully sad, very funny, absolutely true, very grand indeed. I think the difference in mood, tempo, scope, and its appearing in driblets, must have put me wrong the first time.

---

[1] Stanway in Gloucestershire, owned by the Charteris family, where Ann Fleming spent much of her childhood.

[2] PLF means Waugh's 'Sword of Honour' trilogy, of which the first novel is *Men at Arms*, published in 1952. The other two are *Officers and Gentlemen* (1955) and *Unconditional Surrender* (1961).

On 21 April 1967, just a month before a general election, a group of right-wing army officers ('the Colonels') seized power in Greece. The coup d'état, *which followed a period of constitutional crisis, came as a complete surprise. The coup leaders placed tanks in strategic positions in Athens, effectively gaining complete control of the city. At the same time, a large number of small mobile units were dispatched to arrest those suspected of left-wing sympathies, from lists prepared in advance. The constitution was suspended, allowing citizens to be arrested without warrant and tried by military court. By the early morning all Greece's prominent politicians, including the acting prime minister, had been taken into custody.*

To Joan Rayner   La Tartana
27 April [1967]   Marbella
                                                      Prov. de Málaga

Darling,

It seems ludicrous only to be writing now, but everything has been so dislocated and delayed by events inside Greece that mails are ten times slower than they were before. I sent you a telegram from Kardamyli the night before the *coup d'état* (saying I was coming here yesterday), and days later the Post Office people said it had come back from Athens because every telegram in a foreign language has to have a vernacular translation appended. I also sent one from Kalamata, and another from Athens, but wonder whether they ever reached you.

The queer thing about the recent events in Greece is that you probably know more about it than I do. All internal newspapers stopped, Athens radio gave out nothing but official bulletins, no foreign papers came into the country.

I first heard of it at 1 o'clock on the day of the putsch, when Lela[1] came from the village, where she'd gone to get a loaf; dashed up like Cassandra saying a Dictatorship had been declared and that the gendarmerie were bringing down Communists from the mountain villages in handcuffs after arresting them in the middle of the night – two, in fact from Tseria (one of which was that dark Petro, who made such a mess of building the outside stairs. Paraskevá

of Proástion was also arrested. I don't know anything about Capt.
Charn, I hope not). Junior and Petro were enlisted in the T.E.A.
militia,[2] – the former most unwillingly – for temporary service,
probably over now. Absolute calm – indeed stunned bewilderment –
reigned everywhere. For a *coup d'état*, it was ontologically perfect – no
bloodshed, no resistance or time for it, complete *fait accompli*. Nobody
knew anything in the provinces. Athens, when I got there, was a
tangle of mutually exclusive rumours. I got the definite impression
that the Mani and the provinces in general, were *pro* – though
heaven knows what I base this on – and Athens split up into 100
different attitudes.

Shan[3] thought, unwillingly, that it was absolutely necessary, because
of the threat of the big Papandreou[4] rally in Salonica, where troubles
with the police were all laid on, clashes, martyrs, *perhaps* a takeover of
Macedonia in the north à la Venizelos, even invitation to the
thousands of ex-ELAS[5] partisans to cross the Iron Curtain with guns
in hand and then the finally [*sic*] splitting of the country into two
rival halves, hence civil war. A lot of people voice various versions of
this: others say it is balls, and that there is no possible *raison d'état* for
the coup whatever. All the leaders are unknown. Neither the King
nor Kanellopoulos[6] knew anything whatever. There have been no
blows – at least, as far as I know – no bloodshed – at least as far as I
know – or anything like that, but far more arrests than announced: a
whole busload – fifty? – from our hill villages, 3,000 they say from
the whole of Messenia – so from the whole of Greece it must be
enormous; some hazard 100,000.

George [Seferis] was not obtainable in Athens – perhaps away for
the one and a half days I was there before departure, but apart from
Shan all our friends were anti. I had dinner at Magouche's with Nico
& Vana,[7] whose flat had been raided by reluctant soldiers – like the
extremely apologetic soldiery who asked for my papers and possible
sporting guns on the way to Athens. (Getting an exit visa was less of
a toil than I had dreaded.) Lambrakis[8] (*don't tell Nico*) hid out for a
couple of days in the flat. The President of your bank is arrested! – I
mean, the top one. The King and all the regular politicians are dead
against.

I don't know what to think. All my spontaneous sympathies (in spite of my official views generally) are against the coup, largely because those in the provinces who welcome it are exactly the petit bourgeois, extreme right philistine, Poujadist,[9] *bakali* [grocer's]-assistant, philistine, ex-peasant class – the businessmen of Kalamata, in fact – that are the people one likes least in Greece. But, whether the thing is good or bad, the more it is criticised and disapproved of in the foreign press (which they care about like hell), the better, more moderate it will be. The King's being taken as much by surprise as everyone else, and his genuine reluctance about the [illegible], is excellent. *If* it was a temporary measure till the election in a calm atmosphere can take place, there is perhaps a case to be argued in [favour]. But the longer it lasts, the less in favour there is to be said. The dotty sumptuary laws about church, dress,[10] morality in general, strike a chill. It's the quantity of hit and miss arrests and banishment to islands without trial that fill one with the most horror & disgust. There is talk of [illegible] trials and release impending.

I'm so sorry, darling, to give you such a fragmentary and garbled account.

Magouche – revelling in all as you can imagine, half Scarlet Pimpernel, half Pasionaria[11] – but a great boon to many – drove me to the aerodome; and here I am in the calm liberal atmosphere of Spain.[12] I've got to finish this in a rush as Janetta & I are just off to Seville by car to meet Jaime, so I must shut up. It is veiled and cloudy here, but the hint of better weather on the way. I feel rather lone and gloomy, not really in a Spanish mood, but it's lovely to be with Janetta, sweet, quiet & kind as ever. I'm not wild about the slight expatriate group feeling of Marbella. I'll tell you more of all in a few days. Meanwhile, 1,000 tons of love darling, *I miss you like anything*. All goes well in the house.

xxxxxxx
    Paddy

P.S. Could you ask Meyrowitz[13] to make me two prs of half-moon glasses.

P.P.S. Do, if you have time, bring a few lengths of different coloured material – perhaps sari-type stuff from Liberty's or one or more of the many oriental slips for Covering Cushions, as our nice divans are going to need it.

1 Lela Yannakea, housekeeper/cook. She and her husband Petros performed a wide range of domestic tasks for PLF and Joan.

2 The TEA (Tagmata Ethnikis Asphaleias – National Security Battalions), an anti-Communist militia.

3 The former journalist Alexander 'A. C.' Sedgwick (1901–96), who lived in Greece during his retirement. He had been Athens correspondent for the *New York Times* before and after the Second World War.

4 Georgios Papandreou (1888–1968), three times prime minister of Greece (1944–5, 1963, 1964–5), long-serving liberal politician who first served as a cabinet minister in 1923. His dismissal as prime minister in 1965 began the period of political polarisation and instability that led to the Colonels' coup. He died under house arrest a year later. His son Andreas served two terms as prime minister (1981–9 and 1993–6).

5 The military arm of the Communist-dominated National Liberation Front, formed to resist the German occupying forces, which played a part in the Greek Civil War.

6 Panagiotis Kanellopoulos (1902–86), prime minister deposed in the coup.

7 Nico Hadjimichalis, the architect responsible for the house at Kardamyli, and his wife Vana.

8 Christos Dimitrios Lambrakis (1934–2009), owner of one of the largest newspaper groups in Greece. His publications always supported progressive and left-wing causes.

9 The Poujadist movement, named after its leader Pierre Poujade (1920–2003), articulated the economic interests and grievances of French shopkeepers and other proprietor-managers of small businesses disquieted by economic and social change.

10 The new regime banned miniskirts.

11 Isidora Dolores Ibárruri Gómez (1895–1989), known as 'La Pasionaria', Republican heroine of the Spanish Civil War (1936–9).

12 Spain had been ruled by a military dictatorship since a civil war in the 1930s.

13 An old-established Paris opticians.

To Joan Rayner   Kardamyli
undated [autumn 1967]   Messenia

Darling Joan,

Lovely news of your return! I'll be there to meet you, unless something awful happens, probably going a day or two before to Athens, so if in doubt, send times etc., to the O.P.[1] as well as here.

Diana [Cooper]'s visit was a great success. I met her at the airport last Saturday, and put her into your room, and had everything looking very nice. She adored the house, had no idea it was going to be nearly as splendid or attractive. She seemed rather tired I thought, had had a fall or two in Spetsai. I dreaded her wandering off into the rocks and blessed our sea-steps doing their true function!

Next morning – Sunday – there was a terrible noise of a helicopter whirling across the sky. I dashed into D's room – she said that Niarchos had said he might come over with some of Anne Tree's guests, but hardly without announcing it; so, when the thing disappeared N[orth], I forgot about it, [and] went on working: till looking out of the window, I saw Stavro, Anne and Nancy Lancaster[2] wandering about under the trees with the chief of police and the doctor. The machine had landed beside the war memorial in the middle of the marvelling Sabbath strollers. Sensation! The chief got the Dr to drive them up here in his new car. Luckily, I'd got a chicken and lots of grub for Diana, which, with delicious rice, Lela sat about turning into a lovely luncheon. The machine, meanwhile, had gone back to Spetsopoula for the Canfields,[3] and this time, landed just the other side of our little bay, on plot A, among the olives in the field just under Butlins.[4] Stavro said if we needed any extra food or anything, the pilot would go and fetch it from Spetsopoula! Luckily, no need. The admiration of the house was tremendous, specially by Anne, and above all by Nancy Lancaster, who is a great expert. After a very cheerful and good lunch, the pilot took Lela, little Stavro, her mother and me up on a trip round the island, up the hillside over Proástion; it was rather marvellous. They left again about dusk, leaving us all in a state of slight amazement. All Kardamyli, as you can imagine, was set by its ears with wonder.

D. left on Tues. I took her on a lovely picnick to Marvomati,[5] by the Arcadian gate, and she promised to telephone the moment she got to England, after a night on the way at Judy's. She has promised to give me a complete and beautiful set of Kipling that she has – so don't order it!

Darling, no more now. It's much colder, but lovely and bright and clear. I'm on the lower terrace; meanwhile, upstairs, the *gros beton*

[concrete screed] is being flung – fourteen workmen, a
Brueghelesque feast in preparation by the cistern – chaos, in fact!
The cobbling is finished and looks lovely. How lovely going to
Rotterdam. All news on 1st. Hagar is quite OK again, I'm seldom
out of his arms.

Tons of love P

P.S. I really do think that thick dressing gowns will be needed for
the winter. Could you *bear* to bring one? Blue corduroy wool or
something.

Saturday
Lots of cyclamen out . . . Hagar is the most MTF [Master of Truffle
Hounds] cat I've ever met.

  1 Olympic Palace Hotel in Athens.
  2 Nancy Lancaster (1897–1994), American socialite, partner with John Fowler in the
firm of decorators Colefax & Fowler, creators of the influential 'country house look'.
  3 Cass Canfield and his wife, the sculptor Jane Sage White (1897–1984). In 1967
Canfield stepped down from his position as chairman of Harper's, but he continued as
senior editor until his death.
  4 Possibly a private term for the Kalamitsi bungalows.
  5 A village twenty-five kilometres north of Kalamata. The ruins of the ancient city of
Messene lie nearby, and the road north to Arcadia still runs through the Gate, part
of a mighty defensive wall.

On his return to Greece early in 1968 after a Christmas break in England,
Paddy had some news for Balasha . . .

To Balasha Cantacuzène   Kardamyli
26 February 1968   Messenia

Balasha darling,
    There's so much to say and tell that I hardly know where to start!
Too late for happy new year and Christmas, as it's now nearly Lent,
and the children in the village are wandering about in cloaks and
masks with wooden swords and little bells they seldom stop ringing,

getting the best out of carnival till the Big Fast begins, and nothing
but boiled grasses, fish paste etc. – no oil or cheese! – till Easter . . .
It is funny, living in this remote region, the only strangers for
hundreds of miles. I hope all the locals are as fond of us as we are of
them. I adore Greece, with all its changes of fortune, and always will.
My attitude is that we are guests here, and lucky to be so, and as
guests would no more dream of taking sides in domestic differences
of opinion than I would in the family affairs or disagreements of
friends in whose house I was staying. I'm so sorry to have gone on
so long about this very minor matter, darling, but I don't want to
seem even a *worse* correspondent than the bad one well known by
everyone to be. When you write, don't waste any precious space on
all this . . . [1] I don't know what to do about me and letters. Nobody
would ever think it – this is the first I've written for months – but I
simply love it; and that's the trouble. I'm hopeless at postcards, and
very bad at short ones so I go on putting off the lovely *long* letters
that I'm constantly writing mentally, for days and days which, before
I know where I am, turn into months and months. *Hinc illae
lacrimae.*[2] With you, darling, it's especially grave; yours are so
marvellous and thoughtful and funny and beautifully written that
dashing off a short bright answer seems even less possible than at
other times. It's just *because* I've so much I want to say, and because I
want to write something a bit more complete and thought-out than
I might in other cases, that these dreadful gaps occur. I hope no
more will occur – gaps, I mean – but *should* a seemingly heartless
and incomprehensible silence ever crop up again (I'm sure it won't!),
do bear this in mind and forgive if you can, and attribute it to
anything but lack of love or feeling. I talked about this sort of thing
to Lucienne[3] in Paris about ten years ago, and she looked at me with
a pitying smile and said: *Mon pauvre Paddy, tu es velléitaire!* ['My poor
Paddy, you are a vacillator!'] Absolutely right, alas! I've never yet
produced a book that is less than two years overdue, and delay with
articles and reviews etc. in papers or magazines is just as bad. I
passionately love writing but – except when one gets completely
emballé [engrossed] and suddenly, by the pallor outside the window
and a twittering of birds when one thought it was still 11 p.m.,

realises one has been writing all through the night – find settling down to it an agonising torment. No one knows better than I what Valery meant by *'le papier vierge que sa blancheur défend'*.[4]

. . . We went back to London about the 20th of December, rather snowy and windy, but very exciting with Salvation Army bands pounding away at 'Good King Wenceslas' and 'Noel!' under the falling flakes, trombones reflecting the lamplight. I stayed with Patrick Kinross, Joan just round the corner at Barbara and Niko's, all this in 'Little Venice', a charming bit of Paddington with a network of canals. Imagine my delight when Barbara said she had asked Ina and Michel[5] over for a week and taken the pretty little house and studio for them in Jeremy Hutchinson's garden, filling it up with food & drink, as there was no room in her house . . .

When we all got back to London [after spending Christmas at Chatsworth], we went with Ins and Michel to a party of Diana Cooper's and ended up sitting on the floor singing to John Julius Norwich – D's son – playing the guitar (most of the singing done by JJ, Ina and me), to Diana's delight, who adores that sort of thing. Everyone a bit tight in the nicest possible way . . .

There was another lovely dinner at Barbara's, where we all were, and Lucy (B's daughter by Rex Warner,* her middle husband) and a great friend of ours called Lady Smart. (Isn't it a marvellous name? Like something out of Sheridan.) Amy is a Christian Lebanese, ultra civilised, a painter, wildly intelligent and intuitive, captivating and maddening by turns, and has read everything in French and English under the sun. She is the widow of an enchanting man, Walter Smart, a great wartime friend of ours in Cairo, Oriental Minister at his Embassy for years and years, and, with Amy, a great friend of Larry Durrell's – he's the model for Mountolive,[6] transposed – Robin Fedden and, formerly, of Prue's during her Middle East wanderings. They lived between Cairo and Gadencourt near Pacy-sur-Eure, on the edge of Normandy and the Île de France, in a rambling, book-filled, farm-like village house where I, and sometimes

---

* The writer (*Wild Goose Chase*, *The Aerodome* etc.) and Greek scholar-translator of Thucydides, a heavenly man.

Joan and I, lived for two winters years ago, to write . . . After dinner,
almost without meaning to, and no doubt helped on by whisky –
having been slightly teased by Amy about Joan's and my long and
slightly irregular association – I said that we'd been *meaning* to put it
right for years and years, but had both been too diffident to press the
other. (Quite true! We'd toyed with it again & again, firmly planned
to *sometime* . . . Talk about *velléitaire*! Now, Kardamyli made it idiotic
not to.) *So why not now?* Huge excitement broke out, Joan and me
overjoyed, everyone else too. In fact Amy became so possessive and
bossy about it, in her Bashkirtzeff-like ebullience[7] (could have
throttled her!), and although it was all her doing, we almost felt like
calling it off! Not really, of course. But it was the fuss connected
with such occasions that had subconsciously, I think, been giving us
both cold feet for ages. Anyway, a mood of great rejoicing and
hilarity superseded. Ins looked surprised, amused and delighted,
twigged at once our fleeting moment of Amy-induced exasperation. I
rather wanted to send you a joyous telegram at once, but she advised
against it . . .

Getting married, even in a registry office, wasn't quite as easy as I
thought. One has to establish two weeks' residence from the day one
requests it, at Caxton Hall, Westminster. There was a certain amount
of teasing from friends, when it all got about (we tried to keep it
secret to avoid fuss, but no go). My line was that neither Joan nor
I 'believed in long engagements'. On the fateful morning, I waited
for Joan, Barbara (Joan's sponsor), Niko [Ghika] and Patrick Kinross
(mine) in Whites,* swigging brandy and soda till the car arrived with
all of them in. Wheeler, the barman, dashed down the stairs with a
full glass of brandy which he pushed through the window, for us to
sip in turns on the way. ('You'll need it! All the best!') Actually, it all
went off painlessly, nearly as easy as getting a dog licence. We all
went for a recovery swig in a pub round the corner, then back to
Barbara's, where she'd got a lovely luncheon – oysters, delicious
champagne, a marvellous old-fashioned round of beef – and to eat it,

---

* I was put down for this swanky and frivolous haunt years ago without being consulted
by friends who were members, so it's not entirely my fault. Couldn't resist it when
elected, I'm slightly ashamed to admit.

those in the car, us, Amy, Diana Cooper, Maurice Bowra, Cyril Connolly and his wife Deirdre. No family on either side. It was a hilarious meal, very strange and pretty with everything white and gleaming in the garden under falling snow, a log fire blazing in B's pretty house; it might have been in Cracow or St Petersburg. Maurice – you remember what a friend of Guy's he used to be? – drove back to Oxford where he is Warden of Wadham College and vice-chancellor. (He's marvellous. The funniest talker since Dr Johnson.)[8] In the evening, Patrick Kinross (tall, rubicund, jolly, once a journalist under his earlier name of P. Balfour, now a serious writer on Middle Eastern affairs and history, and the biographer of Atatürk) gave *another* feast with all the same people as luncheon plus lots more: Iris Tree (wonderful, I'll write lots more about her another time), her son Ivan Moffat, a tremendous crony of mine, Coote Lygon, Magouche (now back from Florence), Raymond Mortimer, J. Julius, Andrew Devonshire (Debo stuck in Derbyshire, alas) and lots more. (Couldn't find Biddy – she must have been in Scotland.) It all ended up in a golden haze with Iris, Ivan and me doing improvised turns – last of the Romans arguing with the first of the incoming Anglo-Saxons, improvising bogus Latin and A-Saxon etc. Great fun. A lovely day, much dreaded beforehand but all glorious when it actually happened.

A dreaded meal next day! Knowing my mother's unfailing knack of always trying (thank God, unsuccessfully, and almost certainly unconsciously) to make a hash of private concerns of mine – you remember how odd she was – I'd taken jolly good care to keep her absolutely separate from me and mine, though I often see her alone; so Joan and she had never met. Well next day Vanessa[9] (as nice, and as good an ally as ever. She sends lots of love. I'll tell you all about all this in another letter), Mummy, Joan and I had a great banquet, among the Second Empire mirrors and caryatids of the Café Royal. Well, it went off splendidly. Mummy's spiky eccentricity was in complete abeyance and she was like her old amusing, intelligent and charming self: liked Joan very much (J. was terrified at first; same here), and J. liked her too. It wouldn't last through too many frequent contacts – I know Mummy too well! – but spaced out, all should be well. She *is* an odd creature: so bright and gifted and well-read, intelligent and gay in some ways; so terrifying and destructive in others; so full of odd delusions and manias. My solution is to let her have as little to do with my real life as possible, but to be terribly nice in other ways and make her life as happy as I can; it seems to work more or less; any other course would end in chaos. It's all a bit sad. Anyway, *this* occasion went off triumphantly, thank heavens.

In spite of Joan and me wanting everything to pass off normally and quietly and without fuss, the occasion was made the excuse by friends of a series of minor parties until we left . . .

At long last, after a devious journey, we got here and were greeted with hugs and kisses and congratulations by all the village; and every day, after lunch, troops have turned up, bringing loads of sticky cakes and bottles of ouzo as presents. A slightly harrowing ritual follows: on arrival, *just after lunch*, each guest has to be served with a sort of round meringue and a little glass of sweet emerald green or ruby red liqueur made out of bananas, followed *immediately* by mézés of liver and kidney washed down with retsina, a Marinetti repast.[10] But it is lovely to see the big room of the house too full of coiffed crones – rather like a *claca*[11] – papas in tall hats, and all the old and young of the village, all rather formal until we manage to stir them up a bit by clowning about and producing the time-honoured jokes that produce – it doesn't matter how many times they've been told before! – their time-honoured responses. Yesterday, the girls and young women, and one or two old ones, ended up by dancing the *Kalamatiano* [Greek folk dance] to the tune of their own shrill songs. It was very pretty, all in a ring in front of the Băleni-form fireplace.[12] They are very nice – the Maniots, I mean. Not a bit like the Cretans; they are supposed to be very religious, Royalist, rather reactionary, like La Vendée or Navarrois, but this reputation is very exaggerated by non-Maniots. They are tremendously honest, which is rather nice; a bit lost; I think we must seem very odd phenomena suddenly dropping into their midst out of the blue. They have been uniformly nice to us and, I think, love having us here, and are proud of the fact that one has alighted on their village out of all the other villages in the world. I do hope so. The time's a bit out of joint at the moment . . .

There have been scores of interruptions in the last few days, and it's now the 29th instead of the evening of the same day I started this! So I'll keep all else to say for my next one, when I've explored the pyramid ahead. Lots to say, about the house etc. Meanwhile, darling Balasha and Pomme, tons of fond love

    from Paddy

P.S. *Stop Press!* I'd walked down to the village to post this and, lo and behold, two letters from Pucioasa, one dated the 19th the other the 20th – one of them addressed to Joan, opened by me by mistake (not used to change of name yet) with both yours and Pomme's letters to her and to me . . . Joan's up at the house, but will be so pleased – I've reopened the envelope, after rushing through the letters and scribbling this in the *kafeneion*, but must stop it now and post it, as the postman is rolling his eyes and tapping his fingers in mock impatience!

    x x x

1 PLF hinted that under the new regime his letters were being intercepted and read.

2 'Hence these tears' – Terence, *Andria*, line 126.

3 Lucienne Gourgaud du Taillis, born Lucienne Haas (1898–1982), artist, a friend of Balasha's in Paris.

4 'The blank paper defends its whiteness.' It was Mallarmé, not Valéry, in his poem *Brise Marine* ('Sea Breeze').

5 Balasha's niece Ina and her husband Michel Catargi were now living in Paris.

6 David Mountolive is the central character in the novel *Mountolive* (1958), the third book in Durrell's *Alexandria Quartet*.

7 Marie Bashkirtzeff (1858–84), Ukrainian painter and sculptor, who died of tuberculosis at the early age of twenty-five. She is perhaps best known for her lively and readable journal.

8 PLF was being charitable here. Eighteen months earlier (7 November 1966) he had complained to Annie Fleming about Bowra's deafness: 'I do wish he'd wear an aid, as it turns all conversation into one-way-tennis, with all one's own balls lost in the long grass.'

9 PLF's older sister, Vanessa Fenton (1911–87).

10 Filippo Tommaso Marinetti published a *Manifesto of Futurist Cooking* in 1930. Among its stipulations were that the conventional order of courses should be abolished, together with knives and forks; that there should be no more pasta, as it causes lassitude, pessimism and lack of passion; and that perfumes should be used to enhance the tasting experience. Some food on the table would not be eaten, but experienced only by the eyes and nose.

11 A gathering of people, usually older ladies singing and gossiping, to carry out a common task like sewing or dehusking maize.

12 PLF had a fireplace constructed at Kardamyli to imitate those he had seen at Băleni, themselves imitations of one Balasha's uncle had sketched on his travels in Persia.

To Balasha Cantacuzène   Kardamyli
20 June 1968   Messenia

Darling Balasha,

All my letters – that is about every three months *in all*, to *any*one! – invariably start nowadays with an inundation of richly deserved apology. It's really an act of penitence, an *acquis de conscience*, to assuage my own guilty conscience about being such a criminally late letter writer – and is probably utter hell and a bit tedious for the reader (who, anyway, if an old and adored friend, has probably, by the mere fact of one's writing, half forgiven one already!); so, darling, although I've got an enormous amount of things I want to answer when the right moment comes – and a conscience black with guilt! – I'm going to spare you my self-lacerations this time, and simply forge ahead as though I were an angelically innocent party! Anyway, darling Balasha, I know you understand these things . . .

How strange, Balasha, that you should ask me about Iris Tree! The same day a letter came saying poor Iris had died of cancer. It suddenly started about a year ago, and galloped on to its sad close; she knew all about it and faced it with great courage. It was Diana Cooper who wrote with this sad news; sad, but perhaps a blessing too. She – Diana – was with her to the last. It was really a worse blow for her than for anyone else; they had been accomplices, rivals in a comic way, and above all, tremendous friends, ever since they were small girls. She was Iris Tree's youngest sister.[1] I adored her. She [Iris] was so funny and gifted, a very talented poet, Bohemian to the backbone; always broke, never caring a damn, with marvellous huge blue-green eyes, a wonderful snide smile and a laugh rather like a bad schoolboy's, flaxen hair cut like a page's, the figure and the carriage of a young girl, right to the end. She used to dress in rather loose woven dresses, yellow or

turquoise caught in at the waist with the sort of old leather belt a
French porter might wear; the last time I saw her she was wearing a
green tie almost as narrow as a bullfighter's, on which [were] about a
dozen butterflies and beetles and grasshoppers of jewelry or coloured
glass, that looked stunning; usually bare-headed, but occasionally with
a rather wide-brimmed felt hat at a musketeerish tilt, and always
accompanied by a huge jet-black Alsatian called Auguri; an excellent
horsewoman; a lifelong unwilling inflictor and victim of the pangs of
love. Totally independent, living in studios – or derelict towers in the
country – in or near Rome, Venice, Provence, Catalonia. She was first
married to an American painter called Curtis Moffat – their son, Ivan,
about my age, is a great friend, very gifted also – then to a v. tall,
amazing-looking Austrian called Graf Friedrich Ledebur, known as 'the
Uhlan' [cavalryman]. They were divorced and he remarried, but
nevertheless he was always rejoining her for months on end. She had
a slight, very engaging Petrouskaesque clown quality, cultivated rather
as a joke. Marvellous mimic, a wonderfully funny, original and
unexpected conversationalist. She always had the same leather bag
slung over her shoulder, full of paper and pencils, and spent a great
deal of time writing in cafés. A great noctambulist. I often spent hours
wandering from café to café with her, talking all night. Friends with
everyone and completely classless. She had the gift of causing,
unwillingly, comic, charming or unusual events. About ten years ago,
I camped in a colossal half-ruined Orsini castle in the Roman
Campagna I had managed to borrow (all rats and owls, and
uninhabited for 200 years) in order to write. She said she would like
to come out of Rome for a few days to do some work, and cooked
the most marvellous meals. I was driving her back to Rome after
sunset when all of a sudden my battered car ran out of petrol. There
were nothing but dark fields for miles, till at last we spotted a faint
light. I took a lane through the corn, and at last reached a farmhouse,
where a whole family were swallowing spaghetti by lantern-light. I
asked if they had any petrol, and a boy called Silvio, about eighteen,
said he would siphon some out of his motorbike. On the way to the
car, he said that while ploughing the week before, his ploughshare had
bumped against something hard – a headless stone lady, he said, and a

pair of stone feet '*una signora di pietra senza testa ed un paio di piedi*' ['a stone lady without head or feet']. He had hidden them in the cowshed. I got Iris, we walked back, made our way through the horns and the munching of the shed with the lantern, to where he had covered up his troves with hay. We put them under the pump, scraped the mud away, and a beautiful seated statue of headless Cybele[2] emerged (2 feet high), enthroned, holding her disk, with two lions at her feet, beautifully carved folds of drapery; and a ravishing pair of marble feet (half-lifesize) on a plinth, one with a heel lifted, beside the stump of a marble tree on which the vanished statue must have been leaning her elbow; also a handful of coins from the reign of Domitian. You can imagine our excitement! Silvio asked if I'd like to buy them. I said, like mad I would, but neither of us had anything like [the] very low price he wanted for both (about £8). But I got them a month later & smuggled them to England where they stayed ten years (Iris didn't want them – no fixed abode). Now they are here, in rough niches, and look glorious. I've told all this only to illustrate how odd and unexpected things always happened in her company.

A couple of years ago, she, Joan and I were all in Marseilles by chance. One day we went to the Camargue and rode for miles, to try and catch a glimpse of the flamingoes that nest there. The day ended at sunset with us all strolling along the battlements of Aigues-Mortes, a strange town in the delta, its fortifications reflected in the mere – and gazing down at the quay where the 5th (?) Crusade had set sail.[3] There was a statue of St Louis (the commander) on a pedestal, holding a sword and wearing a narrow crown of *fleurs de lys* on his bobbed hair. Iris stopped and exclaimed 'Oh *look! Aren't* they kind? They've put up a statue of *me!*' It *did* look rather like her!

I do hope this is legible, Balasha darling, as I've got to get it off without rereading or correcting as the postman is chafing. I'll write again soon. All my love to Pomme – do both keep in touch about her later plans.

    With tons of love

      Paddy

from Joan too, who will write

¹ PLF means that relations between Diana Cooper and Iris Tree were like those between an older and younger sister. The next sentence refers not to DC, but to Iris Tree.

² Cybele, mother of the gods, goddess of fertility and mistress of wild nature, symbolised by (tamed) companion lions.

³ Louis XI departed from Aigues-Mortes on the Seventh and Eighth Crusades.

For at least five years Paddy had been working on a book based on 'the Great Trudge', his pre-war journey across Europe, undertaken largely on foot. This had begun as an article for an American magazine on 'The Pleasures of Walking', and had become steadily more ambitious as time passed.

To Jock Murray   Kardamyli
late July, alas [1968?]   Messenia

Dear Jock,

The trouble is, that about twenty different people are doing to me exactly what I am doing to you. I know it's no consolation, but if I am causing anguish, anger, sorrow and disappointment in Albemarle Street,¹ the same afflictions are being visited on me here twenty-fold; viz. deadlock on deadlock. The studio for writing in, the power-house for prose about thirty yards from the house in sequestered silence, was supposed to be finished three winters ago. The shell is up, but carpenters, tile makers, plumbers, electricians, glaziers – every single artisan whose combined efforts would make this thing habitable is doing a Leigh Fermor on me – viz. promises, delay, procrastination, augmented by a random scattering of illnesses, strokes, stones in the bladder, melancholia, and they are all interdependent. Occasionally it seems, after endless toil, journeys, pep-talks, threats and prayers, to be going well; then a link in the chain cracks; the cat stops killing the rat, the rat stops gnawing the rope, the rope stops hanging the butcher, the butcher stops killing the ox etc. etc. Each of these breakdowns involves long hot drives – then drinks – to the various villages where these horny-handed sluggards are scattered: to Kalamata and Tripoli, in the middle of the Peloponnese, each temporary remedy calling for a separate system of comminution,

appeal, exhumination, wire-pulling and ruse. I could have settled in
the empty shell, but there is always someone tinkering loyally away
[at] the loam and the rough cast.[2] I am terrified unless I keep at it
that it won't be finished *when winter comes*. It's no joke. No joke,
above all, because all this does in the equanimity and established
routine that I need to get over the style and cook my old man's
dumplings. But I do tear my nose from the wrong grindstone to the
right one. If coming Greece-wards, do *come here*; one more distraction
couldn't do any more harm than the seething mass of it already on
the job; and it would be such fun; and you would understand all
these transitory but infuriating difficulties far better than by reading
this bare outline of them, for there are many others tiresome enough
for us to confront, without burdening you with them vicariously.

I feel better after all this. To hell with them all. The right will
triumph.

Best love from Joan and me,
Yours ever
Paddy

[1] The John Murray building at No. 50 Albemarle Street.
[2] An allusion to *A Midsummer Night's Dream*, V, 1.

*Paddy knew several of the British Ambassadors to Greece, but he was especially
friendly with Michael Stewart, who was in post during the difficult period of
the Colonels' rule, and his wife Damaris.*

To Damaris Stewart   Kardamyli
2 October 1968   Messenia

Dear Damaris,

I've been meaning to write for days to thank you both for letting
me and mine horn in on that gorgeous banquet. It *was* fun, and the
Ghikas adored it. I fear that, maddened with the General's Naxian
wine, I was rather noisy; I feel guilty about booming out those rather
grivoises [saucy] French songs, which the wicked old general, muffled

by his even riper years, treacherously initiated *sotto voce*. He *did* enjoy himself; so did I, and I think everyone. One's only middle-aged once, is my new watchword.

It was a different tale next morning. Before setting off, I slunk round to see Barbara and Niko Ghika and was comforted to discover that the aftermath of the Naxian affected them in the same way, viz. spots before the eyes, racing pulses, headaches like forked lightning. (All well worth it.) It was consoling to pool hangovers in their softly lit quarters.

We called for tamer music and for paler ale.[1]

The Jellicoes'[2] visit was all too brief. George did a tremendous high dive from a rock, which I'll always think of as Jellicoe's Leap, rival to Sappho's in Lefkas.[3] Put on my mettle, I stole there after they left and when no-one was about (in case of funking at the last moment), described (?) the same dread parabola. It wasn't as dread as it looked, but I wish I'd thought of it first.

We – my mason-god-brother and two workmen & I – are busy weaving a huge and beautiful pebble star round the octagonal fountain in the front terrace (placed there entirely due to you for the sake of swallows), to astound Joan with when she gets back from Blighty on the 8th. (I do hope you'll both come and inspect whenever you can.) It is fed by cunning underwater pipes which will spread concentric ripples: beguiling enough, we hope, to lure down even the most jaded northbound swallow next spring. How quelling if they ignore these blandishments!

Yours ever

Paddy

---

[1] 'I cried for madder music and for stronger wine' – Ernest Dowson's poem *Non Sum Qualis Eram Bonae sub Regno Cynarae* ('I have been faithful to thee, Cynara! in my fashion').

[2] PLF's close friend and wartime comrade, George Jellicoe (1918–2007), 2nd Earl Jellicoe, and his wife Philippa. The Jellicoes would become regular visitors to Kardamyli.

[3] Sappho is supposed to have leapt to her death from the white cliffs of the southerly cape of the island of Lefkas, for love of Phaon, a ferryman.

To John Betjeman   Kardamyli
28 September 1969   Messenia

Dear John,

Here are the gloomy London verses, and two more, while I'm
about it[1] with explanatory preceding Arguments. I've just finished
reading St Simeon Stylites;[2] my word, it's funny.

I wish you'd all stayed here longer; it was so marvellous. Lovely
autumn weather now, viz. in Greece, suddenly clean deep earth and
vegetation colours after the rain, lighter veils of shadow cast by solids,
evening air the colour of hock, pale magnesium shadows, clarity of
vision, hence abolition of distance, all the way to Mars. Cyclamen
and lovely smells.

After too much to drink one night before you came, Joan & I
were making up epitaphs, apropos of one I saw years ago in a Devon
(Cullompton) church full of Chichester tombs. One, with a lady very
much overdressed and holding a coronet went: 'Here's Lady Donegal!
To sing her praise // Needs not a wreath, but a whole Grove of
Bays', etc. This is one to Copella, the mule who brings all the sand
for the building here.

> Water with Tears the pebbles of this Strand!
> Copella's shed her final load of sand.
> Her sands ran out. For Mortals, too, alas!
> The Grains grow scarcer in Life's brittle Glass.
> Her life was grasing [grazing], but our Flesh is Grass.

which was followed by several others including both of us, of which
I send Joan's

> Pussies, here Mistress Joan LIES! Offer her
> At least the Incense of a grateful Purr!
> Let Tortoiseshell and Tabby both repine
> That ne'er look'd up in vain at suppertime.
> Some call to mind her Bounty, some her Grace
> And plaintive Mews contort each whisker'd Face

And Kittens, when they see incisèd here
Her name, a fleeting second may forswear,
Their lissom Sport for one compunctive Tear.

Next door to each other in Rousham churchyard, I noticed one
headstone dedicated to Jos. (?) Mason, the other to Ebenezer (?)
Fortnum, both mid eighteenth century, I think. In Tidcombe
churchyard, Wilts, a stone commemorates someone called VIVEASH,
a name I thought made up for Mrs V., in *Antic Hay*.[3]

   Do come back and inspect progress.

   Yours ever
      Paddy

Box, I'm sure, is the name of the Penguin author on Orthodoxy.[4]

O Gemme of Joye and Jaspar of Jocunditie
(Soho Thoughts from Abroad)[5]

Come when the publics are shut and the fish bars are clashing
      their shutters
And the rust and the rain are in triumph and the cats are at
      work on the clanking
Dustbins and vomit cascades in a neonlit gush by the Wimpy
Bar.[6] The greensward is gossamer'd o'er with family planning
      devices;
Nark-time has come to the manor. The narrows are busy with
      wide boys
And the lanes are a-flicker with flickknives and the clip-joints
      cough up for protection.
Unlayable dolls slick their heels in the dimly-lit doorways of
      clip-joints,
And a chucker-out slumbers below in a lair full of beetles and
      coke-lids.
Sid puts the blanks on the twanks and Sam pushes pot by the
      parking

Lot – what a zoom of exhausts as the kids come up West for a
    giggle and
Kicks! Look at Len, Jack and Les going in with the boot by
    the phone-box,
And Pimlico Pete on all fours, spitting half of his gnashers
    down Meard Street,
Poised for a cop in the shelter, a honey-haired plain-clothes
    policeman
Flutters blue lids on blue eyes at an out-of-work actor from
    Ealing
Billed for a run at the Scrubs;[7] the patrol-car glides blue to
    the kerb-stone.
Turbaned in lilac, a Sikh, and a clerk with his heart full of
    Helen
Of Troy, are morosely at gaze, but *Kinky*, *Wank*, *Cute* wink the
    windows
And mugs from the midlands and suburbs slow down at the
    lure of the glow worm
Glow on the jamb by the bell-push, of ill-written cards that
    say 'Edna',
'Mona, young model', 'Sheree' and 'Sabrina' and 'Yvonne,
    French model',
– Dodging a jagload of starlets with poodles in Ogilvie tartan
Jackets, all meat for their masters, the real estate moguls of
    Highgate,
With fruit machine empires and frighteners and candy-floss
    cohorts of call-birds
Taking a tenner a tinkle in Bayswater luxury flatlets –
Sadly they turn from the doors to the doorway of Round-the-
    Clock-Striptease.
Come! 'Tis the time of good cheer! The deep freeze is rife
    with *bistecca*,
Pop goes the grocers' Marsala, the tins are releasing their
    scampi,
Hang up the flitch made of cardboard and roll out the Watered
    Barolo!

Cyprus head waiters are welcoming admen in broken Italian,

And top men unbend from the tension of public relations and
satire,

Carnaby-collared and cuffed, and cleverly quiffed for the
close-ups.

Nasal the note of the noise and nasal and knowing the features

The *crèpe-suzette* lights from below; and fragrant the double
Drambuies

Entwining with jumbo Partagás[8] the fumes of the spoils of the
showroom

A crooner and runaway heiress confer with the Press over
cointreau

And fizz! go the takeover bargains for retreads and camp-sites
and surplus

As Bunny-time looms, as the wipers awake on the windscreens
of Phantoms.

Come! 'Tis the hour of Expenses, TV personalities, flash bulbs!

Hark to the click of the wheel and the murmur in Bow Bells
Parisian:

'Banco!' 'Rien ne va plus.' 'Slip the sergeant a couple of tenners.'

Hark to the deep organ voice and purple heartbeat[9] of Old
England.

---

1 'The Greek Stones Speak' and 'Christmas Lines for Bernard of Morlaix', both printed
in Artemis Cooper (ed.), *Words of Mercury* (2003).

2 A Tennyson poem, first published in 1842.

3 In Aldous Huxley's novel *Antic Hay* (1923), the character of Myra Viveash is inspired
by the society heiress, Nancy Cunard.

4 PLF probably refers to George Herbert Box (1869–1933), prolific author on religious
topics.

5 The title is drawn from a poem by William Dunbar (1465–1520), 'London thou art
the flour of cities all', printed in the *Oxford Book of English Verse*, a volume that PLF
knew well; he had carried a copy in his rucksack on his walk across Europe. The subtitle
is a reference to Browning's 'Home-Thoughts, from Abroad' (1845).

6 A chain of cheap restaurants selling hamburgers.

7 Wormwood Scrubs, a prison in West London.

8 A brand of Havana cigar.

9 A reference to 'purple hearts', a type of amphetamine.

To Niko Ghika   Kardamyli
2 October 1969   Messenia

Dear Niko,

What a lovely evening. Well worth postponing my departure for, *and very nearly my last!* Next day, after thousands of slow hairpin bends south of Tripoli, when I came to the straight bit of road leading into Megalopolis, I must have heaved a sigh of relief and accelerated to much too fast a speed; a back tyre exploded, the car shot along for a 100 yards or so while I just managed to keep it on the road, then its left wheels got into a shallow ditch and whiz bang! *Over* the car turned *completely*, went on a little way like a tortoise on its back, then stopped. I climbed out of the broken window on to the road, feeling blissfully happy and no wonder! Only a small bump on the forehead, like David's sling stone mark on Goliath's forehead – now vanished – and, out of a case of whisky, 2 huge demijohns of Markopoulo retsina, 3 γαλόνια [gallons] of Hercules' blood, 3 of Νεμέα ροζέ [Nemea rosé], and 3 big Aigina pitchers for turning into lamps, not one was broken, not a drop spilt (of either nectar or ichor).[1] I have given up smoking as a penance for simple folly of inappropriate speed, a whole week now; and still feel rather bereaved and at a loss. The faithful Peugeot, which saved me like a loose-fitting suit of armour, is being hammered into shape again by Athenian artisans and will be ready next week.

There is a serious problem down here among the books, i.e. a steadily increasing plague of these destructive little insects known to bibliophiles as 'silverfish'. We are very anxious about it, and I meant, when in Athens, to contact Mr Walton, and get his advice. (There is some very simple petrol-based solution that deals with it.) The awful thing is (don't tell!) that I've forgotten his Christian name, and, as we are on first-name terms, I can't write to him direct (no '*cher ami*' in English!) Could you please most kindly send me his name – also – perhaps, put our problem to him by telephone? It is v. worrying, like a minor plague of Egypt. It would be sad if our slender library dissolved as it assembled!

Do come here, if you feel like a change from Athens. It is

marvellous now, beautiful autumn weather, paler sunlight, warm
bathing, clear air. The new exedra,[2] to the left of the terrace outside
the drawing room, looks lovely. It's nearly finished, same system as
the big one, with a marble balustrade at the end supported in two
squat pillars. The other two pillars are these old rafters from
downstairs embedded, to mark the change from the leaning exedra
back to the horizontal. It looks very nice. Underneath, there is a
broad black stripe (pebbles, etc.) round the table plinth, and then
round the edge, the crest all white except for a symmetrical pattern
of black dots, like the spots on a Hellenistic mosaic leopard.

How is the Corfu house plan getting on?[3] I think one of the
most beautiful things in architecture, gardens, etc. is the descent of
white terraces, balustrades perhaps, all connected by a shallow
continuous staircase – raft after floating superimposed raft, jutting out
over sky and sea – this kind of thing is occasionally seen with two
tricorned figures standing, for scale, in imaginary Piranesi ruinscapes,
or better still, Virgil and Dante in a Paradiso illustrated by Doré –
cypresses, cedars, sea below, cloudburst descending, shafts of sunlight
overhead.

Lela's waiting for this, so I must stop. Do come here if you want
to do some work away from Athens. Many thanks for letting us stay!
Love,
    Paddy

---

[1] The ethereal golden fluid that is the blood of the gods.

[2] A room, portico, or arcade with a bench or seats where people may converse, especially in ancient Roman and Greek buildings. PLF built several exedrae at Kardamyli, one inside and two outside.

[3] The Ghikas were building a house on Corfu, after their house on Hydra had been destroyed by fire – set alight, it seems, by a servant who resented his new mistress. The landscape gardening – the courtyard floor, the stone benches and tables, the fountains – was all done by Ghika himself. PLF sent him suggestions under the title 'Random thoughts about San Stephane'.

To Balasha Cantacuzène   Kardamyli
10 November 1971   Messenia

Darling Balasha,

I can't wait till the whole Peruvian document[1] is ready, before
writing, as it looks as if it might easily be another two weeks or
more! My writing in the tents in the Andes must have been almost
more illegible than it normally is, what with wind and thick gloves
and the cold, and the poor lady who typed it out obviously had an
appalling struggle with it. I've just finished correcting it, as there
were so many misreadings, and have sent it back to England. *Ouf!* It's
not for printing, only for those who were on the trip and three or
four others. It's almost fifty pages of typescript, written absolutely
helter-skelter, but I hope it gives a lively picture of our adventures.
The whole thing was so marvellous and the company so delightful
and amusing and the place so strange and impressive and beautiful
that it *ought* to be readable, in its superficial and slapdash way. So I'll
resist the temptation (once more!) to spoil whatever novelty it might
have by anticipating its unpretentious contents! One moment (which
I forgot to put in the journal) came back to my mind in the middle
of last night: we were high up a very bleak snowy plateau, all of us
huddling in a tent just under the glacier line, dark, with a few streaks
of afterglow (not dawn, alas!) showing sulphurously in the west; a
scene of great desolation. It suddenly reminded me of that Goya
print from the *Caprichos*, with those shapeless creatures huddling as
we were, except that it was the wrong end of the day.[2] I described
it to the others and the sinister import of *¡Si amanece, nos vamos!*
They were all very impressed with the appositeness of the situation
and the quotation, and we started talking about Goya, and *Los
Caprichos* and those awful *Horrors of War*. Robin Fedden remembered
that he'd been to a big comprehensive Goya exhibition at Burlington
House two years ago (which I missed). One of the drawings
represented a brawl involving three men, drunk, he thought. The
captions underneath had Goya's Spanish, and an English translation;
it was the English of this particular caption that had struck Robin. It
was '*Two against one? Stuff his arse with hay!*' Whose? How? Why? We

were all suddenly in fits of laughter about this enigmatic sentence; and also at the boldness of the translation. The phrase became a catchword for the rest of the trip, *à propos de rien*. We wondered what the original had been – *¿Dos contra uno? ¡Henchi su culo con heno!* – or *con pajo?* Simple pleasures . . .

Darling, I've asked Sandoe's to send you a copy of Robin F's book *Chantemesle*[3] – it's about the house he lived in in France, as a child. His father was a painter, and they lived close to the Seine, near Givenchy, in Normandy. I love it, and reviewed it when it came out in the *New Statesman*, and will send the review if I find it.

More about Roman birds: when we got back from the Andes, I went to stay with Andrew and Debo at Chatsworth, and Harold Macmillan[4] (married to A's aunt) was there – an *absolutely charming*, erudite old boy, full of Greek and Latin and the classics. On a long walk through the woods (where everyone else was banging away [shooting] the other side) he told me that the Romans had brought the first pheasants to Britain as pets, and when Honorius recalled them,[5] the birds got loose, took to the woods, and bred. They also brought the first beech trees, which have spread everywhere.[6]

There's been some going and coming here. First of all, Xan and Daphne Fielding. I don't know whether I've told you about him. We were in Crete together through most of the occupation (where he was wonderful) and he has remained my best friend ever since, also of Joan's. He's delightful; wandered about like me before the war, speaks perfect French and Greek & excellent German, extremely bohemian, rather rebellious, very funny, much loved by all for his looks (rather like a slim, v. neat Persian prince), charm and niceness. He's always reminded me of Lafcadio in *Les Caves du Vatican*.[7] Daphne is the daughter of an eccentric Cornish peer,[8] and was married to the noble Marquess of Bath, till they separated and she married Xan (Henry Bath *then* married Virginia, Viola Tree's daughter, who is very like Daphne; so everyone seems happy). She's rather an Augustus John kind of character (and was a great friend, indeed, also of Debo's, Diana Cooper's and Iris Tree), v. bohemian, dashing, and reckless, admired by many. She writes books (*not* v. good) and Xan has become one of the best translators from French.

They've always been v. broke and v. happy, living first in Portugal, then in the Kasbah of Tangier, now in a little farmhouse not far from the Château d'Uzès in Languedoc (once inhabited by your equestrian friend, now redecorated by *La Sardine qui s'est crue sole*),[9] and about ten miles from Larry Durrell – after a short terrible time in a sort of Wuthering Heights in the rockiest, windiest and snowiest slopes of the Cévennes. They stayed two weeks, and it was a great success and I'm so glad they came at last. Apart from them (RUN OUT OF BIG PAPER), Joan's brother came, Graham. I think I've told you all about him – very intelligent, very retiring literary-musical hermit; then Peter Mayne, an old writer friend who has written excellent books about India and one remarkable one about Morocco called *Alleys of Marrakesh*.[10] At the moment Joan's sister Diana is here – at least, not here, as Joan's taken her to Mistra for the night, so I'm in stately solitude. She's very nice, but has not a single interest in common with Joan or Graham, and is v. unlike: shy, tall, v. correct and well dressed in a not very imaginative Knightsbridge way, and stitching away at gros-point. I think Joan finds her heavier-going than I do! . . . Just before this, Aymer Maxwell came for a week, and made me promise to send his love to Pomme, which I do herewith! He was without his boat this time – thank God in a way! – and so everything was much less emotionally strung. In fact, nothing but laughter . . .

It's still lovely here, all washed clean after a few days' heavy rain (perfect for Joan's olives!) and looking gleaming and luminous. We still bathe in the middle of the day, but may have to grit our teeth in a week or so. I've managed to drill myself – in spite of guests – into a sort of trance of work, and, thank God, am getting ahead. Joan and I spend a lot of time in reciprocal boasting about our travels, and the place is littered with books about Scythians, Incas, Uzbeks, Conquistadores, Tamarlane and Pizarro . . .

No more now, darling Balasha, except tons of fond love to you and to Pomme – and I will get the Peru stuff to you the moment it is ready.

Paddy

xxx

1 An account of PLF's Andes expedition, based on his letters to JLF, published as *Three Letters from the Andes* (1991).

2 A set of eighty Goya prints, published as an album in 1799. Print No. 71, *Si amanece, nos vamos* (*When day breaks we will be off*), shows three old hags conferring at night about how they will gorge themselves on their fellow creatures.

3 First published in 1964.

4 Harold Macmillan (1894–1986), Conservative politician and prime minister 1957–63, married Lady Dorothy Cavendish, daughter of the 9th Duke of Devonshire.

5 AD 410.

6 Neither of these assertions is proven.

7 In André Gide's *Les Caves du Vatican* (1914), Lafcadio is a handsome, athletic young man of sixteen. His unorthodox education has made him value independence and originality.

8 4th Baron Vivian.

9 PLF plays on the name of the Marquise de Crussol d'Uzès, née Amieux, the former mistress of the French Prime Minister, Edouard Daladier. The Crussol family owned a sardine-canning business.

10 Peter Mayne, *The Alleys of Marrakesh* (1953).

To Xan Fielding   Kardamyli
21 February 1972   Messenia

Dear Xan,

I'm so sorry being such a sluggard with my pen! I didn't manage to answer your marvellous letter to White's for the same reason that I didn't manage to write a single letter all the time I was in Blighty: viz. overexcitement, movement, excess, the pendulum swing of dissipation and retribution (milder than *nanuère* [formerly], but still far from heart's desire) and general enjoyable disarray. Now, of course, when we're safely back in our hermitage, I discover to my fury that I've forgotten it, with a bundle of letters to be answered, in Niko & Barbara's flat in Athens, where I stayed on return. Damn. I'll recover it in three weeks' time, when we get there again; so this is only really an answer to the second one sent on the 2 Feb.

It would be *splendid* if you both came in late July and August, and we'll have dictionaries & pencils and papers waiting. Any travels between now and June (when the same party as last time heads for the snowy peaks of Kurdistan) are ruled out, alas, as I have a real

chance of finishing this bloody book by then if I stick to it. I'll be in
real disgrace if I don't, specially after that fruity portrait by Derek
Hill (rather good)[1] and Jock Murray's shaming kindness and
forbearance . . . I loved your Rochefoucauld-Vauvenargues[2] maxims.
One might do some bogus Balkan proverbs, on the analogy of the
genuine Bulgarian one: 'An uninvited guest is worse than a Fuck.'
I've just thought of one! viz. 'A cold wife is a belfry without bats,
and an impotent man is a minaret without a muezzin' . . .

Alfays rememper dat Chairmany is de turd of Europe.

I loved staying with Patrick, as usual, and what luck seeing Daph
for dinner the night we arrived. Joan and I diverged over Christmas,
to reunite later, as is sometimes our wont: she to Dumbleton &
Graham, I to Annie Fleming's, where Diana came too. Then, still
under Annie's wing, for two nights in a draughty lough-side schloss
in Ulster called Shane's Castle, inhabited by a seldom seen son called
Raymond O'Neill,[3] a halt on the drive to Donegal, where Derek
Hill lives. We stopped at Londonderry on the way, where, after lunch,
I made my way to the Bogside: rainy, deserted, brick-strewn with
roadblocks made out of upturned cars and oil-drums; through a gap,
past a republican tricolour and, in huge letters YOU ARE NOW
ENTERING FREE DERRY, to the Bogside Inn, full of posters
saying 'Death to all Stoolies', 'End Internment Now' and 'Down with
the Ruling Class', where the nearly incomprehensible N. Ireland
cloth-capped porter drinkers shied away from my Anglo-Saxon
overtures with menacing looks. I managed to talk at last – for one
and a half hours – with a chap called Finn, who seemed to be a
local Provo spokesman. I'm going to try and recapitulate our
colloquy on paper – I should have done it next day – so I won't
attempt it now. But it left me with a feeling of absolute hopelessness.
Three dull thuds, two streets away, of exploding bombs ('There they
go!') reminded me how late it was getting. 'Don't open your mouth
on the way out, for Christ's sake!', were Finn's parting words.
Schoolchildren were gathering brickbats for pelting the evening
patrollers, and outside the Bogside, sections of camouflaged jacketed
Gloucesters with blackened faces were patrolling cautiously, v. young
and, understandably, v. wary looking. A street was cordoned off, hoses

playing on a flaming Spinning Mill [a pub], Annie waiting v. anxiously at the dingy hotel – the only decent one had been bombed out – on the banks of the Foyle River. So, away over the cratered frontier post, to peaceful Donegal. When the bombs went off, all journalists in the hotel bar had streamed out, then a tip-off man had dashed in shouting 'There's been a tarring and feathering!' What's one to do where both sides are hopelessly in the wrong (or, with a change of focus, both right), though, admittedly, one side in the wrong for several centuries more than the other? If only the Normans, after beating the hell out of us in 1066, hadn't crossed the sea and done the same thing in Ireland 101 years later! They didn't know what they were landing us with. It's a bugger.[4]

Just before leaving, I went to Chatsworth for the weekend – it's utterly changed! Debo with unclouded brow, and Andrew, hurling fruit juice down by the flagon, turned from Raskolnikoff into Mr Pickwick.[5] From here I borrowed a car and went across country to Monmouth to stay with Philip [Toynbee], which was marvellous, then back to London, crawling through a snowstorm, then back here. I've forgotten to mention that immediately after Ireland, Joan and I went to Paris for a week and ate ourselves to a standstill.

That brings us up to date. It is now the second day of Orthodox Lent and all the Kardamylians are creeping about like spectres under a giant blanket of Shrovetide hangover, which includes us as, in the morning, Grigori Khnarakis[6] of Thrapsano and three other Cretan warriors followed their whiskers through the door with a γαλόνι [gallon] of *tsikoudiá* [Cretan raki] . . .

Joan sends fond love to you and Daph; also Lela and Peter [Petros] and I.

Πολλὴ ἀγάπη σὰν πάντα, καὶ ὁ Θεὸς νὰ φέρει ὅλα δεξιά! [Much love, as always, and may God bring everything to a happy conclusion!],

    Paddy

---

[1] Jock Murray had commissioned portraits of several of the firm's authors from the artist Derek Hill.

[2] François VI, Duc de La Rochefoucauld, Prince de Marcillac (1613–80), author of

Maximes (1665); Luc de Clapiers, Marquis de Vauvenargues (1715–47), friend to Voltaire and author of *Réflexions* and *Maximes* (1746).

3 Ann Fleming's son from her first marriage to Baron O'Neill, who was killed in action during the Second World War.

4 'Bloody Sunday', one of the worst incidents of the 'Troubles', took place here in the Bogside only a few weeks after PLF's visit: British soldiers from the Parachute Regiment shot twenty-six unarmed civilians taking part in a demonstration against the policy of internment without trial, killing fourteen.

5 Andrew Devonshire had given up drinking.

6 A member of the Cretan resistance who had taken part in the operation to abduct General Kreipe.

Billy Moss had married Sophie Tarnowska, his former housemate in Cairo, at the end of the war. After living in London for a while, they set up house in Ireland where she raised their three children while he pursued a career as a writer; but they separated in 1957. Moss never really settled in the post-war world, and he died in 1965, at the age of only forty-four.

To Sophie Moss   Kardamyli
4 May 1972   Messenia

Darling Sophie,

I've been meaning to write for years and years – but you know what the Road to Hell is paved with! Anyway, here we go!

I've just got back from Athens after the most extraordinary encounter with – guess who? General Kreipe, and all his captors! We had all been summoned there by an extremely enterprising Greek TV personality [Niko] Mastorakis. So there we were all gathered together: Manoli, George,[1] me and all the rest of the survivors – two, including poor Bill, were dead, one had been killed a few months after the operation. Then, onto the stage where the cameras were slowly ambles the General, but walking very well (present age seventy-seven), white-haired, but otherwise unchanged. The greetings all round were terrific, wringing of hands, slaps on the back, and, between me and the Cretans, wild kisses. After the show we all went to an Athenian taverna with twenty more Cretans, where there was tremendous singing, and lyre-playing and Cretan dancing, all ending up pretty tight, and many tears being shed for old times' sake. I had three more meals with the General before leaving, and we talked for ages. I'm very pleased about all this, as the whole odd story seemed unfinished, somehow. I think this reunion was a kind of exorcism. He has a very nice wife, married for fifteen years, and I think she was pleased, too. After all, the old boy hadn't managed to do any harm in Crete before his capture, and I always liked him more than Billy did. I think their *froideur* was largely the result of misapprehension because of the extreme language difficulty. Anyway, they flew back to Hanover last night, and this peculiar chapter has somehow been rounded off.

Manoli and George asked lots about you and asked me to send their love, which I do, along with mine. I'll tell you more details about all this when I come to England in a few months, as it's been far too long. Joan and I suddenly decided to marry five years ago, and, not believing in long engagements, did so within the week, and are living happily ever after here, where I'm busy writing a long book about my early troubles, which goes on getting longer and longer . . .

Do write, Sophie, and tell all your news (I do hope this address is the right one, but I'm sure they'll forward it, if you've moved). It's such an age, and all my fault, owing to living in such a Bacchic whirl on rare visits to England. But I plan to set that to rights. So no more now – this is really just to re-establish contact, and bring, dear Sophie,

  lots of fond love
   from Paddy

[also from Joan]

Have I addressed this correctly? Do instruct.

Balasha's cousin, and my old friend Constantin Soutzo,[2] who I saw two years ago, tells me that a son (or daughter?) of his is now married to some kind of a niece (or nephew?) of yours.[3]

I saw Balasha a few years ago in Rumania, and we are in constant correspondence. She's just as nice in every way as she always was, though fallen on hard times . . .

¹ Manoli Paterakis and George Tyrakis, members of the team that had abducted the general.

² Prince Constantin Soutzo (1912–2004), whom PLF had known in Rumania before the war. He managed to escape when the Communists took over and made a new life in Canada.

³ His stepdaughter Iona had married Jan Tarnowski, the nephew of Sophie Moss's first husband Andrew, whom PLF had known in Cairo.

To Diana Cooper   Kardamyli
25 November 1972   Messenia

Darling Diana,

I've just heard from Annie about your poor hands.¹ I can't *think* of anything more horrible, maddening, frustrating and, I bet, painful too. *1,000 wishes* from Joan and me for a lightning recovery, and I wish I were in London to come and read aloud to you of an evening. I've just been through a bout of Kipling stories, which made one think of reading 'The Drums of the Fore and Aft'² to you in your room in Chantilly, so I could have inflicted more of the like on you. (This was set off by a collection of essays on him, out recently, of which by far the best – on Kim – is by your lover Chaudhuri.³ It's packed with lovely illustrations, and I recommend it strongly.)

I still can't quite take in the Judy tidings.⁴ (I've written one of those tributes for the *Times*, but far too late, and it probably won't get in,* so I enclose a copy. I hope it doesn't look as if I mean that her death was caused by burning the candle at both ends; though, perhaps, indirectly, it might have helped. Colin [Tennant]'s and Ivan [Moffat]'s pieces were excellent, I thought.) She'd been meaning to come here from Patmos. We got an unsigned telegram from Istanbul, thought it was Freya (who was also impending, from S. Turkey), wired back 'Come!'; and of course she never got it; nor Freya . . . When we got back here, three weeks ago, a jaunty card was waiting,

* I wired to Frank Giles to get his backing for this late offering.

sent from Rome ('Missed you! BUGGER! Might you *both* come
here en route for Blighty?' etc.); also an amazing drawing of one of
those verbal misunderstandings between SS. Augustine and Gregory,
our age-old joke.[5] I was just writing back in similar terms, when
Milton's telegram arrived. One will miss her frightfully. I wonder
what will happen to Milton – (Rome? twin-life?) – and poor little
Anna?[6] She's a marvel. It's all bewildering, abrupt and upsetting in
the extreme . . .

Our journey out here – Joan, Graham and me in a new station
waggon – was glorious. At first, sitting behind them both listening to
their blended groans – one alto, the other tenor – about traffic, rain,
etc., I felt almost hysterical; but as we headed S.E. from Paris, the
blasting and bombardiering dwindled and a marvellous and
stimulating seventeen days' sightseeing-plus-gastronomic concatenation
began forming, link by glowing link: Carolingian kings, stone
crusaders and their ladies in Romanesque undercrofts and cloisters,
ombles chevaliers [Arctic char], crayfish tails, pulled in half-mourning,
Lombardic frescoes, white truffles (as at Sybil Cholmondeley's),[7]
little-known Bergamask painters, exploding roast turkey, gorgonzola
washed down by Valpolicella, then Dalmatian ham and slivovitz;
Diocletian's choked palace that you gazed at from the *Nahlin*;[8] streets
of pearl and ivory between symmetrical palaces; scores of Ragusan
oysters, broken minarets, skewered kebabs, and many barbaric
delicacies: Balkan and Byzantine kings – then over the Greek border
into S. Macedonia, Delphi and home, where one is still bathing
twenty days after Guy Fawkes Day.

The olive harvest is in full swing, the groves are busy with mules
and sacks and ladders and huge baskets and shouting and singing,
rugs and tarpaulins are spread, figures crowd the branches as the
berries rain down, coiffed women from the hill villages abound, all
in old and disintegrating dresses, 1,000 times laundered and faded by
the sun to the most subtle and charming hues. With a bit of rain, it
would have been a bumper crop, but even without it it's pretty good,
so it's all smiles under the leaves. Before harvesting, the branches
droop like those on the tree in the Willow-pattern plate; after, up
they go, lopped and stripped like moulted birds. Joan's toiling away

on a lower terrace with a chorus of squaws; it's a job closed to men
– alas or hooray – except for the lopping and pruning; jealously
guarded craft-secrets.

Obviously, pen-grasping's off for you for the moment. I'll write a
bit later on and see how things are going. Joan sends love and
sorrowing commiseration, and tons of fond love, plus hugs

from Paddy

xxxx

P.S. Should the Judy piece ever be used, I wish they'd use your
enclosed copy with its corrections.

1 PLF had slightly misunderstood: DC had sprained her wrist.
2 A story by Rudyard Kipling, first published in 1889.
3 Nirad C. Chaudhuri, 'The Finest Story about India – in English', in John Gross
(ed.), *Rudyard Kipling: The Man, his Work and his World* (1972).
4 Judy Montagu had died on 8 November, at the age of forty-nine.
5 See note 2 on page 227.
6 The Gendels' daughter, then nine years old.
7 Sybil, Dowager Marchioness of Cholmondeley (1894–1989), daughter of Sir Edward
Albert Sassoon and Baroness Aline Caroline de Rothschild.
8 A luxury steam yacht, moored in the port of Galati on the Danube. Built in 1929,
Nahlin had been chartered in 1936 by Edward VIII for a cruise in the Adriatic, with
Wallis Simpson and the Duff Coopers among his guests. The King had all the books
removed from the library to make more room for alcohol. In 1937 the *Nahlin* was
bought by King Carol II of Rumania; upon his abdication in 1940 she became the
property of the Rumanian Ministry of Culture, and was used as a museum before
becoming a floating restaurant.

*Paddy was still working on his book about 'the Great Trudge', but as time went
by the scheme seemed to become more and more complicated . . .*

To Jock Murray   Kardamyli
10 January 1973   Messenia

Dear Jock,

I'm so sorry being such an age writing. I knew it would have to
be a long-ish letter, so kept putting it off till the decks were a bit

clearer of all the ludicrous nonsense that has been cluttering them till
now. I mentioned mysteriously in my last letter a plan I wanted to
put to you . . . I think I told you that, when I went down the
Danube a few years ago, I went to see my old friend Balasha
Cantacuzène (the dedicatee of *The Traveller's Tree*).[1] When she and her
sister were chucked out of their old home in Moldavia by the new
regime, they were given a quarter of an hour to pack – a brisk
deracination after three centuries – and were then herded off to the
west of Wallachia, where they still are (where I went to see them at
dead of night). One of the things salvaged was great lumps of my
diary (covering the period I've written about in the present book),
which I brought back here. The two versions tally pretty well, on
the whole, though there are obviously divergences owing to the
difference between recalling things that happened thirty-nine years
ago – 1934–9 – and scribbling them down on a café table a couple
of hours after. The parts covered are: Slovakia and a bit of Hungary;
then a long gap, caused by an idle summer loitering from schloss to
schloss in Transylvania; then quite a lot of Bulgaria, Bucharest,
Bulgaria again (down the Black Sea coast); and Constantinople. The
emergence of this long-lost document has been a bit of a curse and
a puzzle. It should have cropped up before I started, or when it was
too late. What I plan to do is take details out of it to give the text
more vivifying detail where it is needed. In one or two cases fairly
radical changes will have to be made. This is all to the good, as the
rewritten first part (which I dealt with so cursorily in the first
version) is now expanded to considerable length, and contains a lot
of detail, and this new stuff will give the post Vienna-part a
considerable boost, I hope.

My original plan was to finish the book on board the boat sailing
to Salonica and Mt Athos, from Constantinople. Now a new idea has
begun to sprout.

The diary, after Constantinople, goes on to Mt Athos, in
considerable detail, monastery by monastery, covering about a
month in mid-winter, ending just after my twentieth birthday. The
whole of the diary, I hasten to say, is extremely immature, ignorant,
awkward, pretentious and inhibited by turns, an odd mixture of

pseudo-sophistication and naïveté, and also wittingly and
unwittingly comic, often embarrassing. This summer, as a joke and
an experiment, I read long passages out loud to people staying here,
who insisted on more, so I read the lot. They would agree with all
my comments above, but said that nevertheless it had a sort of
immediacy and freshness that later reminiscence lacks, obviously. So
last time I went to Athens, I got someone to type it out, to have a
better look; and a rereading suggests this: that I might shorten some
of these passages, cut out the awkward or embarrassing bits, and
dock the repetitions, but leave the style unchanged, and insert
them, here and there, after telling the story of the diary's untimely
recovery, as a sort of counterpoint to existing text. It's an odd idea,
and presents the difficulty of entire discrepancy of style (because,
although I'm the 1934 diarist's descendant, I could also be his
grandfather); but, if handled with skill, it might give a sudden new
dimension to the book which would be all to the good; and the
clash of the two styles might have a special point of its own.[2]

Well that's the first idea. The second is this. After Mt Athos, [I]
went to stay with some people in Macedonia, and the Venizelist
revolution broke out, which I managed to accompany on horseback,
on a borrowed steed, and attached unofficially to a Royalist cavalry
squadron, across Macedonia to Thrace; when it was over, after a week
or two, I rode back to the Chalkidiki alone, returned the horse, and
continued my interrupted walk south, through Macedonia and
Thessaly to the Meteora, to Boeotia, through Attica to Athens, where
the walk stopped for good, and an entire new life began, which I
can't write about − Rumania etc.

I've long been wondering what I should do about this first
introduction to Greece, which, after all, has been far more important
to me than any of the other countries the book traverses; and now
the following solution looms: to prune and cut down drastically, to
about an eighth of its present length, the Mt Athos diary; write
another chapter on the revolution, and final chapter covering the
month it then took me to walk to Athens − possibly ending at the
first distant glimpse of Athens from Eleusis; then writing THE END.[3]

With considerable trepidation, I'm sending you a few random

pages of the central European diary, and the whole of Mt Athos.
Bear all my strictures in mind, I implore! Whatever else you think
about it I can guarantee a few laughs, however unintended.

No more now, as this has been quite long enough. It's 11 p.m. and
pouring with rain, a steady windless downpour – music to our ears,
thinking of all the trees – your plane is prospering beautifully – and
the masses of rosemary hedges we have been planting.

Yours ever
    Paddy

---

1 The original dedication had referred to Balasha merely by her initials. PLF added a
note to this letter as follows: 'In any future reprints, should they be made, it would
now be OK, it seems, to put her name in full, viz. BALASHA CANTACUZÈNE.
I think she'd be touched.'
2 This was essentially the strategy adopted by the editors of the posthumous volume
of the trilogy, *The Broken Road* (2013), where PLF's account of his visit to Mount Athos
was published.
3 This intention was never realised.

To Aymer Maxwell   Kardamyli
1 March 1973   Messenia

Dear Aymer,

I ought to be writing this in sackcloth with a rope around my
neck, like a Calais burgher. How this delay has occurred is a mystery;
but please forgive me for being such a swine in not writing till
now . . .

I enclose a letter from Charles Rutland,[1] whom I scarcely know.
It suddenly occurred to me: why not Katounia? So I've written to
him, cracking it and Dirk [Hatterick] up like anything, saying he'd
better be quick off the mark, because of Bill Sterling's[2] yearly
descent, and the panting queue of other aspirants. So I expect he'll
be getting in touch with you. I gave him your address and telephone
number. You probably know him well. My first vision – there have
been few others – was of a very unruly night on King's Guard,
where I was Ian Moncreiffe's guest, and everyone got enormously

tight, and a great deal of breakage and baying for broken glass took place, and in the middle of the wreckage C. Rutland was dancing furiously by himself, wearing one of the lampshades, which entirely masked those lean features.

I – we – wish you had come down here on your flying visit. Since Niko, Barbara and Father Levi,[3] our only visitor has been Coote Lygon (who had been knocked over by a car a month before in London, so was on two sticks) hobbling about the terrace like a wounded admiral on his quarterdeck. Did you see a remark of Osbert Sitwell quoted in one of the Sunday papers, about Dame Ethel Smyth:[4] 'Ethel would look exactly like Wagner, if only she were more feminine'? The other item I've enjoyed most recently is the refusal of Miss Schneider[5] of a large offer by a butter firm for permission to reproduce her picture on every packet. (Could one stamp it on pats?)

It's suddenly freezing cold here.

Keep in touch, and please come here as soon as you get to Greece.

Fond love from both of us.

Yours ever

Paddy

[1] Charles John Robert Manners (1919–99), 10th Duke of Rutland. It seems that he had written to PLF asking about places to stay in Greece.

[2] Unidentified: perhaps Lieutenant Colonel William Joseph Stirling of Keir (1911–83).

[3] Peter Levi, S.J. (1931–2000), poet, writer, traveller and scholar.

[4] Ethel Mary Smyth (1858–1944), composer and suffragette. She had several passionate affairs, most of them with women. Virginia Woolf said that being loved by her was 'like being caught by a giant crab'.

[5] In the Bertolucci film *Last Tango in Paris* (1972) the actress Maria Schneider is sodomised by her co-star Marlon Brando, using butter as a lubricant.

To Balasha Cantacuzène   Kardamyli
soon after Orthodox Shrove Tuesday, 1973   Messenia

Darling Balasha,

   Phew! (I never know how this is spelt, except it's not 'Pshaw!',
which expresses another mood). I've just finished correcting 26,000
words of my new book for a typist in Athens. As I can't read my
own writing, it nearly killed me. I had to copy out whole pages for
the poor girl, and even the uncopied ones are a cobweb of erasures,
balloons, and additions; and I've now got to tackle another 15,000. So
this is in the nature of a wave between the bars of my own literary
prison! I'll try and write more clearly than I've done in my own
MSs. I do envy you, Balasha darling, to have such a lovely clear and
decorative hand. If I manage to change my writing now, I wonder if
it would drag my whole character with it into a different – perhaps
better – shape?

   I wonder how this book will read? Impossible to tell, but it
doesn't seem too bad. The part I have been correcting is Germany
and a part of Austria: the Dutch frontier to Düsseldorf, Cologne,
Bonn, Koblenz, all up the Rhine till I branched off along the Necker
to Heidelberg; then down through Baden and Württemberg to
Stuttgart, across Swabia to Ulm and Augsburg, then into Bavaria to
Munich; S.E. to Salzburg, over the Austrian border, N.E. till I join
the Danube again (which I had crossed at Ulm) at Linz. From there,
along the river to Vienna, which I've not yet reached (I'm halfway
between Melk on the Wachau, and the castle of Dürnstein, where
Richard Coeur de Lion was imprisoned on his way back from the
Crusade). The odd thing about this book is that I began it years ago,
as an article for an American magazine, to be called 'The Pleasures of
Walking'. I dashed across Europe, as far as Arad, in ten pages (it's
now, in the revised version, about 200 till Dürnstein!). Then I got so
fascinated and carried away that I chucked the idea of the article
and let it rip. So all Transylvania, Bulgaria, Bucharest, the Black Sea
Coast of Bulg., Turkey, and Constantinople (where the book ends) is
written out in full – another 200 pages; so now I'm struggling on to
join hands with myself in Arad. This I did ages ago, and will have to

change, here and there, in the light of that diary which you so nobly
rescued from Băleni. So the book will have had a very odd genesis,
and should be very long; I hope not too long! I think there's another
three months' hard work on it. This rainy winter solitude with only
Joan and her pussies has been a great help. *I can't think* what to call
it. While you're reading, *do please* keep your eyes open for any short
phrase that might do. Shakespeare's poetry is a goldmine – 'Brief
Candles', 'All our Yesterdays', 'Antic Hay', 'Handful of Dust', etc.

What a selfish screed! Darling, I do hope your health is not giving
you hell. You know how we wish we could do something. It's awful
to be so powerless . . . You write so stoically about it all . . .

I'm so glad you both enjoyed the Virginia Woolf book;[1] and I
agree with all your verdicts. But, with all their appalling faults, they[2]
fascinate. I'm very glad to have one or two tenuous links with it all
– through Barbara and Mary.[3] Our friend Janetta (now married to
the Spaniard Jaime Parladé) . . . was pretty well brought up by Ralph
and Frances Partridge, and I often went to stay at Ham Spray,[4] full of
Lytton's things, and with Carrington's paintings everywhere. Gerald
Brenan,[5] now eighty, but haring up and down the mountains like a
roebuck, came here for ten days last year, with a beautiful girl,[6] v.
well read and terribly nice ('no sex, alas!' he told me, rather ruefully)
and then back to the little Andalusian village where they live. He
writes marvellously about Spain, specially his history of Spanish
literature. We used often to see Clive Bell, when we lived in the flat
above Mary, in Charlotte St, and Bunny Garnett,[7] frequently in
England now, as he has developed a passion for our friend
Magouche . . .

No more now, darling Balasha. John Donne says, 'letters, more
than kisses, mingle souls'[8] . . .

Tons of fond love to you and Pomme,
     Paddy

[1] Quentin Bell's biography of his aunt, *Virginia Woolf: A Biography* (2 vols., 1972), had
won several prizes, including the Duff Cooper Prize.

[2] PLF is referring to the Bloomsbury Group.

[3] Barbara Ghika and her mother, Mary Hutchinson (1889–1977), née Barnes, who
owned the flat in Charlotte Street where PLF and Joan lived in the early 1950s. Lytton

Strachey, Mary Hutchinson's cousin, introduced her to the Bloomsbury Group. She became friendly with Virginia Woolf, and was also close to Aldous Huxley and T. S. Eliot.

4 Their house near Hungerford, Berkshire. They lived there for almost thirty years until 1961, when Frances sold it following her husband's death.

5 Gerald Brenan (1894–1987), writer and scholar of Spanish history and culture.

6 Lynda Nicholson-Price (1943–2011), poet and translator, who had been Brenan's companion since 1968.

7 David 'Bunny' Garnett (1892–1981), writer and publisher associated with the Bloomsbury Group.

8 'To Sir Henry Wotton' (slightly misquoted).

To Nancy Mitford   Kardamyli
20 April 1973   Messenia

Darling Nancy,

There's a horrible *scirocco* blowing here – ashen sky, mewing cats, slamming windows, and hearts of lead. The villagers, reduced to nervous phantoms by Lenten fasting, with several days to go still – we're halfway between Greek Palm Sunday and Easter – get snappier and snappier; worse than Moors at the end of Ramadan. By the time the paschal lambs are on their spits, they will be beyond everything except gnashing and scowling.

Derek Jackson[1] has just left, after four days here; all alone, which was nice; and you were talked of with great fondness (hence this pen suddenly being put to paper). He was very bland and easy; but, my word, he's very far from usual. Last night I had dinner nearby (they telephoned, but, as they were with a mob of descendants, refused to come here) with Laura Waugh[2] and her sister Bridget. I complained bitterly about the inadequacy and the indiscretion of the diary in the *Observer*[3] – particularly about the idiotic brief biography of Mark[4] – and Laura agrees, saying it was all the fault of Peters,[5] E. Waugh's agent, who had complete rights. She hadn't even read most of it. It all sounds very rum to me, and a bit wet, I must say. All this having been said, it makes fascinating reading. We guess who most of the asterisks are, but one or two are elusive. Laura said 'Audrey' was someone called Audrey Lucas,[6] which rings a faint bell, but v. faint . . .

Joan is a sort of Queen Canute in a rising tide of kittens. I think of little else except yards and yards of rosemary hedge I planted earlier on, and five poplar trees, and am seldom far from a hose. I almost feel that those leaves and shoots are springing from my own elbows, hands on ears, like a nymph seeking refuge in the vegetable kingdom from some lustful pursuer, e.g. Syrinx.[7] When shadows fall, a marten steals down from the mountains, craps on the terrace and steals up into the mountains again. A lot of wild geese flew overhead last week, on their way north from Africa. Hoopoes, golden orioles and bee-eaters are beginning to appear and one often nearly measures one's length over a tortoise; so spring's here at last.

I've just finished Dame V. Wedgwood's *Thirty Years War*,[8] which has always fascinated me. Such an extraordinary cast: the Elector Palatine, the Winter Queen, Maximilian of Bavaria, the Emperor Leopold, Wallenstein, le Grand Condé, Richelieu, Gustavus Adolphus, Mansfeld, Christian of Brunswick, Piccolomini, the Cardinal-Infant of the Spanish Netherlands; half-Velasquez, half-van Dyck figures, with shoulder-length hair, whiskers and imperials, and wide starched or lace collars breaking over black armour inlaid with gold. It's rather how I'd like to go about . . .

We're off tomorrow to stay with the Ghikas in Corfu, where I hope it's more *propre et gai* [clean and comfortable] than here; will probably feast a certain amount with C. and E. Glenconner.[9] Lovely change . . .

Lots of love
Paddy

P.S. Debo and I have a desultory exchange of riddles. I've just asked her (1) why Diocletian, that well-known Dalmatian character, was a schizophrenic and (2) why someone might be depressed sitting down at the dining table at Lismore. The answer to (1) is because he was a split personality[10] and (2) because the outlook is Belleek.[11]

---

[1] See note 3 on page 197.

[2] Laura Waugh (1916–73), née Herbert, Evelyn Waugh's widow. She died only two months after this letter was written.

[3] In 1973 Waugh's diaries were serialised in the *Observer Colour Magazine* prior to publication in book form in 1976.

[4] Mark Ogilvie-Grant, a close friend of NM's. It is not obvious why PLF thought his biography 'idiotic'.

[5] A. D. Peters (1892–1973), literary agent.

[6] Audrey Lucas (1898–1975), daughter of the travel writer E. V. Lucas, had an affair with Evelyn Waugh after the breakdown of his first marriage.

[7] Syrinx, a chaste nymph. Pursued by Pan, she ran to a river's edge and asked for assistance from the river nymphs, who transformed her into hollow water reeds that made a haunting sound when his frustrated breath blew across them. Pan cut the reeds to fashion the first set of pan pipes, henceforth known as *syrinx*.

[8] Dame Cicely Veronica Wedgwood OM (1910–97), who wrote under the name C. V. Wedgwood, author of *The Thirty Years War* (1938).

[9] Christopher Grey Tennant (1899–1983), 2nd Baron Glenconner, and his daughter Emma.

[10] A play on words: Split is the city on the Dalmatian coast where Diocletian died.

[11] A reference to Belleek china used at Lismore.

To Diana Cooper   Kardamyli
17 July 1973   Messenia

Darling Diana,

Here, I say! It really is about time I had some direct news! Roundabout rumours steal across Europe about adventures in Ethiopia; but nary a word from you!

All's well here. Lovely and cool with a mild west wind off the sea which is gurgling fifty yards away. I'm scribbling away under an alfresco ceiling of rush mats raised on stilts on one of the olive terraces just under the house. I hear Joan mooching about just overhead, followed by a mewing crowd, as usual.

For three whole months today, I haven't smoked a single cigarette! Considering I'd been smoking from 80 to 100 a day for the last thirty years: end-to-end – they could have formed a single monster cigarette (which I'd been steadily smoking my way along) stretching from Victoria Station to Brighton. Then came the death-grapple with weight. Phew! It's swung in my favour now, very decidedly, that only by dint of being seldom off the scales: –

'Weighing-machine upon the floor,
Say, who's lighter than before?'

I find it is a great help to pretend as I step onto the device, that it is
a lift, and attended by two Dickensian lift-boys. One is the Fat Boy
from the *Pickwick Papers*; he touches – or rather used to touch – his
cap with a collusive leer, and the words: '*Going up, Sir?*' Thank
heavens, his place has now been taken by his slender colleague, O.
Twist, at his leanest, who just murmurs '*Going down, Sir!*' in tones of
respect and admiration . . .

If there are any about, I occasionally smoke a cigar in the evening,
on the principle that the embrace of a black concubine, in the
French Antilles, was not considered adultery. Otherwise, it's all
snuff-box and beads . . .

We both wish you would come here. *Why not?* Do please ponder
it! It's much easier and more comfortable now. Lela would be
pleased: so would your admirer the Abyssinian cat – you could give
him some home news (us too?); and we would be in seventh heaven.

Tons of fond love & hugs,
From Paddy
Also Joan

*Paddy made his life more complicated than it needed to be by accepting commit-
ments that he could not fulfil, and suffered torment in trying to wriggle out of
them afterwards.*

To Michael Stewart   Kardamyli
25 January 1974   Messenia

Dear Michael,

I'm in an abyss of doubt and anxiety about the Anglo-Hellenic
League, and I'd do anything to get out of it. In the euphoria of
setting off to hunt for antiques in the Portobello Road, I cheerfully
said 'yes': not for glory or gain, but as one might say it to a pal,
consenting to go and *ad lib* for half an hour – eked out with a few

notes and quotations – to his wife's Women's Institute. (I had an ambience of buns and cocoa in mind, in some vague institutional premises . . .)

But I see from your letter that I hadn't got the hang of it at all (my fault); that it's a very serious affair, involving a lecture hall, publicity, a large, critical and very different kind of audience from the one I had vaguely imagined – (I've heard of the Anglo-Hellenic League for years but, oddly enough, never run into it: perhaps, subconsciously, on purpose) – an audience ready to weigh practised academics in the balance and find them wanting. All this doesn't induce a failure of nerve, but a swarm of depressing thoughts. For, though I can be a terrible gasbag in private, I'm incapable of talking extempore to a formal audience; still less to one which would know a lot more about the well-worn themes of Byron than I do. So, for a slow writer like me, this would mean literally weeks putting together a written essay on I'm not quite sure what, still: 'Byron and Common Sense' . . .?

The thing is that I have at last got up a proper head of steam on my book, and I had been keeping all decks clear for these desperately longed-for empty two and a half months of winter ahead – before our solitary laborious winter evaporates into distracting and gregarious spring – to forge ahead like a monomaniac, and get as near as time allowed to the end of this wretched incubus of a book. I hoped to get it into Jock Murray's hands at last for publication this winter. Unfortunately, I seem to be utterly incapable of doing two creative things at once and the preparation of a formal conference on Byron, joined with the absence in London, would take an enormous chunk out of this longed-for and vital period. I know I ought to have thought of all this before consenting so frivolously. But if there were any way of getting out of this predicament, as I now see it to be, with – not *l'honneur*, but without lasting shame – it would be salvation. You know it's nothing to do with cash – it's absolutely adequate, and, apart from the fare, I'd have done it for nothing – only time.

I *have* a saving suggestion. When I was in the British Council in Athens, Peter Quennell came out to lecture on Byron, with special reference to the poet's links with Greece. It was brilliant, erudite, funny, all that a lecture should be. He's one of England's most distinguished Byron scholars, you'd agree. He *must* have text of the lecture still. Would the fee – plus perhaps, what would have been coughed up for my fare? – tempt him? I'm sure it would – he'd merely have to read out the former text, a little reshuffled and updated, perhaps. (He's a great friend of mine, but perhaps it would be better not to mention that I had proved a broken reed on the same theme – only that I had spoken so enthusiastically of his lecture.) If not, what about Doris Langley-Moore? Leslie Marchand? – or Jock Murray: six generations of Byron publishing and links with Greece? (Monty Woodhouse . . . ?)[1]

If there is no remedy, I'd have to do it – *déshonneur oblige*! Of course I'd try not to let you down by producing a public fiasco (but it would be a *private* disaster); but that's my fault for not going into it more thoroughly in the beginning. I'm so sorry for all this, Michael. I'm *utterly* to blame, *mea maxima culpa*, and very many apologies. Let me know if it's thumbs up or down . . .

Yours ever

Paddy

Change of theme. Love from Joan, & to Damaris. Thank you *very* much for those Grass-Green-Incorruptible-Seven-League-Boots. I've been speeding over the sierras in them. I oughtn't to have got them buckshee. Just read horrible news about J. Pope Hennessy.[2]

---

[1] Doris Langley Moore (1902–89), fashion historian and Byron scholar; Leslie A. Marchand (1900–99), editor of Byron's letters and journals; C. M. 'Monty' Woodhouse (1917–2001), politician and scholar of modern Greece, who had served with SOE in Crete during the German occupation: author of *The Philhellenes* (1971).

[2] The biographer and travel writer James Pope-Hennessy (1916–74) had been brutally murdered in his London flat.

To Diana Cooper   Kardamyli
24 June 1974   Messenia

My darling Diana,

It's a day of joy here, thanks to your knock-out American-flight letter. And on legendary St Firmin paper[1] too. I came across a few surviving stolen sheets a couple of months ago, but can't find them to answer in kind. How you have the nerve, Diana, to talk of 'innate lack of confidence', from the best letter writer now breathing, beats me! And all carried off dazzling hell-for-leather style: 'Done in the smack of a whip, and on horseback too,' as Sir B. Backbite said about his friend's silly poem.[2] Apropos of Sheridan, Joanie's [brother] Graham, suffering from the omnipresence of pictures of our recent dictator here, complained about his damned disenfranchising countenance.[3]

Owing to delay in the arrival of newspapers here, and further held up by absence in Athens and then chez Barbara in Corfu, I missed the horrible tidings about Raimund[4] until it was ages late. I knew what a shattering loss this must be for you and meant to write; then something intervened. *I wish I had.* I'm so glad JJ made such a moving address. Unlike you, I thought Isaiah's piece in *The Times* immensely good, especially about R's romantic and Mozartian approach to life,[5] and I thought it implied, even if it didn't mention, his *Tale of Genji* side, that I only knew about from you. I'm glad you're going to Zell am See[6] – hope it doesn't interfere with other plans, *see below* – though it might be a bit upsetting. Oh dear, I can't help wondering what will happen to Liz. I wrote her a pretty feeble line, being hopeless at such things.

Now: Daph's Book.[7] I was vaguely against the idea, in an unforceful way, dreading that Daph might make a hash of it; but, with all its obvious shortcomings, I rather loved it once it had surfaced. It caught a lot of Iris's point though not all; and its faults were so transparently due to D's wild, un-earnest, enthusiastic and flapperish niceness. I selfishly felt – as I suppose dozens of others did – that I could, if asked as of course I longed to be, have brought a bushel or two of grist to the *Schöne Müllerin*[8] wielding the pen: bit about Rome, and the Sabine and the Alban hills, castles, feasts, *trattorias*, Ischia and Provence, as there wasn't enough about her Italian life. The thing is, Iris was the sort of treasure everyone feels proprietary about, and wants a share in. But on the whole I loved it, and wrote and said so. A. Scott-James's review of the book was detestable. It was hideously unfair to break it on the wheel for the reasons she cited.[9]

Plans. I was supposed to be mountaineering somewhere – the Pyrenees, the Tyrol or the Mountains of the Moon – with Andrew for the last half of July, but he hasn't written so I don't know what's on. (At least, he *has* written, but only to ask what to do with my copy of that head that his Claudine of Innsbrück cast in bronze for him,[10] so I said *you* had consented to give it temporary shelter. I hope this is all right.) Joan and I are coming to Blighty for August, so I pray you will be there. We'll stay at Patrick [Kinross]'s if he can have us, so will be nice and handy. I'm going to Brittany for a few days to see an old Hungarian pal called Elemér v. Klobusiçky[11] who is escaping from ghastly drudgery in Budapest to stay for a month with his escaped son, who is Napoleonically wed to a girl called Caroline Murat.[12] (Elemér was a dashing and very funny ex-hussar squire, and I haven't seen him since he was thirty-five and I was nineteen, when we were galloping about the Transylvanian woods together, swimming down poplar-shaded rivers and leaping out to chase nymphs – at their challenge, I hasten to say – who were reaping on the banks; barefoot but dauntless over the stubble fields, till we cornered them by the ricks.) Then, back here. *Any chance of your coming?* You touch on being lame and halt: if there's no attendant yacht to deposit and retrieve you in our bay – I see a Bucentaur[13] ruffling up! – it would be child's play to arrange for a purple palanquin between here and the road. More of this when we meet.

Literary news is that my laggard Odyssey has grown to such a size that the cost of book production may compel Jock Murray to split it up into vols. I feel slightly against this, as, after this awful house-building and bone-idleness-promoted silence, I feel I ought to knock the reader out by sheer weight of pages. But I suppose he's right.

Vol. I would take us across Holland – snow all the way – in

December 1933, then up the Rhine and across Swabia and
Württemberg to Munich; Salzburg, Upper Austria, along the Danube
through the Ledebur-country, cowsheds and castles all the way, and
snow; nineteeth birthday in a beetling Childe Roland keep near the
Vienna woods; Vienna and the Feb. 1934 revolution and sketching
from door to door. Then, the river again, to Bratislava (with an illicit
sidestep by train to Prague); across Slovakia (snows melting, spring
beginning) and a long stay with Minka Strauss's father[14] (a charming
Swann-like figure) in a snug manor beside a Danubian tributary.
Then back to the great river; arrest and release on suspicion of
smuggling while slumbering among the rushes (Vol. I drawing to a
close now . . .); crossing the huge bridge between Slovakia and
Hungary, on Easter Sunday evening, all Hungary waiting the other
side, and the bells of Esztergom cathedral peeling across the flood.
Dreamy halt at midbridge – *CUT!*

Vol. II would thus open with scores of Magyar noblemen, like a
crowd of Prince Igors, in green and scarlet hessians, fur-edged
dolmans, and scimitars, and fur hats with plumes like escaping steam,
with the Cardinal-Prince-Archbishop, Primate of Hungary, clattering
up to the cathedral behind six white plumed greys . . . Then
Budapest; the Great Hungarian Plain half trudging, half on borrowed
steeds, social ballooning alternating still with social frogmanship in
castles and hovels; Transylvania for the nymphing season; W. Rumania;
S. to the Iron Gates; into Bulgaria, crossing and recrossing the Great
Balkan Range and north over the river again to Bucharest at the
turn of the leaf; down the Black Sea coast, arriving at Constantinople
in a light snowfall at the end of Ramadan; viz. New Year 1935. *End
of Vol. II.*[15] I'm now toying with the idea of an unwritten Vol. III
– I'd meant to conclude with the Bosphorus. This hypothetical vol.
would start with arrival by sea at Mt Athos, and January and
February (twentieth birthday) in all the monasteries in deep snow,
and not another soul except the monks. The 1935 Venizelos
revolution; then, two months accompanying the Royalist Cavalry,
again on a borrowed steed, through Macedonia and Thrace. Back to
Salonica on it through the Rhodope Mts, then S. via Thessaly, till the
book would end with a distant prospect of the Acropolis. I am

working very hard on the end of Vol. I. There would be a pause
between I and II – the latter is complete except for the final chapter.

I'm writing this on the lower terrace that you remember, under a
charming and shady pavilion Petro and I have built; 5 yards square,
with pillars of peeled cypress poles, supporting a roof of that criss-
cross trellis work I have such a passion for. It spreads a cool checky
and lozengy carpet of shade, like tartan underfoot, that turns dogs as
they trot through into momentary leopards and bipeds into
harlequins. This autumn we'll plant vines and roses that will surge up
the poles to form a Gérard de Nerval[16] canopy, *la treille où le pampre
à la rose s'allie* ['the trellis where the rose and the vine are entwined'].
I reread his *Filles de Feu* two years ago. It's a very moving and
romantic story, all in the St Firmin neighbourhood, La Route de
Flandres, Senlis, Ermenonville, etc. But you probably know it by
heart.

Petro and Lela scull out every morning to take in the nets they
spread overnight, ascending the sea-steps with baskets full of tangled
Breughel-and-Bosch-like fins, tentacles, spines, gills and accusing eyes.
Shoals are changing the whole time: blue, green, buff, scarlet orange,
deep purple; striped, and fancy. Lobsters are infrequent enough to be
a great treat when they turn up rattling their castanets. Sometimes
there is a *dentice* [sea-bream] – *synagrida* to us – fit for Tobias to be
painted with.[17] So it's fish for luncheon every day. Heaven knows
what it does to the brain.

Cicadas v. loud to-day . . . I spy Joan, three terraces down, filling
a colander with apricots, the ones from the branches for lunch, those
on the ground for jam – pretty dull, she says, but there are so many
one can't just leave them. Also small plums the size of a penny,
green-gold, translucent and delicious.

Apropos of Ledebur country, Friedrich comes for a few days in a
fortnight, on his way to some prosperous Embericoes on an island,
bringing a tall son *d'un autre lit* [from a previous marriage] and his
chum. He likes Daphne's book. We're both looking forward to it, and
I'll grill him for details about Upper Austria.

Darling Diana, this was meant to be a brisk paragraph or two
about plans, so disregard extraneous matter. Your letter was a true

302 PATRICK LEIGH FERMOR

delight to both. One suffers from an intermittent Crusoe-complex on this headland, scanning the waves for bottles with messages and yours was half-genie, half-hippocrene. Joan shouts many tender messages from the apricots and tons of fond love, Diana darling,
from Paddy
XOXOXO

P.S. There's been an intermittent rustling in the long grass all through this letter. I now see it is a very small tortoise.

¹ i.e. the notepaper of Le Château de Saint-Firmin, DC's house in the grounds of the Château de Chantilly.

² In fact it is Crabtree, and not Sir Benjamin Backbite, who says this, in Sheridan's play *The School for Scandal*.

³ 'That, now, to me, is as stern a looking rogue as ever I saw; an unforgiving eye, and a damned disinheriting countenance!' (Sheridan, *School for Scandal*).

⁴ DC's close friend Raimund von Hofmannsthal, who had been married to her niece Liz Paget, had just died.

⁵ 'Raimund von Hofmannsthal was a man of incandescent aesthetic feeling . . . His imagination was shaped by Mozart and Austrian baroque and neoclassicism . . . He seemed to have before his eyes an ideal vision of a Royal Court of unimaginable splendour, ruled by a divinely inspired princely artist, and he tended to romanticize the lives of all those of whom he was fond, which brought many of them much comfort.' Obituary by 'I. B.' [Isaiah Berlin] in *The Times*, 26 April 1974.

⁶ Raimund von Hofmannsthal owned Prielau, a seventeenth-century chateau on the shores of the lake at Zell am See.

⁷ *The Rainbow Picnic: A Portrait of Iris Tree* (1974).

⁸ 'Fair miller-maid': PLF refers to Schubert's song cycle.

⁹ 'She has not been too lucky in her biographer. The *Rainbow Picnic* reads like a profile for the *Tatler* written in a hurry.' Anne Scott-James, 'Portrait of a Golden Girl', *Sunday Times*, 14 April 1974.

¹⁰ The sculptress Angela Conner had made a bronze of AD's head, and would also do PLF himself; PLF refers here to Browning's poem 'My Last Duchess' (1842).

¹¹ Elemér von Klobusiçky (1899–1986) had been PLF's host on his family estate at Guraszáda in Transylvania in the summer of 1934.

¹² Joachim-Napoléon Murat, Marshal of France and King of Naples 1808–15, was Napoleon's brother-in-law.

¹³ The state barge of the Doges of Venice.

¹⁴ Baron Philipp Schey von Koromla (1881–1957), known as 'Pips'.

¹⁵ In fact Volume II in its published form – *Between the Woods and the Water* (1986) – would take him no further than the Iron Gates, on the Bulgarian frontier.

¹⁶ Gérard de Nerval was the nom de plume of the French writer, poet, essayist and

translator, Gérard Labrunie (1808–55). The quotation is from his poem *El Desdichado*, published in 1854. His *Filles de Feu* was published in 1852.

[17] St Tobias is often depicted with the fish he cleaned by order of an angel.

To Janetta Parladé   Kardamyli
7 September 1974   Messenia

Darling Janetta,

I *did* think of you last week! It was the end of the last weekend in England, Whit Monday in fact, when Annie, the Donaldsons[1] (who I scarcely knew, but liked, especially he) and I, set out to meet Francis Watson[2] on the edge of the Carrington country for a lunch in a village you must know well but whose name escapes me, with a very nice old pub, the Something Arms, where we didn't eat, and another one, where we did; a beautiful old rosy-coloured brick watermill converted – perhaps rather spoilt – with tiles of the same hue: you can still see the old mill-race roaring under a kind of glass leper's squint in the floor. We all got noisy and happy and a bit tight, swilling wine down, and gorging like Brueghel reapers on a row of marvellous roast things that one slashed into *ad lib* on a long trestle table. Afterwards, there was some competitive showing-off, jumping from one half-submerged stepping-stone to the next, across the river – the Kennet, perhaps, hallowed by crayfish memories? – that must have turned the mill-wheel of yore. After all this, A. and I drove to Gibbet Hill, parked near those gallows, and set off along the path, with a tall hedge on one side, that runs along the top of a long high ridge. After a while, though I'd never been on the top of it, I felt certain that I knew the country below: surely the great hogged mane of trees sweeping downhill was the Bull's Tail? There was a cluster of buildings below that could only be Ham Spray. It was! Annie turned back here, to get the car and pick me up below, as I was determined to proceed; so I slogged on, not meeting a soul, except two boys flying a kite, as it was quite a windy day, sending big cloud shadows scudding over the fields below. Very few wild flowers, masses of Deadly and Woody Nightshade in the hedges, Jack in the Pulpits with burnt-up cowls turning into

Lords and Ladies, and sprays of elderflower just beginning to turn, they'll all be purple (black?) by now. Came to a crossroads, & shot steeply downhill between v. high banks and hedges, and into Ham, where I mooched about the church and churchyard for a bit, then on to a village green, near a pub (Rose & Crown?), where I fell asleep in the grass till woken up by Annie with the motor. We peered over the fence of Dove House, to see if there were any scampering Rothschildren;[3] then leant over the gate of Ham Spray, looking rather deforested and shaven and shorn; tiptoed a few yards inside and fled at the signs of movement within. We passed the small Inkpen pub where I remember buying fags with you years ago; also the house with the huge copper beech that I think you took for a spell.

It was all marvellous, and full of happy reminders.

I'm not sending any news, as I know Joan's written – only the above, if you call it news; proof, if needed, that you're thought of and missed.

 Tons of love
  Paddy

Also to Jaime

 [1] John George Stuart Donaldson, Baron Donaldson of Kingsbridge (1907–98), soldier, farmer, prison reformer, consumers' champion and politician; and Frances Donaldson (1907–94), née Lonsdale, writer and biographer.
 [2] Sir Francis John Bagott Watson (1907–92), art historian and museum director, who lived after his retirement at Corton in Wiltshire.
 [3] i.e. young Rothschilds.

Paddy's relations with his mother Aileen (née Ambler) were never easy.

To Balasha Cantacuzène   Kardamyli
9 September 1974   Messenia

Balasha darling,
 My weeks [in London] were strangely and, in a way, rather sadly taken up in trying, with some success, to straighten out my mother's

affairs which she manages always to re-entangle with unerring skill, largely due to a confusion between reality and a vivid and usually rather malevolent imagination which impels her to quarrel – quarrels based on fictitious accusations, strongly believed, against absolutely everyone who she comes in contact with – except, so far, me, because I'm so seldom there. I think it's a form of neglected creativeness which has taken a wrong turning, a sort of superannuated spoiled-ness with a touch of megalomania, hung over from early gifts and beauty and success: 'Well, all right, if not love, *hate!*' It's agonisingly painful, and a cause of unhappiness to everyone, and helpless, frustrated goodwill, especially to those nearest to her – Vanessa and Francesca[1] (who both send their love. Francesca remembers you so clearly and romantically as a little girl, in Gloucestershire). So my time was spent between Brighton (where she has been [in] a very nice sort of hotel nursing-home for the last few years, tormenting everyone) and the Herculean task of liquidating the flat she had in London for the past forty years – but uninhabited by her for the last six – sorting out papers, getting rid of and storing furniture & pictures, cleaning the place out. One couldn't move in it, everything was deep in cobwebs and dust and London grime, exactly like Miss Havisham's house in *Great Expectations*: thousands of newspapers piled up, magazines, books in confusion, manuscripts and typescripts of plays[2] – some of them put on for trial runs for a few days in theatre-clubs – programmes, piles of aviation magazines from her 1928–30 passion to learn to fly; masses of dresses that should have been thrown away decades ago; skis, skates, side-saddles deep in mildew . . . moulting fans, dog-eared music, a ukulele. (I only learnt a few years ago that when she and my father set off into the jungle for camp and geological exploration – one elephant, several horses, endless bullock-carts, an army of servants, one bullock-cart always contained a piano for jazz, ragtime, a bit of Chopin, a bit of Rimsky-Korsakoff), countless hats, forty-year-old toques like caved-in soufflés, moth-eaten furs, an artillery busky in a case, buttons of native cavalry and infantry regiments, her brother's and their grandfather's sabres, a lance-pennant; and – anticlimax! – nearly 300 empty milk bottles shoved away in odd corners, and a long-dead pigeon (which must have flown down the chimney),

probably from Trafalgar Square, 300 yards away. There was also a
dried-up husk of a small scorpion in a tin trunk full of letters (why
not a cobra's skeleton?), thousands of them, going back to the 1830s,
faded yellow, and written across twice in spidery writing, and rather
fascinating albums of faded photos of endless Amblers and Taaffes[3]
since the earliest days of photography: races, gymkhanas, picknicks,
pig-sticking, tent pegs, garden parties, cavalcades, steeple chases, polo,
my mother's mother (who was quite a competent portrait and
landscape painter, also born in India) elaborately veiled in a palanquin
between four long-suffering coolies, in identical tunics and turbans, or
riding with my mother and uncle, with faded white plaster mansions
in the background built in a mock-moghul style, with frilly
crenellations, standing among palm trees and banyans. Always hosts of
servants lined-up, innumerable because caste would only let each one
do one particular task, e.g., a groom couldn't sweep, a laundryman
couldn't draw water etc.; so the humblest subaltern seems to have had
a retinue like the Ban of Craiova[4] . . . Strange world, I'll sort all these
out, one day. There were lots of later photographs too, of amateur
theatricals in Calcutta and Simla, round which all social life seems to
have revolved, with my mother invariably playing the lead: St Joan,
The School for Scandal, The Beaux Stratagem, Portia [sic] in Twelfth
Night, Rosalind in As You Like It, etc.

As you can imagine, there was something rather harrowing about
all this. All the verve, fun, looks, high spirits, talents and energy
having, in the end, taken such a bitter turning. The 'spoiled-ness' I
mentioned earlier, I think must have been due − as it is with many
girls brought up in India and, as it must have been with many
tiresome Gone with the Wind beauties in the Southern States in
America − to being over-successful when young in a small arena,
surrounded by a nearly exclusively masculine society and a different
coloured population in a subject position. Well, there we are, and
enough of that. All too sad! If only kindness, mellowness, a humbler
interest in other people had ensued, instead of this fierce conviction
that everyone is wrong and hostile except oneself . . . I've blown off
a lot of steam. Don't mention it too much when you write. I want
to let the whole thing sort itself out clearly in thoughts . . .

***

We – though Joan was most of the time at her brother Graham's in Gloucestershire – stayed with Patrick Kinross by the canal in Little Venice, which was nice. I got to England a day earlier, and rushed across southern England to join Robin Fedden, Annie Fleming and Michael Astor at a pub in S. Wales, for a walking tour. But when I got to Abergavenny, Michael had twisted his ankle, and Anne got the sudden news that her son Caspar had taken an overdose of some wretched drug in Jamaica, swum out to sea, been washed back to the shore, picked up half-dead and flown by helicopter to Kingston, the capital, where he was being brought round (he's in hospital in London, on the way to recovery, thank God). So in the end, Robin and I did the walk alone, through the Black Mountains – green and russet, really – for a few days: lovely wild rolling country of bracken and mountain streams, with only shepherds there, with enormous flocks and wonderfully clever sheepdogs – I think the silent, methodical skill of these animals rounding up great flocks in silence, guiding them into single file, in obedience to an occasional carefully pitched whistle from field to field, and letting them fan out over wild country, never rucking it, then wheeling them back to their byres, is infinitely more proof of an unbroken civilisation than a jet-aeroplane. (When I think of the chaotic bawling, barking, bleating, stone-throwing, crook-flourishing, rage and disorder, incomplete improvisation after thousands of years – that prevails in Greece, I can't help feeling there has been a serious break since the times of Theocritus. But don't tell anyone.) Otherwise, nothing but troops of ponies grazing, thick woods and deep valleys. Lovely seeing full-sized trees again. I also got away from London to Graham's, then to Michael Astor's where David Cecil and his wife Rachel[5] (Desmond MacCarthy's daughter) were staying too; to Ann Fleming's, where pale Caspar was, and a long walk through the Carrington–Strachey country; and a last glorious weekend with Debo and Andrew D., at Bolton Abbey in Yorkshire – not far from Wensleydale! I thought of you and Guy [Branch] – wide rolling dales, the house standing

beside a ruined Augustinian Abbey (like Fountains) on the banks of a
rushing river with a Plantagenet bridge. It was for a grouse-shoot
(A[ndrew] doesn't shoot – nor do I – but he loves arranging it, like
an altruistic strategist) on high dales and moors, with a party of
tremendous shots led by Debo, all v. nice, with troops of loaders and
retrievers and labradors with their tongues out, under a windy sky of
rushing clouds casting their shadows over the dappled country below.
There were great shooting lunches, with masses to drink – hamper
on hamper, hot pots, mulled wine, lots of port. The fact that anyone
was able to hit anything afterwards renewed my faith in providence.
On Sunday, Debo and I drove over to Haworth, where the Brontës'
vicarage is now a museum; a steep bleak little town with the rather
charming vicarage at the top, among tall trees and moss-covered
tombstones, and the moors rolling away rather desolately beyond.
Countless Brontë relics are assembled there – MSs, books, bonnets,
clumsy pictures of their dogs by brother Branwell, so thick with the
atmosphere of those extraordinary sisters, that one quite forgot the
other pilgrims gazing beside one. (I've got a booklet which I'll send.)
The site of Wuthering Heights is only a few miles beyond. But the
weather seemed wrong. Clear blue sky, bright sunshine! Thank God,
a few clouds appeared before we left, even a few spots of rain, a
draught of wind – one's always complaining about the weather . . .

SUDDEN STOP! Continued in our next! – time has passed, and
I'm just off to Patras to meet Pomme & Ins.

Tons of love, darling Balasha,

Paddy

---

1 PLF's sister and her daughter.

2 Aileen participated enthusiastically in amateur theatricals.

3 The Amblers believed themselves to be descended from Sir John Taafe, of County
Sligo.

4 The Great Ban of Craiova was the Viceroy of Lesser Wallachia (in modern Rumania).

5 Lord David Cecil (1902–86), biographer, historian and academic, and his wife Rachel
(1909–82).

To Balasha Cantacuzène   Kardamyli
2 November 1974   Messenia

Balasha darling,

I wonder what it's like at Pucioasa now? Winter has arrived here,
suddenly and prematurely. Last year we could go on swimming till
the 20th of November; now the sea is a great heaving mass of waves
and foam, with the waves leaping to enormous heights, and
completely concealing the island. Pomme, who knows the way it is,
will see how huge they are. There were lovely flawless autumn days,
then a sudden wild west wind with the cypresses bending double,
followed by a monsoon of rain and bubbling torrents rushing down
from the mountains so that when the first storm was over, there
were enormous fans of ochre-coloured silt opening over the grey-
green sea at the end of each ravine-bed. Thank heavens, it is just
what was needed, and all the villagers, from wandering about like
pessimistic spectres, are suddenly garlanded with smiles; and we,
being small-scale olive-owners too, rejoice with them. The only ones
who looked a bit hangdog were the people from the mountain
villages, fearing that the fierce wind would have blown all the
berries off the trees. But I went up to Proástion, and found
everything intact . . .

The house filled up again very soon, with Raymond Mortimer
and Dadie Rylands, and two other chaps who stayed three days.
Some others, however, who had announced themselves, didn't come,
so we had a very happy time with Raymond and Dadie. Raymond
announced that he was in his eightieth year, to our astonishment; he
certainly doesn't look it. Long Crichel, where he lives[1] (3 miles from
Napier's house[2] in Dorset) has always been a sort of Mecca for me;
inhabited by Raymond and Eardley Knollys (painter) and Desmond
Shawe-Taylor the music critic, and, until he died seven years ago,
Eddy Sackville-West: all working hard, as in a lay-monastery, except
for the delicious food and the funny conversation. Dadie Rylands,
Fellow of King's Cambridge for donkey's years, is a mere seventy
something, but unlike frailer Raymond, swims for hours – almost to
the island, like Ins – and gallops across the mountains like a stag.

Both of them constituted a strong breath of all that was most sympathetic in Bloomsbury: v. amusing and loving about 'Virginia' and 'Lytton' and 'Ottoline'. Dadie's a tremendous Shakespeare scholar, and has the most beautiful reading-aloud voice: so we had enchanting evening hours with the sonnets, Troilus and Cressida, Byron, Gerard Manley Hopkins, Browning etc. Raymond (who has always been a great backer and encourager of mine) firmly insisted on my handing over to him some chapters of my present book (which I was too shy to show, until it is polished up, to Pomme and Ina, though I rather longed to, in spite of its imperfections. *I wish I had now!*) They both read it, and were tremendously enthusiastic about it (I was dreading their verdict, as no one has seen it except Joan), far beyond the call of guest-to-host politeness; so I am feeling very boosted up and encouraged! . . .

Two days ago, Joan got a telegram saying that Cyril Connolly was desperately ill with a heart attack, and that things looked very serious indeed, threatening the worst. He's a great friend, partly of mine, but a much greater and older one of Joan's – in fact, [she is] his closest; so she flew off with Graham two days ago. I drove them in, J. very upset and anxious, and saw them off at the aerodome. I *do* hope he'll be all right, but there's not much hope it seems. It would be a terrible loss.[3] Oh dear . . .

So here I am, all alone with the cats, and work, which I have flung myself onto with tremendous verve, after the kind words of these two literary gents! This is an absurd letter, all social doings, but I thought you would like to know what we've been up to. I'll write a proper one later on.

Please give all my fondest love to Pomme, and lots and lots to you, darling Balasha,

from Paddy

[1] Long Crichel House, near Wimborne, in Dorset, shared by Edward 'Eddy' Sackville-West, his partner, the music critic Desmond Shawe-Taylor (1907–95) and the artist Eardley Knollys (1902–91). They formed what was in effect an all-male salon and entertained a wide variety of guests. Later they were joined by the literary critic Raymond Mortimer and, later still, by the ophthalmic surgeon Patrick Trevor-Roper (1919–2004).

With Anna Venetia, daughter of Judy Montagu and her husband Milton Gendel,
at the house Paddy built in Kardamyli. In his right hand is a coolie hat. The picture
was taken in 1969, not long after work on the house was complete.

'Dirk Bogarde, the actor who is doing one in the film [*Ill Met by Moonlight*], is absolutely charming – slim, handsome, nice speaking-voice and manner, a super-gent, the ghost of oneself twelve years ago.'

On location in Africa for *The Roots of Heaven*, Paddy could not resist the temptation to start an affair with the female lead, Juliette Greco.

Lyndall Birch, daughter of Antonia White and Tom Hopkinson. 'I adored my time in Rome and adored you,' Paddy wrote to her in November 1958, 'and greatly miss our secret conclaves.'

'You *are* a lovely present to suddenly get, my darling Ricki . . .' Enrica 'Ricki' Huston, the fourth and much younger wife of the film director John Huston, with whom Paddy began an affair in the winter of 1960–1.

Writing under a makeshift shelter in the garden at Kardamyli.

On the terrace at Kardamyli overlooking the sea.

With Ann Fleming at
Sevenhampton, en route to
a fancy-dress party. Paddy is
dressed as the eighteenth-century
French poet André Chenier.
He is wearing tights borrowed
from a parlour-maid.

'It all went off painlessly,
nearly as easy as getting a dog
licence . . .' The Leigh Fermors
at Westminster Register Office
on their wedding day,
17 January 1968.

'We had both drunk at the same fountains long before . . .' In 1972 Paddy was reunited
with his old foe, General Kreipe, for a Greek television programme.

Paddy with Rudi
Fischer, at Fischer's
flat in Budapest, 2001.

With Lady Diana Cooper in Greece, soon after she was widowed. She and Paddy exchanged long letters until her death in 1986.

'I'm feeling tremendously buoyant and bucked about the whole *In Tearing Haste* project . . .' With Deborah Devonshire at the Old Vicarage in the village of Edensor in 2008, not long after the publication of their correspondence.

In the garden at Kardamyli, December 2001. Note the pebble mosaic.

² Napier Sturt (1896–1940), 3rd Baron Alington, a friend of Balasha's who lived at Crichel House; PLF stayed there several times before the war.
³ He died on 25 November.

To Balasha Cantacuzène   Chatsworth
28 June 1975   Bakewell

Darling Balasha,

Joan's told you all about my temporary medical bother,¹ so no need to go into it, except that all goes well and they are very pleased with progress at the hospital where I go for treatment. The hanging about waiting for one's turn is the most burdensome part of the business. I had a lovely long telephone call with Ins a few days ago, v. cheering and encouraging as she knows all about these woes. What a lovely time she had in Sicily.

I must tell you the recent happy ending of a long Cretan saga. In the summer of 1943, I had assembled about fifty Cretans in the north slopes of Mt Ida, most of them being hunted by the Germans, in order to take them by night marches to the S. coast, for evacuation to Egypt by torpedo boat. There was a sudden false alarm of 300 Germans coming up the hillside. Everyone leapt to arms, I picked up my rifle – which was always unloaded, as I carried the bullets in a bandolier – shot the bolt back and forth and pressed the trigger – 'easing the springs', as they call it; and *bang!* Some students from Herakleion had been playing about with the weapons, loading, unloading etc., and had left a round in the magazine. There was a cry. The bullet had struck my old friend and guide Yanni Tsangarakis, passing twice through his bent leg, striking a stone and ricocheting back and through his body. He died in half an hour, holding my hand – you can guess at the misery! – and we buried him there. I wanted to go to his village in W. Crete, tell his elder brother Kanaki what had happened, but couldn't, because of the embarkation on hand; and all the other guerrilla leaders said: 'Leave it till after the war, say Yanni has left for Egypt, for the accident, by Cretan custom, could start a blood feud, and split the resistance movement.' I reluctantly consented, determined though to seek out Kanaki at the earliest opportunity. Immediately after the embarkation came the Italian collapse, Badoglio,[2] etc. I went to eastern Crete, which was occupied by the Italian Siena Division, and persuaded their General Carta to desert with much of his staff and plans of the defences of Crete; and went with them by sea to Egypt; returning several months later by parachute; and I only returned to W. Crete when we had General Kreipe as prisoner. We went through Photeinou, Yanni and Kanaki's village, where Kanaki asked me if I had shot Yanni. I told him the whole story. He nodded and said, 'That's all I wanted to know,' and wandered off through the olive trees. When I was out of the army immediately after the war, I went to Photeinou on foot in the dusk, and entered Kanaki's cottage – high up on the mountain-side – and he stood up, saying 'What do you seek here, Mihali?[3] We are not friends,' laying his two first fingers on the butt of his pistol in his sash. It was no good, so I left v. sad. Meanwhile, everyone in Crete – where I'm rather a favourite – was trying to persuade him that it had been a mistake: but politically opposite people had somehow poisoned the family into believing that I had done away with Yanni 'because he knew all the secrets of the English'. Can you beat it? (We hadn't any.)

About fifteen years later, Joan and I were going round all our old haunts in Crete, stopping three days in the village of Alones – 7 miles from Photeinou – with Father John [Alevizakis], the wonderful old priest there, a man in a million. When the evening came to go to a farewell banquet in Retimo, one of the priest's surviving sons said, alas, we couldn't: Yorgo, Kanaki's son, had heard I was there, and was waiting on the edge of the forest, with a rifle and binoculars, to pick me off when I left the village. (There was only one way out of this deep black ravine, Yorgo was on one side, our way out on the other.) Yorgo, apparently, was a very wild boy (I'd known him v. young in the war), a great sheep-thief. I asked whether he was a good shot. Levtheri, Fr John's son, laughed and said, 'Yes, the blighter can shoot a hole through a 10 Drachma piece at 500 metres,' which made us all laugh rather ruefully, including Joan (who was marvellous). The only thing to do in such a case is to be accompanied by a neutral figure, head of a rival 'clan' or family, in whose company nobody can be shot without involving the whole tribe. This is the accepted code. So Petro Petrakis, an old friend, was sent for, and under his protection Joan and I crossed the blank hillside, looking across the valley at Yorgo sitting on the rock, binoculars round his neck and gun across his knees; but unable, by Cretan ethics, to blaze away . . .

Another fifteen years elapsed. Meanwhile, the siege to convince the Tsangarakis family that they were behaving unjustly continued in vain. Yorgo, because of various misdeeds, had had to flee his village and got a job as a shepherd outside Herakleion. Three months ago, dear George Psychoundakis ('The Cretan Runner') went to Herakleion, sought out Yorgo, and tried to convince him; but, though he wavered, he said he could never be friends with me: it was his duty to 'get the blood back', as one says in vendetta circles. He also told George that two years earlier, he had gone [illegible] around to Kardamyli but I was away, somewhere; and after a brief stay with a Cretan gendarme there (who said I was a nice chap) left again with his mission unfulfilled. All this was gloomy news: when suddenly – four weeks ago – lo and behold, the telephone rings in Kardamyli and our old wartime leader in E. Crete, Micky Akoumianakis, tells me that my would-be destroyer Yorgo had a nine-month-old unbaptised daughter and he wanted me to stand godfather, and name her – next Sunday. Micky was out of his mind with joy – this is the classical and *only* happy ending to a Cretan blood feud – George's words, and the weight of all opinion in Crete (which is all on my side) had worked at last!

Joan had left for England (this was all only a month ago), so I flew to Crete, armed with a candle two yards long, adorned with a dreadful pink tulle bow (why are Orthodox wedding & baptism things so [illegible]?), a whole baby's outfit, a gold-inscribed cross, ribbon-button-holes, smaller candles, net bags of sugared almonds, etc. There, waiting at Herakleion airport, was Geo. Psychoundakis, Manoli Paterakis, a dozen guerrilla chiefs, old Kanaki who had left his village, 7 miles to the west, for the occasion – now aged and infirm, booted, sashed, turbaned, stooping over a twisted stick; and

Yorgo, a wild-looking chap of forty now, two front teeth knocked out, booted too. I was buried in whiskery and badly-shaven embraces for minutes on end; then I was whisked off to a banquet in the mountains, getting back to Herakleion in time to smarten up for the service; I'd decided to call the child Ioanna, in memory of Yanni, and because of Joan. So there I was, with this pink naked infant in my arms, flanked by a mass of my grown-up god-daughters from wartime baptisms, walking round and round the font, reciting the Creed, blowing away the Devil ('Ftou! Ftou! Apotássomai!'),[4] where a bishop, an archimandrite and several splendidly clad priests, all old chums, officiated and chanted. When I'd placed my new god-daughter, sumptuously clad now, in her mum's arms and been kissed by my new god-brother Yorgo, Kanaki and several hundred other wartime brothers-in-arms from all over Crete, we all gathered at a taverna, where a table was laid for 300, sucking-pigs roasting, wine flowing, *lyras*, lutes, violins playing. It was a giant banquet. I had to lead the dances (plenty of foot slapping!). Everyone was very happy, as it was the happy end of a miserable saga; all wartime Crete rejoiced. Yorgo my god-brother, said, as we sat, rather tight, with arms round each other's necks, 'God-brother Mihali, if you've got any enemy, anyone you want got rid of – *just say the word, god-brother!* You'll have no more trouble!' I hastened to say that there was no one, *absolutely no one!*

All singing, we drove in a cavalcade to the aerodome, and I caught the midnight plane back. It seemed as if the day had lasted a century . . .

I *had* to get back, as next day I was flying to Paris, with Manoli and another resistance figure, Manoussos Manoussakis, to take part in the TV broadcast '*Dossiers de l'Ecran*'. We were put up in great luxury – all paid for, including the journey – in a charming and grand hotel called the Château Frontenac, just off the Champs-Élysées. It was so strange to see Manoli – a mountain chap who belongs to sheepfolds, caves and mountain tops – among those muslin curtains, brass bedsteads, pink lampshades, Empire furniture, watered-silk panels on the walls, gold swan-shaped bath taps, and reproductions of Chardin, Watteau, Fragonard & Vigée Le Brun:

La Cruche cassée, La Balançoire mystérieuse, Embarquement pour Cythère,
Le Baiser volé, etc.

It seems that the programme was a great success. They showed the
whole film *Ill Met by Moonlight* first, then there was a sort of '*table
ronde*' – Me, Manoli, Manoussos, Wavell's chief-of-staff, Gen. Belchem,
Sir Colin Coote (ex-editor of *The Times*) – but, alas, no Kreipe, as he
had fallen ill at the last moment (we talked on the telephone to
Hanover). Instead, a very intelligent German military historian. We all
had invisible interpreters in all four languages used, connected to
hidden earphones, but I spoke in French throughout. The whole
operation was discussed from every point of view – strategic, moral,
tactical etc. – and people were telephoning from all over France,
asking the chairman questions, which he then put to us in turn to
answer. It was v. lively and (as we had plenty to drink!) fluent. The
whole thing lasted three hours. What was extraordinary was that for
the rest of our stay – I took the two Cretans to the Invalides, up the
Eiffel Tower, to Notre-Dame, Arc de Triomphe, etc. (great fun!) –
total strangers kept saying '*Tiens! C'est Manoli le Cretois!*' or '*Regarde!
C'est le Commandant Fermor!*'

***

It's lovely here. I arrived yesterday. Fellow guests, apart from Debo and
Andrew, are A's uncle (married to his father's sister), ex-prime minister
Harold Macmillan, and Sybil, Dowager Dss of Cholmondeley, half
French, very erect, eighty, with hair powdered, looking more like a
French marquise than an English one, sister of Philip Sassoon. *V.*
intelligent. *Hates* Marthe Bibesco. Full of tales of Briand, Herriot,
Clemenceau.[5] Diana Cooper told me the other day that she'd had a
long, v. secret affair with the actor Louis Jouvet,[6] now dead. I've
always liked her. Also Robert and Cynthia Kee, great friends of A and
D, and of Joan's and mine. Alas, no Joan, in spite of pleading, as when
she's in England she never goes anywhere except The Mill House,
which she shares, officially, with her brother Graham.

It's Saturday morning, everyone is outside, strolling under the trees
except 'Uncle Harold' and me, in a sort of big library sitting room.
He came tapping in on a silver-mounted Malacca cane half an hour

ago, saying, 'Just been wandering through the state rooms. I don't
expect I'll see them again.' He's sitting beside the fire now, leaning
back with long legs outflung, reading Thomas Hardy's poetry, the
book held almost touching his nose, occasionally reading out a few
lines – 'Rather good, eh?' – when I break off this letter for a minute
or two's chat. He's marvellously intelligent and alert, and side-
splittingly funny, with a wonderful quiet but *imagé* [full of imagery]
way of reminiscing. Tremendously well read, rather like an eighteenth-
century grand Whig. Brilliant imitations of Curzon, Lloyd George,
Churchill, Lansdowne, etc. He looks v. well – blue eyes, pink cheeks
– occasionally almost *pretending* to be an old man, if you know what
I mean. As the years pass, everyone begins to understand what a
very good P.M. he was. When he finished, he refused any reward –
Earldom, Garter, etc. – and remained a plain Mr, which is very grand.
Not even a Knight![7] He and Sybil Cholmondeley were full of tales of
Talleyrand last night (who is Andrew's gr. gr. grandfather),[8] e.g. the
Prussian Ambassador who was totally bald, had a ballerina as mistress.
He was boasting about her disinterestedness: 'what *can* I give her?' he
asked. Talleyrand's answer: 'just a lock of your hair'.

No more now, my darling Balasha – I'll write all news soon. We
are going to move into a flat of Joan's sister Diana, for the rest of the
treatment. I'm not sure of address. Whites, St James's St, SW1 is safest
for the moment.

Tons of fond love to you and to Pomme,
        from Paddy

---

[1] PLF was being treated for cancer of the tongue.

[2] Proclamation announcing the Italian armistice broadcast on 8 September 1943.

[3] PLF was known as Mihali by his Cretan comrades.

[4] 'Ftou!' represents the sound of spitting: Greeks say this (instead of actually spitting)
in order to avert the evil eye, to which babies are especially prone; 'Apotássomai' means
'I renounce [Satan]', which is said by the godfather during the baptism service, speaking
on behalf of the baby.

[5] Aristide Briand (1862–1932), French foreign minister; Édouard Herriot (1872–1957),
three times prime minister of France; Georges Benjamin Clemenceau (1841–1929),
prime minister of France, 1906–9 and 1917–20.

[6] Louis Jouvet (1887–1951), actor and director, one of the most influential figures of
the French theatre in the twentieth century.

7 In 1984 Macmillan accepted a peerage as Earl of Stockton.
8 Talleyrand was AD's great-great-great-great-grandfather, through his illegitimate son,
Charles Joseph, Comte de Flahaut.

To Xan Fielding   The Mill House
11 July 1975   Dumbleton

Xan, παιδί μου [dear boy],

How rum, ill health smiting us temporarily down suddenly, as
with twin thunderbolts! Yours must have been terribly alarming, both
for you and Magouche! Thank heavens all seems well now, from the
various accounts flitting back across the Bay of Biscay. Ὁ Θεὸς νὰ
μᾶς φυλάξει ὅλους, ἀμήν! [May God preserve us all, Amen!] My
course of therapy is about two-thirds through, and consists in going
to the Royal Marsden Hospital in the Fulham Road every afternoon,
except for weekends, and getting a two-minute deluge of cobalt rays
on the right cheek, like Danaë under the golden shower. It makes
one rather raw, dry-mouthed, shaky and a bit headachy at first, and
not fit, while the treatment lasts, for much physical or mental
exertion. I'm just coming to what they call the 'uncomfortable
cumulative period'; but, I must say, it's not nearly as bad as one
thought it might be, and cramps one's style much less than we had
thought it might. When it's over in a couple of weeks, I have to have
a reassessment in a month's time, so will not go to Greece with Joan,
but hang about in the cool north, to keep out of the sun, which is
supposed to be not good at first. Joan will go back to Kardamyli,
to look after things and people there, and I'll go on a sort of Mr
Sponge's Correcting Tour[1] with my MSs – Ireland, Scotland? –
cadging shelter under friendly roofs. Not too bad!

We stayed at Patrick's for ages at first, then, to be closer to the
hospital, removed to a flat belonging to Joan's sister near the Royal
Hospital, Chelsea, where we'll be another week or so. Everybody's
been *angelically* kind, endless offers of hospitality and help. All hopes
are high, including the Docs.

So much for all that! . . . In spite of the hospital boredom there has been lots of fun involved, much feasting and chat. Daph was here for a bit, taking all recent events lightly and unvehemently;[2] goodwill all round, inevitable cabinet reshuffles that happen to all of us, no question of people taking sides, splitting people up into Montagues & Capulets, as poor Cyril was prone to; in fact, hang right and making things easiest for all. I went to Simpson's in the Strand last week – downstairs – with Ran[3] and Michael Astor, and it was marvellous. We gorged ourselves to a standstill, and I was shocked to discover how unregenerately carnivorous I could still be on occasions.

Joan and I are alone here at the moment – a slightly rainy Sunday, welcome as there has been a drought. We walked in the fields yesterday where we slid on the hayrick twenty years ago . . .

Please give fondest love to Magouche, and ὅ,τι ποθεῖς διὰ σένα, χρυσό μου [whatever you may wish for, dear boy].

Love Paddy

[1] A reference to *Mr Sponge's Sporting Tour* by R. S. Surtees (1849).
[2] Xan Fielding had left his wife Daphne for Magouche Phillips, whom he would marry in 1979.
[3] Randal McDonnell (1911–77), 8th Earl of Antrim.

To Raymond Mortimer   Sevenhampton[1]
19 September 1975   Swindon
                                                   Wiltshire

Dear Raymond,

I *did* enjoy our threefold irruption into the peace of Long Crichel. Miraculously, when there were so many temptations pulling the other way! – I managed to get lots of work done. I think I could play the Dictionary Game forever without getting tired of it. I still can't quite believe in Caleb Simper, that household world to Joan.[2]

She left, alas, on Tuesday, and I came down here the day after, hotfoot from a festive lunch at Diana Cooper's. She was looking marvellous and in great spirits, and only mentioned over coffee when she had run through more pressing topics that the night before she

had had a crash in which her car was 100% write-off. She and
Auntie Nose[3] were inside – not a scratch on either, except a quarter
of an inch of court plaster on Diana's little finger – 'But all our
pockets were full of broken glass and of course the car looked like
a brown paper bag –'

Caspar [Fleming] has taken himself off to a nursing home for a
cure much to Annie's relief. I'm working away hard, and we go
sightseeing in the afternoons – Malmesbury the day before yesterday,
Fairford yesterday, where I could willingly spend a whole day going
over the stained glass inch by inch. I didn't realise it's the only
church in the kingdom where the old glass is absolutely intact.

Dear Raymond, thank you again, and not only for a four-
poster-bed and delicious board, but for being such a help with the
still nameless book (*World Enough and Time?*). It was angelically kind,
and I *know* what a sweat!

   Love to all
   Yrs ever
      Paddy

---

[1] Ann Fleming's house.
[2] Caleb Simper (1856–1942), English composer and organist.
[3] Violet Wyndham (1890–1980), one of the most faithful members of DC's inner circle.

To Diana Cooper   Kardamyli
5 November 1975   Messenia

Darling Diana,

   That *was* a nice feast, with you and Ran *Chez Victor*,[1] the night
before I left. I bet it's the first time *Mandalay* and the *Te Deum* have
ever been sung there, at any rate, on the same night. I'm coming
back some time next week for a few days – the tail end of my
medical imbroglio – so we'll be able to do something glorious.

   Michael Stewart has sent us the *Oxford Dictionary of English Place
Names*, which I've been deeply immersed in for the last two days: all
their derivations, etc. Reading it is like wandering in a rambling

twilight wood with ragged troops of Thor-worshipping Anglo-Saxons in most of the glades – swine rootling, watermills turning, cattle halted by fords and stepping-stones, wolves peering out of alder-clumps at peaceful grazers, a few Normans clanking about, Welshmen brooding on their wrongs beside wishing wells, Norwegians busy caulking and careening, Danes crowding round cooking pots on swampy islets, Corns [Cornishmen] digging for tin, Irish zealots repairing drystone chapels, Romans wearily forming tortoise and assembling and shipping catapults at the double while Picts make off with their poultry, parties of Britons out after flints and woad and mistletoe or hauling on cromlech-ropes, and somewhere, I suppose, huge and shadowy Beaker-men reeling and hiccupping in the bracken. Rough island story, in fact . . .

It's my Greek name day tomorrow – SS. Michael and Gabriel and All Angels[2] – and the whole village comes up here to attend mass at the little rock-chapel. Then they troop along to the house for liqueurs and sweet cakes, followed, in due course, by meat and wine, rather like one of those Futurist meals organised by Marinetti in the twenties. Lela and some crones from the mountains are busy sweeping and garnishing the house, after whitewashing the chapel, and decking it with garlands of olive, bay and oleander.

　　See you next week, Diana darling. Till then, tons of fond love
　　　　from Paddy

[1] A fashionable restaurant in Wardour Street, Soho.
[2] The Feast Day of Saints Michael and Gabriel and All Angels always falls on 8 November, so presumably PLF wrote this sentence two days after starting this letter.

To Frances Partridge   Kardamyli
28 November 1975   Messenia

Dear Frances,

　　I'm labouring under two leaden layers of guilt! I was horror-struck to learn from Janetta that I had got the nights mixed up; and terribly disappointed as I had been *particularly* looking forward to feasting with you and Janetta and Jaime; worst of all, seeming so rude and callous. But at least, I thought next day, after many attempts to telephone – always when you were out – a letter may result in eventual forgiveness. So I did my best, put two 7d stamps on it – nothing smaller was available. Then the normal processes seemed too slow, so I drove at full speed across the park, stopped the taxi – arriving from the east – at the great pillared doorway *beyond* No. 15, left the letter on the hall table, and went on my way with my conscience several ounces lighter. When, meeting Janetta on Tuesday night for a drink in The Star Tavern, I learned that you had never got it, and that I must have left it at No. 14 instead of No. 16, I was convinced that there was nothing for it but the River. We peered through the glass beside the doors: no table in your house, so it must still be on the one in No. 14, which we descried but couldn't reach, owing to all doors being shut. Well, I <u>AM</u> sorry, Frances, and I really will pull my socks up and do better next time, *should* I ever be asked again, so *please* don't cross me off your list, as they used to say!

Joan and I do wish you would come and inspect this place some time. It's not at its best at the moment, as rain is coming down in buckets. It's the sort of weather that people posted to the Sudan used to pine for: 'really wet green days!' Joan's* many cats slink up and down under the arches, peering at each other in wild surmise, the young ones that is. The older ones sit meditatively in front of the fire, rather like your painted one, the correct winter posture for pusses of riper years.

With many apologies again, and love from us both.

Yours ever
Paddy

* I spy her picking tangerines at the bottom of the garden, under an umbrella.

Dadie Rylands wrote to Paddy after the publication of A Time of Gifts *in
September 1977.*

To George 'Dadie' Rylands   Kardamyli
10 December 1977   Messenia

Dear Dadie,

It *was* cheering, getting your letter on the night of the party, and I
feel very sustained by the kind things said. Yes *of course* you are right
about the second line of Petronius.[1] It was all right on the last
proofs. What demons of destruction can have appended that
meaningless '*-es*' on to '*major*', ruining sense and scansion in a blow?
Thank goodness I *didn't* notice it at once; I was already writhing
and groaning about misprints – turning Grendel's mother from a
'water-hag' to a 'water-hog', 'ghostly' into 'ghastly', 'prince' into 'price'
to name a few – and I think '*majores*' would have done for me, I
don't know *what* to do about my habit of 'than' with the accusative,
I thoroughly disapprove. I *don't* like it when I see others do it; but
seem cruelly blinded to this beam in my own eye. I would like to be
a staunch maintainer of the decencies – like that Roman soldier in
Sir Arthur Poynter's picture ('Faithful unto Death'?) standing
impassive among the falling lava and Scoriae of Pompeii[2] – and here
I am, the fugleman of drift.[3] I wish I could have an instrument like
those frogs' legs of Galileo or Volta, wired to a battery, which would
make my right hand leap painfully from the page each time, until I
was cured. But I *do* plan to reform.*

It's pouring with rain here at the moment, & wind, waves half a
mile high, thunder and lightning, rather splendid. I've got the first
cold of winter. Joan said this morning 'Have you been taking your
Redoxon?' I said '*Ad absurdum*,' quick as winking. It was an opening
I had been waiting for for ten years, and it has put me thoroughly
on the mend.

---

* Also the equestrian Duke, on page 203, is Newcastle, not Manchester. The fact that
this is my fault – confusion between unvisited industrial cities – makes it all the more
bitter. But I should have remembered the V. Woolf's essay [Virginia Woolf's *The Common
Reader* (1925)] on the bluestocking Dss of N [Duchess of Newcastle].

We go to Barbara and Niko for Christmas. What a pity you won't be there! It would be a great joy if you came here whenever you were able. Joan sends much love and joins me in wishes for a Happy Christmas – premature ones, on the New York Rabbi principle (see P.S.) – and every kind thought from

Yours ever

Paddy

P.S. It seems that a young New York Rabbi is in the habit every year, *weeks* before the Day of Atonement, of promenading before his synagogue with a sandwich board which says REPENT NOW AND AVOID THE YOM KIPPUR RUSH.

¹ PLF had quoted some lines of Petronius as one of three epigraphs to *A Time of Gifts*.
² PLF is thinking of (Sir) Edward John Poynter's painting *Faithful unto Death* (1865).
³ A fugleman is a highly trained soldier posted as a model before soldiers conducting exercises.

Following the publication of A Time of Gifts, Paddy received a letter from a stranger living in Budapest: Rudi Fischer, a naturalised Australian of Transylvanian origin who worked as a languages editor for the New Hungarian Quarterly. Fischer's letter was appreciative, but not uncritical, and he drew attention to several mistakes in the text. It was obvious from his comments that Fischer's wide knowledge was matched by meticulous attention to detail. Paddy determined that the book's sequel should not be published without Fischer's scrutiny.

To Rudi Fischer   Kardamyli
7 July 1978   Messenia

Dear Mr Fischer,

Thank you very much indeed for both your letters and please accept my humble apologies for being so late in answering them! What happened was this – I went to stay with friends in Corfu in April, so missed your *first* one, which somehow got stuck here

without being reforwarded. From Corfu I went on to England, and
only got back to my base here the day before yesterday, and found
your second letter waiting alongside the first.

I hate the idea that you thought I might have been offended! On
the contrary, I'm deeply grateful for all your very useful and
constructive suggestions, all of which I will most joyfully take into
account when a reprint is due. I have corrected a few already. Your
emendations about the difference between a *Reichstadt* and a
Kaiserstadt will be particularly useful for the German translation,
which is being made by Dr Richard Moissl of the Müller Verlag in
Salzburg. It is nearly finished, and he will be sending it to me for
vetting.

Your researches in Slovak-Magyar toponymy were fascinating and
rewarding – especially your triumphant running to earth of Nagy
Magyar and the location of Tövecces. I must certainly get hold of the
Austrian 1:200,000 map – I believe it is the one I *had*, given me by
Baron Schey; but the few tatters that have survived the passing of
decades are quite useless now . . .

I wonder if I am right in assuming from your name that you are a
Siebenbürgischer Sachser?[1] I have always wondered what history-co-
mythological basis – as apart from the real historical one – there was
for the Hamlin origin of the Transylvanian Saxon in the closing lines
of Browning's 'Pied Piper'.[2]

I particularly regret not having got your first letter when I should,
as I stayed on a few days in Budapest on the way to England –
mainly to see my old friend – not seen by me since August 1934 in
Transylvania, but recognisable at once even after forty-four years
– Elemér Klobusiçky, who now lives by translating government
scientific documents, in 127 Pasareti Ut. I hired a car and we drove
on a rainy Sunday, with him and his sister Ilona and a nice
ex-sculptress called Mrs Strásser – to Esztergom & Visegrad, spending
hours looking at the pictures in the palace I hadn't seen for nearly
half a century. I also gazed at my old Buda abode – 15, Úri Utca
– and looked up a more recent friend, you may know, Dr István Gal,
a charming man, and a great authority on historical, especially
Renaissance, Anglo-Hungarian links. Another more recent friend,

Géza Kepes, very good on both modern and ancient Greek poetry, was in London, but I saw him for a moment when I got there.

As you can imagine from the above, your letter gave the greatest possible pleasure and help. If I get stuck in my detail about Hungarian history, I hope I may make so bold as to write and ask your help. I also plan to plague my other Hungarian friends on their particular fields – but as you are all polymaths, it will be a hard choice!

With very many thanks again, and all kind wishes,

Yours ever

Patrick Leigh Fermor

[1] One of the ethnic German (and German-speaking) minority in Rumania.
[2] 'And I must not omit to say
That in Transylvania there's a tribe
Of alien people who ascribe
The outlandish ways and dress
On which their neighbours lay such stress,
To their fathers and mothers having risen
Out of some subterraneous prison
Into which they were trepanned
Long time ago in a mighty band
Out of Hamelin town in Brunswick land,
But how or why, they don't understand.'
        Robert Browning, 'The Pied Piper of Hamelin'

To John Julius Norwich   Kardamyli
Twelfth Night, 1979   Messenia

Dear John Julius,

V. many thanks from both of us for the smashing Cracker![1] I love the Strachey description of Cardinal Wiseman.[2] I read somewhere that Manning hated Newman so much that he went to great lengths to get a butler called Newman, whom he was constantly calling for: 'Newman! Newman! What can that idiot be about? Newman? The man's a cretin', etc. I wish I knew where I'd learnt this. Apropos of the splendid epitaph of Dr Horne, here's an odd non-scanning

epitaph – 'a quaint epitaph' quoted by Horace Walpole, and found
among the MSs of Sir T. Carew of Ushington, on a member of the
great Genoese family of Pallavicini, who made a fortune by
collecting funds for the Pope in the Reign of Q. Mary (of Calais
memory), some of which he gave, later, to Q. Elizabeth, and bought
a prosperous manor at Babraham,* where he died, a knight, and
presumably Protestant, in 1600:

> Here lies Horatio Palavazene
> Who robbed the Pope to lend the Queene,
> He was a thiefe. A thiefe? Thou lyest,
> For whie? He robb'd but Antichrist,
> Him death with besom swept from Babram
> Into the bosom of Old Abram.
> But then came Hercules with his club,
> And struck him down to Belzebub.

You will be glad to hear that Theophilus Field, Bishop of Hereford,
later contributed to a compilation called 'An Italian's Dead Bodie
stucke with English Flowers, Elegies on the Death of Sir Oratio
Pallavicino'.

You may wonder how I come by all this abstruse lore in the depths
of the Mani. Last year Jock Murray suddenly told me that about £200
had mounted up from *Violins* (opera)[3] royalties; so I blew the lot on
the DNB [*Dictionary of National Biography*] which is still coming out
here in dribs and drabs, almost complete: so give me a few minutes'
notice, and I can be pretty knowing about almost anyone in England
– (before 1900) – up to William Tytler (1711–1792); but am still steeped
in murk about Petruccio Ubaldini . . . It would be hard to find a
more fascinating and time-wasting acquisition.

I long to know more than the DNB can tell about Sir Robt-
Shirley's distant relation, *also* Robt (1581–1628) who spent years at
the Court of Shah Abbas, married a Circassian, and always thereafter

---

* ' . . . Strong men have cried like babes, bydam
  To hear what happened at Babraham . . .'
  [From Robert Brooke's 'The Old Vicarage, Grantchester']

wore Persian dress, even at the English Court. There are two
charming Van Dyck pictures of them at Petworth, in full eastern fig.

I'm becoming illegible. Must pull myself together.

Three or four years ago, in a book by Mary Stewart[4] called *The
Ivy Tree* (thriller, hotly recommended, like all her books) the
following quotation comes: 'Time hath his revolutions, there must be
a period and an end to all temporal things, *finis rerum*, an end of
names and dignities and whatsoever is terrene, and why not of De
Vere? For where is Bohun? Where's Mowbray? Where is Mortimer?
Nay, which is more, and most of all, where is Plantagenet? They are
entombed in the urns and sepulchres of mortality!' No author was
mentioned, and these haunting lines started a fruitless search through
quotation dictionaries, *Urn Burial*, *Religio Medici*, *The Anat. of M.*,[5]
Milton's prose, Sydney's *Defense of Poesy*, Donne's *Sermons*, etc. – till
at last, in despair, I wrote to the author, and, at last learned that the
quotation is from the closing speech of Lord Justice Coke, in the
reign of James I, in some claim concerned with the all-but-extinct
Earldom of Oxford.[6] In order to avenge myself, I made up a
spurious seventeenth-century page concerning judges, and slipped it
nonchalantly in my answer; and she went through a similar torture,
till I owned up. I *was* pleased. (She must be extremely nice, lives in
Edinburgh, married to a geologist called Sir Somebody Stewart and
is née Rainbow.) I was doubly bucked when Dadie Rylands asked
whether it was a missing fragment of *Hydriotaphia*; perhaps to give
pleasure, which it did.

Anyway, the *Cracker* is a great delight, and if I'm burdening you
with these enclosures, it's your fault for starting hares! V. many thanks
and love from both of us, and Happy New Year, a trifle late, to you
and yours.

Yrs ever

Paddy

P.S. I am writing this in a grey-green Harris tweed jacket, good as
new except for leather sleeves, which Leslie and Roberto made for
your father in June, 1936. You must be almost coevals – perhaps the
coat a bit younger.[7]

1 JJN's annual *Christmas Cracker*, 'a personal collection of quirky quotes and literary odds and ends', which he sends to his friends instead of a Christmas card.

2 In Lytton Strachey's *Eminent Victorians* (1918).

3 PLF's novel *The Violins of Saint-Jacques* was turned into an opera, with a score by Malcolm Williamson and a libretto by William Chappell, first performed on 29 November 1966.

4 Mary, Lady Stewart (1916–2014), née Mary Rainbow, developed the genre of romantic mysteries. She married the geologist Frederick Stewart, who was knighted in 1974.

5 Sir Thomas Browne, *Hydriotaphia, Urn Burial, or, a Discourse of the Sepulchral Urns lately found in Norfolk* (1658) and *Religio Medici* (1643); Robert Burton, *The Anatomy of Melancholy* (1621).

6 Actually from a speech given by the Lord Chief Justice Sir Randolfe Crewe, in the reign of Charles I, to his fellow peers sitting in judgement on the rival claims to the peerage, between Robert de Vere claiming as heir male of the family, and Lord Willoughby de Eresby, claiming through a female, as heir-general to the late earl. Judgement was given in favour of de Vere, but he died without leaving a male heir, so the title became extinct.

7 JJN was born in 1929.

To Xan Fielding   Athens
May Day 1979   Greece

Darling Magouche/Xan,

Please forgive this scrawl, scribbled with one foot in the stirrup, on the way to Jordan in three hours, where we hope to see Janetta on the plane, but, alas! neither of you.

Recent news *here* on the disagreeable side.

(1) With the backing of the Embassy, I've been trying to get that bronze memorial tablet[1] stuck up at Arkadi, as Tom [Dunbabin] and Fr. Dionysius[2] wanted it. Monks very hesitant and wet, but I went, there was a half-hearted banquet, and a suitable place chosen. A car turned up with four 'journalists' next day, who threatened and frightened the monks into withdrawing permission. Exactly the same thing happened at Preveli. Then Yerakari[3] bravely said *they'd* put it up. There are no Communists or even left-wing people in that bit of Crete, and the C[ommunist] P[arty] in Herakleion, responsible for everything, were thwarted. The next move was on Orthodox Easter Sunday night. Joan and Barbara were woken by a great bang at

1:30 a.m. but neither Niko nor I. Someone rushed down next morning with the news that the car had been blown sky high. There it was indeed, with the whole front scattered for acres all round, 10 yards of burnt, slow-burning fuse underneath, and a red poster with hammers and sickles. (They mistook the Feast for Ascension Day.) Everyone locally v. ashamed and apologetic, masses of telephone calls and wires including one of five pages from Chanea – all our pals' signatures, so moving it was almost worth it.[4] Not quite, as insurance pays nothing for Malicious Acts; but the Ambassador may shame the Ministry of the Interior into compensating for it, or something. The CP are only a small minority in Herakleion: but it shows what hatred and organisation can do. They are trying to explode every trace of Anglo-Greek friendship, and rewrite history in their own version, which, thank God, is not working, except with isolated brutal acts and a stream of poison.

The other disagreeable thing is that Bandouvas[5] has written his memoirs, with the sole purpose, some think, of shuffling off the responsibility of the Viannos massacres on to me, saying I'd given him *carte blanche*, 'The Green Light', etc., at the time of the Italian surrender. I'll have to refute it some time. The odd thing was he insisted on coming to Arkadi with me from Herakleion – huge kisses and, that evening in Herakleion, a sheep roast whole. The book appeared a week later . . . All very strange.

No more now, *mes enfants*. We are terribly excited at our departure. Please forgive the rather breathless tenor of this letter. Joan sends all her love to you both, so do I, also Barbara and Niko.

      Paddy

      xxx

[1] A plaque to the Allied servicemen and Cretans who had died in the Cretan resistance to German occupation.

[2] Pro-Abbot of the monastery of Arkadi, Crete.

[3] The highest village in Crete, on the southern end of the pass at the north-western end of the Amari.

[4] 'Dear Mihali, We read an unbelievable piece of news in the papers yesterday STOP. Your friends in Chanea and the villages cannot find words to express our anger for this most uncharacteristic act STOP. Thirty-eight years ago you came to Crete to share

with us the four darkest years of recent history, gambling heads and tails with your life every day and being always the first to set an example in the most daring missions STOP. With your leadership were written some of the most brilliant pages in the resistance of all Europe STOP. With your kindness and your dashing spirit you won forever the hearts of your old brothers-in-arms, and not the passage of time, or absolutely any other factor can diminish in the slightest degree the love we all feel for you STOP. With the certainty that history will write you down among the most ardent and tried Philhellenes, we grasp your hand.'

5 Manoli Bandouvas, a resistance leader in Crete, whose pre-emptive raid against the Germans in 1943 had provoked terrible reprisals in the Viannos area, in which over 500 people were killed.

To Diana Cooper   Kardamyli
28 August 1979   Messenia

Darling Diana,

I'm feeling rather amazing and marvellous. I suddenly thought, rightly, I was too thick and heavy – all the aftermath and the revenge for having a lovely time in Blighty – [so] that yesterday, the first day with no guests or visitors since we got back, I determined to put *your* device for sylphdom into practice, viz. to skip all meals and intoxicating drink, for twenty-four hours. Started yesterday morning, no brecker, worked all morning, basked on beach in lieu of luncheon, walked six miles, three cups of tea, hid while Joan supped to be far from temptation, then played Word Making and Word Talking till midnight, slept like seventh Ephesian,[1] woke with the sun, toast & tea at 9, and it's now 12.30 and I feel light as a feather, all evil shed away, a pulse in the eternal mind no less.[2] The shed evil is actually over 3 kilos – the same as three thumping vols. of the *Dictionary of Nat. Biography* (just weighed them). But I know these shed kilos are hovering in the air hard by, scowling and snapping their fingers with frustration, planning early re-entry . . . But still, the feeling of buoyancy and beatitude is almost supernatural.

Just to top everything, when I dived into the sea, at the end of that bracing walk yesterday, on surfacing I very nearly collided with a kingfisher which was flying low over the water. It settled on a sharp rock in the entrance to a cave. I swam towards it slowly and almost without moving and got within almost touching distance, hovering in the shadows while it twiddled its head about, peered for tiddlers and preened its marvellous coloured wings in the sun, pecking about in its armpits, and blinking. It flew off after about twenty minutes, and I hope it will be there when I go there in an hour. But no diving. I'll slide in like a burglarious merman.

This letter is a sprat to catch a whale, i.e., a long account of your Tuscan travels.

Tons of fond love, darling Diana,
from Paddy and from Joan

[1] PLF refers to the story of the seven sleepers of Ephesus, Christians in the pagan Roman Empire, who sought refuge in a cave rather than recant. There they slept for 150 years or more (the period is disputed), until they awoke to find that Christianity was no longer persecuted.

[2] 'And think, this heart, all evil shed away,
    A pulse in the eternal mind, no less
    Gives somewhere back the thoughts by England given;
    Her sights and sounds; dreams happy as her day;
    And laughter, learnt of friends; and gentleness,
    In hearts at peace, under an English heaven.'
        Rupert Brooke, 'The Soldier' (1914)

Paddy and Joan spent Christmas 1979 with Xan and Magouche Fielding in their new house in Spain. 'Their abode above Ronda has become delightful,' Paddy wrote to Debo Devonshire, 'with thick walls, blazing fires, mountains all round, twenty minutes' walk to the amazing town, where a wonder-bridge spans a deep chasm full of swallows. One day we climbed up into some mountains and looked down on Gibraltar and the Mediterranean & the Atlantic hanging in space, with Jebel Musa, the other pillar of Hercules, on the Moroccan side; then the Riff Mountains; then the faraway glitter of the Atlas . . .' (In Tearing Haste, pages 179–80). In mid January the four of them set out from Ronda by car, driving through the cork woods of Estremadura to the Atlantic coast, and then across the Tagus into Lisbon. They toured Portugal, zig-zagging north until they crossed the Spanish border into Galicia, and reached Santiago de Compostella, where the party broke up: Paddy and Joan flew on to Madrid, and from

there to Barcelona, while the Fieldings drove on to Leon and Salamanca, and
then south.

To Magouche and Xan Fielding   Kardamyli
1 February 1980[1]   Messenia

Darling Magouche, Ξάν, παιδί μου [Xan, dear boy],

Well, that *was* terrific. There is so much to chew on, and we're
chewing on it like pepped-up and uncharacteristically competitive
ruminants; dead-beat dashes for the *Encyclopedia Britannica* – vols
PAY-REE and SHU-TOM – and unseemly tugs of war at bedtime
over Rose Macaulay. I wish cats didn't turn into cradles for me, the
initial gear change from 2nd to 3rd seems to be a kind of *wiegenlied*
[lullaby]: z-z-z-z sets in. I can't think, this being so, how I can
possibly be so glutted with visual impressions. Perhaps I have a
subliminal knack of waking up in the nick [of time] – aided by
a solicitous prod now and then – whenever anything this terrific
looms. Selective Slumber in Portugal . . . I can't get over what can
be done with granite, viz. to Escorial. I wish we'd heard *12* strike!
It still reverberates . . . [2] I think they should let one nearer these
kneeling gilt figures, Charles V, his Empress, Ph. II. etc. What about
that magical Beckfordian moment, in the painted chamber
underneath the pretty theatre? Icy Avila, where we cowered over
the brazero in our hostelry reading Ford[3] aloud, sticks in my
memory like a sort of Castilian Troy. Eighty-eight Towers! Priam's
seven-gated City . . . Anyway, thanks to my everlasting diary (three
months filled in with days of the week now in advance) and its
contents copied down from Magouche's and Joan's, copied down
from mine, we can now gloat over each step of our marvellous
journey and sojourn in retrospect, like counting over the plum-
stones on one's plate and remembering how delicious each one
was . . .

Joan's told you how we fared in Madrid – another feast at Botin's,
a visit next day to my Hispano-Rumanian pals, nice supper at Jijou's
– not bad at all for an informal snack, my solitary visit to appalling
Apocalypse Now.[4] We were feeling pretty forlorn at the idea of the

missed plane in Barcelona, and having to hang about five hours in
Ciampino airport,[5] getting to Athens at nearly midnight when Joan
had the brilliant inspiration of cutting our losses, staying in Barcelona,
and catching the same plane we had missed next day. Our spirits shot
up as we made for the *Oriente*, where we were given a huge suite
full of discarded clothes horses, where only half the taps work, not
much of the heating and few lights; but it's failed to dampen our
spirits, nor the discovery of hidden mousetraps in the dark corners,
and mounds of nibbled biscuits. We had drinks in the lanes at a nice
place called The 4 Brothers. There is a slightly *típico* restaurant called
the Curallos, which I liked more than Joan. After ages with Picasso
and a twilight prowl round the crypt of the Sagrada Família[6] – I'm
sorry to see they have got rid of the bats, which squeaked and
wheeled overhead at my only other visit by the hundred while the
priest intoned vernacular vespers in Catalan: 'Priei, Hermans' instead
of '*Orate Fratres*' – we had a smashing dinner at the Amaya on the
Ramblas. When Joan had retired, I set out to rove the town, headed
straight for the lanes and was given a free *fine-à-l'eau* [brandy-and-
water] by the v. nice owner of The 4 Brothers. I was strolling back
along the same lane when the sound of rhythmic clapping from one
of the many bars beckoned me inside. I was the only customer
except at the far end a turtle of locals, some of them gypsies having
a lovely time drinking, singing and swigging, and clapping, a couple
getting up now and then to stamp and twirl. What luck I thought,
and ordered a beer, and watched from the bar at a respectful distance.
I was sipping my [illegible], when a seedy, bald, polite slightly fishy
old boy came up and asked where I was from, and gave me a
friendly pat on the back when I told him. He owned the bar, he
told me, and pointed to a huge rather moth-eaten stuffed bull's head
on the wall over crossed banderillas and said he'd once been a
matador, and had killed that very bull in the ring in Valencia thirty
years earlier. Quick as lightning, D in the Afternoon in mind,[7] I said
¿Entonces, se ha cortado la coleta?,[8] with a swinging gesture; he laughed,
slapped me on the back and said how splendidly I spoke Castilian
(he was from Madrid) and left me. After half an hour I thought I
might as well push off somewhere else, and put down a 100 pesetas

note for the beer and waited for the change. At this the barman flew into a temper and said it was 270 pesetas for a beer.[9] I said the equivalent of what rot. He began to shout like a lunatic and soon all the people from the other end of the room were milling around shouting and waving their fists. I shouted *¿Donde está el Señor Matador que ha dado muertea un toro a Valencia?*[10] There was a sudden bewildered pause in the shouting, everyone crying *¿Qué Toreador? Qué toro? Qué Valencia?*[11] etc. and I spotted the bald man at the back of the room expostulating with the others. He'd obviously invented the lot. I shouted to him *¿Donde esta il pundonor Castiliana?*[12] and this was taken up by all the rest. *¡¿Que pundonor Castillano?!* etc., and much else, when suddenly I saw the barman stoop down his side of the bar, and emerge again, a screaming Jack in the Box, brandishing a heavy wooden club over my head like a lunatic. I managed to capture the throng's attention for a second by pointing to the club, and saying: *¿Usted quiere tocar me aqui?* – pointing to the crown of my head with my forefinger and not knowing the Spanish for 'club' (the same?) – *¿Con esta pieza de leño?*[13] The clubman had burst into a sort of war dance, but the bar was safely between us. I pointed accusingly at this pseudo-matador, saying *¡El pundonor castillano e muerto!*[14] and turning on my heel, as they say, strode to the door like Regulus,[15] shouting *¡No esta terminado!*[16] There was still the hell of a row, but nobody stopped me. Two people came out not to crowd me but to reason with me, but I marched off in a fury, and at the next corner, came on three officials in uniform. Police, I thought, and dragged them back with [me]. The owner and one or two others were called out into the street, v. quiet and respectful now, while I went on about having been threatened: *¡Me ha amenazado con un grand leño!*[17] etc. Apparently these particular officials were not allowed into premises but said I should go to the police station and report it. The others ('Bar Andaluz?') v. conciliating and I strode off, but cooled down before I got there (I suppose I was a bit tight as well) and thought, 'What the hell?' and headed for the Ramblas again, and ended up in a 'drugstore', bursting with people, where I drank a beer at the normal price, full of amazing tarts of both sexes. A rather splendid-looking girl, as I went past, pointed [at] the very tough pals who were standing on either side of her, and said ¿Which do you want? ¿Him – or him? ¿Or me? When I got back to the *Oriente*, Joan was heading through my part of the suite, clambering like a sleep-walker to the only loo through the assembled hat-stands, mousetraps and towel horses, so I had a splendid small-hours tale to unfold. I must say, the whole experience made me feel young again . . .[18]

I haven't yet said thank you for that marvellous hol – a whole nosegay of roses and not a thorn in the lot – and for all the feasts and wonders and fun. But I do so now, and tons of fond love to you both,

from Paddy

I've found the Rumanian poem[19] about the wind in the different flutes, and will send it in a few days. Did you note down the two *Enc. Brit.* mentions, from the Index, about the White Ship? Worth a mention. I'll see if I can find anything here. I have a feeling there was something else I was going to hunt up. But can't remember – do let me know if you can – and anything else.

You must have seen how excited we both were about the book.[20] It's absolutely tip-top and will be a great triumph.

Do write to George Bug [George Psychoundakis] after another look at his book.

[1] Misdated 1970.

[2] 'Have you seen it?' PLF wrote to Debo Devonshire. 'Bleak and splendid is the word, half palace, half monastery, all granite, full of dead kings, with a bell that goes on vibrating half a minute after each toll.'

[3] Richard Ford (1796–1858), author of books on travelling in Spain.

[4] Francis Ford Coppola's film *Apocalypse Now*, set during the Vietnam War, had recently been released.

[5] They were due to change planes in Rome.

[6] The extraordinary cathedral-sized church designed by the Catalan architect Antoni Gaudí (1852–1926), still unfinished more than a century after construction began in 1882.

[7] PLF is thinking of Hemingway's book about bullfighting, *Death in the Afternoon* (1932).

[8] 'Has he cut his pigtail?' Matadors use the phrase 'cutting your pigtail' to mean retiring from the bull-ring.

9 About £1.84 – perhaps £7 in today's value. In a letter to Diana Cooper describing the same incident, PLF reports that the barman demanded 500 pesetas.

10 'Where is the matador who once killed a bull in Valencia?'

11 'What bullfighter? Which bull? What about Valencia?'

12 'What happened to the famous Castilian honour?'

13 'Are you going to hit me with that piece of wood?'

14 'Castilian honour is dead!'

15 PLF perhaps refers to Roman general Marcus Atilius Regulus, who was taken captive by the Carthaginians and returned to Rome on parole to negotiate a peace. He urged the Senate to refuse the proposals and then, despite the protests of his own people, fulfilled the terms of his parole by returning to Carthage, where he was promptly tortured to death.

16 'This is not over!'

17 'They threatened me with a big stick!'

18 He was a fortnight short of his sixty-fifth birthday.

19 *Mioritza* – see *Between the Woods and the Water*, pages 235–8.

20 A reference to Fielding's manuscript of a book about the winds.

To Diana Cooper   Kardamyli
25 February 1980   Messenia

Darling Diana,

    You'll never guess what I've been up to! At last I've pulled myself together and assembled all your letters. I think a few are missing, and will probably turn up, slipped down the backs of drawers or left in books etc. But there's plenty to chew on, almost 200 pages of different sizes. Most of them were still in their envelope, so even if undated could be placed by the stamps outside, and even if the envelopes *were* missing, can be pretty accurately placed by the drift of the contents. As I had to go to Athens last week, I took this great stack of treasure with me and got them photostated, page by page, dishing them out to the chap in the Xerox shop, piling them up as they came out, feeling like Gutenberg or Caxton. Then I re-sorted them, and reread; and, of course, they are utter glory. I read some well-chosen ones – Coronation Nile journey, the Atlas, El Glaoui, Iris, etc. – to Joan, that is, and Barbara and Niko Ghika, and they were bowled over, just as I was: fascination, laughter, damp eyes and sighs, but always recovering into some marvellous light touch or

simile – in fact your own marvellous self shines through like a
beacon and illumines all. I will send this precious collection to you
when I can find a suitable messenger: some time within the next
two to three weeks I hope, for you to go over & select as you see
fit, and let Philip Ziegler[1] borrow, if he still wants to use them – he
said he did last year – I'm sure that some of the descriptions of
travel, adventure etc. come into letters to other pals, as they do in
mine (I dread to think of some of the near duplicate of letters of
mine that must be gathering dust in scattered drawers). Anyway,
darling Diana, here they are – or rather, will be. I was very moved
reading them, by this record of shared delights and trust, confidence,
warmth and loving friendship, and can't believe my luck, unfaltering
for all these years, and still prospering in such a marvellous, happy
and treasured bond, light as garlands,[2] as lasting as those hoops of
Polonius.[3]

   After thoroughly embarrassing us both, I'll charge on.

   Last week, we were summoned to Athens by the Ghikas for an
intriguingly mysterious evening two days ahead. We'd got a sort of
an inkling what it might be from a hint or two, and it turned out
to be what we'd thought, and very exciting, too; viz. getting elected
to the Athens Academy, as what's called a Corresponding member,
which is the most a non-Greek is allowed to be; and as it's the
local equivalent of the Acad. Française, it's considered a great
honour. Joan, Barbara and I were waiting in the flat, when Niko
telephoned to say it had gone through with thirty votes out of
thirty, with one absentee blank – i.e. jolly well, and before we
could say knife, he was back in their flat with a kind of Comus
rout of delightful fogeys, corks began flying, beakers brimming and
many embraces; ninety-year-old sages dashed at one with a hop,
skip and a wince. Then lots of other friends rolled up, the cork-
fusillade went on into the small hours, and there was not so much
as a flicker of hangover next day. Well, that *was* nice. Another nice
thing was the end of a long toothache. A charming lady-dentist
discovered a sort of Polyphemus's cavern in a back tooth,
measureless to man,[4] in which a flock might snugly winter, but too
late now: walled up . . .

No more now, darling Diana, except tons of fond love & hugs from
    Paddy

P.S. I'll find a way of getting the precious bundle of letters to you – perhaps via Michael Stewart, who is coming out in three weeks time to Athens with Mr Macmillan, who is getting a prize for being president of an Acropolis preservation committee, awarded by the Onassis Foundation to whose prize-giving committee, he and I both belong. It's rather fun. They pay for stately travel and hotels whenever a three-day meeting crops up. G.B., the Meurice in Paris, Sachers[5] one day perhaps?

P.P.S. Darling Diana, Do go through all the letters carefully before handing over, as there are obviously lots of things not for strangers' eyes – cheerful mocking of friends, now and then brief exasperation with loved ones, which, in cold blood to the uninitiated, might leave scars.

I'm sure it's all right with Philip Ziegler, he seems a very nice chap indeed; even so, unexpected dangers yawn. I was horrified by some of the things that appeared – and by Laura's[6] guilty frivolity in handing them over unread – when Evelyn's memoirs or letters appeared in a Sunday paper with clumsy and harmful editorial comments in the guise of elucidation.[7]

Letters and talk should *always* be free and reckless between friends, according to Castiglione in *Il Cortegiano* – it's a quality he calls '*sprezzatura*', the point being that *among* friends, if they are the sort he is writing about, *nothing* can be taken the wrong way. But outside the magic circle, in the coldness and impersonality of print, *beware*, is his drift; and I'm sure he's right. P.
    xxx

---

[1] Philip Ziegler's *Diana Cooper: A Biography* was published in 1981.
[2] 'For men acknowledged true desires
   And light as garlands wore them.'
            Bayard Taylor, 'A Paean to the Dawn'
[3] Polonius's advice to his son, Laertes: 'Grapple them to thy soul with hoops of steel.'

4 'In Xanadu did Kubla Khan
    A stately pleasure-dome decree:
    Where Alph, the sacred river, ran
    Through caverns measureless to man
    Down to a sunless sea'
                        Coleridge, *Kubla Khan*
5 All luxurious hotels: the Grande Bretagne in Athens; Le Meurice in Paris; Sacher in
Vienna.
6 Waugh's widow.
7 See pages 292–4.

To Niko and Barbara Ghika   Kardamyli
undated [probably February 1980]   Messenia

Dear Niko, Darling Barbara,

This is not a bread-and-butter, but a Nectar-and-Ambrosia letter!
What a lovely stay that was, and that miraculous red-letter day of
the Academy! Unforgettable. Thank you both so much for all the
immediate toils and worries that had to be contended with to
make it possible *at all*, what with breakdowns, and dilatory
plumbers and electricians; for that wonderful champagne, of which
even thirty or forty beakers full failed to produce even the flicker
of a headache; and above all, Niko, for the generous thought, so
many months ago, of getting me hoisted into your august assembly,
wreathed and blushing, and for the toils and patience of seeing that
it really did come true. Not only the champagne overflowed, but
hearts too, and still do. We came back in a haze of well-being,
elation, and gratitude.

I wonder what it's been like in Athens since we left? Here bright
summer days are accompanied by Arctic, bone-biting cold (with
nights when the stars look like chips of icicles) and very slightly
warmer days, but dark with endless drizzle and forbidding grey skies.
It's like that today, and Joan's reclining with a bit of flu – perhaps
something different, as it doesn't seem to be catching – under her
manifold blanket of cats. I have meals on a little table at the bottom
of the bed, a blazing fire heaving, and after dinner I've been reading
Chaucer out loud, pronounced as modern English, with only a faint,

almost unuttered 'er' or 'o' sound for those final vowels which have since dropped away, like the simian tails of our forefathers when no longer needed, and it makes it very easy to understand, especially with a glossary on the opposite page for the really difficult words. It's a sort of private breakthrough, like my secret decision, at the age of about twenty, always to pronounce Latin, to myself, not in either the 'old', the 'new' or the 'Erasmian' way, but simply as Italian. It turns it into a living language at once, instead of a stone-dead inscription on blurred and overgrown marble. Alas, alas! It can't quite be done with ancient Greek, because of the metrical quantities in scanning. They all say it was a matter of pitch, as in Chinese; but nobody has ever managed to give a convincing or even melodious demonstration.

No more now, except a billion thanks again, and bless you both forever.

With lots of love,
    Paddy

To Diana Cooper   Kardamyli
19 July 1980   Messenia

Darling Diana,

What a lovely evening, that dinner in your house, our last night in Blighty! (I wish I'd written next day to say so). I love Tom Stoppard[1] saying 'It's the sort of evening I always hope I'm going to have, but never do.' Do you see what I mean about his having more than a hint of *un*-gross and un-fleshy Oscar W about him, depending largely on fine, large and friendly eyes, and a soft and many-curved formation of the mouth? He seemed quite exceptionally nice the two times I met him, the first at the Lit. Soc.,[2] and the second, more protracted, thanks to you. Anyway, it was *lovely*, full of amusing discussion, quotation, reading aloud, and plenty of laughter, sitting up in the glow until the last possible moment, before flitting off into the night. It reminded me of many a happy evening in the black-and-white-floored chamber at Chantilly.

> 'And there they loll till far into the night
> Toying with heresies by candlelight',

as I remember Peter Q. and I improvising, after innumerable glasses, just before tottering bedwards. It was snowy and frosty weather, and next morning he and George Gage[3] and I walked across the white park, had a look at the statue of Anne de Montmorency and those marvellous stables and then thought: why not a nip at the Tipperary (or was it the Piccadilly?) bar, that haunt of jockeys in the main street which you always dreaded, as it made guests late for luncheon.

I still can't get over the splendours and delights of the Raymond Asquith book.[4] I bet the reviews will be *quelque chose*. I haven't seen any of them yet, except a short and charming one, half interview, by Philip Howard, ending in so splendid a Danaë shower of dewdrops that I felt like standing up and cheering. I expect they've found someone infinitely better qualified than I to review it for the *Times Lit. Supp.*; but I've just written to John Gross, the v. nice editor, to see if they will let me do one of those ad. lib. commentaries on the middle pages, devoted to anything they want. What I'd like to point out, is the enormous amount of buried quotation there is in the letters book to K. H.[5] and to you, which must mean a vast quantity of shared poetry which was in daily use, and pointless if the other correspondent couldn't spot it – no helping inverted commas; e.g. like R. A.'s saying a German artillery barrage had done no harm (none killed that time), seeming to aim at a million but missing one unit, which prompted us, helped by faint memories, to run it down, and read out in *The Grammarian's Funeral*.[6] I remember thinking at Chantilly, looking at that girlish album of yours, with favourite poems engrossed in a careful hand, how very similar yours had been to mine; Sir Thomas Wyatt's (my favourite of the lot) make me nearly jump out of my skin. Browning, Tennyson, Swinburne, and Meredith are the ones I remember best. What others? Could you have a look at them – but of course, no need – and roughly let me know? Were you sixteen or eighteen when you made that amazing pilgrimage to Box Hill?[7] How astounded Meredith must have been.

It's suddenly very hot here, but I write, I am there now, in a sort of arbour through which a breeze always seems to blow, on the olive-terrace under the window where you stay (whence I suddenly heard the click-clack of that invading helicopter); and I manage to make the thick-walled studio as cool as a sepulchre by closing all the grey shutters, so that only a restful penumbra reigns within. Cicadas scrape away on every twig. During our absence, a rumour started here, and in neighbouring villages, that I had died while on furlough. It was rather fun, for a week or two, climbing into the higher villages, and watching their jaws drop and eyes shoot out on stalks at what must have seemed like the vision of a spectre, or Lazarus risen from the tomb, and assuring them with a light laugh that the rumour was exaggerated . . . [8]

A dragon-fly has just settled on this page, of so enormous a size and with such unwieldy drooping and rainbowy wings, that I don't see how he's ever going to take off again.

With tons of fond love & hugs, darling Diana,

    from Paddy

(Joan sends hers too)

[1] Tom Stoppard (b. 1937), dazzlingly clever playwright and screenwriter.
[2] The Lit. Soc. (normal abbreviation), founded by William Wordsworth and others in 1807, meets once a month at the Garrick Club.
[3] George John St Clere Gage (1932–93), 7th Viscount Gage.
[4] John Jolliffe, *Raymond Asquith: Life and Letters* (1980).
[5] Katharine Frances Horner (1885–1976), whom Asquith married in 1907.
[6] 'This high man, aiming at a million,
  Misses an unit'
       Robert Browning, 'A Grammarian's Funeral' (1855)
[7] The novelist and poet George Meredith (1828–1909) lived at Box Hill, in Surrey.
[8] Mark Twain, 'The reports of my death have been greatly exaggerated.'

To Diana Cooper   Kardamyli
9 February 1981   Messenia

Darling Diana,

After Christmas, we – us, that is, and Xan and his mate –
suddenly decided on Syria, so hastened to Athens and took wing.

Well, Damascus looks a slum at first, especially under rain and
slime, but, bit by bit, its hidden splendours dawn. The Great Mosque
is the eighth Wonder of the World. Out of doors, it encloses a vast
courtyard full of dazzling Byzantine mosaics and pigeons; inside are
endless hushed vistas of columns and acanthus leaves from the
Roman temple to Jupiter that it has usurped. Dwarfed by muffling
acres of carpet, little groups are dotted about, conversing quietly or
prostrating themselves towards Mecca on a sudden impulse. Cross-
legged, doddery, steel-spectacled Imams in snowy turbans and robes,
rather like archdeacons or minor-canons of a Mohammedan
Barchester, whisper the Koran to themselves from low, inlaid folding
lecterns, or just roam about vaguely. On several days I sat there too,
hours of vacant bliss leaning against a column's base, lulled by the
tick of a nearby grandfather clock (with Arabic numerals, but made
in Coventry in 1852). Moslems love them. Rather surprisingly, they
also love the head of St John the Baptist, jealously enshrined and
revered in a very ornate crescent-topped tabernacle half-way down
the aisle. There were marvellous temples and burial towers at
Palmyra, dead beautiful cities like Resafa,[1] long, reedy moments by
the Euphrates, and dramatic dawns and sunsets across the desert:

'. . . And when the deep red eye of day is level with the lone
    highway
And some to Mecca turn to pray, but I toward thy bed,
    Yasmin . . .
Shower down thy love, O burning bright! For one night or
    the other night
Here comes the gardener in white; and gathered flowers are
    dead, Yasmin'[2]

Hassan to the rescue! Aleppo was a warren of lanes and caravanserais like a tangle of Oxford colleges; Crusader castles – e.g. Krak des Chevaliers, fierce as a gauntlet, complex as The Maginot Line – scowl from many a mountain; and there were scores of wonderful and enormous ruined Romano-Byzantine basilicas. The biggest and noblest, larger than Ely, was built round the stump of a column once 60 feet high, on top of which St Symeon Stylites perched for forty years, unsheltered and unplumbed. The faithful domed him over in the end – perhaps to his rage. I hope they left him a loophole for the splendid view over the Alawite mountains. The Djebel Druze, covered in snow, looked like the North Riding, and not far off was Bosra, with the biggest and most complete and sparkling Roman theatre ever seen, embedded in a giant Saracen fort and only revealed a couple of decades ago: black basalt with an apricot Corinthian proscenium and a colonnade round the top. We had luncheon at Dera'a, where T. E. Lawrence was thrashed and violated by the Turkish bey. We peered at the building where it must have happened – if it did: it may have been wishful thinking by hindsight, if I may use the expression – and fidgeted uncomfortably . . .

Back in Damascus was an enclosed tomb with a bulbous green turban: *Saladin's!* Only a month before, we had been gazing at the recumbent effigy of his foe and friend, Richard Coeur de Lion, at Fontevrault, south of the Loire;[3] and our minds flew to *The Talisman*[4] . . . There's a fine old *hammam* [Turkish bath] a few lanes away, built in the same reign by Nur ad-Din el Shahád el Mansúr[5] (may his bones rest in peace!) and I slunk off there with Xan on our last afternoon. When the steam, the clanking of brass bowls, the thumping and the bone-cracking were over, we were swaddled like mummies in many layers of linen sheets and towels and finally, in mantles of cloth of gold, our heads swathed, we were led away, bobbling and nearly insensible, to recline on divans that looked up into vaults of basalt and a vast, dim dome, and down on to softly lit fountains; slowly coming to. Then, as we bubbled away at hookahs over bitter desert coffee spiced with cardamom, we could just hear, as we sipped, the muted wail of a *muezzin* from a minaret hard-by (recorded, of course: convolvulus-horns sprout from their balconies).

Fragrant and disembodied – the cleanest people east of Suez and north of the Hedjaz – we issued forth at last into the twilit *souks*, followed by the black and burning glances of the Bedouin that swarm along the Street called Straight . . .

Well, it was lovely. We are now buried in Doughty[6] and the *Seven Pillars* and the *Letters of Gertrude Bell*. I found these *Letters* one of the most brilliant and exciting books I've read, and very funny too. I long to read her other books: have only read *Amurath to Amurath*.[7] She was Ed Stanley's & Judy's great aunt; also, rather unfortunately, Molly Buccleuch's.[8] You *must* have known her – we all *could* have. Sylvia Henley[9] comes in a lot. *Do write* about this, what she was like, etc. She's become a sort of craze with us: an extraordinary mixture of guts, brains, humour, and niceness too, and one can't get better than that.

No more for the moment, Diana darling, except pining for news – nobody writes – and tons of fond love

from Paddy

P.S. What news of Annie? I'm just about to send her a very similar letter – so don't let on!

P.P.S. The food was very good, but might pall. Ask JJ if he has kept his sense of hummuz.

[1] An archaeological site, known in Roman times as Segiopolis.

[2] James Elroy Flecker, 'Hassan's Serenade' (1922):

> 'But when the deep red eye of day
> is level with the lone highway,
> And some to Mecca turn to pray,
> and I toward thy bed, Yasmin . . .
>
> Shine down thy love, O burning bright!
> for one night or the other night
> Will come the Gardener in white,
> and gather'd flowers are dead, Yasmin!'

[3] The Royal Abbey of Our Lady of Fontevraud or Fontevrault is a complex of religious buildings in the Loire Valley, near Chinon. Henry II, his wife, Eleanor of Aquitaine, and their son, Richard I, were all buried there, though it seems that their remains may have been destroyed during the French Revolution.

4 Walter Scott's 1825 novel *The Talisman* is set in the Third Crusade.

5 Ruler of the Syrian province of the Seljuk Empire from 1146 to 1174 AD.

6 C. M. Doughty, *Travels in Arabia Deserta* (1888).

7 Gertrude Bell (1868–1926), traveller, archaeologist, mountaineer and diplomat. *Amurath to Amurath* (1911) traces an expedition to Mesopotamia.

8 'Molly', Duchess of Buccleuch (1900–93), née Lascelles, had been one of Duff's mistresses, known collectively by Diana as 'the dairy' because their names were reminiscent of cows' names – Molly, Poppy [Baring], Daisy [Fellowes], Biddy [Carlisle], etc. 'Please keep out of the dairy,' she would say to him.

9 Gertrude Bell's cousin Sylvia Laura Henley (1882–1980), née Stanley, accompanied GB on her last visit to Iraq.

To Diana Cooper   Kardamyli
15 April 1981   Messenia

Darling Diana,

I wonder if you fully realised that Harun al-Rashid[1] sent an elephant called Abulahaz as a present to Charlemagne in AD 802? I've just come across it in a forty-five-year-old notebook, and had clean forgotten it. I've looked it up in a wonderful old eight-volume book called *Italy and her Invaders*[2] that Freya gave me last winter, and it's quite true. The poor creature was killed in 810, in a battle against the King of Denmark: what a shame! Up till then he lived in the park of Charlemagne's palace at Aachen (Aix-la-Chapelle to us). I wonder which route he took? Baghdad – Palmyra – Aleppo – Antioch, then by sea, probably, to Bari, and along the Appian Way to Rome; then north, over the Alps at the Brenner, across Germany and up the Rhine? Or Venice, perhaps, then Vienna, and along the Danube? I like to think that *perhaps* the Caliph sent him *via* the Hellespont or the Bosphorus and through the Byzantine Empire – they were on fairly good terms till the *end* of 802. But then they would have had to cross the new Bulgarian state, reigned over by a horrible Khan called Krum, who, at banquets with his boyars, used to drink out of the skull of his defeated enemy, the Byzantine Emperor Nicephorus, bisected and lined with silver.[3] They were a rotten lot. I bet if they had spotted Abulahaz, they'd have eaten him. But *if* they had got through Bulgaria all right (travelling after dark, perhaps), things would have been better in what

later became Hungary, because Charlemagne had defeated the beastly
Avars there, and scattered them eight years before. There would have
been a few Slav settlers gaping in the doors of their huts as the little
troop went by: Abulahaz, his mahout and grooms, and probably an
escort of Bedouin lancers. The Hungarian Plain was ideal elephant
country then – all swamp and forest, unlike now. (One is so prone to
forget that a squirrel in the reign of King John could travel from the
Severn to the Humber without once touching ground.) I do hope
the elephant went that way, because it's just the way I went, and am
writing about; I could have come nose-to-trunk with his phantom on
the banks of the Tisza (a Hungarian tributary of the Danube) as he
squirted cool jets all over himself among the reeds . . .

I meant to start with saying how sorry I was to read about Enid
Bagnold,[4] knowing what an old pal of yours she was, marbles or no
marbles. Dauntless Annie says she *may* come here with Patrick
Trevor-Roper next month, *in spite* of all the afflictions that beset her.
I do hope things turn out all right. It really is unfair. Debo keeps me
more or less posted. Annie writes that *you* are well, which I was
pleased to hear, as never a word from source. I *would* like a bulletin.

Joan is back in Blighty for two to three weeks, with brother
Graham, and I go for ten days, over the Orthodox Easter, to Barbara
and Niko in Corfu, address (written in hope): c/o B[arbara] G[hika],
Kanoni, St Stefano-Sinies, Corfu, taking one's work with me. It's
going fine.

So happy Easter, Diana darling, and tons of fond
    love from Paddy
    xxx

---

[1] Harun al-Rashid (786–809), 5th Caliph of the Abbasid Caliphate, a vast Islamic
empire comprising Arabia, Persia and much of North Africa.

[2] Thomas Hodgkin, *Italy and her Invaders* (8 vols., 1880–99).

[3] The Emperor Nicephorus I was killed, supposedly on a dunghill, at the disastrous
Battle of Pliska or Battle of Vărbitsa Pass in AD 811.

[4] Enid Algerine Bagnold (1889–1981), a writer best known for *National Velvet* (1935).
In 1920 she married Sir Roderick Jones, chairman of Reuters, but continued to use
her maiden name for her writing. Their great-granddaughter is Samantha Cameron,
wife of the former Conservative Party leader and prime minister, David Cameron.

To Ann Fleming
15 June 1981   Corfu

Darling Annie,

I'm *so sorry* you've been having such a mouldy time,[1] and wish I
were on the spot to cheer you up – *not*, so I learn from Pat [Trevor-
Roper] and Debo, that you are not reacting to all these wretched
nuisances with all your indomitable spirits. Actually, I *do* hope to be
in Blighty early in July for a short time, so there I may loom.

I wish you had been at Kardamyli at the same time as Pat. It was
lovely seeing him, in spite of some very slightly lowering though
sympathetic presences. We were both struggling with speeches we
had to make, he to the leading eye-experts of the planet, I to a
swarm of Cretans. He hasn't told us how *his* went: I'm sure
dazzlingly well. I followed his advice to the letter, and it seems that
it did the trick, i.e. a double whisky immediately before, neither
more nor less. I administered this (from a miniature bottle in my
pocket) in the loo of the Defence Minister Averoff's private bomber,
which carried us, and some ministers and ambassadors, to Herakleion.
There were about 3,000 old Cretan pals roped off, a regiment of
Greek soldiers, a bevy of bearded archbishops and archimandrites
enclouded in incense. When the loudspeaker summoned the Def.
Minister to unveil the monument, he called for me, and we paced
solemnly to the ten-foot-high monument, tugged on two ropes, and
down flopped the Greek flag and the Union Jack while three Scots
Guard pipers blew solemn pibrochs. Then a Maori sounded the Last
Post. Averoff made a short address, then waved me to the rostrum,
when, thanks to Pat's formula, I let fly with vigour and thank God,
no mistakes in the Greek. Hardly a dry eye! It ended with what
seemed a million whiskery embraces from my shaggy old chums and
their descendants, and was followed by a giant banquet with scores of
lamb roasted whole, and stringed instruments and dances and songs.
Everyone clanking with medals, which was fun. I think the rather
prim but nice lowland Scots Ambassador and his wife were amazed
by these ogre-ish revels of old guerrilla chiefs. They were even
surprised when an old god-brother of mine, next night, in the

luxury hotel where he was feasting us, got up in the middle of the
singing, pulled out an enormous revolver, fired four bullets through
the central window-pane, then four more very neatly, in the smaller
surrounding panes and then pushed the smoking gun back in his
breast pocket, and resumed his seat as cool as a cucumber . . . I was
almost a stretcher-case from banqueting by the time I got back to K.
It was the fortieth anniversary of the Battle of Crete.[2]

The day before leaving, we went to a green lawn-like plateau just
under the Idaean cave (where Zeus was brought up) just under the
peak of Mt Ida, still covered in snow. More feasting and lyra-playing
and singing and *feu de joie* with all the shepherds there, all old
friends. There was dripping mist and clouds when we got there but
they all blew away, leaving nothing but clear blue planetary air and
hovering eagles, and, on the green plateau below, all the ewes lining
up to be milked, four hundred bells jangling as they headed across
the sward to the prehistoric goat-fold. Marvellous!

We arrived in Corfu two days ago, and here we sit, opposite
forbidden Albania,[3] only twenty minutes away if the channel were
grassed over; but it might be 1,000 miles. The Acroceraunian
mountains flash in the sun, swallows dart under the branches. We saw
seven families of nearly full-grown storks on the way up here. Jacob
Rothschild[4] left last night, leaving Serena; Dadie Rylands reads
Phineas Redux out loud – beautifully – to Barbara and Joan, while
Niko paints away in his shady studio and I sit under the criss-
crossing swallow-droppings writing to you. A fine burly Croatian
cook is approaching under the arbour with *taramasaláta*, glasses, ice
and ouzo-bottles, so no more for the moment, darling Annie, except
tons of love from
    Paddy

and see you soon.
    (Love from others here.)
      xxx

My pen is breaking down, I'm so sorry about the illegibility.

1 She was fatally ill, and died only three weeks after this letter was written.

2 The Battle of Crete lasted from 20 May to 1 June 1941.

3 Albania was then under the iron grip of the Communist dictator, Enver Hoxha. It was the most isolated and poorest country in Europe.

4 Barbara Ghika's son, Jacob Rothschild (b. 1936), married to Serena Mary Dunn.

To Xan Fielding   Kardamyli
19 July 1981   Messenia

Xan παιδί μου [dear boy],

First of all, many, many thanks to you both for giving me the freedom of Bruton St! Of course, I didn't go in the end, and there is the key waiting at White's! Have you got another? In case *not*, I'll enclose a word to the Hall-Porter asking him to hand over any small parcel addressed to me, possibly containing a key, and with a Spanish stamp on.

I was only going back to Blighty in the hopes of catching a last glimpse of Annie; but, sadly, I was too late. I can't believe one will never see her again . . .

Jock only began to read The Winds[1] on the last morning, and cagily said 'A very interesting idea', as he pored over it. Of course Joan and I cracked it up like billy-o and rightly.

I'm sorry being so slow with the typescript. I hope I haven't been too free with emendations and loppings. If I've knocked off any bloom or dew, simply put it back. I tackled it exactly as if it were my own stuff, disentangling and simplifying where I felt it might make things clearer. I think it's tip-top; but there are one or two ways where it might be even tipper, and, if I may put it so, topper; and these are they. I think there is a tendency to *over-explain*, and stress the point when it has already been made. A succession of very short paragraphs now and then makes it a bit jerky and choppy, and I feel some of them could be merged. Perhaps illustration and quotation are piled up a bit too lavishly, and can be pruned, to the bits that are undiscardably germane. I feel 'dwelling' too long lets the tension drop, and your text should sail along with the unencumbered freedom of its theme. Fruitiness pops up its head for a moment now and then. I can speak with feeling about all these things, as they are exactly my own faults, and I recognise them at once. Alas, Dr Johnson was right in his advice to us: 'Read over your compositions, and wherever you meet with a passage which you think is particularly fine, strike it out.' I find this a very consoling thing when I feel constrained to any verbal blood-letting.

Do send any other parts where I can come in handy as a second opinion – I'm perfectly ready to go over all, if wanted. I'm so sorry about the thick pencil: it's the only one in the house. I've used brackets – round or square – for passages or words that you might consider excising, and have sometimes actually erased. If entrusted with other parts, I will promise to be more systematic, and neater, and to write more clearly. I don't know what's happening to my writing, it gets worse and worse. I've just read, in the Lyttelton Hart-Davis letters, that 'inaudible speech, like illegible writing, is the nadir of bad manners'; so I plan to reform, starting now . . .

Feel dreadfully bowed down by the loss of Annie and Philip:[2] too much for a single month . . .

Lots of fond love to Magouche and you from both of us

[1] XF's book, eventually published posthumously by a small private press in 1991 as *Aeolus Displayed: A Book of the Winds*.
[2] Philip Toynbee died on 15 June 1981.

To Artemis Cooper   Kardamyli
23 February 1982   Messenia

My dear Artemis,

How very kind of you to send that review of Clive James' about Diana.[1] It's absolutely tip-top, and fills exactly the void I was grumbling about at that lovely dinner party. I've stuck it, and your letter, in the back of Philip's book, a mild form of Graingerising[2] I've taken to recently, and I wish I'd started years ago: i.e., the addition of relevant things to books. My system is to cut the flap off an envelope, then stick it with UHU inside the backboard of the book, with the now un-flapped opening facing *upwards*, but *inwards*, so that the contents can't fall out. It makes the book much more interesting later on, is great fun to do and fills one with a feeling of achievement; and it is hard to imagine a more insidious and time-wasting excuse for postponing what you really ought to be doing. Start today.

But don't let it delay the editing of the letters![3] They will be breathlessly awaited and just the thing to set the stagnant air blowing in the right direction again. I know the feeling about recapturing lost voices, what one would give for a few seconds of it. Lists of uneavesdroppable interlocutors leap to the mind, if such a ghastly conjunction of words were capable of leaving the ground.

Very many thanks again, dear Artemis, and much love to your dear ones from us both

love Paddy

I do envy your beautiful clear writing, mine sinks fast into Linear B.[4]

---

[1] 'Mrs Stitch in Time' (a review of *Lady Diana Cooper* by Philip Ziegler), *London Review of Books*, 4 February 1982.

[2] Named after the Scottish doctor, poet, translator and collector, James Grainger (*c.*1721–66), who is credited with introducing the idea of interleaving the printed text of books of history and topography with prints.

[3] AC was editing her grandparents' letters, published in 1983 as *A Durable Fire: The Letters of Duff and Diana Cooper, 1913–1950*.

[4] A script used for writing Mycenaean Greek, dating from about 1450 BC, notorious for being indecipherable: though discovered in the late nineteenth century, it was not deciphered until the early 1950s.

To Diana Cooper   Kardamyli
28 May 1982   Messenia

My darling Diana,

I'm just back from such a queer journey. I suddenly felt I *must* have a glimpse of the country I travelled through in 1936 in Hungary and Rumania (for Vol. II): one remembers the foreground and the storyline, but the middle distance gets a bit blurred. So, I

took wing to Budapest, hired a car, and set out over the Great
Hungarian Plain.

I had ridden over the first 150 miles of it (of yore, I mean) on a
borrowed horse, and, retracing the journey it all came flooding back,
the vast rolling fields, the bits of bleak heath, the swing wells,[1] the
processions of poplars, white cattle with nearly straight horns, the
lilac everywhere, and hollyhocks and peonies in the villages, storks
on the chimneys and cuckoos everywhere . . . I caught glimpses of
castles and *gentilhommières* where I had dossed down on my original
trip, with the families of the *grafs* and *freiherrs*, all vanished long ago.
At least, all except one, at a place called Körösladány, which used to
be inhabited by a morganatic Habsburg called Ct Meran, with a
beautiful wife and three charming children. I had stayed a few days
in the large and rambling baroque *kastély*. Well, the *village* was still the
abode of one of the children, Hansi Meran. He had been twelve
when I was last there; he's now sixty, a huge, grizzled handsome chap
in a loden jacket, married (and widowed) to a peasant girl, after
returning from the war, and being arrested for no reason by the
Russians and sent for ten years to Siberia. I found him in a cottage
with a visiting sister from Vienna (thirteen years old when last
sighted, now a gr. grandmother). I was surprised by how clearly they
remembered my ancient visit! 'You see that table?' they said, pointing
to a Biedermeier desk salvaged from the castle (now a school). 'You
used to sit at it all day writing in a big green book' – (I've got it
beside me now). He was now a retired pensioner, after working as a
farm-labourer on his own confiscated acres. There were a few
rescued odds and ends, portraits of gr. gr. gr. gr. grandma Maria
Teresa, and aunt Marie Antoinette. We all sat sipping whisky and
reminiscing in the dusk, with cattle mooing past the windows . . .

I climbed over the walls of several minor Bridesheads and slunk
about the grounds. The largest, O' Kigyós, was now a school, but all
the exotic trees were as I remembered, box hedges neatly trimmed,
magnolias and tulip trees shedding their petals and millions of
doves . . . No need for secrecy in any of these cases. Here the old
Slovak gardener remembers the Wenckheim[2] I had played bike-polo
with, practically, [with] tears in his eyes.

Back in the capital, I flew to Bucharest, as it was difficult to take a Hungarian hired car into Rumania, and hired another, and went and stayed twenty-four hours with Pomme (sister of Balasha Cantacuzène,[3] loved by me of yore), talked day and night, then sped on to Transylvania, to follow my old tracks along the leafy and beautiful valley of the Maros, beset with more Bridesheads – nineteenth-century, baroque, Palladian, one late Renaissance – where landowning Hungarians had stayed on after Transylvania had been handed to Rumania after the Great War. They, too, were turned into loony-bins, so I found myself strolling along shady paths, and up branching balustraded stairs surrounded by vague figures who smiled and mopped and mowed like characters out of the last scene of *The Duchess of Malfi*. The last one I saw, and the oldest, formerly owned by a friend called Elemér von Klobusiçky, was now a nursery plantation for bamboos, and other experimental growths. Great thick walls and steep tiles and pillared balconies and vast chestnut trees covered with moulting pink and white candles. I spent a month there in July 1934. It was dusk, so I tapped on a lighted window, and a v. nice peasant woman came out with a nice daughter. I said I was a friend of the former owner and they were very excited. I said I'd seen him in Budapest the week before. They had heard all about what a dasher he had been, and what fun. 'Come and have some brandy made from Mr Elemér's plums.' We sipped on the terrace, looking out over the overgrown tennis court, nightingales starting up in the forest, the Maros curving away. 'We feel guilty living in a confiscated house. Please send him our respects . . .'

So, on to all the old towns of Transylvania. There are some beautiful 'Saxon' ones with fortified steep roofs, spires and Gothic churches, the houses, it is said (including by Browning: see the end of the poem), of the children who were led into the mountainside by the Pied Piper. This is where they surfaced again.

No more now, Diana darling, except heaps of fond love
    from Paddy (also from Joan)
    xxx

Peter Q. says a book is being done about Annie.[4] Is it a bit early? What about Hugh Gaitskell, & Caspar?[5] It's a strange craze.

[1] A well with a hinged arm, a bucket at one end and a counterweight at the other, common on the Great Hungarian Plain.

[2] Count Józsi Wenckheim.

[3] Balasha died of breast cancer in 1976.

[4] Mark Amory was editing Ann Fleming's letters.

[5] Ann Fleming had an affair with the Labour leader, Hugh Gaitskell, who died in 1963. Her son Caspar suffered from depression, and committed suicide in 1975.

To Michael Stewart   Kardamyli
29 June 1982   Messenia

My dear Michael,

You really are the most marvellous fulfiller of promises, however slight and uncommitting! I can't tell you how I rejoice in this splendid quartz watch, with its handsome black case, its unfaltering needles, its mandible tick and the discreet but merciless challenge of its alarm! It arrived a week after the final breakdown of the kitchen clock and half a day after Joan had lost her wrist-watch on the beach; so its advent with Graham was timely in every sense. *Very many thanks indeed.*

I rang up Hará.[1] No, she hasn't forgot Bean's *Beyond the Maeander*,[2] and would love it and was tremendously pleased and touched by the idea. What a nice girl she is.

On a sudden inspiration, Joan and [I] motored to Gythion, caught the night ferry to Kastelli-Kissamos in W. Crete, and spent a week tooling all over the island. It really was terrific. They made a great fuss of us in all our old haunts – mostly high up in the mountains – and we had to have about fifteen meals a day. One or two people I hadn't seen for thirty-eight years said, when we first arrived, 'How thin you've got!' Similar old friends, at the end of the stay, said 'How fat you've got! Po, po, po!' The car filled up with gifts – millstone-cheeses, demijohns of wine, wicker-covered gallonia of *tsikoudia* and mulberry-*raki*, raisins, almonds, walnuts, shepherd's crooks . . . They really are a marvellous lot, quite unlike anyone else, and funnier, higher-spirited, more musical and alert and affectionate and nice-looking. My god-daughters, all matrons now, are a fine lot. The wine is delicious and, in the villages, absolutely pure, which is extremely rare, so, however much we swallowed, which was a great deal, there was no trace of a hangover next day; and the lamb is so marvellous — it almost has a thyme and heather taste from what they graze on — that it almost converted Joan — did, temporarily — into a carnivore. She adored every moment of it. At Retimo [Rethymno], the hotel sent us a complimentary bucket of champagne. We *were* pleased.

Corfu was very quiet and satisfactory. Barbara, Niko, Dadie Rylands, Diana Gage and us, with Dadie reading his annual Trollope aloud, this year *The Prime Minister*, very good, but not quite up to last year's *Phineas Redux*, we thought. We were glued to the wireless for Falkland news[3] and there was great rejoicing at the upshot.

The Turkish project is very exciting and tempting. I do hope it would involve being on the move — that is what one needs after a few static gulf-tide months at Kardamyli!

I've just been going through old letters for Annie Fleming, requested by Mark Amory, who is doing a life of her, a bit early perhaps. I was tackled for the same thing by Mark Bonham Carter,[4] but oiled out of it, as (a) too much on hand and (b) I don't think I could be much good at it. The letters are tip-top — full of dashing *sprezzatura*, exactly as she spoke, and often very funny. You get several very warm mentions.

No more now, Michael, except many, many thanks again for that smashing clock, and fond greetings from all under this roof, and to Damaris.

    Yours ever
      Paddy

---

1 Hará Kiosse, Nico Hadjimichalis's companion after he left his wife Vana.

2 George E. Bean, *Turkey Beyond the Maeander: An Archaeological Guide* (1971).

3 On 2 April 1982, Argentina invaded and occupied the Falkland Islands in the South Atlantic, in an attempt to establish its long-standing claim to sovereignty. The British government dispatched a naval task force to retake the islands. The conflict ended with the Argentine surrender on 14 June 1982, returning the islands to British control.

4 Mark Bonham Carter (1922–94), Liberal politician and publisher.

Jessica Treuhaft, known as 'Decca', second youngest of the Mitford sisters, was compiling a volume of memoirs of Philip Toynbee, and asked Paddy (amongst others) to contribute his own recollections of his old friend. The book was published in 1984 as Faces of Philip: A Memoir of Philip Toynbee.

To Jessica Mitford
16 September 1983   Chatsworth

Dear Decca,

Here I am for all too brief a moment, got here last night, off tomorrow. Andrew was off to a wretched banquet in Brixton, true torment, so Debo and I had a hilarious time here, jolly tales about your youth, and some song.

This is in haste, one foot in stirrup, pricking Spainwards. About including the 'working' part of letters in the final text, the only thing that worries me is things that you might – or I might – think merely a lark can sometimes cut to the quick, without one's knowing. So *could* you let me have a look, I promise not to hold things up, and whizz back at once to you. In a fortnight's time will be % Senor Jaime Parladé (viz. Janetta), Terre de Tramoros, Benaha – viz. Prov. de Malaga, Spain; and a fortnight after that, home.

(2) I came across this, by me, but P. T. *soi-disant* speaking, must date from late forties or early fifties.

> 'When I was in love with a Liberal Girl
> 'I was a swine and she was a pearl.
> 'I'm still a swine, sir, but fancy-free
> 'And many a liberal Girl loves me.'

Thought for the week.

Please forgive haste, and 1,000 salaams, as an Anglo-Indian uncle of mine used to say.

Yours ever
Paddy

Bit of a lapse here Claudewise, alas . . .[1]

Later: WRONG! He came back here from the races where his favourite steed cracked, & was put down, but NARY A SIP. NOTHING BUT NICENESS.

P.S. Decca – I brooded in the night, and felt racked with foreboding about my off-the-cuff-and-record ramblings that went into all the stuff about Philip, and wondered if I'd made clear *how* racked I was. So, up at dawn, I hared down to the lodge (where letters rest before departure), extorted mine from the chap who dwells there, and reopened it. Totally unnecessarily, as it turns out, so this is only to explain why the contents of the envelope have been untimely ripped, and Scotch-taped up again.[2]

Went to a marvellous sheep sale yester'een with Debo, it was wonderful, faces like the whole of Gilray and Rowlandson, and an auctioneer haranguing, in what sounded like Finnish but was just rustic north country.

This is the sort of whirl I like to live in.

---

[1] PLF means that Andrew Devonshire had lapsed into drinking excessively, a weakness of his. 'Claud' was Debo's nickname for her husband.

[2] PLF alludes to lines from *Macbeth*, V, 8 ('The Scottish play'):

> 'Macduff was from his mother's womb
> untimely ripped.'

Like Paddy, Gerald Brenan had immersed himself in another culture: a scholar of Spanish history and culture, he had lived much of his life in Spain, latterly in the village of Alhaurín, near Malaga. Paddy would often call on Brenan when visiting Janetta and Jaime Parladé or Xan and Magouche Fielding, both of whom lived nearby. Brenan and Janetta Parladé shared a close friend in Frances Partridge.

In 1984 he was moved in controversial circumstances to a nursing home in Middlesex, but he returned to Spain after the authorities there made special arrangements to provide him with the nursing care on which he depended.

To Janetta Parladé   Kardamyli
15 July 1984   Messenia

Darling Janetta,

I think that snap of Gerald in *The Times* two or three weeks ago,
with the accompanying description of the Mayor of Alhaurín coming
to take him back from Pinner to his village again, and the
municipality taking on the housing and nursing – in recognition of
Gerald's great services to Spanish literature – is one of the most
moving things I have ever seen. It justifies all Gerald's theories about
the intrinsic nobility, style and *pundonor* [point of honour] of the
Spaniards in a strangely satisfactory and surprising way, and seems a
sort of vindication of all his life's work. I was struck so forcibly by
this that I almost wrote to *The Times* and said so there and then. But
I didn't, (a) because I'd recently written a letter to them about
something or other, and I think it shouldn't become a habit, and (b)
because there are so many others who would be more suitable. I
thought at once of Frances, V. S. P.[1] and you – v. old friends and ones
who had toiled away so splendidly to help Gerald. I thought of
writing to Frances and V. S. P., and suggesting they should write a
letter, paying a glowing tribute to Alhaurín and its inhabitants, so that
it would be translated in the Spanish press, and all should see that
their magnanimous gesture has not gone unobserved.

Do you think you could possibly write with this suggestion to
F[rances Partridge] & V. S. P.? I mentioned it in a letter to Stephen
[Spender], about something totally different, and if the letter needed
signatures to give it body, as it were, I bet he would like to append
his, as an old Hispanophile (ours too, and yours, unless you do the
whole thing). I do hope there are not wheels within wheels, and that
all that glows here really *is* gold. I really think it is the most
extraordinary and inspiring event.

It would be simply lovely if you sat down and wrote us all the
details of the Gerald saga after we separated. We pine to know!

No more now, darling Janetta, except tons of love from both of us,
and to Jaime,

Paddy

Exchanges in the Press between foreign countries – and often between England and Spain – are so often bitter & sneering that to have something that is exactly the opposite would be a glorious change. What I find so nice about it is the Mayor and Corporation *realising* what a treasure they have been nursing in their midst!

¹ Frances Partridge and V. S. Pritchett.

In writing his account of his 'Great Trudge' half a century later, Paddy was obliged to confront several problems. One was the issue of authenticity. Which should he strive for: the truth, or what he remembered of his walk so long after? Because the two were not always the same. He outlined his thoughts on this subject in a letter to Rudi Fischer in 1979. 'Yes, I did go back to Esztergom last year, and noted the forlorn state of the Bridge. I had already written the next bit – also Esztergom – before going there, and certain details had changed, both in fact and in my memory. I don't think I'm going to change them, certainly not the actual changes, which not only don't matter, but nor will I clean up the inaccuracies of memory, unless they become ridiculous and flagrant. One's first glance at something, one's age, and make-up at the time, have their rights too, and also the way the first glances have matured since or even gone off the rails here and there, have claims which might make later rectifications tantamount to doctoring! It's a delicate point; but there is a case to be put . . .'

Another issue was discretion. Paddy mentions fleetingly meeting a 'very pretty and altogether unusual' young woman called Xenia near the Transylvanian village of Zám; and describes several encounters with 'a pretty and funny girl in a red skirt called Angéla', with whom he has an affair. In fact these two were the same: a young Serb woman called Xenia Csernovits, unhappily married to a Hungarian husband.

To Rudi Fischer   Kardamyli
22 November 1984   Messenia

Dear Rudi,

I wish I could think of an attractive name for ex-'Angy'[1] – thank
you for rescuing me! I'll call her 'Y' for the time being; 'X' and 'Z'
are both unsuitable . . .

You know that 'Y' is just what she seems, but the uninitiate reader
doesn't; hence, there's no anomaly about Zám and its incumbent,
followed by Y's entry. But perhaps I *should* say a bit more about
Xenia, as I do want her to come in: I didn't know it then, but Zám
was my first Transylvanian sojourn, & she was kind to me and I want
to set it on record. Y must appear as a totally different person, as,
under a different name, she can; hence the infliction of schizophrenia.

You wrote: 'I think you ought somehow to overcome the problem
that there is honest-to-goodness sex with Rumanian peasant girls,[2]
but only *minnedienst* [courtly love] where *ladies* (your italics) are
concerned. If the *ladies* are unrecognisable anyway, why can't they be
tumbled in feather beds, if not the hay?' Well, nobody who has read
these chapters so far has been in any doubt that sex *was* involved,
both with Y and Iza,[3] and with Safta and Ileana it wasn't much more
explicit, and they thought the passages were well managed, neither
wallowing nor evasive. The thing about *ladies* and feather beds in
country houses is that it is very predictable and humdrum, and
usually pretty fatuous in the telling. (A. Devonshire says that in his
grandfather's day, there used to be a 5 a.m. 'sorting bell' rung at
Chatsworth every day during house-parties & shoots so that
adulterous couples, flitting along the passages like discreet ghosts,
could re-cohere before daybreak.) There *was* more hanky-panky on
my journey than I have mentioned; omitted for the reasons above.
As for the distinction between the literary treatment of *ladies* and
peasant girls, for once, surely class-war has no excuse for rearing its
ugly rear. It was those two nice girls who made the running! As we
were stark naked we weren't discernibly members of *any* class. They
had no idea who Elemér was, let alone me. The encounter was equal
on both sides, set off by their teasing, furthered by our response,

starting up as a sort of impromptu spontaneous joke; great fun, absolutely charming, and, it seems to me, exempt from all sociological blemish, however deplorable to a moralist. Nothing to do with *droit de seigneur*, or any rot of that kind. Gyula Illyés[4] would have acquitted us on the spot.

I wish I had written to you before setting off for Turkey, because the 'Y' business *does* need some explanation, and, as we know, there is more to follow. I very much wanted to bring all this in, as it seemed the high point of that extraordinary summer; I don't want to lose myself in all the subterfuges and hazards due to the need for secrecy, but wanted to bring out the amusing aspects that were *caused* by this necessity. The most salient points – a fugue in a borrowed car, the dodging of familiar faces, a borrowed house, a race with the train and then goodbye to Transylvania – are, *mutatis mutandis*, as told, see below.

As this point of the story approached, I realised how urgently I wanted to write some more about Transylvania. It had always been a mysterious name to me, and it still is. Until we started corresponding, I had thought – all these years – that I *had* been in Transylvania ever since crossing the frontier at Curtici (Decebal!); then learnt from that I had only been in Arad and the Banat; the actual sojourning in Transylvania being only while I was at Zám and Gurasada. Your letters, Sigerus's *Siebenbürgen*,[5] and Makkai's History[6] made me long to write about the region, to touch on the Szeklers,[7] strike a blow against the cheap exploitation of Dracula – Vlad Tepes;[8] and to write something about the Saxons and their history because they are going through a bad time now, and, very much, because your belonging to that community has made it seem so much more real. In autumn 1934, after arriving in Bucharest, I spent a week at Sinaia with some of the people mentioned in Chapter V, as Toncsi Mocsonyi's guests[9] . . . We drove to your birthplace and on, through Fagaras, which I failed to take in properly, to Hermannstadt, having marvellous meals in Gasthäuser that might have been in Bavaria or Austria.

These places were all I had seen of Transylvania (bar Z and G and a bit further in) when we parted at the aerodrome two years ago when I left for my Brideshead Revisited journey. I was tremendously smitten with Alba Iulia, Torda, Kolozsvár, M. Vásárhély, and, above all, Segesvár and the Saxon villages and churches, the latter seen for the first time since those fleeting glimpses in autumn 1934. I was determined to drag all this into the book. But how? After all, when this part of the book was finished, I would have shot my bolt, and the chance wasn't likely to occur.

At this point my literary guardian angel – or rather Satan wearing his mask – whispered in my ear the solution which you see demonstrated in Chapter VI. *Dichtung* [literally, Poetry, here used to mean Art], as you very charitably put it, intervened. I knew that if I wrote ten or twenty pages into the book about Transylvania, based (as it would have to be) on hearsay and mugging up, it would have had no life in there and would probably have to be cut, in the end. The highly improper idea occurred to me of planting my 1984 Transylvania into the 1934 triple fugue, as a means of recapturing my latter-day journey, while drawing on many conversations, your letters, Sigerus, and my own many memories of Rumanian pre-war travel – fairs, etc., trusting to luck that they tallied – and backdating it all from the very drab and rundown externals of life that I met in 1982, to the much livelier, more colourful and certainly happier, ambience I recollected from old wanderings in Transylvania, Moldavia, Wallachia and Bucovina – before the deluge – even Bessarabia, tho' that hadn't much relevance. My 1982 route was pretty well what we – 'E', 'Y' and I – had planned in 1934, until that telephone conversation came and buggered it up; which was why I went the way I did on the later solitary journey. The landmarks of our v. limited 1934 journey – the borrowed horse already mentioned, 'Y' wrapping her hand in a scarf, bathing in the Maros and the final hectic dash to Deva – fitted the later journey, as now narrated, like a glove. (The ducklings in a basin, the electric weather and the storm, all belong to the later trip.) The Hotel New York (now boringly rebaptised Continental) was where I stayed, hence the wealth of detail about the décor. (It looked as unchanged – not that I had seen it – as was Capsa's in Bucharest, except, in the latter, commissars had replaced *boieri mari*).[10] Sighişoară is the place I would have been most loth to omit. It fitted in

perfectly with the mood of our escapade and furnished the ideal
excuse to digress on your fellow Saxons. I do hope I haven't
misrepresented them, and that you will put me right if I have gone
astray.

This extremely immoral procedure seemed to make everything
drop into place, as though preordained, especially the few fragments
of conversation, even if they were uttered elsewhere. If this high-
handed treatment of *Wahrheit* [Truth][11] had been undertaken for base
reasons – to distort history, to boast, to pay off scores or for
propaganda of some kind – there would be no excuse for it. (Of
course, the longing to write a successful book is bound up with
writer's vanity.) But the aims here aren't ignoble: nor, of course,
particularly praiseworthy. But my conscience isn't very hard boiled;
and I am surprised by the comparative lack of twinges, tho' I know
that one always lets one's self down lightly for what one would
condemn in others. I tell myself that a kind of transmuted *Wahrheit*
can emerge from its combination with *Dichtung* in cases like this.
Would it be hypocritical to plead the intervention-rights of Art? Yes,
it would.

Well, there's my guilty secret, which you are the only other living
soul to share. The trouble about Chapter VI – or the reverse – is that
all who have read everything up to date like it the best, Dimitri[12] in
particular, in spite of the mild demur already mentioned. My moral
decline is such, that in this particular case, I am rather shocked to
discover that I don't really give a damn about my misconduct; it has
enabled me to include so much I would have hated to jettison, while
doing nobody any harm at all. These readjusted two days' travel have
done the trick, and I don't think I can change it now. In fact, in
very bad company, 'ὃ γέγραφα γέγραφα' ['What I have written, I
have written.'][13] Do, please, consider all I have written in this letter
as absolutely in confidence and *sub bulla* [under seal] – indeed,
carburendum [burn on reading]! I would hate this evidence of
wickedness to be extant. Dr Johnson says that nobody writing
lapidary inscriptions is on oath. I would like to extend it to *certain
categories* of events, *under very special circumstances if they are half-a-
century old* . . . When Joan and I were setting off for the Far East

a number of years ago, a great pal at the British Embassy said: 'I bet you'll want to send some things back – lamps, rugs, etc. – but the customs' duties are frightful, so send them to me by [diplomatic] bag, but *don't overdo it*; for, tho' I've no principles whatever about breaking the law, I have the strongest possible principle about being found out.'

Hear, hear.

This book's main difficulty has been that it all happened fifty years ago. My patchy and spasmodic notes, sometimes very full, are scattered with gaps, and my memory swings very erratically from the lucid to the nebulous and back. In some ways, I was better off with *A T. of Gifts*, when all records had vanished: the newness of this experience had fixed long sequences in my mind indelibly. When I started to write the book, and found myself in doubt, I would always append 'at least I think it was so', or 'unless my memory fails' to such a degree that the text became a tissue of weak and halting passages and hedged bets. The moment I cut them out – which I did, almost entirely – things went a lot better. Bold statements, every time, rather than hesitation – *unless it can do harm*. The part of the journey covered in Chapter VII is very blank in my diary, only odd notes and half a dozen place names pencilled in the back (I had still not shaken off the sloth of those lotus-eating weeks), and I am certain that the ill-recorded and recollected stages of the journey are probably in the wrong order, though some emerge with great clarity . . .

TRAVAILS OF A WRITER

This second part of *A T. of G.* has been an absurdly long pull, partly because of the time-gap, partly because Vol. I struck lucky, and I didn't want the second to be an anti-climax; and partly because I was determined to try and capture the glow of happiness and excitement that suffused this stretch of the journey. I was worried – still am – about the scope having narrowed to a particular rut – i.e. Hungarian landowners, to the exclusion of so much that is exciting and interesting. This vol. is, in this matter, nothing like Vol. I, and, no doubt even less like the sequel to come: Bulgaria, Turkey, etc. (with a brief *boevese*[14] interlude in Rumania). Because of all your kindness, help, interest and knowledge, the one reader I wanted – and want – to please most, is yourself. I think, perhaps, the wisest course for me, rather than foisting unsolicited wads of the book on you while it was still being written, would have been to have waited till it was finished and then asked your opinion, when I could look on the thing with detachment. I was a bit concerned when – apropos of the first chapters, you wrote that it was an excellent draft (superseded in a later letter, to my relief!) but that it had somehow lost the 'fictional' quality of the first volume. I knew you meant the feeling of freshness and excitement which *A T. of G.* seemed to have – not a shift into *Dichtung!* – and I fully understood, and agreed; but felt rather downcast and hoped that the lost quality would return. (I don't know whether it has or not.) Those few who have read it seem to like it; they know nothing of the subject, so their approval doesn't cut as much ice as it should. You had done exactly what I asked – *you* had suggested nothing more than a final vetting for mistaken accents and obvious howlers, and unlimited help on the way; and, as requested, you gave me your honest opinion, with which I entirely agreed. One thing I am quite sure of: your help, comments, advice, generosity with time and research will have steered the book clear of hundreds of pitfalls and – if anything could – may have supplied a depth and dimension it could *never* have aspired to without. If it falls short of what it should have been, it won't be from lack of help from you!

I would be enormously beholden to you for even something more. Could you, as it were, take a sponge and momentarily wash all our correspondence from your mind, pretend the book is by a total stranger, then report and advise? Except for major howlers or injustices, I feel I *can't* rewrite large sections, and that such virtue or consistency as the book possesses might leak away in the process. I'm into the last chapter now, so please don't worry about affecting my spirits during 'work in progress'.

I long for the whole book to be finished! It's used up a lot of my life and I should have been shot of it years ago. Cyril Connolly said that all autobiographical writing was settling a debt with the past, and I pine for this one to be paid. The way ahead – Bulgaria, Turkey etc. – stretches like a mile of oakum.[15] But my feelings here are nothing like so deeply involved, so perhaps I won't make such heavy weather of it. I may carry on after Constantinople, to Mount Athos in winter, where, immediately after (ship to Salonika), I trudged to every single monastery and kept an infinitely fuller diary than any of the earlier ones. I had my twentieth birthday in St Panteleïmon, the great Russian foundation. Then I might end up with the Venizelist revolution of spring 1935, which I followed with a squadron of Greek cavalry, all through Macedonia and Thrace, once again on a borrowed horse, this time borrowed from an old friend called Petros Stathatos, who had a large farm on the Chalkidiki peninsula. I saw him two weeks ago in Athens.

Rudi, I apologise for inundating you with all this! I'll stop now, as it is 3.30 a.m. I bathed till a week ago, now rain is coming down in buckets – *il pleut des hallebardes* ['it's raining spears'], as the French say. It would have been pure gold a month ago, as no olive-conscious villager fails to mutter; but too late now – only silver.

Yours ever
Paddy

love to Dagmar

Next morning
I found the letter totally illegible, and have copied it out.

[1] Angéla – see introduction to this letter.

[2] PLF refers to an incident when he and his friend Elemér von Klobusiçky (disguised under the pseudonym 'István' in the book) are discovered swimming naked in a river by two lively peasant girls, Safta and Ileana.

[3] 'Y' is Xenia Csernovits; 'Iza' is probably Ria Bielek; see *Between the Woods and the Water*, page 95.

[4] Gyula Illyés (1902–83), left-wing Hungarian poet and novelist.

[5] *Siebenbürgisch-Sächsische Burgen und Kirchenkastelle* (1900) by Emil Sigerus (1854–1947), Transylvanian ethnographer, collector, historian and writer.

[6] László Makkai and Erdély Öröksége (eds.), *Erdély Története* (*History of Transylvania*) (10 vols., 1941–2).

[7] Broadly speaking, the original Hungarian-speaking population of Transylvania. See *Between the Woods and the Water*, pages 165–6.

8 Vlad the Impaler (1431–76/7), the historical figure upon whom the fictional Dracula is supposedly based.

9 Antoniu Mocioni de Foen ('Mocsonyi' in Hungarian) (1884–1943), Great Chamberlain to King Carol II of Rumania.

10 Great boyars, or 'grand aristocrats'. A boyar was a member of the highest rank of the feudal Bulgarian, Moscovian, Kievan Russian, Wallachian and Moldavian aristocracies, second only to the ruling princes or tsars.

11 PLF here refers to Goethe's autobiography *Dichtung und Wahrheit*.

12 Prince Dimitri Obolensky (1918–2001), Russian-born historian who settled in Britain and became Professor of Russian and Balkan History at the University of Oxford. He was knighted in 1984.

13 Pilate's answer in John 19:22.

14 A tale of exile and return: a reference to the story of Boeve de Haumtone, known in English as Bevis, one of the most popular ballads of the Middle Ages.

15 Uncoiling, unravelling, unpicking and shredding 'oakum' (rope covered in tar) was a common form of punishment in Victorian prisons.

As this letter and its two follow-ups to Pamela Egremont demonstrate, Paddy would go to extraordinary trouble to chase down a detail – which he might then not use.

To Pamela Egremont   Kardamyli
1 December 1984   Messenia

Dearest Pamela,

S.O.S.! Help needed! I desperately want the name of the man wolves had sniffed at, and some rotter has gone off with our copy of *The Unbearable Bassington*,[1] or it's fallen behind something! He crops up in a deeply moving paragraph about the Carpathians in the last chapter of the sequel to *A Time of Gifts*. Thank God, the book's drawing to a belated close, but it's only the second of three vols. on this wretched journey, and, when it comes out sometime next year a third vol. – Bulgaria, E. Rumania and Turkey – looms like a mile of oakum. The present vol. is to be called *Between the Woods and the Water* (any good?), the 'woods' being Transylvania, and the 'water' being the Danube, beginning at Esztergom, and rejoined, after the Gr. Hungarian Plain, Transylvania and the Carpathians, at the Iron Gates.

We are back from a marvellous Asia Minor journey, joining Xan

Fielding & Magouche at Salonica, driving to Adrianople & Constantinople, then Nicea, Brussa, Bithynian Olympus, Sardis, Aphrodisias, Theyma, Ephesus, Smyrna, the Maeander Valley, the Troad & Troy (deeply moving in spite of the jumble). When we got to Çannakkale – the 'Chanak' of the Dardanelles campaign – I had a shot at the Hellespont, & *just* made it – would have been a lot less slow if I'd been put in a mile further upstream. There's a frightful current amidstream and I got whirled along – behind Joan in the stern of a skiff shouting directions and sitting on her hands to stop wringing them. The normal time for proper swimmers, put in at the right place, is about an hour. I was *2 hours 55 minutes* (3 or 4 miles), and crawled out into Europe in the end, exhausted but jubilant. Limbs turned to stone, back in Chanak in the afternoon, so I slunk off to a *hammam* and re-emerged light as a feather and settled down to a thoughtful *narghilé*, and bliss . . .[2]

I hoped to come to Blighty for Christmas, but daren't face Jock without the whole thing being perfect so will skulk here toiling, and come back some time in the New Year, and we must have a lovely feast.

V. many thanks in advance for the wolf man's name!

love Paddy

Also from Joan. *How is Sachie* [Sitwell]? Do give him my love, also Kisty [Hesketh].

I sent a gloating post-Hellespontive card to Michael & Damaris [Stewart] – but all of these boast-cards seem to have been chucked away by the hotel unposted.

---

[1] 'Saki' (H. H. Munro), *The Unbearable Bassington* (1912). The name PLF was searching for is Tom Keriway.

[2] PLF was then sixty-nine.

To Frances Partridge   Kardamyli
20 December 1984   Messenia

Dearest Frances,

Thank you so much for the magnificent *Country Life* piece about
Gerald [Brenan] and many apologies for being such a long time
answering. It's beautifully done, you do write gloriously and it hits
every nail on the head, one after another. I hope it was translated
and published in Spain. Bravo! In fact, *arci-bravo*! (i.e. double strength,
like an archdeacon), as Don Giovanni rather unexpectedly says to
Leporello at one point. It made me very homesick for Spain, your
text and the illustrations, an emotion I'm not really entitled to, as I
know it so little: but they – the text and pictures – set wickedly
disloyal thoughts about Greece furtively stirring.

I've been so long answering because Joan and I have been going
through a minor *saison en enfer*[1] over paying the tax on our car,
which is *twice the purchase price* in Greece, viz. a tidy sum. We've
scraped this appalling Danegeld together and we humbly hang about
outside office after office in Kalamata then Athens like Calais
burghers *trying* to pay it; but endlessly interlocking formalities
concatenate like a sequence of bureaucratic tortures – the Rack, the
Strappado, the Boot, the Maiden, the Thumbscrew, the Scavenger's
Daughter; and it finally comes to light that some trivial but
apparently vital document from the Peugeot factory outside Paris is
missing. As we'd left things to the last minute (hoping to oil our way
out of it all in some way), each extra day exposes us to some
hideous fine, and the missing document can't be got to us before
three weeks. Yesterday, the authorities granted us a reprieve till Jan.
10th; but it's too late. We have aged beyond recall . . .

Rather sadly, we are lurking here over Christmas – or rather,
driving to Pylos for two days – instead of returning to Blighty
– because I daren't show my face there, let alone in Albemarle Street,
without my last chapter finished. Thank God, it won't be long. The
wretched book has now been split into three parts. *This* one is
Hungary, B'pest, the Great Plain, Transylvania, the Carpathians and
back to the Danube at the Iron Gates: all to be called *Between the*

Woods and the Water. And then Vol. III looms like several furlongs of oakum.

We had the most wonderful journey in Thrace and Asia Minor with Xan and Magouche – do give them our love – and we were surprised by the unexpected niceness of the Turks and, quite often, by the delicious food; and the beauty and wildness of the regions we traversed were totally unspoiled; you often find yourself wandering among pillars and aqueducts and forums and theatres all plumed with leaves and grazed by flocks as though you were a Piranesi figure merely placed there for scale.

Many thanks again, dear Frances, and tons of love from us both,
Paddy

Riddle:
Q: What is the slowest event in the Hellenists' stadia?
A: The egg-and-dart race

¹ *Une Saison en Enfer* is the title of an extended prose poem by Arthur Rimbaud.

To Rudi Fischer   Kardamyli
9 January 1985   Messenia

Dear Rudi,
I feel very ashamed of myself for not sending enough seasonal greetings, but I do in retrospect, and I do hope 1985 turns out to be a marvellous year for you and yours. We meant to go back to Blighty for Christmas, but I felt I *couldn't* face Jock without the whole book buttoned up. All sorts of things have interrupted the last chapter, but the end is in sight. I can't thank you enough for all your corrections and suggestions. They have been of the greatest possible help, and you will see on very many pages – as you must have already – the results of your intervention. I dread to think what the book would have been like otherwise. When I'm finished, I'm going to go through all your carefully kept letters, taking notes.

I'm so glad you took my rather shifty behaviour in Chap. 6¹ with

such tolerant understanding. It was a great relief. But please lock it
in the casket of your breast; otherwise, *brutta figura* ['a bad mark'] for
me! Apropos: at a grand reception in the Embassy in Paris, Diana &
Duff Cooper were standing at the top of the stairs receiving guests,
and he was wearing the scarlet ribbon of the *Légion d'Honneur* across
his chest. Randolph Churchill whispered, as he shook hands:
'Advertising Cordon Rouge, Duff?' to which Duff whispered:
'Mumm's the word.'

Further, apropos of morality and expediency, I once asked Dom
Gabriel Gontard, Abbot of Saint-Wandrille, what the difference was
between moral and ontological good. (I was dabbling in theology a
bit in those days.) He thought for a moment, and said, '*Supposons que
vous voulez tuer quelqu'un. Votre bras est fort, vous trouvez votre bon
homme est mort. Voilà! Votre action, est* ontologiquement *parfaite – mais
moralement, très très mauvaise.*'[2]

This is not a proper answer to your letters, but I'll be sending one
soon. For some reason, I find it a bit hard to describe the course of
things with the prototype of Angéla, but I will tell you when we
meet.

Instead of going to England, Joan and I slunk off to Pylos and
stayed at a small hotel there, and spent most of the time in bed
reading, as it never stopped raining. It was rather nice; when one
could see anything outside, the whole Bay of Navarino lay out our
window, with the island of Sphakteria barring it to the west. There
are points where you can still see the timbers of sunk men o' war,
deep down.[3] A few bangs and broadsides and powder magazines
blowing up would have rather cheered the scene. For New Year, we
went to stay with an old American pal called Hod Fuller[4] on Spetsai
(an ex-Marine commando from Boston who used to be married to a
great pal called Dozia Karaiskáki, gr. gr. granddaughter of the Greek
klepht from the Eikosi-Ena,[5] now dead alas). Then back here, and
to work. For a fortnight early in December Bruce Chatwin came to
stay for two weeks, and liked it so much that he has taken rooms
nearby, dining with us every night, and is now meeting his wife and
mother in Kalamata, as he has taken rooms for them too. He was
keen to get his mother here, as his father, with three hands, is sailing

across the Atlantic in a pretty small boat. He plans to stay till March,
finishing a book on Nomadism, which has always obsessed him. We
go for energetic walks every afternoon.

Back to the grindstone! And all fond wishes to you and Dagmar,
however belated!

Yours ontologically

Paddy

1 See letter to RF, 22 November 1984.

2 'Suppose you wanted to kill somebody. Your arm is strong, you find your opponent
is dead. So, your action is *ontologically* perfect – but *morally*, very, very bad.'

3 At the Battle of Navarino (1827), during the Greek war of independence, an Ottoman
armada was destroyed by an Allied force of British, French and Russian vessels.

4 The son of a Harvard archaeologist, Horace 'Hod' Fuller served with the French
Army as a volunteer in 1940, and then joined the US Marines before transferring to
OSS. As a special forces commando, he fought with the French resistance in the
Pyrenees against the German occupiers, and was awarded both the Silver Star and
the Croix de Guerre for his courage.

5 Georgios Karaiskakis (1780/1782–1827) was a famous Greek *klepht* (brigand), and a
hero of the Greek War of Independence against the Ottomans. 'Eikosi-Ena', meaning
twenty-one, refers to the starting date of the Greek War of Independence (1821).

To Pamela Egremont   Kardamyli
18 January 1985   Messenia

Dearest Pamela,

You were a brick to leap so nobly into action! (Please thank Tony
Quinton and other literary Good Samaritans for their help.) Alas, it's
not Ulrich v. Gradwitz or George Znaeym from 'The Interlopers,'[1]
I'm enclosing the relevant page where the gap yawns (as well as the
two preceding ones, as it doesn't make sense without the run-in),
and, as you see, the I's[2] – and the marvellous 'Wolves of
Czernogratz'[3] – are there already. The odd thing is that I thought *you*
had quoted the line about the sniffing wolves, hence my cry from
the depths, and I then remembered it – or thought I did – too. I
thought the occasion for the phrase was this: Miss de Grey? or van
something? the nice girl that Bassington was rather negligently

wooing, goes for a ride by herself to think things over. Alarmed (for her horse) by the appearance of a travelling wild-beast show, she puts into the yard of a farmhouse till it passes. At the farm is staying a farmer traveller, whom ill health has condemned to inactivity. Here is where the missing phrase came, so I thought. X. then goes on to describe the plots and intrigues and feuds of this farmyard in terms of a mediaeval state – the cattle, flocks, poultry, dogs, cats, lurking foxes etc., a brilliant flight. But *now*, all of a sudden, I begin to wonder: could it have been in 'When William Came'? Unfortunately, this too is in the lost or rifled vol. – could you bear to peer into it, when next it's handy? Looking through the *Short Stories*, I suddenly thought I was on the right track in one called 'Cross Currents', whose main figure is called Alaric Clyde. I drew a blank. My chap is a sort of Wilfrid Thesiger, but on ice instead of sand. I started rereading the stories – they are as good as ever. Of the two recurring dandified figures, it occurred to me that Reginald is a sort of Hamish Erskine,[4] and Clovis Sangrail, Alan Pryce-Jones.[5]

We've just been having the worst storm for a hundred years – thunder and lightning like the end of the world, Old Testament deluges and deafening gale winds churning up the sea and uprooting trees and scattering tiles like confetti. We lost two tall cypresses last night, and a splendid olive, and have just been taking advantage of a lull to saw them up (with Bruce Chatwin, who is staying) for much needed firewood. I'm rather looking forward to being seventy in a fortnight.

Thank you so much, dear Pamela, for taking all that trouble about Mr X. I feel guilty at inflicting new travails!

love

Paddy

Is the envelope correctly addressed? 'Dowager' sounds rather stately, and the Christian name a shade fast. What happens in the unlikely case of a parish nobleman, who has married a duchess and become a duke, divorcing? Does he become *Gonzalo*, Duke of Plaza Toro? Or a Dowager Duke, when widowed?

1 In Saki's story 'The Interlopers', two enemies are trapped together beneath a fallen branch in the forest. Gradually they realise the futility of their quarrel and end their feud. After shouting for help, they perceive figures approaching. The story ends as one of them realises that these are wolves.

2 i.e. the Interlopers which give the title to the story.

3 The title of Saki's story is 'The Wolves of Cernogratz'. PLF misspells it here and in *Between the Woods and the Water.*

4 Erskine was notoriously narcissistic.

5 Both Reginald and Clovis Sangrail are malicious dandies in the Saki stories.

To Pamela Egremont   Kardamyli
7 March 1985   Messenia

Dearest Pamela,

I've just written to Mr Webb to thank him for taking all that trouble over Bassington, commenting on his interesting 'Kipling in France' paper and sending a Kipling Soc. application form duly filled in and stumped up for. I'm *delighted* to join; I'd often thought of doing so, being such an addict. All this, of course, is the result of your monster surprise envelope, which arrived this morning. You *are* a brick to have done so much and set so many wise and distinguished heads to work sniffing out the missing wolf-sniffed one, and finally delivering his head on a charger. Many many thanks!

You are quite right about the name Keriway. It's simultaneously arch and lowly, *exactly* like a pop-drummer or Fielding ostler, possibly in league, what's more, with a rather seedy highwayman. Or a building society: 'Buy your home the Keriway'. I think I shall just put, 'The broken traveller in the U.B.'[1]

I'm so sorry to hear about the visits to Royal Marsden. I do hope all is as you say. I am full of fellow feeling whatever it is, as you can guess. It's a wonderful place and I think of it with the utmost gratitude.

We might be coming to Blighty in April sometime, I'm not sure, all depends on finishing this book, so plans are what I believe is called aleatory (first trial run of this word, so common and useful in French – 'aléatoire' – but sounds awful in English so will withdraw it).

But, if plans fit, do come here whenever you can. It's pretty spartan as far as comfort goes, because the couple who have looked after the house for twenty years [Petros and Lela] have suddenly opened a taverna in the village, so we only get the time they can spare from their booming business. Rather a swizz. But it's looking marvellous at the moment, clear cold blue skies, olive terraces all bright green still, covered with asphodels, anemones – Adonis blood everywhere[2] – daisies, star of Bethlehem, celandine, small geraniums, gromwell, and, up in the mountains, snowdrops and primroses that nearly make exiles like us faint clean away. Bruce Chatwin is finishing a book too, next door, and we go for huge strides across the hills every afternoon, and he and Joan concoct delicious dinners every other night or so. Joan and I are reading Dostoïevski's *Smoke*[3] aloud in the evening.

Many many thanks again, dear Pamela, and tons of love from us both.

Paddy

---

[1] 'An old addict, I had been re-reading Saki just before setting out . . . I had always been struck by the broken traveller in *The Unbearable Bassington*, "a man that wolves have sniffed at"' (*Between the Woods and the Water*, page 195).

[2] When Adonis lay dying in the arms of Aphrodite, after being gored by a wild boar, she created the anemone flower from his blood.

[3] A slip for Turgenev's novel *Smoke* (1906).

Paddy had first met the Byzantine historian Steven Runciman (1903–2000) in Sofia in 1934. Afterwards he remembered Runciman and his companion Roger Hinks as 'impeccable in Panama hats and suits of cream-coloured Athenian silk and their bi-coloured shoes were beautifully blancoed and polished'. To Paddy, still only nineteen, their conversation seemed 'dazzlingly erudite and comic'. In contrast, Runciman remembered Paddy as 'a very bright, very grubby young man'. Their paths crossed again after the war in Athens, where Runciman, Paddy's boss, dismissed him from the British Council, complaining of 'Paddy's little irregularities': too many parties, too few repaid loans. But Paddy could not hold a grudge long, and in later life the two men were friendly, though not close.

To Steven Runciman   Kardamyli
5 April 1985   Messenia

Dear Steven,

Thank you so much for the paper about Byzantine ladies – which
I have sent on to Niko Ghika – and for the very nice joke about
Leandrine feats.[1]

I am on the last bit of the sequel to *A Time of Gifts*. It ends at
Orsova and I am in a bit of a fix. I had written breezily about
Sigismund's crusaders advancing down the Danube from Belgrade,
and suddenly thought: what were they treading on? I made a dash
for *The Kingdom of Acre*, page 458,[2] and every encyclopaedia and
history book I could find, and all agree. But, as far as I can
remember, on the *right* bank, the rock falls sheer all through the
Kazan defile, with only those slots in the rockface for the brackets or
whatever they were, that supported the planks over which Trajan's
army marched to the bridge at Turnu-Severin. On my two visits to
it, the only way along the left bank was that marvellous road
engineered out of the rock by the orders of Ct István Széchényi (I
suppose in the 1840s). As far as I can remember, the rockface of both
banks drops sheer several hundred feet, and for quite a few miles.
The only alternative, on that bank, would be N. to Temesvár, Lugos,
Caransebeş, then round the Banat Carpathians, and finally, down the
Cerna to Orsova; or perhaps by some mountain passes closer to the
river. If the Hospitallers had come to ferry them downstream, it
would solve all. I wonder if I have gone blind retrospectively and
there is some obvious solution . . . [3]

Isn't it horrible to think that the whole of Kazan pass, Orsova,
Ada Kaleh and the Iron Gates have all been plunged many fathoms
underneath by that wretched dam, like Ys,[4] or Kitezh, a city near
Nizhni-Novgorod that vanished during Batu's invasion, whose bells
can still be heard at the bottom of a lake.[5] Dimitri Obolenski is my
source for this.

I am on the last stretch of this sequel to *A Time of Gifts*, and hope
to return with it inside a month. What a relief. I daren't think of Vol.
III – Bulgaria, Wallachia, Bulgaria again, Turkey and *END* . . .

Καλὸ Πάσχα [Happy Easter] I feel very guilty bothering you with all the above – there's probably no answer anyway!

　　Yours ever

　　　　Paddy

P.S. I have reopened the envelope to copy a bit out of my 1905 Baedeker: 'The Danube (in the Defile of Kazan), here 180 ft in depth, is confined to a width of 180 yards by huge perpendicular cliffs. Before the construction of the Széchényi Road, the defile was unpassable on either bank.'

---

1 SR had written to PLF to say that he had been 'fascinated and awe-stricken by the story of your swim. It's a heroic tale (no, perhaps Leandrine rather than heroic), and I am delighted to have your account of it.' This is a play on the word *heroic* – alluding to the story of Hero and Leander in Greek mythology. Hero was a priestess of Aphrodite; her lover Leander would swim the Hellespont every night to be with her.

2 SR's *A History of the Crusades*, Vol. III, *The Kingdom of Acre and the Later Crusades* (1954).

3 'The long and winding procession of the Crusaders . . . levitated just above the turbulent currents by sorcery. *There was no other way*' (*Between the Woods and the Water*, page 273).

4 A mythical city on the coast of Brittany that was swallowed by the sea.

5 A mythical city beneath the waters of Lake Svetloyar in central Russia. In 1238, during the Mongol invasion of Europe led by Batu Khan, Kitezh is believed to have submerged before the attackers could take it. Old Believers say that the life of the city continues beneath the water: in calm weather one can sometimes hear the sound of chiming bells and people singing; the most pious individuals may see the lights of religious processions and glimpse buildings in the deep.

To Joan Leigh Fermor　　　　　　　　　　　　　　　Grand Hotel
5 November 1985　　　　　　　　　　　　　　　　　　　　Sofia

Darling Joan,

　　I suddenly had the notion of getting out for a night at Eisenstadt in the Bussenland (seeing it in the railway map in the *Westbahnhof* [station]) and having a look at the great Esterházy palace there, and the houses of Haydn & Liszt; but it wasn't allowed, so I went straight through to Budapest where it was pouring with rain. I tried to get

onto that nice woman I stayed with last time, but she had changed
her address, another lady Dr of Economics said on the telephone,
and so I drew [a] blank. After one or two shots, I found a rather
dilapidated Hotel Metropole in the Rákóczi Ut., a semi-brothel with
endless passages, the rooms giving out into a bleak rainy well of
moulting walls. Took a sleeper [a sleeping-pill].

Next morning the search for Elemér began: ringing every ten
minutes, but no reply. The only thing was to take a taxi. His address
was at a complex of workmen's tenement-rookeries, almost in the
fields on the extreme eastern edge of Budapest. The monoglot
driver had never heard of it; but we got there in the end.
Everything was shut and unresponsive to my battering on the
shutters. There were two other names on the door in paint, and
Elemér's, hand-written and blurred on a bit of peeling adhesive tape,
below. It was rather desolate. Threadbare trees, a pram without
wheels, and graffiti, and nobody there. At last an old woman from a
nearby block appeared, also only speaking Magyar; the name
Klobusiçky didn't mean anything to her but she brightened at his
Christian name – 'Elemér bácsi' – viz. 'Uncle Elemér'. I gathered he
had broken his leg in July and been taken to a hospital. Which one?
She'd no idea – there were dozens. So I gave her Rudi's telephone
number, and set off – in the gloaming by now – for sodden
Budapest, wondering what to do. I rang up Rudi, and he came
dashing to the Metropole, and I told him about it all, and he started
telephoning everywhere, but in vain. Then, in a pause, Dagmar
(Rudi's wife – like him, she's a Transylvanian Saxon, and very nice)
rang saying that they had telephoned from Elemér's complex – it
was a v. pretty girl from the next flat, secretary to the local
Communist cell, Elemér had told me, and utterly devoted to E.,
in spite of his constant jeering at her tenets. I had taken her out to
luncheon with the two of us at Gödöllő, last time I was there – a
treat for her – at Elemér's request, so she knew all about me, and
said he had been for weeks and weeks in a military hospital (as a
honvéd ['defender of the Fatherland'] hussar from the Great War,
presumably!). Dagmar said she would drive me there when she
finished work, in a little car she has. Rudi and I had a cheerful

dinner together, talking late and drinking lots of red Médoc from Eger till late.

I pottered about, saw the Bornemisza–Thyssen exhibition[1] up in the palace, had something to eat in a bar full of Arabs, smugglers it is thought, or terrorists, where Dagmar picked me up, and we drove miles to the west of Budapest, nice leafy hills, as far from his quarters as Hampstead is from Gravesend. I took lots of goodies, also flowers and pears, whisky and all spare books – only to learn that he had been shifted to an Old Folks' Home in Budapest, as far away this time as Fulham. We gave three nurses a lift into town, they all knew Elemér well and loved him – (Uncle E., again) – and they thought his leg was on the mend, but said he couldn't really look after himself. In the rain, the place looked like a Victorian prison, but was not nearly so bad inside. Dagmar and I found his room, which he shared with five other old boys (all rather nice). It was dark again. E. was asleep, so I had difficulty in finding which he was. When I woke him, he looked v. drawn, top teeth out, white stubble, but still recognisably good looking and aquiline. The sad thing was he didn't recognise me but when I talked about Greece, he said 'In Greece lives Leigh Fermor, my good friend.' 'But Elemér, *it's me!*' 'No, you are too young. You give him my love.' Dagmar had stolen off by now. We talked a long time, but he wasn't *absolutely* sure it was me, and kept referring to me in the third person, as though I were absent. I asked about his sister Ilona, who lives in Szatmár. I'd forgotten her married name – so had he – and her address, and his son Nicholas's, in Düsseldorf – he has changed address – I've only got his old one. He [Nicholas] hadn't been to see him, but his French daughter-in-law ('Caroline Murat, a wonderful girl') had. (I got their addresses later from the Communist girl by telephone, via Dagmar and Rudi, and will write.) Poor Elemér wasn't taking in much, so I had to tear myself away after a time. We embraced and he hung on to my wrist; but I felt I was tiring him so had to bugger off, feeling terribly wrung. The eclipse of a *honvéd* hussar. I have a terrible feeling that he won't emerge, or last very long. Alas! *I'm so glad I saw him.* The nurses were v. nice.

The place was miles from anywhere, & it was pouring cats and d., no taxis till an hour later. I fell asleep in a wicker chair in the janitor's lodge, pitch dark by now. I had a jolly Transylvanian dinner in R. and D.'s flat, sat up ages, then back to the Metropole, slept till 4.30 a.m., then taxied to the airport.

***

At Sofia airport, they said my visa was only valid for twenty-four hours – they directed a taxi to the Min. of Foreign Affairs. I paid the fare with 1 dollar (officially 1 dollar = 1 leva, unofficially 3 or 4). He buzzed off, I tried to leave my luggage with the security guard, while I went in; but it wasn't the right place, the British Consulate was, so I had to leave my bags on the pavement, while I ranged in search of a taxi, found one at last, went to the Consulate, where the polite but apathetic staff said I should go to the Aliens' Office – no, it was forbidden to leave luggage. They advised me to stay at the Sofia Hotel, perfectly reasonable; so I clocked in, and utter hell began.

The Aliens' Office is a Black Hole of Calcutta, two girls dealing, through niches in a frosted glass screen, with 100 Arabs, Angolans, Namibians, citizens of Niger and the Haute Volta, scores of Africans, many of them conversing with each other in Fr. or English; woolly heads *à perte de vue* [as far as the eye can see], all here on crash destabilisation courses, perhaps. It took an hour, nearly fainting, to wrestle to one of the cubby holes, where the harassed girl, speaking a bit of English, took my passport, kept it an hour, then gave it back and said 'Come back at 2.' I did, then was told, come back at 4, and just before the place closed, got it back with a chit to the bank, where I could buy a prolongation to allow me to stay ten days and change money at a very slightly less extortionate rate. 'Take it to the bank tomorrow morning.' She had forgotten it was Friday night; for when I went next day, it was shut till Monday, so was the Aliens' Office. It looked strange without its swarm of Africans.

Meanwhile this hotel was getting crusty about my staying on with my papers still not right. A period in limbo began. I could do nothing till Monday. I retired with *Radetsky March*[2] to my claustrophobic room, where most of the floor space is taken up by an empty mini-bar full of spiders' webs; the lights weak but elaborate; there was a downpour outdoors. I set out to buy a paperback novel; went to *twenty* bookshops, *not a single foreign book except Russian.* Bulgarian-English phrasebook? *Not one.* Oh, for the P. Highsmith, Mrs Gaskell and Huxley, which I had left with Elemér! – he'll never read them (we had reverted to German). There's only *Radetsky*, so I am spinning it out. Every official is gruff and unfriendly – except with sudden shining exceptions – I think through political fright of hobnobbing with pariahs from the West. Some ghastly National Day is in the offing. Acres of scarlet hoardings are going up with the faces of the Zhivkov president[3] and Gorbachev, larger than tennis courts. Pilgrims buy single gladioli, and troop in Indian file into Dimitrov's Lenin-style Mausoleum,[4] and out again, schoolchildren are dragooned about in noisy troops, all with red flags. I got thoroughly demoralised and trod on my specs in the dim bedroom – fortunately, only bust one lens, so I can read with my head on one side – better so, perhaps, for I mustn't rush the only remaining pages. I know, if I still smoked, I would have set the building on fire. Still, I can always leave the bath on and forget it . . .

On Sunday morning I went to the Victorian Byzantine Cathedral of Alexander Nevsky, well remembered and rather fine. There was an Orthodox mass of great splendour – infinitely better than anything on our journey, infinitely better than in Greece, all booming in Russian-style bass voices; troops of deacons in green & gold dalmatics, all blue with incense; but not many people there, and half of them foreigners. I suspect it's half a tourist-draw, and half a cover-story. Most of the foreigners were Unesco delegates who fill this, and all the other hotels: the scum of the earth, they seem to me. Mooching about outside the cathedral, I was approached by an affable chap; any dollars to change? 3 leva a dollar. 'Traveller's cheque?' '*No problem.*' I signed one for fifty on the rump of a marble lion. He gave me 150 leva for 50 dollars. He had no change for a 200 leva note, so I gave him 50 levas and went on my way rejoicing; but I only rejoiced until I tried to pay for lunch: 200-leva-notes were all withdrawn in 1980; nothing higher than 20 leva is legal currency now . . . *Vai de mine* [woe is me].

The town is unrecognisable: ghastly Russian-style blocks, Balkanic back streets with gap-toothed cobbles, yawning manholes, façades under repair, all masked with cardboard. There are endless trudges for everything, ending in total failure to get it. On Saturday, I took a bus to a village on Mt Vitosha, a splendid well-remembered range above the capital, for a solitary lunch – slivovitz, kebabs – then to the Golden Bridge, a huge glacier-moraine in the forest, like a river of granite boulders, each the size of a bus, an extraordinary sight. Went for a marvellous windy trudge through the steep beech woods (also birch, oak and poplar). The wind – west – was so strong it tore leaves down by the thousand. *I saw exactly what Shelley meant.* 'Beech leaves, when driven along in thousands, seem to stand another time and scuttle in chaotic mobs'? – 'stricken multitudes as from an enchanter fleeing'[5] – (what is the adjective? 'Calamity'? Can't be 'panic' – torture). I spent most of Sunday (after my reverses) in the museum, which is splendid. Saw all the gold rhytons, heads, etc. from Panagyurishte,[6] with more time and elbow-room than in London, and countless other wonders. They have a large statue of Cybele the size of ours, tho' headless, armless and Lion-less. But the robes and girdle are identical, also the throne and *one give-away lion's paw*; so I wrote to Dimitri's Thracological professor[7] here (now Minister of Education – more later) saying that the present label – 'Statue of a seated woman' – can be removed, and 'Cybele' put there instead. I sent off Dimitri's letter (it is now Wednesday), and on Tuesday got a message asking me to call later in the week).

When Monday came, I went to the bank and paid what I had been told to pay for an extension – $40 – and then back to the Aliens' Office, which was a Zulu kraal once again. I gave my passport to a different lady. After an hour, she told me to come back at 2 p.m. I flung up my arms in such despair that she finally had pity, and I was given a grudging card, allowing me to stay and change money for a fraction more. Two surprises back at the hotel. (A) The 'down' charge for the hire of a car, *the daily fee*, all to be paid for in dollars, with coupons obtained in the suburbs, would have amounted to 100 dollars for a 200 kilometre day; 8 or 900 for the trip I had in mind; and (B) the girl at the Consulate had said the hotel was cheap. I asked how much when I got to the hotel, and understood to my delight, it was 8 levas – cheap for propaganda purposes, I assumed, and said 'Eight?' The doorman said – 'No. Eighteen' or so I thought. I now learnt it was eighty . . .

All this was something of a relief. I realised that, what with the weather, the general charges, the reserve, the unhelpfulness, the fright of the officials, and the expense, that I'd have to wash the whole thing out and come back (with you, if you could face it) by car, which apparently is easy. Then, the problem was I felt I couldn't go back to Kardamyli before my nameday. So I have decided to go to Salonica and see if I can go to Mt Athos for a few days, but I believe permission is difficult. Might try through the museum, staying the night at last year's hotel, telephoning you at Graham's meanwhile, and to Barbara and Niko. There are no Olympic flights from Sofia, only infrequent Bulgarian ones, the train takes eleven hours (several of them waiting at the frontier) but I found a bus left on Wednesday for Salonica, leaving at 3.30 p.m., arriving at 10 – about the distance of Passau to Linz – so hope to leave on that.

On Monday night I took a taxi to a restaurant they had recommended at the Consulate. It was miles out in the country, given over entirely to tarted-up folklore, sharp yells, shouts, stamps, twirled handkerchiefs – dances that I'm sure have never been danced. Ate from hand-made knobbly plates, drank out of earthen mugs, rubbing shoulders with Cubans and North Koreans and anti-Solidarity Poles. I couldn't help wondering how Graham would have liked it. Last night I went to *Rigoletto* at the Opera. Sung in perfect Italian to my surprise (scarcely any foreign word is spoken here, except Russian) – and very good indeed. This was a great joy. Sustained by it, I went back to my room, poured out some whisky from my Vienna bottle – there was none there. I thought those buggers in the hotel had pinched it; then remembered I'd filled the plastic half-bottle [with whisky] once or twice – perhaps more often than I thought – so perhaps they were innocent after all. The elderly maid was one of the only nice people I have seen for what seems like eternity, so was relieved.

Wednesday

All packed; bill paid; and D.V., Salonica tonight. The place glows in my mind like Eldorado or Avalon. Thelema[8] and Cockaigne.[9] I've got five pages of *Radetsky* to go. I hope it's end of Lucky Jim week . . .

Thursday

I sat beside the nice driver and the road followed the Strouma river – poplars, tobacco, vines – till it got dark at the frontier and it started raining over No-Man's-Land. The toothcomb treatment of luggage in both frontier posts took two hours, but at last the joyful moment of leaving the Iron Curtain came, and we crept on through the dark. It was much further than I had thought – getting to Salonica at 11, after a 3 o'clock departure in Sofia. No taxis, owing to a strike, but I found a rather nice dilapidated hotel ('Pallas') next to the bus station, and v. close to our last year's hotel . . .

I'm in a taverna on the waterfront, lovely sunny day, glittering sea, bus in half an hour to Ouranoupolis in the Chalkidiki, then by boat tomorrow to the little Athonite port of Daphni, unseen by me for fifty-one years . . .

Tons of love darling and hugs too. I long to see you.

xxx Paddy

P.S. Forgive incoherence. No time to reread. I bought a small knapsack and some serious boots this morning. If it's not too much of a bore an anorak like yours is my present dream.

[1] An exhibition from the Thyssen-Bornemisza Museum in Madrid.

[2] Joseph Roth, *The Radetzky March* (1932).

[3] Todor Hristov Zhivkov (1911–98), General Secretary of the Central Committee of the Bulgarian Communist Party, 1954–89.

[4] Georgi Dimitrov Mikhaylov (1882–1949), General Secretary of the Central Committee of the Bulgarian Communist Party, 1946–9.

[5] 'O wild West Wind, thou breath of Autumn's being,
    Thou, from whose unseen presence the leaves dead
    Are driven, like ghosts from an enchanter fleeing,
    Yellow, and black, and pale, and hectic red,
    Pestilence-stricken multitudes'
            Shelley, 'Ode to the West Wind' (1819)

⁶ Thracian treasure dating from the 4th–3rd centuries BC excavated in 1949 near the town of Panagyurishte.

⁷ A contact given to PLF by Dimitri Obolensky.

⁸ A set of religious beliefs, tabulated by the occultist Aleister Crowley (1875–1947), allowing the believer to 'do what thou will'.

⁹ The land of plenty.

To Xan Fielding   Kardamyli
3–4 December 1985   Messenia

Xan παιδί μου [dear boy],

Shattering news about poor old Manoli. Changebug [George Psychoundakis] rang me up and said had I heard anything, then broke the news that he had fallen in the mountain above Koustogerako and got killed. So I rang up Manoussos [Manoussakis] and learnt that the funeral was next day, dashed to Kalamata, got the plane, and flew to Canea next day, where Manoussos met me at the airport. He drives v. slowly, so we went in the taxi which was taking a gigantic wreath from Kosta Mitsotakis, and got there in one and a half hours. (They knew we were coming, and held things up.) There were about 100 cars and trucks in the village, which was packed. Poor old Manoli was laid out in his coffin in the house, top of head covered in a white cloth, obviously rather bashed, but face all right, and looking very calm. Eleni, and all the family were swollen with weeping, the house crammed. M. and I put our bunches of flowers with the others, kissed Manoli's brow (cold as the clay), and then climbed to the churchyard. Lots of Resistance movement wreaths on ribboned poles. Outside the church, just before the burial, someone made a short speech, and Geo. Psych. recited a marvellous short poem hastily written the night before. Afterward, when we went to condole in the receiving line, Eleni and all the others seized me like bears and hugged and hugged, all in floods, and in the end I felt myself shoved in the receiving line too, like a relative, receiving the condolences of scores of people I'd never met. It was all very moving and harrowing. I said I was there on behalf of all allies & friends and especially you. Afterwards, under a walnut tree, Kosti and Antoni told us what had happened.

Some young chap in the village had teased Manoli (not spitefully): Ἔ, μπάρμπα Μανώλη, δὲν μπορεῖς νὰ κυνηγᾶς τ᾽ ἀγρίμια ὅπως στὰ νιάτα σου! ['Eh, Uncle Manoli, you can't go hunting wild goat like you used to in your youth!']! He said, you wait, took his gun next morning and set off for the high peaks. The others, following, lost sight of him, stalking high above, heard two reports, and went home, thinking he'd taken a different path. When he failed to return next day, a search party went up, couldn't find him, only a large ibex with long horns on the edge of a deep cliff; and at last, spotted M's body 200 or 300 yards below, at the bottom of a deep chasm – too steep to climb down. A helicopter was summoned from Canea, and M. was hauled up with a grapple at the end of a long cable – killed outright, thank God. He must have been hoisting the ibex on his shoulder, slipped or lost his balance – they are nearly as heavy as a small pony – and crashed into the void.

I can't get used to the idea that he has vanished, although we had a scare four years ago. The only thing is, he vanished in his own mountains, like an eagle, engaged on something dangerous and of course, forbidden. There is a sort of fitness . . . Manoussos wrote a very good piece about him – I'll send you a Xerox, if he hasn't.

***

I think Joan has told you my adventures in Hungary and Bulgaria and Mt Athos – especially the tracing of Elemér – my partner in chasing reapers on the banks of the Maros in Transylvania, called István in the book.

The evening before I left Budapest, I was crossing a huge underground crossing, like Piccadilly Circus, under a square called Déak [Ferenc]tér, where about a million people, just having knocked off work, were milling in all directions. I wanted to go to a place called Vörösmarty tér, so timidly approached a young man in horn-rimmed specs and said, 'Vörösmarty tér, kérem szépen' (please). He said, 'Do you speak English?'

'I am English.'

'Really?' he was fluent, nearly perfect. 'Do you know Kent? I've been there.'

'Yes, a bit. Where?'

'A village called Headcorn.' (Costa's village.)

'Near Ashford?'

'Yes, and a still smaller village called Grafty Green.'

'I know that too. I even remember the name of the house I stayed in there.'

'What was it called?'

'Fermor Cottage.'

'How do you spell it?'

'F.E.R.M.O.R.'

On this I produced my passport. We both remained rooted to the ground, and then made our way to Vörösmarty tér in a slightly haunted state. Admit it was odd.

How marvellous, Magouche and you – and J[anetta] and Jaime! – coming for Christmas! I do hope it's lovely bright weather, like today. We'll go for some marvellous walks, work off the turkey and p.p. [plum pudding].

We still haven't fully digested our *Barockfahrt* [journey into the Baroque], but gloat over the p.c.'s and guidebooks like misers with their gold.

Tons of love to you both

  Paddy

  also Joan

P.S. When I got back and saw that *Spectator* piece,[1] I thought at first it was a leg-pull of some kind, and felt rather embarrassed. Then the next envelope revealed that it was by Patrick Reade, my godson! God-filial piety, bless him.

---

[1] 'An Extravagance of Curiosity', a profile of PLF in *The Spectator*, 7 September 1985.

Early in 1986 PLF received a postcard, franked in Middlesex, which read:

'Kind Sir!

I was thrice fortunate on my trip to the erstwhile capital of the BRITISH EMPIRE. I discovered the velvety smoothness of Guinness, the exquisite taste of gourmet steak and kidney pudding and your magnificent magnum opus, A Time of Gifts. *You will perhaps be surprised to hear that my late maternal grandfather Alois Schoissbauer figures in it. Indeed, he was none other than the pimply youth who 'borrowed' your rucksack rife with manna in Munich.[1] He is clearly recognisable for he often told me the tale. You will no doubt be interested to know that it (the rucksack) later concealed all his belongings when he fled across the Alps from Tyrol to Switzerland when the Nazis wished to incarcerate him in a KONZENTRATIONSLAGER, not as a Jew (which he was not, being a Bavarian and a Roman Catholic), but as an anti-social element. I later inherited the rucksack and carried it all the way across Asia to Peshawar where it was stolen by an Australian hippie, at least so I have been led to believe.*

Respectfully your obedient servant,
    Dr Franz Xaver Hinterwälder,
        Professor of Farsi and Pashtoo, Fridausi School of Oriental languages, Kirchstetten, Nether Austria

P.S. As an attentive reader I was able to discover from A Time of Gifts *that your LXXI birthday is approaching next Tuesday. Permit me to take the occasion to wish you the compliments of the season.'*

---

[1] See the passage in *A Time of Gifts*, pages 95–7, which describes how PLF's rucksack, containing his passport, money and diary, was taken from a hostel while he was in a state of 'hoggish catalepsy' after a night's drinking in a Munich *Bierkeller*.

This was of course a hoax, concocted between Rudi Fischer and Xan Fielding in the Travellers Club, but Paddy fell for it, 'hook, line and sinker'.

To Franz Xaver Hinterwälder   Kardamyli
18 February 1986   Messenia

Dear Dr Hinterwälder,
   Thank you for your postcard and the news of the fate of my
rucksack in Munich half a century ago. I am glad that it helped
your grandfather to escape from the Nazis. I wonder if my passport
was any use in getting across the frontier. The loss of the rucksack,
the newly arrived £4, and the passport didn't matter, as they were
all made good within twenty-four hours. But the thing I *did* miss
was my notebook, full of my travel journal. It had my London
address inside – it would have been kind of your ancestor to have
posted it. I am sure you would have mentioned it, if by any chance
it had survived. It would have been a great help to me in writing
the book.
   Thank you for your kind wishes, and the best of luck.
   Yours sincerely,
      Patrick Leigh Fermor

To Rudi Fischer   Kardamyli
2 [?] February 1986   Messenia

Dear Rudi,
   I was absolutely amazed by the news that F. X. Hinterwälder
doesn't exist! The hoax was entirely successful – I was fascinated and
a bit horrified by the complacency of the thief's descendant – the
tone was so exactly right! . . . *Of course*, I should have suspected
the writing – but I didn't! . . . Bravo!
   Yours ever
      Paddy

Between the Woods and the Water, *the second volume in Paddy's trilogy about 'the Great Trudge', was published in October 1986.*

To Rudi Fischer   Kardamyli
10 November 1986   Messenia

Dear Rudi,

As you see, we have run out of the usual paper, so here goes in leading strings.[1] Perhaps it will make me more legible!

I do apologise for being such a bad correspondent while in Blighty, but you will soon see why, and condone. I scribbled a note to you just before leaving, promising to send a clump of reviews when I got here, and posted them off registered to you yesterday. I v. much want you to see them, as I strongly feel that much of the credit for the book's success is due to your marvellous help. The reviews are all good except for the one in the new *Independent*, who couldn't bear the book.[2] The best is, rather unexpectedly, the *Guardian*, which really does get the point of what I was trying to do.[3] Jan Morris, who I admire very much, has written a very friendly, percipient and slightly worrying one.[4]

We broke our journey to England in Amsterdam, which I'd never been to, where we met an old friend called 'Coote' (Lady Dorothy) Lygon, or rather, since last spring, Heber-Percy, as, both of them in the mid-seventies, she was married last spring to Robert H. P., usually known as the Mad Boy, who was left beautiful Faringdon House in Berkshire, by an admirer for many years, Lord Berners. But he seems to have turned into a monster of selfishness and she has moved out again to her nearby cottage . . .

We saw all the Rembrandts within miles, starting with the Rijksmuseum, and then visiting the Hague and Haarlem, also in pursuit of painting. The red light quarter was just as dramatic as you painted it on the telephone – corsetted sirens in window after pink-lit window, a seething public, and suddenly, trumpets and drums and flags as a formation of the Salvation Army marched along the canal-bank, took up position on one of the bridges, and burst into brass-backed hymns, banners waving. It was like a scene out of a Passion play, especially with that enormous Gothic church looming over all.

In London we stayed with our old friend Janetta, not far from Sloane Square. Jock Murray had worked out the most intricate plan of campaign. Before it started, I went down to Canterbury for a night, after being wooed by letter by the school, to talk to the sixth form and other local worthies. They knew all the details about the sack including the heroine's name (Nellie Lemar) and all about her. It seemed very strange. I stayed with the headmaster, Canon Phillips. All very odd.

Jock's promotion campaign started with signing 1,100 copies in a fantastic Clerkenwell Dickensian warehouse, piled high with Byron, Macaulay and Scott and all subsequent authors. I rather enjoyed this, drawing back between each hundred, and looking out over Wren churches. There were signing sessions in the following days at several giant bookshops, with buyers lining up, in each case followed by a feast: Hatchards (twice), Heywood Hill, Sandoe, Harrods, and many others. In each case, windows were filled with copies of the book and snaps of the author . . . I secretly revelled in these displays, but was alarmed by the idea of being caught gazing in, like a nipper outside a sweetshop. Everyone likes the cover, which I was rather disappointed by at first, but have got used to now. I insisted on Jock's people inserting a loose addendum slip in all signed copies, with corrections of a few of the worst mistakes. There are plenty, alas; some publisher's blunders, some due to my proofreading blindness. Anyway, the thing seems to have sold like billy-o: a second printing was followed by a third, and when I left, a shop [assistant] said to Joan, when she asked how *that* book (pointing) was going, 'like hot cakes'. Jock had also fixed up BBC talks (I missed hearing them, alas!), also one in Greek from Bush House, followed by a Rumanian interview in the same building. To my relief, the Rumanians there had read it *and* were v. enthusiastic; I dreaded their thinking I had taken too neutral, or pro-Hung. line over Transylvania,[5] but no. I even muttered a few lines of Mioritza,[6] which they were very keen on. They were all violently against the President (C),[7] & hate the regime . . . John Julius Norwich and I did a long interview for TV, not shown yet (don't know when), but I don't expect you get that in Hungary. (By the way, did Murrays send you an extra copy of the book, and *A T. of Gifts*, in case they wanted you to translate it? *More important still*: did I send you an inscribed copy, as would be my delight & duty if I haven't? I ask because I signed and handed out so many, that I might easily have got in a muddle. Please put me out of my agony, so that I can act at once, or *not*, as needed.) Next day. I see my writing has degenerated again. There was one day that I dreaded: being guest of honour, and *making a speech*, twice on the same day, once to the Anglo-Hellenic League, after a huge lunch at the Travellers in the library, and, much larger, in the evening, at a dinner of the Special Forces Club – SOE, Commandos, SAS etc. – in the D. of York's headquarters, everyone in full fig with decorations. I'd got this one typed out, and, thanks to oceans to drink all through dinner, it went off well, and all ended up in a cheerful and drunken blur, with Xan Fielding, Geo. Jellicoe and others. The first speech was about Anglo-Greek memories, the second about picturesque SOE characters.

Jock drove me down to a vast book emporium at Henley, where there was a great signing session, then lunch with Steven Runciman, and after that we went to see Bruce Chatwin, who is very ill and thin, with a disease that apparently only usually affects young whales in the South Pacific. But he was very cheerful in spite of that. We continued on to the painter John Piper and his wife Myfanwy, [illegible] by Betjeman in her salad days. They live in a sort of tithe-barn in the middle of the woods.

The only weekends away from London were both to Chatsworth, the first with Joan and Janetta, while Debo was in America for some exhibition, the second, and last, when she got back . . .

It seemed very strange to get back after these hectic weeks; now, from here, the weeks seem stranger still. A huge round of correspondence was waiting, with lots of letters to write. This is the first!

Joan sends her greetings, and please give my love to Dagmar, and forgive these illegible self-centred pages. I've only gone into all this at such length because a great share of the credit belongs to you!

Yours ever
Paddy

Now for Vol. III! Andalusia for Christmas.

1 The letter was written on lined paper.

2 'Every girl is pretty, every man dashing. Horses are strong, dogs eager', the end result being 'a quite ruthlessly pleasant journey'. Graham Coster, *Independent*, 16 October 1986.

3 Tim Radford, 'Recalling Perfectly', *Guardian*, 17 October 1986.

4 'Mr Fermor is beyond cavil the greatest of living travel writers.' Jan Morris, 'Jaunts in the Balkans to the Land of Dreams', *The Times*, 24 October 1986.

5 The rival claims for Transylvania by Hungary and Rumania were a recurrent problem for PLF.

6 An old Rumanian ballad, quoted extensively in *Between the Woods and the Water*.

7 Nicolae Ceauşescu (1918–89), General Secretary of the Rumanian Communist Party 1965–89, head of state 1967–89. He was overthrown in the revolution of 1989, tried and executed by firing-squad.

To George 'Dadie' Rylands   Kardamyli
27 October 1987   Messenia

My dear Dadie,

This letter is written in sackcloth and ashes.

Have you ever written a letter, stuck it up, stamped and posted it – and then realised, later on, that you have done nothing of the sort? It happens to me from time to time, and it has happened now, hence this deeply apologetic letter. James Stourton's[1] invitation to your birthday party[2] arrived a few days before our return to Greece and I wrote to him at once, in a hurry, saying, alas, we would be back here; but put off writing to you till the morrow, in the hopes of sending you a proper letter, full of thanks for being bidden and tons of seasonable thoughts and bitter regrets at missing the feast; whereupon a tidal wave of packing, movement, change, complication and departure swirled us away and it is *only now* that I realise, with a thrill of guilty horror, that the letter was only written in imagination. (Or so I think. If I did write, and have been equally forgetful about the deed, please discount all this. But I don't think so.) Hence the deeply contrite mood of these lines. I haven't dared mention my hideous oversight to Joan. As I was to send all her wishes as well, she would swoon with horror . . .

I do hope it was a splendid banquet and worthy of the occasion. Many, many thanks for asking us and I do wish we had been there too.

I am writing this at 7.30 a.m. in a dressing-gown. It rained heavily last night, so I got up as soon as it was light and set off after mushrooms, sure I would come back with a record-breaking basketful. I combed all the groves within a mile, and found *not one*. Worse still, there was a sudden lightning-flash, then a crash of thunder like Waterloo, Borodino and King Lear rolled into one, followed by a soaking downpour like massed hosepipes. Hence the dressing-gown. Mushrooms have been a great disappointment this year, either rotted away, poisonous, or not there. Otherwise, lovely October weather, and I think we will be able to go on bathing for two or three weeks more. Meanwhile Vol. III proceeds, rather ploddingly, but I feel it will soon break into a trot, then a canter.

Many apologies again, dear Dadie. Joan would send lots of love as well as me, but she's still fast asleep, and I'm *not sure* I'll apprise her of my grave omission.

Yours ever
Paddy

P.S. Here are two frightful riddles.

1) What would be a suitable name for a country nook where Dukes of Sutherland might recover from all the ceremonies of a coronation?

2) The title of what book by a famous nineteenth–twentieth-century novelist might also apply to vomiting induced by an oyster?

(Answers inside envelope.)
1. 'Dunrobin'.[3]
2. *The Return of the Native.*

[1] The Hon. James Stourton, art historian.
[2] A party to celebrate Rylands's eighty-fifth birthday on 23 October.
[3] Dunrobin Castle is a family seat of the Dukes of Sutherland.

To Jock Murray   Serres
29 August 1988   Macedonia

My dear Jock,

   I feel a bit strange, after driving incredible distances (for me) and
have halted for the night in this town (not slept in by me since April
1935), and am scribbling under a huge plane tree strung with lights,
not many furlongs from the Struma river – Strymona – which I
tried to cross on a horse in the same month. Thank God the wise
beast turned back soon after he was out of his depth, peering
reproachfully back at me like an indignant chessman. I'd read about
'swimming horses across rivers' – it's not so easy as it sounds. My
steed and I had begun to revolve in the current, and I had visions of
us both being whirled out to sea – it was a mile from the mouth –
like the head of Orpheus down the current of the Hebrus, only two
rivers from the east, still singing it seems, altho' torn to bits . . .[1]

   My aim on this journey is to fill in the *middle distance* – it's purely
a visual thing. One remembers pretty clearly the foreground, also the
skyline, especially if it is, as it usually was, a violent zigzag of peaks.
It's been so *hot* in Kardamyli, one melted like a midsummer
snowman. I rather pine for those Rhodope and Balkan canyons, and
vast cool forests of beech and pine.

   Love to all,
   yours ever
      Paddy

[1] According to Ovid, Orpheus was torn to pieces by the women of the Cicones after
he rejected their advances. His head and lyre, still singing mournful songs, floated down
the swift River Hebrus to the Mediterranean, and there, the winds and waves carried
them to the shores of Lesbos.

To Michael Stewart   Kardamyli
15 December 1988   Messenia

Dear Michael,

We've been having a strange time here, the last few days. All of a
sudden in the middle of the night a huge wind blew up, clashing
shutters and doors, rattling windows, and soon, puncturing the hours
of darkness with sounds which turned out next day to be falling
trees. (We lost one tall cypress.) Rain came down as though from a
hosepipe, turning our gallery into Venice, and terrific seas crashed,
accompanied by hours and hours of thunder and lightning. All this,
with telephone poles down between here and Kalamata, plunged us
into darkness and silence. When Petro came next morning, he had a
terrible tale to tell. Three young policemen were on the jetty, half in
and half out of a car (why, nobody can discover) when a gigantic
wave swept them into the sea. One fought for a while, a rope was
thrown, he was dashed on the rocks, and soon dead, but eventually
hauled out. The other two vanished, and for the next two days, a
helicopter was slowly clattering up and down the coast, peering
down, boats zig-zagged about the bay, frogmen flown from Euboea
worked their way along all the submarine caves. They were found on
two succeeding days, many fathoms down in chasms on either side
of the island, tangled in yards of seaweed . . . The first to go was a
Cretan called Strati, extremely nice, and the son of a chap from the
Amari in Crete, between Ida and Kedros, who had been a great help
to us all in the war, and especially when the General was being
smuggled west. A week ago we were drinking *tsikoudia* here and
talking about all this – prehistoric legend for him, of course. All
these things have cast a pall of mourning over our bit of coast.

Joan and I fortified ourselves in her room, lit blazing fires and
hurricane (or rather, butane) lamps. It felt very primordial and cut
off. But after dinner I read Curzon's *Monasteries of the Levant*[1] to her
– and then we remembered your bottle of Dow's vintage port in the
cellar; and as we sipped warmth and cheer began to spread, and it
has transformed every succeeding evening. I felt I had to write and
tell these tidings.

Corfu, alas, is off, so we are meeting Xan and Magouche in
Marseilles, to wander about Provence, and spend Christmas under the
roof of Dominic de Grunne,[2] whom Joan and I scarcely know; but
he's kindly welcoming us.

Happy Christmas to you and Damaris, Lucretia and Olivia![3] We'll
toast our benefactor in tonight's blushing glasses . . .

> Yours ever
> Paddy

---

[1] Robert Curzon, *Visits to Monasteries of the Levant* (1849).
[2] De Grunne lived in a house tucked into the hillside below the château of Ribes,
not far from Le Puy.
[3] Their daughters.

To John Julius Norwich   Kardamyli
19 February 1989   Messenia

My dear John Julius,

Many, many thanks for *Byzantium: the Early Centuries*.[1] I've darted
about in it everywhere, and it reads beautifully. I can't sail formally
through, as I would like to have done, and will do, because Joan has
taken it, and is doing just that, and enjoying it enormously. But she
said, towards the end of dinner last night, rather sadly: 'The only
trouble is, it's *no use* my reading history now, especially at night,
I simply forget it all in the morning.' Then, after a pause, she said, 'I
suppose I ought to be reading *Black Beauty*'; a second pause followed,
then, 'except that it makes me cry . . .'

My turn next.

I'm so glad you approved of the *S. Bank Show*.[2] I can't make up
my mind about it. I thought there were many lost opportunities, and
sequences where, because of cutting, the original purpose got
somehow lost. I rather thought *Jock* stole the show, a wonderful Phiz
or Cruikshank illustration, and beautifully modulated *début*. Xan
looked nothing like himself, and I thought I was pretty odd most of
the time. It was a bit hazy, so I had to sit for innumerable hours, eyes
screwed up like boot-buttons as they stared into the glare. It

somehow turned the mouth to a sneering slit, with glimpses within
of an elegiac country churchyard; while Melvyn sat questioning
under low cool fronds, fingers elegantly weaving, and as cool as a
cucumber. The drawback was that he didn't really *know* anything
about it. I sighed for you, who do, and thought of how swimmingly
and painlessly that easy-going session in Blomfield Road[3] had gone,
and how splendid the result. Ah well. David[4] was terribly nice,
occasionally burying his head on Joan's shoulder, and saying 'Why are
they all so *beastly* to me!'

Elizabeth Chatwin is staying here for a bit, busy in the window-
seat filling in hundreds of *faire-parts*.[5] I've just written a piece about
Bruce for *The Spectator*,[6] after having done another about a Polish
SOE pal three or four weeks ago. I'm turning into a memorialist.
I'm *now* struggling with one for a sort of florilegium [collection of
excerpts from other writings] for Julian Jebb. I want to end it with
some lines, *not* written by his grandfather, or, he thought, M. Baring.
He used to recite them when he'd had a few, and they have always
haunted me – You probably know them:–

    'He loved her to distraction
    'As I've often said before,
    'And they went pit-pat, pit-pat, pit-pat
    'Round the kitchen floor,
    'All covered with oom-tarára, oom-tarára, oom-tarára,
    'Round the kitchen floor . . . '

Any ideas?
    Very many thanks again, from both of us and love to Molly
    Yrs ever
        Paddy

I would have begged to review Vol. I, though all unqualified. But I
took vows, some months back, to do no outside work till I get to
curtain point in my Vol. III, and, except for obituaries, it would cause
mortal offence to people I have been firm with. But I'll leave no s.u.
[stone unturned] to get Vol. II when it appears.

P.P.S. If, in a later vol., you want to bring out how deep ran
nineteenth-century lack of interest in Byzantium, you have only got
to mention O. Wilde's Hawthornden Prize *Ravenna*.[7] Nearly 1,000
lines, and *not one mention* – as far as I can remember – can't find
– only Dante and Gaston de Foix get a look in, and of course Lord
Byron and, up front, Victor Emmanuel and the Risorgimento (tho' I
don't think he mentions Anita Garibaldi dying there).[8]

But, of Just: Theod: Belis: Narses: Galla Placidia: Theod:
Amalasuntha:[9] and the rest of our little group, not a whisper . . .

[1] JJN's book of this title, covering the period AD 286–802 and the first volume of a
trilogy, was published early in 1989.
[2] The ITV arts programme *The South Bank Show*, presented by Melvyn Bragg
(b. 1939), had made a film about PLF, first broadcast on 22 January 1989.
[3] JJN had interviewed PLF for an earlier television programme on the same subject.
[4] David Cheshire (1944–92), television director.
[5] Partly printed letters (presumably responses to letters of condolence).
[6] Bruce Chatwin died of an AIDS-related illness on 18 January 1989.
[7] Oscar Wilde won the 1878 Newdigate Prize – not the Hawthornden Prize, which
was not established until almost twenty years after Wilde's death – for his poem 'Ravenna',
which reflected on his visit there the year before.
[8] PLF's memory of the poem is largely accurate; the Risorgimento is alluded to,
though not named, and nor is Garibaldi's wife Anita.
[9] The Emperor of Byzantium, Justinian; Theodora (his wife); the generals Belisarius
and Narses; Galla Placidia, daughter of the Emperor Theodosius I; Amalasuntha, daughter
of Theodoric the Ostrogoth.

To Rudi Fischer   Kardamyli
30 June 1989   Messenia

Dear Rudi,

Just got your marvellous letter about the great rehabilitation
ceremonies in Budapest.[1] It really *is* extraordinary. Would you ever
have foretold it a few years ago? Whatever one's reservations, I think
we must all raise a cheer. Thank you, too, for your amusing
elaborations on the theological aspects of *Gluttony*. I was given the
choice between that and *Lust*.[2] A lifelong martyr to the latter, I
chose the former.

I've got in such a tangle about correspondence that I can't remember whether or not I have told you about the Yemen. If *not*, let me know, and I'll remedy the gap . . .

I wasn't asked to do a review of Bruce's last book, and I'm rather glad, as I've done two about Bruce, & the obituary bit, in the last two to three years, and it would be rather a *réchauffée*. In the same way, I now find it very hard to write about Greece or Crete. (I'm enclosing an article about the latter, from an English Language monthly in Athens, which is less embarrassing than most.)

Just before we went to the Yemen, Elizabeth Chatwin flew out, and (as I think I wrote to you) said it was Bruce's dearest wish that his ashes should be buried beside a small church of St Nicolas about two miles up the flank of the Taygetus, near the village of Exochori (which we walked to after plunging into the deep canyon between it and Tseria). It's on a spur of the mountains, very small and old – tenth or eleventh century, & v. bat-haunted – with fragments among the stone-and-tile Byzantine masonry, probably meaning there has always been a shrine on the spot. We often picknick there, among the v. steeply perched and narrow ledges, covered with olive trees and very tall oaks. As you know, B. had become an Orthodox – he wanted to meet me at Chilandar on Athos, on the way back from Bulgaria, to keep him company while he was received by the Serbian monks there. But things had gone too far for travel, even in a wheelchair. When I got back, I asked our vicar (Fr Dimitri) if it was all right and he said yes indeed, and he would sing a mass if we liked. But as there had been two already, one in France, another in Moscow Road,[3] Eliz. thought not. She flew over here three weeks ago, and she, Joan and I drove up there with trowels, and spade, then Eliz. emptied the casket in, we filled it up, uttered silent prayers and poured on some wine as a libation; then feasted under the branches.

With any luck, I'll just catch the last outgoing post of the week – viz. Friday morning – so I'll put a sock in it now, dash down, and do better in my next!

Love to Dagmar

Yours ever

Paddy

P.S. Sunday night (1.7.89), I've reopened this to append that the
excellent translator of *Mani*[4] has broken the government impasse here
by getting elected caretaker PM of government till new elections in
Oct. He's a delightful man, *honest* (v. important), religious,
commission in Navy when Colonels came in, Minister of Works
under Karamanlis. He's gt. gt. grandson of Zanetbey Grigorakis of
the Mani[5] (see Book) and translated it in political exile in Kythera.

[1] On 16 June 1989 a ceremony took place to honour those executed by the Communist regime in the repression that had followed the Hungarian uprising in 1956. As
many as a quarter of a million people lined the routes and crowded into Heroes' Square.
Speakers denounced the Soviet invasion of 1956 and called on Soviet troops to leave
the country.

[2] See page 202.

[3] St Sophia Cathedral, the Greek Orthodox Church in Bayswater, London.

[4] Tzannis Tzannetakis (1927–2010) resigned his naval commission on the day after the
1967 *coup d'état*. He was imprisoned and later exiled by the military junta for his
resistance activity. When democracy was restored in 1974, he joined the New Democracy party of Constantine Karamanlis, and served as Minister of Public Works and
Minister of Tourism. In 1989, after the socialist leader resigned in response to corruption charges, Tzannetakis became prime minister of a coalition government for the
ensuing few months of political crisis. He later served as Deputy Prime Minister
(1990–93), Defence Minister and Minister of Culture.

[5] Though appointed bey of the Mani, Zanet Grigorakis conspired with agents of
Napoleon to mount an uprising against Ottoman rule with French support.

To Michael Stewart   Kardamyli
21 July 1990   Messenia

Dear Michael,

This is just a brief message to say that Joan and I had a great treat
last night *entirely thanks to you*. We uncorked and decanted the
magnum of Château Fombrauge early in the afternoon – two and
three-quarter decanters-full – and gave it a long breather while Joan
prepared a marvellous plain chicken and *pommes vapeur*. I went for a
long swim in the gloaming, then ascended and laid the table for two
at the top of the stairs. Then, after a preliminary swig or two of
Glenlivet, and a cleansing munch of brown bread, we settled down to

it. The wine was absolutely magnificent, with a fascinating and transporting bucket (if that's the English for *bouquet*), and a smooth and insidious texture that cocooned us in happiness. We didn't rush it, but we were soon on to the second decanter, which was accompanied by some excellent Shropshire Blue I had brought back from Blighty a few days earlier. We didn't finish it – too good to gulp – but hope that, firmly stoppered, it will relaunch us again tonight.

I went to Blighty for four days for the most frivolous of reasons, viz. to go to a marvellous twenty-firster for a grandson[1] at Chatsworth. No hopes of persuading Joan – though she egged me on, in her usual splendid way – so I was by myself, drove north with Janetta and Jaime, who I stayed with, and it really was wonderful [illegible] – 250 to dinner, 1,000 guests. There were acres of tent, a number of wild and shaggy contemporaries of the birthday boy (who has the fine architectural name of Wm Burlington), but, luckily, lots of contemporaries too, and plenty of tiaras, starting with Debo's which was like Cybele's mural crown, with a sweeping strawberry and raspberry-coloured dress. Soon after dinner, when everyone was getting very cheery and rather blurred, there was a masque of B. Jonson on the steps of the fountain, with dresses and scenery taken from designs of Inigo Jones in the library there, then to the soaring Beethoven's 5th Symphony, a cumulative display of fireworks such as I have never seen, all dropping reflected in the lake. Everything then all melted into a golden Turneresque haze of semi-oblivion, until the beginnings of daybreak: a full moon with a few decorative alabaster clouds, and figures wandering about in a trance under the oak trees . . . As nobody failed to say, one will never see the like again.

Back to the grindstone! Only a few hours to go before drinking yours and Damaris's health in the last of the Saint-Émilion.

Love from us both

Yrs ever

Paddy

---

[1] William Cavendish, Earl of Burlington (b. 1969), son and heir of Peregrine 'Stoker' Hartington, later 12th Duke of Devonshire.

To Jock Murray   Kardamyli
5 January 1991   Messenia

My dear Jock,

Many thanks for your letter and for the fascinating *Robert Byron's Letters*.[1] I've only read a few pages after luncheon today, but Joan has been deep in them for days, absolutely hooked. What an extraordinary bird he was, incredibly and precociously gifted to an amazing extent. His mother must have been marvellous, too, to have evoked these letters. I wish I'd known him properly. I remember having a long chat, but totally tight, when I was eighteen in a nightclub – was it 'Frisco's the Boogie-boogie' – too early – or 'The Nest'? I met him after my travels, once when he and several other of the Georgian Soc.[2] were assembling for a meeting – Jim Lees-Milne,[3] R. B., Michael Rosse?,[4] and, perhaps, John Betj., but not sure. (This was in Catherine d'Erlanger's house in Stratton St; she had taken up painting, and I was her sitter.)[5] Then again with Sachie Sitwell, and again with Bridget Parsons, in early 1940, when I was a soldier. I heard about his death in Cairo from his then brother-in-law Evan in Rustum Buildings, the SOE hang-out.[6] What a help he might have been in Greek affairs!

What I meant to say was, yes, of course I'll do a review somewhere. His books were one of the things that prodded me to set off for Constantinople.

Yesterday, as it was a blazing sunny day, Joan and I had a picknick high up on the edge of a wood at a village on the coast called Platsa, at the monastery of St Nicholas Kampinar. The grass was covered with blue, purple and mauve anemones. After a blissful nap under the pines, I set off on foot, Joan planning to meet me by car in an hour's time, as I wanted to walk down by a steepish winding path. The usual path was blocked with piled thorny branches to stop sheep getting along it, and also some new wire-netting, so I strolled on downhill, waiting for another path, and went badly astray. The descending path got steeper and stonier and the olive terraces were more and more neglected, till at last I was so far down as to be beyond the point of no return to the monastery, now far aloft in the distance. I thought there must be a path soon, but instead a deep ravine yawned, which logically had to descend to the sea. The going was worse and worse. An abandoned hamlet – three to four houses with no roofs, only rotten beams – was entirely covered in brambles and ivy; the once stepped, now gap-toothed path getting steeper and worse, now so overgrown and deep as to be much darker, old fungus, toadstools, rotten trees, *maquis* [densely-growing, evergreen shrubs] and sudden cataract drops leading to frightful cliffs, so I tried another direction, saw a tiled roof to the north. On arrival, it was a totally abandoned chapel. The sun was setting by now. I had a moment of threatened panic, thinking of Joan waiting at the car, struggled on in the gloaming, down a few overgrown olive terraces, then maquis closed in again, cliffs' edges were muffled with bushes and undergrowth, frightful drops looming when I poked with my stick and peered down. Thank heavens, though it was dark now, it was a clear starry night. I thought I could see a gap, too hard to discern, and finally slid down onto what proved to be two truck-ruts of a seldom-used road. Oh the relief! I trudged on with a lighter heart, but couldn't think what to do at turnings. I tried two, one led steeply down to an abandoned farmstead, then fumbled steeply up again. A second led, as far as I could see, to a full cistern; only Orion reflected in it stopped me from stepping straight in . . . At last I seemed to be on a more sensible track. I could see all the lights of the coast twinkling below and *at last*, three hours after I should have been there, got to the path leading to our rendezvous tower, and there was a wavering torch coming towards me – it was Joan, on her way to ring Kardamyli and organising a search party. She was right! One could have bust a leg (or one's skull) on one of those hidden precipices. Imagine the relief! Great embraces. We were in a frightful state, hearts pounding, I soaked in sweat, shanks criss-crossed with bramble tears in the manner of Grünewald.[7] We dashed gratefully home, and double whiskeys, hot baths, delicious soup and Nemean wine, followed by glasses of port brought here by Coote, Bella and Frieda, and R. Byron and Saki in front of blazing logs, did their healing work . . .

Poor Joan! She was just what one should be in such cases, and more.

All greetings to you and Diana.

Yrs ever

    Paddy

[1] Robert Byron (1905–41), traveller and travel writer, best known for his *The Road to Oxiana* (1937). John Julius Norwich has described him as 'one of the first and most brilliant of twentieth-century philhellenes'. Byron died after his ship was torpedoed by a German submarine in the North Atlantic. His letters were edited by his sister Lucy Butler and published by John Murray as *Robert Byron: Letters Home* (1991).

[2] The Georgian Group, founded in 1937, campaigns for the preservation of historic buildings and planned landscapes of the eighteenth and early nineteenth centuries. Robert Byron was one of its founders.

[3] The architectural historian James Lees-Milne (1908–97).

[4] The Irish peer Lawrence Michael Harvey Parsons, 6th Earl of Rosse (1906–79).

[5] Baroness (Marie Rose Antoinette) Catherine d'Erlanger (1874–1959) (née de Robert d' Aqueria), a society hostess, wife of the French banker Baron Emile d'Erlanger. They lived at No. 139 Piccadilly, the former home of Lord Byron, on the corner of Stratton Street.

[6] SOE's Cairo headquarters, in the Rustum Buildings, known to Cairene taxi-drivers as the 'Secret Building'.

[7] PLF is referring to the German Renaissance artist Matthias Grünewald (*c.* 1470–1528), whose religious paintings often depicted a scourged Christ.

To Janetta Parladé   Kardamyli

22 May 1992   Messenia

Darling Janetta (change of bowstring:[1] pen conked out),

    It's monstrous that I'm only writing now, after dwelling in your shell for such an age like two hermit crabs; and what a swizz missing you all the time. I can't tell you what a true blessing and boon it was. The new end-room, Jaime's study, is lovely, and I even managed to get some work done, occasionally usurping your stately table upstairs.

    I went to Sandringham[2] under Debo's wing – apparently Andrew hates staying there so much that he fled to Jerusalem – and very much enjoyed it, mostly because of (a) the novelty, (b) the luxury and delicious food, but mostly (c) because of the transparent niceness and goodness and the charming manners of the host. The people there I knew were Derek Hill, Candida Lycett Green, Billa Harrod, Angela Conner and her hubby.[3] The others were a couple who live near Tidcombe (name gone), the painter Kitaj and a beautiful wife (or girl).[4] There was a great deal of sight-seeing: Houghton and Holkham, both marvels I'd never seen – all v. queer re. the first, and v. nice, viz. someone called David Cholmondeley[5] and his pals. Then there was a marvellous ruined Norman Abbey,[6] perfect for me; and several small and beautiful churches. I had a small whitewashed room with a brass bed, which had been the P. of Wales's when a boy, so he told me, and on these different window-panes: 'Nicky Oct and Vth Dec, 1897' and on the next, 'Georgie (Greece) 1900 Nov., 1904 (Nov) and 1911 (June)' and finally, 'Axel (Denmark) 1909 Feb.' The first were the last Tsar and Tsarina, murdered in the Revolution; the second, King George I of Greece, was assassinated in Salonika two years later. The last died in his bed.

Next weekend was with Geo. and Philippa [Jellicoe], who come here in a few days. She and I went for a tremendous long ride – looking down from the Bull's Tail on Ham Spray, then to Coombe where Hendersons and Moores[7] were gathered under Michael Stewart's roof for a lot of drinking. Neither of the horses had been ridden for six months, one not for three years, with the result that from the waist down I turned to stone, as tho' a gorgon's head had been waved. The last weekend we went to Crichel,[8] which was lovely, with a great feast at Cranborne,[9] and a dinner at Jochen's in Peter Heyworth's old house,[10] with Pat, Desmond, & Cressida Ridley.[11] I feel very braced, the way she keeps me on tiptoe. Then we took wing here, but not before having a long feast of oysters etc. at the Poissonière[12] with Francis Bacon, with lots of laughter; only to learn the sad subsequent news[13] when we got back . . . Magouche sent on all the cuttings which we read through slowly & gloomily, thanking our stars for that last meeting . . .

No sooner back here, I fell down that flight of stone steps, rushing for a book from Joan's room in the pitch dark, and turning right too soon. I got quite a battering but nothing broken, so tottered to Paris leaning on the handsome gold-handled ashplant. There Editions Payot had brought out no less than three books in two weeks, which meant endless interviews and unblushingly organised ballyhoo, followed up by a monster assembly of travel writers at St Malo, with much feasting and a book fair, a vast acreage of marquee built out from the huge machicolated keep that dominates the port.

It's rather muggy weather here, with that glare that seems to put everything a bit out of focus, spring flowers all gone, rank grass shooting up and withering but masses of birds and plenty going on in the branches: Jochen is staying, a very easy and helpful guest, and a surprisingly interesting one. Jellicoes come next week and also the still-unmet by you Gowries,[14] who are on the same prize-giving jury we all seem to do time on. I'm getting on with my work, largely egged on by a review in Le Monde which described me, because of my awful slowness in writing, as 'L'Escargot des Carpathes'.[15] I forgot to say that Joan's puss, Gisella, who slouched in out of nowhere last year as an unknown kitten, has just had five of her own, on the bottom shelf of the linen-cupboard. This morning I followed the cat Johnny – also a last year's stranger – into the room on tiptoe, and caught him standing on his hind legs, rubbing muzzles with Gisella, who was leaning out. No more, except tons of love & thanks to you and Jaime from both of us.

Come soon,
Paddy

1 'Darling Janetta' was written in blue ink; the rest of the letter in black.
2 The royal retreat of Sandringham in Norfolk, where PLF was a guest of Prince Charles.
3 The fashionable painter Derek Hill (1916–2000); the writer and campaigner (and daughter of John Betjeman) Candida Lycett Green (1942–2014); the conservationist Wilhelmine 'Billa' Margaret Eve Harrod (1911–2005); the sculptor Angela Conner (b. 1935) and her husband, the photographer John Bulmer.
4 R. B. Kitaj (1932–2007) and his second wife Sandra Fisher (1947–94), both American artists living in London.
5 David George Philip Cholmondeley, 7th Marquess of Cholmondeley (b. 1960), whose family seat is Houghton Hall, in Norfolk.
6 Possibly St Benet's Abbey on the River Bure.
7 The diplomat Sir Nicholas Henderson (1919–2009), his wife Mary and their daughter Alexandra, Lady Drogheda, with her husband, Henry Dermot Ponsonby Moore, 12th Earl of Drogheda (b. 1937), a photographer known professionally as Derry Moore.
8 Long Crichel House – see note 1 on page 310.

9 Cranborne Manor, home to the heirs of the Marquess of Salisbury.

10 Peter Lawrence Frederick Heyworth (1921–91), American-born English music critic and biographer, lived with his companion Jochen Voigt in Dorset.

11 Patrick Trevor-Roper, Desmond Shawe-Taylor and the amateur archaeologist (Helen) Cressida Ridley, née Bonham Carter (1916–98), who excavated sites in Crete, Euboea, Greek Macedonia and Turkey.

12 A restaurant in Chelsea, which closed in 2015.

13 Bacon died of cardiac arrest in Madrid on 28 April 1992.

14 Alexander Patrick Greysteil Ruthven, 2nd Earl of Gowrie (b. 1939), usually known as 'Grey' Gowrie, and his wife Adelheid (b. 1943).

15 PLF was very tickled by this appellation, which he quoted in letter after letter.

Marie-Lyse Ruhemann, née Cantacuzène, was a cousin of Balasha's. When Paddy was at Dumbleton he would often come over to a cottage on the Sudeley Estate which she and her husband Frank rented for their holidays.

To Marie-Lyse Ruhemann   Kardamyli
10 January 1994   Messenia

Dear Marie-Lyse,

The book's[1] arrived safely, and v. many thanks! It seems very well done, and it's a very good thing that it has all been set down before it vanishes from everyone's memory. I've been reading it all the afternoon in front of blazing logs in the fireplace remembered from the one at Băleni, copied out of your father's Persian sketchbook, certainly now lost in Rumania; if so, here it survives, at two removes, like part of one of those traditions in architecture brought back from the Crusades, and subsequently slightly garbled.

I was glad to see Balasha and Pomme there – 'Marie Blanche' and 'Hélène' – but it was a sad little entry, like most of them, *et pour cause.* How I wish that Balasha, when told to pack at Băleni – one suitcase only, and in quarter of an hour by the people in the Securitate truck – as well as finding my old voluminous notebook, on which everything I'm writing is based, had happened to remember her own memoirs.[2] She was putting them together all through the year before the war, especially in winter 1938–39. She wrote beautifully and, if saved, it would have been a marvellous record.

There were lots of memories of her grandfather 'The Kniaz' [prince], and all the stories she had heard for the last two or three generations. Very interesting, very moving sometimes, and often funny. I wish one could hope that they might turn up somewhere but I very much doubt it! A sudden Dark Age descended that nobody was ready for.

Many thanks again, Marie-Lyse, and all wishes for 1995
    love Paddy

---

[1] She had sent him a book by another cousin, Jean-Michel Cantacuzène, *Mille ans dans les Balkans – Chronique des Cantacuzène dans la tourmente des siècles* (*A Thousand Years in the Balkans – Chronicle of the Cantacuzène in the Turmoil of Centuries*) (1992).

[2] On the night of 2–3 March 1949 Balasha and her sister had been evicted by the Rumanian secret police from their family home, the manor-house close to the Bessarabian border where PLF had lived with her before the war.

Another Cantacuzène, Prince Michel Cantacuzène-Spéranski (1913–1999), of the Russian branch of the family, asked Paddy to write a foreword to a memoir, The Cantacuzène-Spéranski Saga.

To Michael Cantacuzène   Kardamyli
17 March 1994   Messenia

Dear Michael,

Thank you so much for your letter and that fascinating copy of the *National Geographical Magazine*. It reminds me very much of my prehistoric trudge along the Danube.

I'm feeling very guilty about being so slow about the foreword. There have been a mountain of things to cope with, but I think I am beginning to see daylight, then I really will buckle to! Please forgive!

What a long time since Balasha and I came to see you and your parents at Sandricourt![1] And how charming you all were. Balasha was tremendously bucked to find such delightful kinsmen, however far away.

I think the book will be a moving tribute to your family, and especially your branch of it, and fascinating recapitulation of a great

sweep of history. I wish Balasha and her sister Pomme could have
seen it – too late now, alas! – as they were always fascinated by
Russian Cantacuzènes, of whatever branch. Her grandfather was
always known as 'Le Kniaz'; he spoke Russian and French long
before he spoke Rumanian, and a very elegant uniform of *Maréchal
de la Noblesse* for Bessarabia – or some of it – still hung in a
cupboard. We used to use it for dressing-up parties. Just before the
war, we went, largely on horseback, to see a lot of Cantacuzène and
Krupensky relations beyond the Prut River along the Dniestr in
Bessarabia, and feasted under the trees at Novoe Usadba, the house
of a dear old General Volodia Kantakuzin – *Croix de Saint Georges,
quatrième classe*? – before moving on to another crumbling Krupenski
gentilhommière called Lamashnitza. Happy days!

    Love to you both,
    Paddy

¹ A nineteenth-century chateau about fifty miles from Paris; PLF and Balasha went
there in 1937.

To Janetta Parladé   Kardamyli
4 October 1995   Messenia

Darling Janetta,
    I'm so terribly sorry about those spectacles! I can't think how I
managed to do it: viz. to pinch, and lose, the good pair, and keep the
cast-off stand-by we sent back. I've hunted every pocket and nook
and cranny and flap and lining, and cracks between chairbacks and
cushions and dark bottoms of cupboards; and all in vain. Please
forgive! I plan to get several brightly coloured semilunar specs in
Athens – hideous, but detectable if astray, and unconfusable with
anyone else's; and I must get you a sumptuous pair, spectacles to end
all spectacles . . .
    We were expecting Magouche to be here by dinner time, but she
rang from Athens an hour ago to say the Kalamata plane for once
had left on time, so she missed it (they shouldn't have sold her the

ticket, if this could happen), so she's bowling through the night in a ruinous taxi, and will be here for a delicious roast chicken about 11 o'clock. Then, after three days of bathing and mountain walks, off we go to Crete for poor Xan's final scattering,[1] right up in the White Mountains, which will be much better than from an aeroplane. A few hectic days will follow, then straight to Athens, as Johnny Craxton and another chap (John Leatham)[2] and I have to do an hour's 'conversation-round table broadcast' about Niko Ghika in Greek. It sounds absolute hell . . .

Joan and I gobble up all the reviews about *Carrington*,[3] which, on the whole, aren't bad at all. I long to know what Frances thinks of it, and you. I bet they've got Ralph wrong, as usual. I do hope we see it some time – obviously, there will be cassettes.

There was quite a healthy rain a few days ago, so Joan and I went mushrooming. *Not one.* I do feel guilty about cluttering your cupboard with that jacket – the tweed's so loud that if you hear groans and oaths and sighs in the shadows, you'll know what they come from.

8:15! Time for Famous Grouse!

love and penitence

from Paddy

---

[1] Xan Fielding had died of cancer more than two years earlier.

[2] John Leatham (1924–2003), intelligence officer, writer, translator and philhellene, who had lived in Greece since 1969.

[3] A film about the life of the painter Dora Carrington (1893–1932), written and directed by Christopher Hampton, and released in 1995.

Paddy generously encouraged many younger writers, as William Blacker (b. 1962) would gratefully acknowledge in an address he gave at Paddy's memorial service in 2011. In November 1996 Blacker had written to Paddy to say that he was just setting off to spend the winter in the Maramures, a mountainous and forested region in northern Rumania close to the Ukrainian border, famous for its old wooden churches and medieval way of life.

To William Blacker   Kardamyli
11 December 1996   Messenia

Dear William – if I may make so bold –

I can't think of anything more exciting than your imminent
prospect – and well done starting in winter. (a) You have the whole
world to yourself, and (b) inhabitants never take summer visitors
seriously. Winter is a sort of Rite of Passage. Do take down any
songs or sayings, above all *descântice* – spells, incantations, invocations,
etc. I bet Maramures is full of them. Also, as much wolf and bear lore
as possible – and remember, *never* drink rainwater that has collected
in a bear's footprint, however thirsty.

Happy Christmas, *La Mulţi Ani*, and best of luck

Paddy L-F

*The suggestion arose that Artemis Cooper should write Paddy's biography jointly
with her husband, the military historian Antony Beevor, whose book* Crete:
The Battle and the Resistance *had been published in 1991. In the event she
would undertake the book alone.*

To Artemis Cooper   Kardamyli
17 June 1999   Messenia

Dearest Artemis,

The arm that holds this pen is stiflingly tubed in sackcloth, but
you can't pick out the warp from the woof, it's so heavily caked
with ash . . . I can't *think* how many days have passed since getting
your marvellous letter without blushing under my double layer of
textile and volcanic dust. My only explanation is that I was fidgeting
about too much in Blighty, and, when we got back here, so alarmed
at the Pelion and Ossa[1] accumulation of stuff to be answered that
soared on my desk, that I sort of seized up and I haven't answered a
single one; but I have a kind of a feeling that this letter will get
everything on the move again. Please forgive.

The joint book by you and Antony is a wonderful idea, and it's
most brilliant and generous of you both to think of it. I'm rather pro

lives *not* being done in the person's lifetime, and I think you both are too. Look at Diana's![2] I'll try and put together a sort of *curriculum vitae* with dates and movements, parents, family, schools, travels, friends, adventures, mishaps, war, etc. And, of course, books. There are quite a lot of letters which have mounted up. A huge pile of ones *to* Diana, of course, which you angelically dealt with and returned and even, when illegible, made spotless fair copies of. There are lots of articles that might need a glance, any amount of oddments, bits of verse, jokes, etc. There's quite a lot of Diana's correspondence at The Mill House, which I've often meant to have Xeroxed, *haven't* of course, but will. Also many to and from Joan. Some amusing ones from Annie Fleming, and various other friends. These are in some sort of order, the main ones, anyway: otherwise, rather higgledy-piggledy. It's rather a curse that *both* Joan and I are very untidy. Things are often mislaid, turning up after a year. The only thing which consoles me is the memory of a photograph – I don't think I ever actually saw it – of Iris Murdoch's & John Bayley's interior set-up, which was as though tossed by a hurricane. But I will try and get things a bit more in order. Joan and I have given this house to the Benaki Museum,[3] after we vanish, so we'll give them great instructions for you to have the run of the place, and all that's in it, if we're both suddenly run over, or eaten by sharks. But I hope you'll both be here lots of times before.

Anyway, it's a splendid plan.

One day, at Asolo, I was reading a marvellous book in her [Freya Stark's] library, *Italy and her Invaders*, eight vols., hefty ones, by Thomas Hodgkin, Vol. I starting – after Rome from the time of Augustus – with the Visigothic invasion, and goes on through the Ostrogoths, the Lombards, the Huns, etc. ending up with the Empire of Charlemagne – literary atmosphere of the Court, Alcuin of York,★ etc. Seeing how much I was enjoying the book, she said, 'I'll leave it to you in my will.' Then said, 'No, perhaps I'll go on living for ages.

★ To give an idea of the cheery atmosphere of Charlemagne's Court, where they all had nicknames. Charl, one day said to Alcuin, who was sitting opposite '*Quid te separat a stulto?*' ['What makes you different from a stupid man?'] Quick as lightning, Alcuin answered '*Stultus*' ['He's stupid.']

But you must come and get it.' So I did. She wrote in it: 'Handed on to Paddy with love, Freya. Asolo 6/12/1980.' She was v. keen on my handing it on, so I'll write in it 'Handed on to Antony and Artemis with love from Paddy and Joan, 17/6/1999.'

(pause of three minutes)
In fact, I've just done it, and will slip it back into the bookcase, duly earmarked, in the classics corner, on the terrace side of the drawing room, second bookcase on the left, just before the pillars, seventh shelf from the bottom. At the bottom, remembering what was written in each of our cubicles at school, I have added NUNC MIHI, MOX HUJUS, SED POSTMODO NESCIO CUJUS?[4] It occurred to me, putting it back, that it's more John Julius's period than yours – but perhaps he's got it and you could borrow it. Further inspiration! We'll leave him the two wonderful leatherbound Nonesuch vols. of Pope's Iliad and Odyssey, marvellously printed on special paper and given by Diana in memory of Duff – allowed to choose – with that lovely new moon bookplate.[5]

I must dash down with this in the hopes of catching the last Friday post – à *la recherche* etc., with knobs on to both, love from Paddy and Joan

[1] Pile Pelion on Ossa – an expression originating in Greek mythology, meaning to add one difficulty to another.

[2] See note 1 on page 338.

[3] The Benaki Museum in Athens, established and endowed in 1930 by Antonis Benakis in memory of his father, houses a collection of Greek art from prehistoric to modern times.

[4] 'Now mine, soon to be his or hers, afterwards who knows whose?' – see the footnote on page 38 of *A Time of Gifts*.

[5] Duff Cooper's bookplate, designed by Rex Whistler, depicts a bust of his wife surrounded by flounces, champagne bottles, scrolls and boxes.

To George Jellicoe   The Mill House
7 September, 199[9?]   Dumbleton

Dear George,

I'd meant to write ages ago, but I've plunged into such an Augean
stable, clearing away all the literary impediments, causes of delay,
mental blocks, prefaces, obituaries – beginning to stand thick as time
wanders on – and all the things that have stopped me doing what I
ought to be doing – viz. *finishing a book* – that I haven't been able to
move an inch. No feasts, no Chatsworths, no Tidcombes,[1] nothing!
It's *morally* rewarding – halfway there! – but otherwise pretty
constricting. Most of my letters begin with an apology. So please
forgive.

Apart from this death-grapple, there is nothing going on here,
except croquet, at which I get steadily worse, and shorter and shorter
trudges in the hills all round. Two house-martins have got a nest in
the eaves just above my window, and they never stop going and
coming, and each time they do, their shadows cross this page (twice,
since the start of this). The other major excitement is the arrival of a
small flock of jet-black Welsh sheep, grazing on the long grass of the
orchard below this window. Their ringleaders are two sturdy rams,
black as soot, and with long twirling horns, the sort that Joshua used
for bringing down the walls of Jericho.

My favourite reading is now Lemprière's early nineteenth-century
classical dictionary.[2] Here is what he has to say about the Emperor
Heliogabalus:

> Heliogabalus often invited the most common of the people to
> share his banquets and made them sit down on large bellows full
> of wind, which by suddenly emptying themselves, threw the guests
> to the ground and left them a prey to the wild beasts.[3]

Lemprière also says that Talassius was a young Roman who carried
off a Sabine virgin, crying out 'Talassio, which meant that she was
now for Talassius' (dative case?). 'But it is more probable that the cry
"Talassio", which was used at Roman weddings, is related to our

"Tally Ho".' Sounds a bit far-fetched.[4]

It's suddenly pouring with rain. Foul weather for old drakes. We slink back to Kardamyli in a few days. Joan is playing chess against herself downstairs, a schizophrenic contest.

Fond love to Philippa!

Yours ever
Paddy

[1] The Jellicoes lived at Tidcombe Manor in Wiltshire.

[2] The *Bibliotheca classica* or *Classical Dictionary containing a full Account of all the Proper Names mentioned in Ancient Authors* (1788) by John Lemprière (*c.*1765–1824) was a readable if not absolutely reliable reference book on mythology and classical history. As he wrote in his preface, Lemprière wished 'to give the most accurate and satisfactory account of all the proper names which occur in reading the Classics, and by a judicious collection of anecdotes and historical facts to draw a picture of ancient times, not less instructive than entertaining'.

[3] Marcus Aurelius Antoninus Augustus (*c.*203–22), commonly known as Elagabalus or Heliogabalus, was made emperor at the age of only fourteen. His eccentricities made him notorious; Gibbon wrote that he 'abandoned himself to the grossest pleasures and ungoverned fury'. His behaviour provoked public outrage, and at the age of eighteen he was attacked and killed by members of the Praetorian Guard.

[4] 'One, conspicuous amongst them all for grace and beauty, is reported to have been carried off by a group led by a certain Talassius, and to the many inquiries as to whom she was intended for, the invariable answer was given, "For Talassius". Hence the use of this word in the marriage rites' (Lemprière).

Michel Cantacuzène-Spéranski still hoped for a foreword from Paddy, though by the end of the century he was seriously ill. This letter was written to his (second) wife Pamela; she replied with a letter describing her husband's peaceful passing.

To Pamela Cantacuzène   The Mill House
7 February [?] [misdated 7 January] 2000   Dumbleton

Dear Pam,

I'm so sorry to keep on delaying, it's far from being on purpose! I'd set this sojourn aside and look what happens.

I was asked to go and stay at Chatsworth, which I adore, and I saw myself scribbling away, but, as an 'old friend', I'd got a miserable room with a tiny table and a depressing window outlook into the rain-and-wind-lashed inner courtyard, as there were so many people staying. (Joan had oiled out of it, not caring for such gregarious occasions as much as I.) So I was constantly downstairs, having fun. (The one quiet writing corner in that vast place was under repair, and swathed in sheets.) But there were all sorts of treats. The P. of Wales was there, and he'd brought a stack of caviar he'd been presented with, so we wolfed it down as abundantly as cornflakes; and, to compensate for my grim quarters, I was shoved next to the P of W's love,[1] whom I'd never met, and enjoyed that enormously. She's immensely nice, non-show-off, full of charm, and very funny, so that was a real treat. They set off with their boxed horses next morning, in full fig, to join the Meynell Hunt at their second covert, avoiding the meet and journalists and saboteurs, and had a wonderful day. The weather was very fierce – *des vents à décorner les boeufs* ['winds to blow the horns off cattle'] as they say, howling through the woods like something out of the Brontës. All this turned back into a pumpkin when I had to leave for a doctor's appointment in London, where it was discovered that I had cancer of the tongue (I'd had this twenty-five years ago, when it took ages of elaborate treatment), but I was whisked off to the Lister Hospital and the thing was sliced off with a laser beam next day, and I was out quite soon, feeling rather groggy and living off bouillon and yoghurt and bread and milk, and am still, now four days after, very lethargic and scatterbrained as one is after general anaesthetics, and probably writing drivel.

Worse still, Joan has got to have a slipped retina operation in a few days' time. We were expected back in Greece three days ago. What a hope.

My original idea in taking up my pen was to [write] about Alan Pryce-Jones's death[2] – I learned about it at Chatsworth, and now I've got to prepare a speech for his memorial service in two to three months, at his son David's request. *But not till I have done yours.*

Did I ask you if you had read Dimitri Obolensky's book,[3] which I think awaits you in Greece? If not I will send you a copy – it has had golden reviews.

I hope you are both well!

Love Paddy

¹ Camilla Parker-Bowles, later Duchess of Cornwall (b. 1947), married the Prince of Wales in 2005.

² Alan Pryce-Jones died on 22 January.

³ *Bread of Exile: A Russian Family* (1999). After Obolensky's death in 2001, PLF wrote that he had been 'an enchanting companion on the hills of Euboea, in the meadows near Oxford, or in the foothills of the Mani in the southern Peloponnese' (*Daily Telegraph*, 7 January 2002).

Paddy agreed to write a foreword to a Folio Society edition of Ill Met by Moonlight. *Then he withdrew in favour of the SOE historian M. R. D. Foot: the matter was 'too delicate' for him to tackle. A week later he telephoned to say that he had been thinking about it, and felt that there were things he would like to say: the coup had, in his view, been diminished by being reduced to the level of a 'tremendous jape', and he hoped to restore the balance by providing something of the context for the enterprise. He did not wish to interfere with Foot's foreword (now redesignated an introduction), but would contribute a 'short' afterword, describing his own experience. It would be 500 to 1,000 words. It eventually emerged at 6,500 words, all of which, as the editor at the Folio Society has recalled, 'had to be wrested from him in hand-to-hand combat, so anxious was he that nothing could be misinterpreted'.*

To Sophie Moss   Kardamyli
4 April 2001   Messenia

Dearest Sophie,

I'm so sorry and contrite about being so late in writing and answering you and Gabriella and Pussa.¹ Please transmit my contrition to them. Lovely letters waited for me here with glorious drawings of Polish architecture and fauna – and here I am writing over a month late.

I was terrifically relieved to hear from that nice lady at the Folio Society that the foreword to *Ill Met* was not in a terrific hurry. It was a great stroke of luck because all of a sudden people started dying all over the place, and I seem to be turning into a sort of latter-day Bossuet, with the *Oraisons Funèbre*s. I had begun the foreword but have put it off for a month (thanks to Folio) until the decks are clear. I want it to be all right, and not done in a hurry. My writing gets steadily slower. What makes it even slower, is that much of it has to be in Greek, which seems to get more clogged with the passing years, instead of flowing like spring-water.

It's been wretched weather here. Joan and I feel like Mr and Mrs Noah in the ark. Rain coming down for forty days and forty nights, with no sign of a dove with a twig in its beak, let alone a distant glimpse of Mt Ararat to perch on, and only two members of the animal kingdom, two tabby cats who love Joan but can't make up their minds about me, after five years. The villagers, of course, love this downpour – it means no drought in August – so the longer our faces, the wider their smiles.

Please give love and apologies all round, and tons of love
   from
      Paddy

---

[1] Her two daughters, 'Pussa' being a family name for Isabelle.

To Pamela Cantacuzène   Kardamyli
22 April 2001   Messenia

Dear Pam,

I was very upset by your letter, and rightly, as I am entirely to blame, while you have been an angel of patience. This is only a short letter, which I got very late owing to mov[ing] about, not because there's little to say – there is lots – but only to let you know how very sorry and penitent I am about my failure to pen down the foreword.

It's not through idleness or anything like that; it's from letting myself get bogged down by a score of things.

The point is, I want this foreword to be very good, or as good as I can make it, because of our mutual concern and involvement in the Cantacuzène family. I have made several false starts, none of them seem to gel properly, so I've put it off each time to have another shot. I suppose I don't write as quickly or as readily at eighty-six as I did in earlier years. I suppose having a pacemaker last year is an indication of slowing up. But I do feel the same about the foreword, and I really will do it. I wish it were now, but I am heading for a book launch – *Time of Gifts* in Magyar – in Budapest, and almost as soon as I get back the 60th Anniversary of the Battle of Crete looms where I have got to write ghastly speeches as Vice-President of the UK Veteran Soc.

But I have great hopes of this summer. Meanwhile, don't lose hope and please forgive

    love Paddy

Rudi Fischer had written to PLF commenting on the attacks by the terrorist group al-Qaida of 11 September 2001, and the response to these.

To Rudi Fischer   Kardamyli
10 October 2001   Messenia

Dear Rudi,

My papers are in an even worse turmoil than usual, with the result that I can't remember whether it [RF's letter] contains some specific questions that need answering. Anyway, I bet it will turn up the moment I have posted this!

We got back here three weeks ago. It seems like the day before yesterday. Have you noticed that when one gets to a certain age, a month only seems to last a week?

Shortly before we left London, I discovered that two pairs of sailcloth trousers I'd bought in a hurry at Captain Watts's Nautical Shop,[1] next to my publishers in Albemarle Street, are several inches too long. I took them back one afternoon to see if I could change them, but it seemed that it would take a week or two. Could anyone *alter* them? They suggested the huge shop John Lewis, tailoring department, in Oxford Street. The lady in charge there said they couldn't alter *outside* clothes, as I had suspected. But she recommended some small jobbing 'seamsters' at 20 Haunch of Venison Yard, not far off. I found it at last, through an archway leading into a dark, cobbled [word missing], full of broken crates and rubbish, and odd and empty houses, some windows broken, some boarded up – nothing to do with the smart Bond Street-Mayfair world in which it was embedded. No. 20 opened after much tugging on a bell. Inside, one iron staircase led up into a long noisy room, with about ten wild-looking men who had dropped their stitching and slicing to listen to the strident voice, punctuated with martial music, on the loudspeaker. It sounded like Arabic except that there was no glottal stop, as in cockney and Glasgow and Mecca. I asked what it was and after a pause, one said, half-heartedly, 'Persian'. A bearded elder took the trousers over and said 'tomorrow'. When I got back to Janetta's flat in passionate Brompton,[2] Joan told me the afternoon's frightful news from New York. When I went back to H. of V. Yard, the wireless was even louder, a sort of braying, with more martial music. I said: 'Persian, again?' and they said, with wide smiles, 'No, next door.' 'Syria?' 'No.' 'Lebanon?' 'No.' 'Pakistan.' 'No.' 'AFGHANISTAN?' 'YES!' They all started laughing. I said, 'What's going to happen?' And they all pointed to the ceiling, said 'Allah knows!' The trousers had been beautifully altered.

All very queer! I don't have any opinion about routing out bin Laden,[3] let alone his being handed over. The whole key to South Afghan life is the code called *Pakhtunwali* or *Pashtunwali*, which revolves round the sacredness of [the] guest, especially if they are on the run or hiding . . . It's like the code of *bessa* in Albania, *omerta* in Sicily and *bushido* in Japan. I quite agree with your thoughts on 'cowardly' attacks, for kamikaze onslaughts.[4] What a gaffe, too, to go on about 'Crusades' . . .[5]

Θεὸς μαζί μας! [God be with us!]

Please forgive this rotten scrawl. I'll do better next time. Joan sends her love to you both, and so do I.

    Paddy

---

[1] Captain O. M. Watts, ships' chandlers, was at No. 7 Dover Street, W1.

[2] In the nineteenth century the Brompton area of west London became known as 'passionate Brompton', on account of the large number of actors who lived there.

3 Osama bin Laden, al-Qaida's leader.

4 RF had suggested that it was mistaken to label those who were launching suicide attacks cowards.

5 President George W. Bush used the word 'crusade' on the day of the attacks, and again on the national day of mourning a week later. His use of the term raised fears among Muslims of a Holy War.

Emma Tennant is Debo Devonshire's eldest daughter. In her reply to this letter, Lady Emma wrote 'Lovely to hear from you & specially on the gripping subject of the Agenbite of Inwit / Inbite of Agenwit, one of the best word jokes ever made' (ET to PLF, 24 April 2002).

To Emma Tennant   Kardamyli
2 April 2002   Messenia

Dearest Emma,

Help needed! Years and years ago, walking beside the Derwent, you asked me if the Inbite of Agenwit, mentioned in the early paragraphs of a book I had just published called *Roumeli*, had anything to do with the Agenbite of Inwit,[1] and I said yes, it was a sort of joke, based in the I. of A., and applied to the tedium of officials stuck for years in the same provincial outpost and having to listen to each other's jokes for year after year; what one might just as well call Conker-bane.[2] You obviously knew all about the I. of A., fresh from Oxford and Eng. Lit, and I *suppose* I must have done too, or else I couldn't have made misuse of it as I did.

Well, Joan was reading *Roumeli* yesterday, and asked what the A. of I. was taken from; and I had clean forgotten too. I've been hunting through dictionaries of quotations, *Webster['s]*, the *Oxford Companion*, and the 11th edition of the *Encyclopaedia Britannica*, and I've drawn a total blank. Then I thought of looking up 'Inwit' in the *Shorter* (but pretty large) *Oxford* dictionary, which did at least mention the word 'Inwit' ['Iywit'?] and 'Conscience', but nothing which was any help about the source, except, bleakly, the word 'Wyclif' in small capitals; and hope sprang! It meant it was much later than I had been thinking. I'd imagined it must have been a century or two earlier, but it was obviously part of the Lollards' hatred of the Latin mass and Bible, a vernacularisation of *remorsus conscientiae*. I made a dash for 'Lollards' in the *Encyclopaedia* and found masses of fascinating stuff about their dissident literature but not a word about the A. of I.! What can it have been – an essay, a book? You are the only person who has ever mentioned it, or asked what I meant by the I. of A., or knew anything about it. Hence this appalling rigmarole. Do, please, send a brief word, and unpucker our brows.

No more for the moment – too serious! – except many thanks in advance, and all hail to you both.

Love, Paddy

P.S. T.B.Y.F.:[3] I remember where I first set eyes upon the words, and I have just looked it up. It's *Ulysses*, J. Joyce, page 14 of the Bodley Head, line 9. 'Speaking to me. They wash and tub and scrub. Agenbite of Inwit. Conscience. Yet here's a spot.' (He wasn't giving anything away!)

I believe there is another equally brief mention, much later. Needles in haystacks.[4]

---

[1] *The Agenbite (or Ayenbite) of Inwyt* (meaning the 'again-biting of inner wit', or, in modern parlance, the Prick of Conscience) is the title of a confessional prose work written in a Kentish dialect of Middle English in 1340 by a Benedictine monk, Michael of Northgate.

[2] 'If a joke is worth making, it is worth making often, think some; other more fastidious ones suffer more acutely from the Inbite of Agenwit' (taken from the opening paragraph of *Roumeli*).

[3] 'Think Before You Flush', here meaning, I should have thought of this before writing.

[4] The phrase occurs three times in the text of *Ulysses*.

To Sophie Moss
24 January 2003

The Mill House
Dumbleton

Dearest Sophie,

Thank you so much for your letter and lovely card – most of them are rather depressing. And all wishes to you, and to Gabriella and Pussa for 2003. *I'm so sorry* being such a sluggard with the pen, but everything will get a bit clearer later on, and we'll have a lovely feast in London. I had a lovely Christmas at Chatsworth, just like something out of Dickens, including a whole troupe of carol singers from the village with lanterns, singing all one's favourites, including one that Xan was very attached to, viz. 'The Holly and the Ivy'. My favourite too.

Since then, everything has been rather turmoil. Joan and I are like two old motor-cars being serviced. On my last trip, to see an oculist, everyone had to change out of the Paddington train at Oxford, thanks to the flooding of the Thames, and go on by bus to Didcot, then into a train again; then out because of further floods at Reading. And during all this shemozzle, my briefcase got lost, I think pinched: there are notices saying THIEVES OPERATING NOW! BEWARE! One might be in Khartoum. Like a lunatic I had masses of documents in it, licence, passport, chequebook, and worst of all, a forty-year-old address book, so I'm back to the start. Can you imagine anything worse? Thank God, I've got yours, in a forty-year-old disintegrating and ragged survivor with a few very, very, early entries. Getting passports, birth certificates, etc., makes one feel one is not yet fully in existence.

This scribble must stop. It's only to send lots of love and wishes to you all, and apologise. Please forgive!!

Paddy

To John Julius Norwich   Kardamyli[1]
6 June 2003   Messenia

Dear John Julius,

I expect Artemis [has told you] about the frightful blow that has fallen here. Yesterday morning I was chatting and laughing with Joan, having her breakfast in bed. An hour later Elpida the maid[2] came running, in floods, saying *Kyria Ionnna*. She had slipped in the bathroom, lost balance, fell, and struck her head so fiercely on a sort of low step that it killed her outright. No pain, thank heavens, except for survivors.

Thank heavens Olivia Stewart[3] was here, the model of speed and efficiency and organisation. With the result that we, with poor Joan, duly looked after by summoned experts, [are] flying to Athens and driving to Dumbleton, where a service will take place. Not quite sure of the day, but I'll [illegible].

Terrible that this angelic figure – the one who could least be spared, has suddenly been carried away.

No more now, JJ, except love to both, and please tell Anne.[4] I'll be in touch again.

Will be going straight to Dumbleton, where a funeral service is already being arranged – naturally accompanied by 'Fight the Good Fight' by John something something Monsell,[5] also sung at their funerals,[6] a great favourite of Betjeman.

I suddenly came on the end of the block of writing-paper, [illegible] of letter from Diana, headed 'Laeken Palace, Brussels',[7] with 'stolen stationery', pencilled underneath by Diana.

---

[1] Using writing paper from Château de Saint-Firmin, Vineuil, Oise.
[2] Elpida Beloyannis, the Leigh Fermors' cook/housekeeper, who was devoted to PLF.
[3] The younger of Michael and Damaris Stewart's daughters, a regular visitor to Kardamyli in her own right, who was particularly close to Joan.
[4] John Julius Norwich's former wife.
[5] John S. B. Monsell, 'Fight the Good Fight' (1863).
[6] i.e. those of Joan's parents?
[7] The official residence of the King of the Belgians.

To Sophie Moss   The Mill House
20 June 2003   Dumbleton

Dumbleton

Dearest Sophie,

I was – am – very moved by your lovely letter. All the last days have been a sort of trance, it was all so sudden and unforeseen . . . It culminated a few days ago in the small, late Plantagenet church here, with sunbeams pouring in through stained glass, and the sound of flocks and birdsong from outside drifting in and seeming to form a part of the liturgy, from the hills and fields.

Here's the liturgy, itself, with a couple of paragraphs from Sir Thomas Browne we both loved, and a strange and marvellous fragment of one of the apocryphal gospels which we were put on to by the poet Seferis.

Please give my love to Pussa and Gabriella. I'm going to write soon. It's rather a consolation to be doing it! And tons of love to you, dearest Sophie, I'll be in London soon and will be in touch –

    Paddy X

Andrew Devonshire died in 2004. Janetta Parladé had been a lover of the Duke's and had remained close to him until the end. Paddy attended the funeral at Chatsworth, and afterwards felt that he should inform Janetta how the Duchess had reacted to her letter of condolence.

To Janetta Parladé
12 May 2004

On Chatsworth writing paper, marked 'In the train to Paddington'

Darling Janetta,

This letter is likely to be very wobbly because the train jerks from side to side at a terrific but irregular rate.

Debo was very moved by your letter, which she read to me at the earliest opportunity. It was perfect, absolutely right in every way, not a false note anywhere. I meant to creep away and telephone you at once, but for some reason, failed totally, I got through to Alcuzcuz[1] who gave me a space-garbled Madrid number which I finally got through to and then you were heading for Alcuzcuz again, and finally I thought I'd better write. (I've become a bit more legible for a moment, because we are stationary in Derby for a moment.)

I came up on (we're off again) Tuesday morning, after getting to Dumbleton after a rather hectic drive from K[ardamyli], and a Saturday devoted to a military function in Athens with Geo. J. and Philippa and a 5 p.m. next day flight. Debo said to come so I went,

and I'm v. glad I did, after driving up there with Jeff the gardener
and his girl. After a buffet lunch, the gathered family and a few
friends moved off towards the church, which was tolling loudly every
few seconds. This part moved at a slow foot pace after the car-hearse,
as the whole mile was lined along both sides of the road with estate
people, game-keepers, gardeners, maids in spotless aprons and
Derbyshire yeomanry in old-fashioned scarlet and helmets, then a
company of Coldstream Guards. All in the greatest quiet and
solemnity, except that the solitary knell had changed to a sequence
of slightly faster descending scales. I was in the car with Christian,[2]
and in church, beside beautiful grandchild Stella[3] (who I hadn't seen
since she was five in the Lowlands, carrying a speckled Prussian hen
under one arm, and one of its eggs in the other hand telling Debo,
triumphantly, that it wasn't a cockerel, as D. had thought when
giving it to her, but a hen). She has turned into a rather shy and sad
raving beauty, with a tear track over red cheeks when we all got up
to go out to his churchyard, where Andrew was laid to rest among
the trees and the Last Post was sounded. D. had planned every detail
of the order of service and ritual, and it somehow managed to be
simultaneously magnificent, rustic, and simple. There were huge
marquees by the big fountain outside the house, and a mass of
people, a mixture of a vicarage garden party and the Field of the
Cloth of Gold. Only Debo and Sophie[4] left next day, and me largely
wandering about hoping I wasn't in the way, but I don't think I was.
We went for a huge walk (for me) after tea. Rather marvellous it
was, and made me very glad to have gone. I talked a lot about you.

Now I'm heading for two days in London under Magouche's roof,
then she is coming south for the weekend and Cressida and Charles[5]
coming over on Sunday, which will be lovely. It's now getting about
too wobbly to write, so I'll finish this, and get it off from the
Travellers or Whites. I forgot to say that it was a wonderful summer
day yesterday, [illegible] and nearly static alabaster clouds and
bluebells and hundreds of other flowers bursting out in those steep
woods.

    tons of love
    Paddy

¹ The house belonging to the Parladés in San Pedro Alcántara, in the province of Malaga, southern Spain.

² Dr Christian Carritt (b. 1927), described by DD as 'a selfless, funny and charming London GP loved and relied upon by all her patients, many of whom became her great friends' (*In Tearing Haste*, page 313, note 1).

³ The model Stella Tennant (b. 1970).

⁴ Lady Sophia Louise Sydney Topley (b. 1957), second daughter of the Duke and Duchess.

⁵ Cressida Connolly (b. 1960), daughter of Cyril Connolly, and her husband Charles Hudson.

To Tzannis Tzannetakis   Kardamyli
20 June 2004   Messenia

Dear Tzannis,

Please forgive me for not writing earlier to thank you for your marvellous words the other night at the Gennadius Library. Everyone was struck by your talk, and said it was the most marvellous piece of writing. The only sad aspect of it is that I am getting so deaf that I couldn't catch whole pieces of it, and this makes me very sad, though eternally grateful. I *have* a hearing machine, but it seems to deteriorate and fail to transmit when I need it most. Of course I long to know what you said. The mere fact of your composition and delivery fills me with gratitude but I would give *anything* to follow your speech in its entirety. Would it be possible for me to have a copy? I long to read it and I would treasure it forever. I know how good it was from what everybody else said of it. I do hope my request isn't an awful nuisance for you, but I would be grateful forever!

It was a wonderful evening, and I am still overcome by it. It was a great joy to see you and Maria, and I wish I had managed to talk to you both, as we used to in Kythera, years ago, that splendid couple of weeks when we were both going over your glorious translation.¹ It was a very happy time. This is the third time that you have put me in your debt, for literary help. I could hear every word of your speech at the other book launching. I wish Joan had been there!

With much love to you both from your grateful
Paddy

¹ Tzannetakis had translated PLF's *Mani* while in political exile under the Colonels' regime.

More than a decade *after he had undertaken to write a foreword to Michel Cantacuzène-Spéranski's book, Paddy had still not done so. 'I have, over the years, made a few tentative starts to the former, but they weren't quite right; so I put them aside till the right one occurs, as when it does – and I'll make sure it does do so – I really will get at it,' he had written to Cantacuzène's widow in 2003.*

To Pamela Cantacuzène   The Mill House
18 January 2007   Dumbleton

My dear Pam,

Thank you very much for your very kind letter. I feel very guilty and downcast about my disappointing conduct about the book. I'm ashamed to say that the list of unfulfilled plans grows longer. I find writing more and more difficult. Literally and physically on one level. I'm slowed up by a wretched affliction called 'tunnel-vision', which makes putting pen to paper result in a tangle like barbed wire entanglement, which is why I am writing on this unattractive lined stationery, which does more or less make the result semi-legible. But the thought process that sets writing in action seems to become slower and more hopeless as time passes. I do hope I am wrong, but the outlook is bleak and upsetting. I wish I had either managed to produce what was needed, or confessed to the gloomy predicament earlier on. I am not absolutely in despair about all this, and hope for a change. It's not very encouraging to say that you are at the top of an unfulfilled programme. But that, alas, seems to be the situation, and I am deeply sorry and penitent about behaving so hopelessly.

The tone of your letter is very kind, forgiving and generous, and I am deeply grateful and hopeful that things will change, but not very sanguine. I'm in England at the moment (Mill House, Dumbleton, Evesham, Worcestershire), but returning to Greece soon.

It seems ridiculous, things being as they are, to hope for a change, but I do.

Meanwhile, kind Pam, very many apologies and love.

Paddy

I will be ninety-two next month . . .

Paddy had spent New Year 2007 with his old friend Debo Devonshire, who had moved out of Chatsworth after her husband's death, and was living at the Old Vicarage in the nearby village of Edensor. Also staying were two old friends, Robert Kee and the former diplomat Sir Nicholas Henderson, who noticed that Paddy seemed very 'down in the dumps', but that he rallied when Debo produced a box of his letters for the party to read. Both welcomed Henderson's suggestion that their correspondence should be published. Debo asked her niece Charlotte Mosley to act as editor. That summer Charlotte visited Paddy in Kardamyli to discuss the book. Afterwards she wrote to Debo to say that she thought it had given him 'a new lease of life – he feels appreciated, and it has taken his mind off Vol. III, which is clearly never going to appear. He reads out passages from his own letters (& sometimes yours) and roars with laughter.'

This letter was written while Paddy was back in Dumbleton, two days after Debo had been to see him there. In another letter to her about the book, Paddy confessed that he was editing his letters: 'I have tempered one or two bits of ardour in case the reader would conclude I was a bit of a rotter, if you see what I mean; but crushes are hard to make look different!'

To Deborah Devonshire   The Mill House
September 2007 looming   Dumbleton

Two days after your departure

Darling Debo,

I'm feeling tremendously buoyant and bucked about the whole *In Tearing Haste* project. Your letters are wonderfully full of life and sparkle and jokes – and moving depths of feeling too. I'm deep in the last third at the moment and most of the difficulties seem to have centred on you, and you handled them brilliantly, thanks to being clever, kind-hearted and as good as gold. What agony a lot of it must have been!

Do *feel free* to hack about in my parts, whenever you think it's soppy or embarrassing or ghastly in any other way. I'm still a bit worried about W. S. M.,[1] and my rather tearing him to bits on the grounds of his rather eerie appearance. I ought to have another look sometime when we can still change a word or two.

What luck having someone as quick, clever, patient and kind as Char[2] in the middle of things! And Helen at the Old Vic![3]

I'm now about to have a bash at those few words to be uttered at Canterbury.[4]

Please keep in firm touch. I brood a bit on the cover. I wonder if [illegible] battlements of Lismore on one side, and sea-girt olive groves and peaks of the Mani, both floating on stage, as it were, on opposite sides, with a few birds and clouds knocking about in the offing, might be any good. I expect inspiration will come crowding in.

Tons of love, darling Debo
  from Paddy

I sat down to a dish of Rhubarb-Crumble with lots of plums afterwards, a perfect feast for Charlotte. I'd never had R-Crumble before. It sounds, somehow, like a contradiction. Rather good . . .

Rita[5] can't stop talking about you all. Nor can I.

P.P.S. That nice Wykehamist poet[6] is keeping me company to Greece on the 18th Sept. Do try and come back sometime.

---

[1] (Willie) Somerset Maugham. PLF's attempts to soften his comments on Maugham when this letter was published in the volume of his correspondence with DD were resisted by the editor.

[2] Charlotte Mosley.

[3] DD's secretary, Helen Marchant, who worked at the Old Vicarage.

[4] On 9 September 2007 PLF opened a new boarding-house at King's School, Canterbury, replacing the one where he had himself boarded.

[5] Rita Walker, the Mill House cook.

[6] Hamish Robinson (b. 1964).

Colin Thubron (b. 1939) is a highly regarded travel writer and novelist.

To Colin Thubron

undated [early 2008]

The Mill House

Dumbleton

Dear Colin,

I had a rather gloomy moment over the New Year, or just after; *viz.* a long piece in the *Daily Telegraph* listing all the worthwhile writers over the last half-century, and the gloom of a streaming cold sent me hangdog to bed, as an absentee from the list.[1]

But all changed next morning. Someone sent me the *New York Review of Books* with your marvellously generous and inspiring article,[2] and I have been walking on air ever since, as though I had been relaunched by a magic dock leaf, if you will forgive the mixed metaphors.

Many, many thanks.

It seems ages since you came to Kardamyli with Anne.[3] Please do it again whenever it's convenient. I'm going back in about a month, having lately become ninety-three years old. Or if you are ever anywhere near, do come here. I'll be dashing to London and back pretty frequently to see doctors. I apologise for this writing – it's barely legible, even to me, the result of an official affliction called 'tunnel-vision' (Simplonitis, to me).

I am about to read *To the Last City*,[4] which has miraculously made its way here, and I note with excitement a number of Quechua place names[5] scattered about the pages.

(Beginning to go off the rails!)[6] Must stop.

Yours ever, Paddy

---

[1] 'The 50 greatest writers since 1945', *The Times*, 5 January 2008. Thubron himself appeared at No. 45 on the list.

[2] In 'A Prince of the Road', *New York Review of Books*, 17 January 2008, Thubron described PLF as 'the greatest travel writer alive'.

[3] Anne Norwich, mother to Artemis Cooper and former wife of John Julius Norwich.

[4] A novel by Thubron, first published in 2002.

[5] The Quechua are an indigenous people of the South American Andes.

[6] The letter was written on lined paper.

To William Blacker   Kardamyli
July 2009   Messenia

Dear William,

I feel very upset. I finished your glorious book[1] yesterday and
tried to get to Mark Amory at *The Spectator*, in order to review it;
couldn't get through, so telephoned Debo Devonshire, to see if
she could get through *on the spot*, as it were. She got through, and
Mark got through with the v. upsetting news that it had already
been reviewed. I got the *Spec.* this morning, a well-written
absolutely favourable review, but I feel *more frustrated than words
can tell*. If ever a book was written to be read and reviewed by
me! Mark said he would give me as much space as I wanted. But,
unfortunately, the review is v. good, and neatly blocks all the
points that I now can't make. DAMN! I asked him (Mark, a
friend and a very nice chap) if he could find someone else who
would welcome a review from me, and he said he would look
round, and keep in touch.[2] So that, maddeningly, is how things
are. The book is glorious, and I long to write about it. I go to
England Aug. 1st, Mill House, Dumbleton, Evesham, Worcs: tel:
01242 621225. I'll be there about a month. Frustration rages across
the Morea.

   Yrs ever,
   Paddy

---

[1] William Blacker, *Along the Enchanted Way: A Romanian Story* had just been
published by John Murray. It was reviewed in *The Spectator* on 8 July 2009 by John
de Falbe.

[2] PLF's review appeared in the *Sunday Telegraph* on 30 August 2009.

To Deborah Devonshire   The Mill House
20 January 2010   Dumbleton

Darling Debo,
It's too queer. The day before yesterday the entire landscape was
wrapped in snow and ice with deposits of snow 2 feet thick piled on
everything, and the only things that seemed to be moving were
smallish dark birds that shot past the windows too fast to be
identified. All was hushed and immobile. Then yesterday, the whole
landscape was bright youthful green – not a speck of white
anywhere, everything back to normal, traffic surging past at the
crossroads, animal life back to normal. Now today, it's half-and-half,
and v. unsatisfactory.

While I was writing, the telephone suddenly rang. It was Christian
Carritt full of arrangements for next week, in a hurry, no other bumf
in sight, so I scribbled this extraneous matter down, now enclosed.
Apologies for intrusion.

But, to continue, I found myself sneaking away from the Antarctic
scenery outside by dipping furtively into *In Tearing Haste*, and
enjoying it *almost* as if it was a total stranger and laughing at all the
jokes. Does this sort of thing happen to you at all? Do tell.

Jeff[1] is about to drive down to Winchcombe for shopping, so I'll
give him this.

Forgive haste and muddle,
tons of love,
    Paddy

[1] The gardener.

Olivia Stewart was a regular visitor to Kardamyli and a stalwart help to Paddy in his last years.

To Olivia Stewart   The Mill House
20 January 2010   Dumbleton

Darling Olivia,

Thank you so much for this lovely present [an alpaca jersey]. It really is a beauty. I've already walked down [to] the end of the drive, an impossible undertaking two days ago: the house and everything visible round it has been caked in snow and ice and not only that, but I was still too aching and stiff from my midnight fall to do anything more than totter. But now there is much more green than white in the surroundings, and I am loosening up a bit at last.

The only figure from the outside world was Pamela Egremont, who managed to drive here through snow and ice in a sturdy car from Sussex Street SW3, and is now ploughing through the slush to the Lake District.

I've managed to do some work, on the third closing volume of my youthful trilogy. I was feeling rather apprehensive about picking up after a long pause. I've been v. worried about this, but to my great relief, the part already written of this last stretch is not nearly as hopeless as I feared it might be, so perhaps it will all be OK in the end. I wish my writing had not deteriorated so.

Right at the beginning of this scrawl, I should have thanked you for your angelic help in all the arrangements for my arrival and return. I wonder where you are now – one of the great capitals of Europe, I enviously expect. I can't tell you what a help Christian has been too – in fact everyone – Rita, Jeff, Hamish . . .

Jeff is just off to the post, so I'll glue this up.

Tons of love
    Paddy

Please forgive this frightfully untidy and *unreadable* letter!

In the spring of 2011 Paddy was diagnosed with cancer of the throat. An operation was performed at a hospital in Athens to remove the tumour. By then ninety-six years old, he chose to refuse further treatment. He was able to return to Kardamyli, and talked excitedly about resuming work on the third volume of his trilogy, completing the story of his great walk begun in A Time of Gifts. But only a few weeks later another operation proved necessary. On 9 June, Paddy left Greece for the last time, hoping to see his friends in England before the end. He arrived at Dumbleton that night, and died the next morning.

DRAMATIS PERSONAE

John Betjeman (1906–84), popular poet, writer, broadcaster and advocate for Victorian architecture, knighted in 1969. He married Penelope Chetwode in 1933, but the two became estranged after her conversion to Catholicism in 1949. As a schoolboy at King's School, Canterbury, in the 1930s, PLF had heard Betjeman lecture long before they met.

Lyndall Birch (b. 1931), daughter of the journalist Tom Hopkinson and the novelist Antonia White. She had married Lionel Birch, Hopkinson's successor as editor of *Picture Post* (a man only five years younger than her father), but the marriage failed after only a few months. When she first met PLF, in 1958, she was living in Rome.

Sir (Cecil) Maurice Bowra (1898–1971), classical scholar and Warden of Wadham College, Oxford, renowned as a wit, often vicious. He was devoted to Joan but not as friendly towards PLF.

Marie-Blanche ('Balasha') Cantacuzène (1899–1976), artist, a princess from one of the great dynasties of eastern Europe. Her family owned a house in Bucharest and an estate in Moldavia, near the Bessarabian border. In 1924 she had married a Spanish diplomat: he had abandoned her while serving as ambassador in Athens, where PLF met and fell in love with her in 1935.

(Charles) Bruce Chatwin (1940–89), travel writer, novelist and journalist. He had known PLF and Joan slightly since 1970, and they came to know each other well when he visited Kardamyli in the winter of 1984/5 and stayed for seven months. After his death from an AIDS-related illness in 1989, his ashes were buried at a chapel nearby, at his own request.

Cyril Connolly (1903–74), a close friend and admirer of Joan's. PLF referred to him satirically as 'The Humanist'.

Deborah ('Debo') Vivien Cavendish (1920–2014), née Mitford, the youngest of the six Mitford sisters, who married Andrew Robert Buxton Cavendish, later 11th Duke of Devonshire (1920–2004) in 1941. PLF had first spotted her at a ball in 1940, though then she had scarcely noticed him. In the post-war years they became close friends, and he was a frequent visitor to the Devonshire seats, Chatsworth in Derbyshire and Lismore Castle in Ireland. The correspondence between DD and PLF over a period of more than half a century was published as *In Tearing Haste*, edited by Charlotte Mosley, in 2008.

Artemis Cooper (b. 1953), writer, daughter of John Julius Norwich and granddaughter of Duff and Diana Cooper, married to the military historian Antony Beevor, whose books include *Crete: The Battle and the Resistance* (1991). Her biography of PLF, *Patrick Leigh Fermor: An Adventure*, was published in 2012.

Diana Cooper (1892–1986), née Lady Diana Manners, famous beauty and socialite, the youngest daughter, in theory, of the Duke of Rutland (in fact, daughter of the Hon. Henry 'Harry' Cust). In 1919 she married the Conservative politician and writer Alfred Duff Cooper, who was appointed British Ambassador to France in 1944, and eventually made Viscount Norwich; she preferred to remain known as Lady Diana Cooper, claiming that Viscountess Norwich sounded too much like 'porridge'. She and PLF became close friends in the early 1950s. In the words of PLF's biographer, 'Paddy and Diana each discovered that the other was the sort of person they liked best.'

Alfred Duff Cooper (1890–1954), 1st Viscount Norwich, politician, diplomat, author, and British Ambassador to France, 1944–7.

Lawrence Durrell (1912–90), poet, novelist and man of letters. Though British, he lived most of his life abroad, in Corfu, Crete, Egypt and

France. He came to know PLF during the war, while serving as a press attaché to the British embassies in Cairo and Alexandria.

Pamela Egremont see **Pamela Wyndham-Quin**

(Henry) Robin Fedden (1908–77), writer, diplomat and mountaineer. In the 1930s he served as a diplomat in Athens and taught English Literature at Cairo University. Henry Miller thought him effete. After the war, he worked for the National Trust.

Alexander ('Xan') Fielding (1918–91), writer, translator, journalist and traveller; met PLF while serving behind enemy lines in Crete during the war, and they became close friends. Before his marriage to Magouche Phillips, he was married to Daphne (1904–97), née Vivian, ex-wife of Henry Thynne, 6th Marquess of Bath.

Agnes ('Magouche' also known as Magouch and Magoosh) Fielding (1921–2013), née Magruder, then Gorky, Phillips and finally Fielding, was the daughter of an American admiral and widow of the Armenian-American artist, Arshile Gorky.

Rudi Fischer (1923–2016), editor and scholar, a naturalised Australian of Saxon Transylvanian origin who was living in Budapest and working as an editor for the *New Hungarian Quarterly* when he first made contact with PLF in 1978, to draw his attention to errors in *A Time of Gifts*. 'My debt to Rudolf Fischer is beyond reckoning,' PLF would write in *Between the Woods and the Water*. 'His omniscient range of knowledge and an enthusiasm tempered with astringency have been a constant delight and stimulus during all the writing of this book; his vigilance has saved it from many errors, and I feel that the remaining ones may be precisely those when his advice was not followed.'

Ann ('Annie') Fleming (1913–81), née Charteris, granddaughter of the 9th Earl of Wemyss. Her third husband was Ian Fleming, later the author of the James Bond novels. They lived at Goldeneye, a house in Jamaica, and Sevenhampton, in Wiltshire. A renowned society hostess, she had friends in politics and in the literary world, and became one of PLF's closest friends and most regular correspondents.

Nikos ('Niko') Hadjikyriakos-Ghika (1906–94), artist and sculptor generally considered among the best Greek artists, from a wealthy Athens family. He and PLF became friends after the war, and in the early 1950s Ghika allowed PLF to stay for long periods at his house on Hydra. After this house was destroyed by fire, Ghika built a house on Corfu. He married first Antigone Kotzia ('Tiggie'), and then, in 1961, Barbara Hutchinson.

Enrica ('Ricki') Huston (1929–69), née Soma, socialite, model and ballerina, born in New York of Italian-American parents. She became the fourth and much younger wife of the film director, screenwriter and actor John Huston (1906–87). She died in a car accident at the age of only thirty-nine.

Barbara Hutchinson see **Barbara Warner**

George Katsimbalis (1890–1978), poet and raconteur, a dominant figure in Greek literary life, immortalised in Henry Miller's *The Colossus of Maroussi* (1941). PLF met him in an Athens nightclub in 1940.

Patrick Kinross (John Patrick Douglas Balfour) (1904–76), 3rd Baron Kinross, historian and writer, specialising in Islamic history. He came to know PLF while serving as First Secretary at the British Embassy in Cairo during the war.

Elemér von Klobusiçky (1899–1986) was PLF's host on his family estate in Transylvania in the summer of 1934. In *Between the Woods and the Water* PLF concealed his identity under the pseudonym 'István'. 'I admired him very much,' wrote PLF, 'he was tremendous fun, and we became great friends.' They had several adventures together, including a frolic with peasant girls who discovered the two young men swimming naked in a river. PLF especially liked the fact that 'István' had run away to join a hussar regiment during the First World War.

Lady Dorothy ('Coote') Lygon (1912–2001), fourth and youngest daughter of the 7th Earl Beauchamp, the doomed family on whom Evelyn Waugh is said to have modelled the Flytes (Lord Marchmain) in his novel *Brideshead Revisited*. She was a spinster until her unexpected, late marriage to Robert Heber-Percy in 1985, two years before his death.

Sir Aymer Maxwell of Monreith (1911–87), baronet, elder brother of the writer Gavin Maxwell. He had inherited estates in south-west Scotland, but preferred sailing round the Greek islands to more conventional country pursuits. While PLF was waiting for the house at Kardamyli to be built, Sir Aymer let him use his own house in Euboea.

Jessica Mitford (1917–96), known as 'Decca', writer and civil-rights activist, the second youngest of the six Mitford sisters. Her left-wing sympathies were in sharp contrast to those of her sisters Unity and Diana, who married the Fascist leader Sir Oswald Mosley. She lived in California, where she met and married the American lawyer and civil-rights activist Robert Treuhaft.

Nancy Mitford (1904–73), novelist, biographer and journalist, eldest of the six Mitford sisters. After the war she lived in France. She had married Peter Rodd in 1933, but the marriage did not survive, and she formed a long-term liaison with the Free French officer Gaston Palewski.

(Charles) Raymond Mortimer (1895–1980), literary critic and literary editor of the *New Statesman* 1935–47.

W. Stanley ('Billy') Moss (1921–65), soldier, writer and traveller, PLF's second-in-command in the operation to capture General Kreipe. He wrote an account of this operation, *Ill Met by Moonlight* (1950), which was made into a film (1957) by Michael Powell and Emeric Pressburger. In Cairo during the war he met the Polish Countess Zofia ('Sophie') Tarnowska (1917–2009), whom he subsequently married.

John ('Jock') Murray (1909–93), publisher, the sixth John Murray in the illustrious family firm, and a patient friend and supporter of PLF.

John Julius Norwich (b. 1929), diplomat, writer and broadcaster, 2nd Viscount Norwich, son of Duff and Lady Diana Cooper.

Mark Ogilvie-Grant (1905–69) was posted to Greece with the Special Operations Executive in the Second World War, but was taken prisoner in the Mani soon after landing. After the war he settled in Athens, where he worked for BP.

Janetta Parladé (b. 1922), née Woolley, a close friend of Joan's, and of Frances and Ralph Partridge, much admired for her beauty and intelligence. She was married to Humphrey Slater, Robert Kee and Derek Jackson, who left her for her half-sister, Angela Culme-Seymour. Eventually she would marry a Spanish aristocrat, the interior designer Jaime Parladé.

Frances Partridge (1900–2004), née Marshall, was married to Ralph Partridge (1894–1960), and lived at Ham Spray, where, before marrying Frances, Ralph had lived in a *ménage-à-trois* with Lytton Strachey and Dora Carrington. Ralph and Frances were close friends of Joan's and Janetta Parladé's.

George Psychoundakis (1920–2006), Cretan resistance fighter, shepherd and author. PLF translated his memoirs into English and then helped to arrange their publication with John Murray under the title *The Cretan Runner* (1955). Later Psychoundakis translated the *Iliad* and the *Odyssey* into the Cretan dialect.

Peter Quennell (1905–93), writer, editor and man of letters, knighted in 1993. He was editor of the *Cornhill* magazine, and co-editor of *History Today*. Once described as 'a rampant heterosexual', he married five times. An urbane and witty companion, he joined PLF on a walking tour in Italy.

Joan Rayner, later Joan Leigh Fermor (1912–2003), née Eyres Monsell, photographer and muse, the second of three daughters of Bolton Meredith Eyres Monsell, MP, who became Conservative Chief Whip and then First Lord of the Admiralty, and was ennobled in 1935 as 1st Viscount Monsell. In 1939 she married the journalist and typographer John Rayner, but the marriage did not succeed, and they were living apart by the time she met PLF in Athens at the end of the war. She and PLF formed a lifelong partnership, despite his affairs with other women. Joan was devoted to her brother Graham, who succeeded his father as 2nd Viscount on his father's death in 1969. Their mother, Caroline Eyres, had inherited Dumbleton Hall in Gloucestershire, a mid-Victorian pile said to have been considered as a refuge for the House of Lords during the war. This was sold after her death, and thereafter Joan and Graham shared The Mill House on the Dumbleton estate.

George ('Dadie') Rylands (1902–99), literary scholar and influential theatre director. Elected Fellow of King's College, Cambridge, in 1927, he lived there for the rest of his life.

Edward ('Eddy') Sackville-West (1901–65), 5th Baron Sackville, novelist and music critic. He converted to Roman Catholicism in 1949.

Georgios Seferiades ('George Seferis') (1900–71) was a poet and career diplomat, a major figure in Greek letters, awarded the Nobel Prize for Literature in 1963. Seferis served as Ambassador to the United Kingdom from 1957 to 1962. He took a stand against the dictatorship of 'the Colonels' who took power in 1967, and by the time of his death he had become a popular hero in Greece for his resistance to the regime. His close relations with PLF were strained by the tensions over Cyprus in the 1950s.

Sir Sacheverell ('Sachie') Sitwell, 6th Baronet (1897–1988), art critic and writer on architecture, one of the three Sitwell siblings. In 1925 he married Georgia Doble (d.1980). They lived at Weston Hall, a Jacobean house in Northamptonshire. PLF was taken up by them in the late 1930s.

Amy, Lady Smart, painter, Lebanese wife of Sir Walter Smart. PLF had come to know them both in Cairo during the war. In the 1950s PLF was often a guest at Gadencourt, their house in Normandy.

Sir Walter Smart ('Smartie') (1883–1962), diplomat and scholar.

Freya Stark (1893–1993), explorer and travel writer, had met PLF in Egypt during the war. She was awarded a CBE in 1953 and made a dame in 1972.

Sir Michael Stewart (1911–94), diplomat, British Ambassador to Greece 1967–71. He and his wife Damaris (née du Boulay) became close friends of the Leigh Fermors, as did their daughter Olivia.

Philip Toynbee (1916–81), writer and journalist, an old friend of PLF's and an exuberant drinker.

Iris Tree (1897–1968), poet, actress and muse, daughter of actor-manager Sir Herbert Beerbohm Tree. As a young woman she had been sought after as an artists' model, being painted by Augustus John, Duncan Grant, Vanessa Bell and Roger Fry; sculpted by Jacob Epstein; and photographed by Man Ray. She was first married to the New York artist Curtis Moffat; their son Ivan, a successful screenwriter, was also a friend of PLF's. Her second marriage was to the actor and ex-officer of the Austrian cavalry, Count Friedrich von Ledebur-Wicheln. After their divorce they both appeared in the 1956 film, *Moby Dick*. She also appeared in a cameo in Federico Fellini's *La Dolce Vita*.

Barbara Warner (1911–89), née Hutchinson, had been married to Victor Rothschild, 3rd Baron Rothschild, and Rex Warner before marrying Niko Ghika in 1961.

Rex Warner (1905–86), classicist, writer, poet and translator. As director of the British Institute in Athens, Warner had been PLF's boss for a brief period after the war.

Janetta Woolley see **Janetta Parladé**

Pamela Wyndham-Quin, later Egremont (1925–2013), society beauty, wife of John Wyndham, 1st Baron Egremont (1920–72), and a long-standing friend of PLF's.

ILLUSTRATION CREDITS

Unless otherwise stated, the original letters and photographs are reproduced by permission of the National Library of Scotland.

Additional Sources: Alamy: 6 below left/Ivan Vdovin. AP/Press Association Images: 16/Thanassis Stavrakis. Courtesy of the Benaki Museum – Ghika Gallery, Photographic Archive, Athens: 7 below. Evening Standard/Hulton Archive/Getty Images: 13 below. Joan Leigh Fermor: 12 below. Bridget Flemming: 15 below. Courtesy of Dagmar Ingrid Fischer: 14 below. Milton Gendel, Fondazione Primoli, Rome: 9, 12 above. Courtesy of the Estate of Enrica Soma Huston: 11 below. The Murray Collection: 6 above/watercolour by Peter Todd Mitchell, 6 below right. Moviestore Collection/REX/Shutterstock: 10 below. Courtesy of Lyndall Passerini-Hopkinson (photograph by Josephine Powell):11 above.

Every reasonable effort has been made to trace copyright holders, but if there are any errors or omissions, John Murray will be pleased to insert the appropriate acknowledgement in any subsequent printings or editions.

INDEX

Notes: Page numbers in **bold** indicate the first page of a letter to a correspondent. Titles of rank are generally the highest mentioned in the letters and notes.

BEAUMONT LIBRARY
PLEASE RETURN

Patrick Leigh Fermor

In December 1933, at the age of eighteen, Patrick Leigh Fermor walked across Europe, reaching Constantinople on the last day of 1934. He travelled on into Greece, where in Athens he met Balasha Cantacuzène, with whom he lived – mostly in Rumania – until the outbreak of war. Serving in occupied Crete, he led a successful operation to kidnap a German general, for which he won the DSO. After the war he began writing, and travelled extensively round Greece with Joan Rayner whom he later married. In 2008, he published *In Tearing Haste*, a collection of letters with Deborah Devonshire. Towards the latter part of his life he wrote two books about his early trans-European odyssey, *A Time of Gifts* and *Between the Woods and the Water*. He planned a third, *The Broken Road*, which was published posthumously in 2013.

Adam Sisman

Adam Sisman is the author of several biographies, most recently of John le Carré. His *Boswell's Presumptuous Task* won the prestigious US National Book Critics Circle Award for Biography. He is also co-editor of *One Hundred Letters from Hugh Trevor-Roper*. Adam is an Honorary Fellow of the University of St Andrews and a Fellow of the Royal Society of Literature.